The Haunting of
Twenty-First-Century America

William J. Birnes

Worker in the Light: Unlock Your Five Senses and Liberate Your Limitless Potential

Journey to the Light: Find Your Spiritual Self and Enter into a World of Infinite Opportunity

Space Wars: The First Six Hours of World War III

Counterspace: The Next Hours of World War III

The Haunting of America: From the Salem Witch Trials to Harry Houdini

The Day After Roswell

The Riverman: Ted Bundy and I Hunt for the Green River Killer

Signature Killers: Interpreting the Calling Cards of the Serial Murderer

The Star Trek Cookbook

Star Trek: Aliens and Artifacts

UFO Hunters: Book One

Dr. Feelgood

Wounded Minds

Hearts of Darkness

The Haunting of the Presidents: A Paranormal History of the U.S. Presidency

The Haunting of Twentieth-Century America

Joel Martin

We Are Not Forgotten: George Anderson's Messages of Love

Love Beyond Life: Healing Power of After-Death Communications

Our Children Forever: George Anderson's Messages from Children on the Other Side

We Don't Die: George Anderson's Conversations with the Other Side

The Haunting of America: From the Salem Witch Trials to Harry Houdini

The Haunting of the Presidents: A Paranormal History of the U.S. Presidency

The Haunting of Twentieth-Century America

William J. Birnes
and Joel Martin

The
Haunting
of
Twenty-
First-
Century
America

A Tom Doherty
Associates Book
New York

Scripture quotations taken from *The Amplified Bible*, copyright © 1954, 1958, 1962, 1964, 1965, 1987 by the Lockman Foundation. All rights reserved. Used by permission.

A Forge Book
Published by Tom Doherty Associates, LLC
175 Fifth Avenue
New York, NY 10010

www.tor-forge.com

Forge® is a registered trademark of Tom Doherty Associates, LLC.

Library of Congress Cataloging-in-Publication Data

Birnes, William J.
   The haunting of twenty-first-century America / William J. Birnes and Joel Martin. — First Edition.
      p. cm.
   "A Tom Doherty Associates Book."
   Sequel to: The haunting of twentieth-century America / Joel Martin.
   ISBN 978-0-7653-2837-3 (hardcover)
   ISBN 978-0-7653-2885-4 (trade paperback)
   ISBN 978-1-4668-2803-2 (e-book)
   1. United States—History—21st century—Anecdotes.   2. Spiritualism—United States—Anecdotes.   3. Ghosts—United States—Anecdotes.
4. Parapsychology—United States—Anecdotes.   5. Popular culture—United States—Anecdotes.   I. Martin, Joel, 1945–   II. Martin, Joel, 1945– Haunting of twentieth-century America.   III. Title.
   E893.B57 2013
   973.93—dc23

2013022086

Forge books may be purchased for educational, business, or promotional use. For information on bulk purchases, please contact Macmillan Corporate and Premium Sales Department at 1-800-221-7945, extension 5442, or write specialmarkets@macmillan.com.

First Edition: December 2013

Printed in the United States of America

0 9 8 7 6 5 4 3 2 1

Let us go then, you and I.

—T. S. ELIOT, "The Love Song of J. Alfred Prufrock"

Man is the only animal for whom his own existence is a problem which he has to solve.

—ERICH FROMM, *Man for Himself*

Why, sometimes I've believed as many as six impossible things before breakfast.

—LEWIS CARROLL, *Through the Looking-Glass*

Contents

Authors' Note

We have made every effort to present historical facts as accurately as possible. However, in the course of researching and writing, we sometimes discovered variations in details such as dates, locations, events, dialogue, and even spellings of names and places. To the best of our ability, we have consulted several authoritative references to provide the greatest historical accuracy possible. However, some variations proved unavoidable and are a reflection of incomplete, inadequate, or contradictory historical record keeping.

In some instances, some names have been changed to protect privacy. However, while certain identifying characteristics have been altered, the incidents and experiences described are genuine.

Acknowledgments

We acknowledge the hard work and courage of those thinkers who, in the face of withering criticism from skeptics and debunkers, forge ahead to establish new frontiers for exploring human experience and spirit. From the beginning of human history, they have been derided, shunned, or even burned at the stake, but they persisted in encouraging others not to accept the obvious, but to explore the alternatives.

—WILLIAM BIRNES

With gratitude to our editors at Forge Books, Bob Gleason and Eric Raab, and to our publisher, Tom Doherty. Thanks to Kelly Quinn for editorial assistance and her patience.

Many thanks to all those who helped this book become a reality, especially:

Margaret Wendt, long my partner and close friend who has guided our journey to discover the "Spiritual Truth."

Kristina Rus, reference librarian, East Meadow (New York) Public Library, for her tireless and meticulous reference and research skills.

Catherine Erdelyi, my assistant, with deep gratitude for her organizational and computer skills—both remarkable gifts.

Elise LeVaillant, with special thanks for sharing her enormous spiritual knowledge.

Roxanne Salch Kaplan for our enduring friendship and shared interest in parapsychology.

Gaylon Emerzian—everlasting gratitude for bringing Bill Birnes and me together to collaborate as authors.

And, of course, Bill Birnes, who has my deepest thanks for co-authoring and bringing to our readers his vast knowledge and insights about the paranormal and its place in American history and culture.

My special thanks to Donna DiBiase, Patricia Ippolito, Nancy Kaiser, Arlene and Michael Rosich, Dick Ruhl, Vladimir Rus, Ph.D., Thomas Santorelli, John Smith, Max Toth, Neil Vineberg, and Robert Petro, the first great psychic I met, as well as TV/video producers Ryan Katzenbach (*Shattered Hopes*) and Eric Walter (*My Amityville Horror*).

All my love to my wonderful grandchildren, Cambria and Caleb Weintraub, whose generation will someday lead—with wisdom and justice, we pray.

In loving memory to my dear friend parapsychologist Stephen Kaplan, John G. Fuller, Sadie and Charles Cohen, Shirleyann Martin, Evelyn Moleta, Mary Moleta, Father John Papallo, and D.C. (Ben) Webster.

And finally, my appreciation to the following libraries and collections: East Meadow (New York) Public Library; New York Public Library; West Babylon (New York) Public Library; American Society for Psychical Research; Axinn Library of Hofstra University, Hempstead, New York; Parapsychology Institute of America.

—JOEL MARTIN

Introduction: The Paranormal and the Attack of the Debunkers

It would be very handy if cultural and intellectual movements conformed to the calendar, demarcating them by January of each year, January of each new century, or, in this case, January of each millennium. But that's not how it is. Imagine sunset on Venice Beach, California, December 31, 1999. As the sun begins to dip into the Pacific Ocean, strange-looking painted people begin a wild dance. Somewhere along the sand a chorus of drummers begins an incessant beat, throbbing as the dancers gyrate against the huge red ball of sun, now halfway into the ocean. If you weren't a rational person planning your New Year's Eve celebration, you might think, from watching the neo-pagan ceremonies taking place in the fading light, that it was the end of the world as you knew it.

Slowly the sun disappears from view and the drumming becomes more intense. Then there is an eerie gloaming, a rim of light below the ocean horizon line with the first hints of twilight overhead. A darkness is coming over the land, a darkness not just of the old year, old decade, or old century, but a darkness of the passing millennium.

A thousand years earlier, early medieval religious thinkers, those keeping count of a calendar, saw the year 1000 CE as the time when the Messiah would return. Islam was a little over three hundred years old, the Catholic church was witnessing the growth of the monastic movement, and the chaos of the Dark Ages was passing into the beginning of the Middle Ages. It was a time when there was a recognition that things were changing in the Western world and that there was a return to the fervent spirituality that inspired the evangelism of early Christianity.

In 1999, however, things were different. This time there was a fervent spirituality of a new age when New Age thinkers were standing at the threshold of discoveries that turned the paranormal into the normal. Modern experimental and theoretical science, which had dominated the twentieth century and had brought us not only the understanding that things unseen were as real as what was seen, but also the realization that we had the capacity to wipe ourselves off the face of the planet with the flick of a few switches, the implementation of sets of mathematical codes, and the transmission of electrical signals along hardwired optical filament strands to arm and launch flying weapons of mass destruction that would rain down on us from out of the skies.

But toward the end of the twentieth century, a new movement was growing. Spurred in part by the research in psychic spying in the second half of the twentieth century, the United States military and intelligence services began to experiment with something called "remote viewing (RV)," the deployment of trained individuals to pick up on coordinates in a partner's mind and perceive where those coordinates led. It was not really a form of mind reading as much as it was a focus to locate a spot that someone in intelligence services wanted located. It didn't always work, but when it did it worked well and for some in the military it indicated that there was, indeed, a sixth sense. The paranormal, the government project seemed to show, was real. In other words, what began at the outset of the twentieth century—the intellectual appreciation of the unseen to be as real as the seen—now was turning into government military policy at the end of the twentieth century.

The twentieth century had also borne witness to another phenomenon, the possibility that craft from another planet, or planets, were visiting Earth. Actually, UFO incidents, as they were called, were as old as human civilization itself. As glyphs of flying craft and human figures in atmosphere or hazmat suits cut into the stone walls of ancient architectural structures seemed to attest, Earth had been visited by some type of humanoid species tens of thousands of years ago. Even the Bible spoke of strange creatures whose children intermarried with the children of Adam and Eve. From a mysterious crash of a flying craft—we believe now that it was a metal-clad balloon—to the fabled encounter of German World War I flying ace, Baron von Richthofen, the Red Baron, with a UFO, the twentieth century was dotted throughout by stories of flying saucer or UFO sightings. Eyewitnesses in Texas in 1897, photographic evidence, physical trace evidence, and even government documents all seemed to point to the strong possibility that something was out there and it didn't belong to us.

Almost as a counterpoint to the rise of New Age culture, spirituality, and an enthusiasm for discovering what, if any, the truth was about UFOs during the twentieth century was the growth of a movement beyond healthy skepticism. By the early 1950s, seemingly as an outgrowth of the passage of the National Security Act of July 1947, our new intelligence organizations began to find ways to locate and commission so-called debunkers to find, by any means possible, holes in any belief in spirituality and to tarnish the careers of those who ascribed to any belief in spirituality, including UFOs.

To be sure, until 1976, debunkers in this country weren't very well organized, unlike psychic researchers who'd formed groups in America and England by the 1880s. Debunking, less organized than today, had been around for a while. The first skeptics of psychic phenomena were probably heard from on the same day eons ago when the first paranormal or supernatural incident was reported. By the time of ancient Greece and Rome, skeptics were not shy about speaking out. In ancient Greece, the famed dramatist Euripides in the fifth century BCE offered the cynical opinion, "The best of seers is he who guesses well."[1] Later, the ancient Roman statesman and author Marcus Tullius Cicero (106–43 BCE) commented, "I wonder that a soothsayer doesn't laugh whenever he sees another soothsayer."[2]

Throughout medieval times, the Roman Catholic Church did not doubt psychic abilities; it just questioned their origins. If they occurred to anyone outside the church, they were demonic or heretical. At the same time, those bestowed with sainthood by the church often demonstrated remarkable paranormal gifts.

America's first self-appointed psychic skeptics and debunkers were on the scene just as soon as the Fox sisters kicked off the Age of Spiritualism in 1848 when they reported spirit rappings in their Hydesville, New York, home. And they've been a presence here and in Europe ever since to dispute paranormal claims.[3]

But, although several organizations for the scientific investigation of psychic phenomena formed—notably the Society for Psychical Research (SPR) in England, and the American Society for Psychical Research (ASPR) in America in the 1880s—there was no strong organization to debunk psychic claims until relatively recently. The first efforts only occurred in the 1970s. A Buffalo, New York, philosophy professor, Dr. Paul Kurtz, an avowed atheist and self-professed rationalist, joined with several like-minded associates to form the Committee for the Scientific Investigation of Claims of the Paranormal (CSICOP) in 1976. Its early forays to debunk astrology as an "irrational belief" backfired when Kurtz could not discredit it as easily as he expected. He then attempted to cover over results that contradicted his presumed conclusion, only to have them uncovered by an honest member in what became known as the "Starbaby scandal," when Kurtz felt his only choice was to lie. Remember, debunking all paranormal and religious claims was their goal. How they reached it was of less consequence.

When CSICOP was formally organized, Kurtz had several close colleagues who shared his ultrarationalistic worldview. One of them was James Randi. But CSICOP was misnamed. There were no scientific investigations or research facilities, and the group was not dedicated to objective inquiry about paranormal evidence. CSICOP's overriding purpose was to debunk psychic phenomena, and brand all psychical claims as "pseudoscience" and "irrational." There was no need to seriously examine psychic phenomena because, as the group's premise set forth, since parapsychology did not exist, all paranormal claims must be considered fraudulent. This same out-of-hand dismissal of all psychic or paranormal claims—prima facie don't exist so why bother to investigate?—continues to this day.

The obvious weapon of choice for Kurtz and company to mount their propaganda war was the media. Of course, psychics are no longer burned at the stake as witches or heretics. We've grown too civilized. Ironically, had it been several centuries ago, CSICOP officers and members, as atheists, would also have been executed unless they recanted their atheism. But, in their version of the Inquisition, debunkers held fast to their own intolerance, as they doggedly pursued a campaign to denounce psi experiences in any way they could, while chipping away at their true adversary: religious beliefs.

To many members of CSICOP, there wasn't a whole lot of difference between Bigfoot, the Bible, UFOs, astrologers, mediums, or miracles. Weeping icons or Wicca, it was all irrational, superstitious nonsense, or "junk science." What's more, there was no God. Therefore there could be no souls, angels, or an afterlife. Magicians and skeptics held the answers, not mediums—or the clergy.

CSICOP, however, knew how to manipulate the media to create doubt and confusion, and often did that superbly. Its members were frequently called upon to refute parapsychologists and psychics on TV programs. Although their explanations about the paranormal were predictable—unfailingly negative—they were never at a loss for words. From the point of view of TV producers, they made articulate guests, and also provided "balance." CSICOP cultivated powerful media friendships, and convinced many TV personalities and news reporters that skepticism was the intellectual and scientific high road when they presented anything about the paranormal.

CSICOP was not beyond intimidation as a tactic, complaining loudly and bitterly as TV networks devoted increasing amounts of time and attention to psychic phenomena and ufology, from the 1970s onward. Debunkers voiced their grievances on those talk shows they deemed "friendly," within their magazine, *Skeptical Inquirer*, and other publications. CSICOP members wrote many books published by Prometheus Books, a company launched by the group's founder, Paul Kurtz. Prometheus Books was ostensibly dedicated to "rational and humanist" positions, and its titles included many that were against the paranormal. Kurtz once went so far as to lodge a formal protest with the Federal Communications Commission (FCC), complaining about a program NBC television aired about psychic phenomena that CSICOP considered unduly favorable to the subject, perhaps concerned it would cause viewers some form of psychic mind pollution. Wisely, the FCC rejected the Kurtz complaint in favor of the First Amendment.[4]

For more than twenty years, from 1962 to 1986, Merv Griffin hosted TV talk shows that broke the taboo on the paranormal, often devoting entire programs to various psychic topics, and never denying his personal curiosity or interest. It was especially courageous in the 1960s and 1970s, and Griffin drew loyal audiences, to the frustration of skeptics and debunkers. Inventive and astute, Griffin went on to develop such long-running hit TV shows as *Jeopardy!* and *Wheel of Fortune,* and became one of the wealthiest people in show business. Apparently, whatever Griffin's belief was in the paranormal, it did not dull his creativity or business acumen, to the dismay of debunkers who hoped to convince America that interest in psychic phenomena could lower one's I.Q.

What amounted to nothing less than a war between spiritualists and debunkers burst most notably into the public consciousness in the latter half of the twentieth century with the arrival on the scene of the celebrated psychic Uri Geller and his nemesis, the debunker—also a celebrated stage magician—James Randi.

1

Uri Geller, the Paranormal, and Psychokinesis

Perhaps nothing illustrates the conflict between believers in the paranormal and debunkers of the paranormal so clearly as the dispute between celebrated psychic Uri Geller and celebrity stage magician and paranormal debunker James Randi. From the middle of the twentieth century through today, researchers across the great divide between hard-core debunkers and true believers in the paranormal have engaged in a battle for the hearts and minds of the general public. The story of Uri Geller and James Randi, best represents a microcosm of this battle.[1]

For many years before Uri Geller appeared on the scene, psychokinesis (PK), or mind over matter, was of serious interest to researchers such as Dr. J. B. Rhine at the Duke University Parapsychology Laboratory. In 1944, Rhine wrote in the *Journal of the*

American Society for Psychical Research, "Thought, define it as you will, exerts a control over material things." Rhine experimented with PK by "investigating claims of a gambler that the state of mind can influence the fall of dice." He concluded that PK was "closely related to ESP." But then, as now, there was no scientific theory or evidence to explain what might cause PK, since it "operates without leaving any conscious record of its working," Rhine said. "Common physical laws do not govern the operation of the psychical processes that produce the test results." Some of that would change in the 1980s, however, according to army remote viewer Paul H. Smith in his book *Reading the Enemy's Mind* (Tom Doherty Associates, 2005), when the scientists at Stanford Research Institute found themselves searching for a hard science explanation as to how remote viewing worked. Prior to that, RV and PK were considered "pseudosciences," which many skeptics still consider them to be.[2]

Between the 1930s and 1980s, though, professional parapsychology journals of both the ASPR and the SPR periodically published papers about PK. *The Journal of the American Society for Psychical Research* reported that between May and December of 1946, "three extensive series of PK tests were undertaken in which 132 subjects performed a total of 76,032 die throws." But the exact mechanism for how PK operated could not be determined.

Ironically, around that same time, in December 1946, Uri Geller was born in Tel Aviv, in what was then still considered Palestine, but which became Israel after the declaration of the State of Israel in 1948. Friends and family remember he brought the hands on watches and clocks to a dead stop without touching them, even when he was a young boy, and throughout his growing-up years. He was also able to bend spoons although he barely laid a finger on them. Some who remembered him as a toddler and witnessed his demonstrations were convinced he was gifted with an inexplicable ability.

The first incident occurred when Geller was only three years old. As he held a soupspoon, it bent and broke. Uri's mother assumed there was something defective in the metal that caused it to separate into two pieces. She never dreamed her young son could be responsible. Might Uri, as a child, have had the cunning of a skilled magician to create such effects? It seems highly doubtful that he or anyone that age would be able to. When he was six, Uri made a friend's watch move forward a full hour, according to one account. How was a youngster capable of causing that?

"It wasn't something he could really do, but rather something that was happening to him," Jonathan Margolis quoted a childhood friend of Uri's as saying.[3] Years later, the friend still held the same opinion "that what Uri showed him was an example of a true psychic gift rather than a rehearsed trick." It would be an important point when Geller was an adult and an acclaimed psychic performer. He was accused by avowed debunkers of manufacturing a phony psychic act when he was in his twenties, and only after he'd read a book about magic. That allegation could not have been accurate if, in fact, Geller had been displaying psychokinetic ability since early childhood. There is another incident Margolis reported in which Uri once repaired a teacher's four broken watches by simply passing his hands over them. Years later, when Uri was famous, one of his teachers wrote to say she remembered that when Uri was twelve years old, he demonstrated bending forks and even mind reading. Uri demonstrated this same feat in 2007 when he repaired watches and clocks while on a live *Coast to Coast AM* radio show with George Noory.

As are all able-bodied Israelis, Geller was required to serve three years in the Israel Defense Forces (IDF) from the time he was eighteen until he was twenty-one. While in the army, he did his best to maintain a distance from anything that would brand him a magician, such as card tricks, at which he was quite accomplished. As for purported psychic feats, he demonstrated few during his service, some of which was spent as a paratrooper.

In the summer of 1967, Geller met a youngster who would become a very important part of his life and career. His name was Shimshon Shtrang, but he was always called Shipi, and he was only thirteen, about eight years younger than Uri. At the time, Geller was recuperating from wounds he suffered after being shot in Jordan during the Six-Day War. It was a wound he remembers well because he often told the story of encountering a Jordanian soldier on the West Bank. They both shot at each other. Uri was wounded, but he killed the enemy soldier. During his recuperation, he took a position as a children's camp counselor.

Shipi attended the camp and was enthralled by Uri's flair for storytelling, mostly tales of science fiction. The boy also was fascinated by Geller's demonstrations of telepathic ability. For example, Geller would invite the kids to draw or think of something. Invariably, he would know telepathically what the children had thought of. The mind reading never failed to hold the group's attention, especially Shipi's.

Geller also discovered that Shipi had a remarkable psychic rapport with him. If Uri wrote down numbers and placed them in sealed envelopes, Shipi knew telepathically what they were. In turn, when Shipi drew pictures, Uri could psychically describe them. Geller also showed the children his ability to bend metal, and insisted that his skills were enhanced when Shipi was nearby.

Their psychic interaction, while mutually advantageous, resulted in considerable controversy for Geller in the years ahead. Shipi would become Geller's business manager, closest friend, confidant, and later brother-in-law, when Geller married Shipi's pretty sister, Hannah, six years older than Shipi. But debunkers would repeatedly attack Geller for having Shipi close by, alleging that Uri could only perform metal bending, telepathy, or any other extrasensory perception (ESP) ability if Shipi was present. This implied that Shipi was Uri's confederate in some way, although it was never made clear how. Perhaps they had a secret code or a set of signals between them? This would cast doubt on a paranormal explanation for Geller's ability.

Debunkers have persisted in that fallacious version of events, despite the fact that Uri can and does demonstrate mind reading and PK even when Shipi is not nearby. What's more, debunkers ignored Geller's childhood abilities, claiming the two had dreamed up Uri's "psychic act" only after they read a book on magic the summer they met.[4]

By the time Geller was twenty-two years old in 1969, the slender, good-looking young man with dark hair and piercing eyes was employing his paranormal abilities as a "professional performer" in Israeli nightclubs, private parties, and the kibbutzim. And he quickly became a "psychic superstar" throughout the country. Even the late and renowned Israeli prime minister Golda Meir, once asked by reporters to predict the future of Israel, quipped, "I don't predict. Why don't you ask Uri Geller?"[5]

In fact, Geller had purportedly foretold the death of Egypt's leader Gamal Abdel Nasser, shortly before it occurred in 1970, a major event throughout the troubled and politically volatile Middle East. As you might expect, Geller's prognostication attracted widespread attention in Israel.

We should hasten to add that not every Israeli was enthralled with Geller. He had his share of critics and skeptics who denounced him as a fraud, even a "menace." One of Israel's popular magazines skewered Geller in an "exposé," claiming his psychic abilities were a hoax made possible by the use of some chemical that bent metal. Only much later did the magazine back down from what were outright falsehoods and unsubstantiated allegations.

It was during the summer of 1971 that an eccentric American

physician and parapsychologist named Dr. Andrija Puharich (1918–1995) visited Tel Aviv and first observed Geller's performance. Puharich had already been responsible for bringing the Dutch psychic Peter Hurkos to the United States in 1965, who became well known for working with law enforcement in criminal and missing persons cases. But now Puharich was ecstatic. He exclaimed that he'd spent years searching for someone like Uri Geller. The two men quickly formed a professional relationship. Puharich tested Geller's abilities and, once convinced that his psychic powers were authentic, helped Uri and Shipi come to America. Puharich's goal was to arrange funding for Geller to be scientifically examined here. Uri understood the significance of this, and that if he were successful, it would add greatly to his credibility as a psychic. However, should he fail in America, his career would likely suffer a fatal blow. His opportunity soon came, and the pressure on him must have been intense.

By November 1972, Geller was at the Stanford Research Institute in Menlo Park, California, located only several miles from Stanford University in Palo Alto. There his task would be to demonstrate, under tightly controlled test conditions, his psychokinetic power to bend metal and other ESP abilities, including telepathy. The Stanford Research Institute, commonly known as SRI International, an "independent nonprofit corporation," was one of a handful of facilities across the country where the paranormal was being seriously investigated. Experimentation was also conducted at SRI in physics, bioengineering, electronics, and remote viewing under contracts with government and industry to the tune of tens of millions of dollars annually.

At SRI, Geller would meet scientists with substantial credentials. One of them was Dr. Harold Puthoff, a physicist in his mid-thirties with a PhD from Stanford University. Puthoff was an expert in laser physics research, held several patents, had also been in naval intelligence, and worked with the top-secret National Security Agency. After researching biofeedback, Puthoff became interested in psi—the preferred word for parapsychology—by the 1970s, especially among scientists. For the record, psi is the twenty-third letter of the Greek alphabet. (The word *psi* is pronounced as if it were spelled "sigh.") Puthoff teamed up with a colleague, Russell Targ, also a physicist and an inventor with a curiosity about the paranormal. He had another interest that would prove useful in psychical research. Targ was an ardent student of stage magic. The pair, along with their early test subject and consultant, psychic Ingo Swann, later became well known in their own right for extensive CIA-funded research about remote viewing, for which they achieved impressive results. Among these results, according to one of the original remote viewers, army major Paul Smith, would involve being able to perceive events taking place in the future. In effect, the remote viewers had discovered a method of psychic time travel.

Meanwhile, Targ and Puthoff turned their attention to testing Uri Geller's alleged abilities. They observed Geller's psychokinetic (PK) power to bend and even break metal, although he had not applied any "direct physical pressure," in their words, and dubbed what they saw as the "Geller effect." They also extensively studied Geller's facility for mental telepathy. Former astronaut Edgar Mitchell, who had a strong interest in parapsychology since the late 1960s, oversaw some of the Geller tests. By then, Mitchell had conducted his own ESP experiments from outer space.

The Geller tests at SRI continued for nearly six weeks, and results depended on who reported them. Targ and Puthoff, among other scientists, pronounced them successful, and Geller considered that the experiments validated his PK and ESP powers. But debunkers spun the outcome differently. They regarded the experiments as inconclusive or a failure in proving Geller was a genuine psychic, attacking SRI's "research methodology," that is the way Geller was tested, and further impugned the scientists' reputations, suggesting one motive was to enhance Targ and Puthoff's status as parapsychologists, possibly to gain them more funding.[6]

Uri Geller was an immediate sensation in the American media, as more people became familiar with his purported psychic powers. There was something fascinating about watching him on TV barely touch a spoon or fork, and then seeing the utensil bend, curl, or break as if it had been heated by some potent but unseen energy. He also demonstrated the same PK effect on keys and even metal nails. In fact, when he appeared on British television, it was not unusual for viewers to claim they, too, experienced similar PK effects at home on their silverware and house keys. Had Geller somehow transmitted his ability to those watching? What explanation might there be for viewers who insisted their broken timepieces and clocks began working again?

Geller's stunning celebrity success had not gone unnoticed by a variety of skeptics looking to debunk any claims of the paranormal. Among the skeptics who raised serious doubts about Uri's ability was the celebrated stage magician James Randi. Born Randall James Hamilton Zwinge in Toronto, Canada, in 1928, he changed his professional name to The Amazing Randi, and built a career dazzling worldwide audiences with stage illusions and escape artistry on many network TV programs, on late-night talk shows such as *The Tonight Show Starring Johnny Carson*, and on college campuses. Randi insisted that Geller was a magician or conjurer, not a true psychic with paranormal abilities, something he said he wanted to demonstrate. He persistently and publicly discredited any claims people made about Uri's gifts.

Debunkers can be in their own ways very deceptive, as was Harry Houdini when he sought to debunk the paranormal after his fight with Sir Arthur Conan Doyle. The late Phil Klass was also deceptive, going to great lengths to discredit any UFO sightings and the witnesses who reported them. Debunkers, whether through their own rigid system of disbelief or whether they're paid by some other entity, like agencies of the government, tend to start from their belief first and then force the facts to fit their belief. In some cases, the distortion is so intense that it looks, upon examination, like the debunkers themselves are bending the truth to fit their arguments.

Few would argue that an open-minded watchdog or consumer advocate isn't useful to protect the public from the charlatans posing as psychics and mediums that have long bilked the gullible, parting them from their money. What easily come to mind are the "1-900" psychic phone line operations that reached their peak in the 1990s, and then seemed to collapse when investigated. Skepticism is healthy, even rigid skepticism. But debunking for the sake of discrediting someone without looking at one's own motives skeptically is a different story.

Perhaps Randi, practicing the art of illusion and stage magic, saw himself as a modern-day Houdini going after every paranormal claim in any way he could. But debunkers, who long ago elevated Houdini to a mythic status as their hero, have misrepresented the great illusionist. Houdini had not denied the possibility that an afterlife existed. His bitterness arose from the frustration of never finding someone who could communicate with his mother in the hereafter.[7] That's a far cry from debunkers who seek to lash out at anything smacking of a supernatural character, including psychic phenomena in any form encompassing, but not limited to, a spirit world.

So it was that Randi appeared to have become obsessed with Geller's reputation as a representative of a true supernatural world, a world he could enter and exit and a world whose existence Geller could demonstrate. Perhaps it was Geller's seeming effortlessness in his demonstrations that provoked Randi to try and expose what he saw as Geller's ability to create a grand illusion. Ironically, it was the conflict between Uri's demonstrations and Randi's challenges that cast Randi into a spotlight.

In point of fact, Randi was nowhere near SRI when Geller was undergoing tests there in late 1972, and again the next year. It seemed that Randi drew his own conclusions about what went on at SRI, conclusions that, predictably, were negative. Perhaps, they had to be because Randi, often described in the media as a skeptic, behaved, for all intents and purposes, like a debunker and was one of the founders in 1976 of a national organization of psychic de-bunkers, called the Committee for the Scientific Investigation of Claims of the Paranormal, often referred to as CSICOP.

What is the difference between a skeptic and a debunker? They are not the same. A skeptic is one who doubts psychic phenomena. He or she will question or investigate fairly before arriving at a conclusion. Debunkers have no need to query or consider paranor-mal claims. Their goal is to deny all psychic events, arguing that psychic claims have no real test of evidentiary credibility. By seek-ing to duplicate a psychic event, debunkers claim that conventional explanations trump psychic explanations. Thus, by eliminating even the remote possibility of psychic causality, the debunker's conclu-sions have already been drawn, and any evidence to the contrary is discounted.

According to debunkers, paranormal phenomena do not exist. They maintain psi is the product of hallucination, superstition, ir-rational thinking, pseudoscience, outright trickery, deception, or fraud. Never mind that many millions of psychic events occur, and have played a role in every society and culture since human beings took their first steps on earth eons ago. At the very least, that sug-gests the history of psi should be of interest to psychologists, sociologists, and anthropologists. CSICOP maintains it has never found or validated even one psychic experience, which seems unbelievable and statistically untenable until one realizes that CSICOP sets the rules and then establishes which alleged psychic or paranormal event satisfies those rules.

The attitudes of debunkers raise the question, "Why would there be such hostility and negativity to even the possibility that the paranormal exists?" The answer may be deceptively simple. In large part, debunkers are secular humanists or atheists. For them, therefore, God does not exist, and religious beliefs are "irrational," even dangerous. Consider the many centuries of wars, killings, and repression in the name of one religion or the other. Look at the religious wars taking place right now in the twenty-first century and by the way, here in the United States, so-called religious values become political policy for candidates running as conservative fundamentalists. It's not surprising skeptics blame religion for the world's ills.

Nevertheless, according to the debunkers' credo, psychic phenomena and New Age beliefs are just other forms of religion that cannot be accepted or condoned by such self-proclaimed, clear-headed, and rational-thinking people, as the members of CSICOP and "The Amazing Randi."

Randi first met Uri Geller at the New York offices of *Time* magazine where Randi and a colleague pretended they were reporters, with the help of a friend who worked for the publication. That gave him an opportunity to observe Geller demonstrate his metal-bending ability.[8] It didn't take Randi long to reach his conclusion. Randi said what he saw was a "transparent sleight of hand performance." What's more, he said that Geller was not a "psychic superstar." What was he? "Geller is a clever magician, nothing more and certainly nothing less," Randi wrote. Then, assuming a more self-righteous tone, he continued, "I am proud of my profession [performing acts of magic]. I am even jealous of it and resent any prostitution of the art. In my view, Geller brings disgrace to the craft I practice."[9]

Essentially, Randi's long-held contention was that the paranormal is not scientific. It is entirely a trick. Therefore, why bother scientists? All you needed was a skilled magician—especially The Amazing Randi—to reveal the deception perpetrated by Uri Geller and his ilk. Randi said he could not "forgive the damage done to respectable men of science and the press who chose to board [Geller's] comet and who may well have to face, in the end, the ridicule of their colleagues."[10]

What Randi overlooked in his highly exaggerated and dire prediction about "damage to respectable men of science" were the opinions of the scientists, themselves. Apparently, those who examined Geller and found evidence of genuine paranormal ability had all been fooled, according to Randi. In fact, because scientists were so intelligent, schooled, and trained, it was easier for them to be duped by a phony masquerading as a psychic. "No matter how well-educated, alert, well-meaning, or astute men of science are, they are certainly no match for a competent magician. Fooling people is his stock-in-trade," Randi proclaimed.[11]

Dr. Andrija Puharich was a brilliant engineer and physician, not withstanding his eccentricities and some genuinely strange conspiracy theories involving UFOs and the CIA.[12] After he'd tested Geller informally, and to his satisfaction, he'd arranged through his connections in intelligence circles for Geller to be tested at SRI.[13] For a long time, no one was certain who paid for those tests. Years later it was revealed that it had been none other than the Central Intelligence Agency (CIA). The tests were conducted toward the end of 1972, and again the following year. Largely, they centered on Geller's purported telepathic abilities.[14] Although Harold Puthoff, Russell Targ, and other scientists at SRI witnessed Uri's metal bending, those experiments had not been conducted under what Puthoff and Targ considered sufficiently strict scientific controls. So, when the "SRI Report," as it came to be called, was released, Geller's metal-bending prowess was only mentioned, but not detailed. However, the SRI Report was published in the prestigious British scientific journal *Nature* in October 1974.[15]

Limits on space prevent repeating the full report here. However, some highlights should give you an idea of the tests Geller underwent. To determine the extent of his telepathic ability, Geller was placed in a "double-walled steel room" that was shielded from exterior sound, sight, and anything conducting any electrical signals. Parapsychologists know it as a Faraday cage, an enclosure that is used for testing subjects. The tightly sealed steel room was set up for only one-way audio communication, from Geller to the experimenters outside.

The Faraday cage, made of copper mesh with double walls, is designed to prevent any interference from magnetic fields or radio waves. It is named for the great British physicist Michael Faraday (1791–1867), highly regarded for his dazzling scientific findings concerning electromagnetism and chemistry. Although Faraday created the concept for the cage, on the subject of psychic phenomena, he was deeply skeptical all his life.

In one SRI-conducted test, Geller was instructed to draw the same pictures the scientists had, without seeing them, of course. He was also asked to apply his telepathy to draw pictures that were kept in the memory of a computer. Another test required Uri to replicate drawings in sealed envelopes that the scientists conducting the tests had not seen. Every precaution was taken to prevent any deceit or trickery, or accidentally providing Geller with any visual or verbal cues or clues. The tests lasted a full week and consisted of thirteen drawings.

When Geller's telepathic accuracy was evaluated, it showed his correct answers far exceeded that which could be obtained by chance or guessing. There was a one in a million chance that Uri could have guessed accurately. In other words, because Geller's results were more than 50 percent accurate, the preponderance of evidence indicated that he was performing beyond the level of chance and was most likely using a mental power. This was tantalizing scientific evidence that Geller had demonstrated genuine telepathic ability.

Another round of tests were set up to determine Geller's clairvoyant powers. Apparently, in these, he scored no better than chance, meaning the results, statistically, were no more or less than someone who had guessed the "test object," whatever it might be, such as a drawing, numerals, something written, or a photograph, and so on. Unlike telepathy or mind reading, in examining for clairvoyance, the test object is completely unknown to all the participants, scientists, and subject. Thus, if the subject—in this case Geller—is accurate, the information had to be psychically transmitted or communicated in some manner other than telepathically. In Uri's case, the SRI results showed he was more telepathic than clairvoyant.

Geller was also tested with dice, the purpose being to determine if he could ascertain the face of a single die placed in a sealed steel box, and shaken by the person conducting the test. That individual had no idea what number would show face up. Geller responded accurately eight out of ten times. Twice he "passed," meaning he chose not to answer, remarking that he was not psychically perceiving the die. But of his eight predictions, he was correct all eight times. The statistical probability of chance on Geller's part was one in a million. The die test was later repeated, but "informally," and Uri was correct ten out of ten times, a one in a billion chance.

Based on the more than five weeks of tests in late 1972, SRI released a press statement that said, "We have observed certain phenomena for which we have no scientific explanation." That was a tempting tease for the media. When in October 1974, *Nature* published the SRI Report about Targ and Puthoff's tests of Uri Geller, the magazine anticipated a controversial response among scientists. That prediction did not require any psychic ability. But *Nature,* in an editorial preceding the SRI Report, reminded readers that despite the sharply disputed scientific opinions about psychokinetic and telepathic abilities, the magazine felt it was incumbent upon it to publish "the occasional 'high-risk' type of paper," and opt to "stimulate and advance the controversy."

The editorial went on, "The issue, then, is whether the evidence is of sufficient quality to be taken seriously." Puthoff and Targ's paper was criticized as "weak in design and presentation [and] details given as to the precise way in which the experiment was carried out were disconcertingly vague." But the magazine hastened to add that Targ and Puthoff were both "qualified scientists writing from a major research establishment."

Nature made an important point reminding readers that the SRI paper would motivate those scientists interested in parapsychology to discuss and debate ESP, allowing those who were interested in "researching this arguable field" to assess the "quality of the Stanford research," and determine "how much it is contributing to parapsychology." Finally, there was the following caveat: just because the paper about the paranormal was published did not mean *Nature* was giving the subject its "stamp of approval."

As the *Nature* editorial candidly pointed out to the scientifically conservative, phenomena such as telepathy—or any other manifestation of ESP—"is beyond the laws of science, and therefore necessarily unacceptable." That about summed up the attitude of traditional scientists to parapsychology in the 1970s, and if it was possible to ignore the entire field, they would.

The Stanford Research Institute also released a film of the Geller experiments with demonstrations of his psychokinetic abilities, including spoon bending. The visual depiction elicited the same response; each side saw what it wanted to. Probably, few minds were swayed, even by the film's ending, which showed curled utensils.[16]

All the while as this flurry of activity was going on around Geller, The Amazing Randi was eagerly in pursuit. He complained that neither scientists nor Geller wished to have him present during their experiments because he was a magician, and he pronounced the SRI test controls, "flimsy." Randi's conclusion was to suppose that Geller had somehow cheated, perhaps he received "hand signals" from Shipi. There was also an accusation from Randi that in the SRI's film, Geller employed a tiny hidden magnet to cause a compass needle to move. "The Geller tests at SRI were utterly useless except as examples of inept and biased research," Randi unhesitatingly announced.[17]

Remember that Randi had seen Uri demonstrate at *Time* magazine's New York office, and pronounced Geller's abilities tricks that any competent stage magician could duplicate. What most *Time* readers were likely unaware of was that *Time*'s then science editor, Leon Jaroff, was a friend of Randi's, and a die-hard skeptic. Therefore, it was no surprise that *Time*'s story about Geller and the SRI tests was brutally critical. But you have to wonder how many *Time* readers—it is an influential newsmagazine—believed they were reading an objective article about what went on at SRI, rather than a preplanned hatchet job to debunk Geller.

Other print media weren't quite as harsh. *Newsweek,* for example, was more temperate as were several important newspaper articles. Geller, meanwhile, continued his meteoric success in the United States. Metal bending was a big hit. There were network TV appearances, newspaper and magazine interviews, public appearances—at up to five thousand dollars a shot—and enough street buzz, academic interest, and scientific debate so that Uri virtually became a household name. Bending spoons and keys, and stopping and starting watches was paying off handsomely for Geller, who was seeing his dreams of wealth and fame come true.

But the question everyone wanted answered was how did Uri do it? Did Uri have genuine psychic powers, or was The Amazing Randi onto something when he flatly accused Geller of being a charlatan? One theory that long made the rounds of skeptics was that Geller engaged in some form of mass hypnosis to convince observers that they'd witnessed something they had not. But upon closer examination, it was a specious argument. For one thing, subjects cannot be hypnotized unless they are willing. In fact, many who've studied the subject consider hypnotism simply the "power of suggestion," and that Geller could not have accomplished it upon those not amenable. There's also a certain irony about claiming hypnosis as an answer for Geller's feats, since some of the most intractable debunkers have argued that there are no such states as hypnosis or trances.[18]

Besides Randi's relentless pursuit, Uri had another problem—and potential embarrassment—to deal with. That was his mentor and friend Dr. Puharich, a Chicago native of Serbian ancestry whose hero was the equally eccentric inventor and scientific genius Nikola Tesla. There was no question about Puharich's accomplishments in electronics, in transistors, and as an inventor; one of his creations was a "micro-hearing aid." However, as time went on, his ideas veered further from the mainstream to what many considered the far fringe of the paranormal. For example, he had taken a serious interest in a largely spurious practice called psychic surgery, through his examination of the Brazilian peasant Arigó, whose feats as a psychic surgeon leave more questions than debunkers care to admit.[19]

After studying Arigó, who accurately predicted his own death in an automobile crash in 1971, Puharich next discovered Uri Geller. Without Puharich, who knows where Geller's destiny would have taken him. For all his eccentricities, Puharich brought scientific and public attention to Geller that might not otherwise have happened so that by 1974, a London *Daily Mail* poll found that 95 percent of readers believed Uri had "psychic powers."

It was hard enough convincing Americans that Geller had genuine PK and telepathic abilities. But in 1974 Puharich wrote a book titled *Uri,* in which he claimed that Geller's abilities had originated with extraterrestrials, and they communicated to both him and Uri here on Earth. Puharich also added another psychic talent to Geller's repertoire. He insisted Uri could levitate, although no one had ever witnessed him performing the feat. None of this helped strengthen Geller as a credible psychic. His actual abilities were hard enough for many to swallow, without Puharich adding what sounded like unbelievable science fiction tales. Uri remained loyal to Puharich, but the flights of fantasy created by the good doctor were not helpful. Puharich increasingly spun stranger and stranger stories; and they fed right into the hands of the debunkers who hoped that the less credible Geller appeared, the more his popularity would sink, and that he'd be gone from the media spotlight.

When you met Puharich, who lived at one time in a lovely house in Ossining, New York, in affluent Westchester County, a suburb of New York City, he was bright, complex, and gracious—that is, until you disagreed with him. Then out came his increasingly paranoid conspiracy theories, and the possibility he'd accuse you of being a CIA spy or operative who was out to get him. In fact, he became convinced the CIA and Federal Bureau of Investigation (FBI) were following his every move. His thinking had become increasingly bizarre, "neurotic, and obsessive; even self-destructive," author Jonathan Margolis noted. Even his appearance changed, from neat and precise in the 1960s to somewhat less so a decade later, when he resembled a disheveled Einstein-cum-hippie with his unruly hair and mustache.

Puharich never intentionally meant to hurt Uri or his career, but the potential was there unless Uri tactfully distanced himself. Puharich had an enormous ego, and no matter how far beyond reality you concluded his ideas were, at some level you had the distinct impression that he actually believed his stranger theories. For example, after he'd personally tested Uri and became convinced of his genuine PK and telepathic powers, Puharich hypnotized him in late 1971. That's when Puharich claimed extraterrestrial intelligences spoke to him through Geller, and said they would guide his career in the years to come. Puharich was fascinated by the hands of his watch reacting to Uri's PK powers, which he believed had some form of extraterrestrial connection. Puharich's experiences with Geller, including their alleged teleportation, were told in *Uri*, the book based on Puharich's meticulous note taking, but the weighty manuscript was difficult to decipher, and it strained credulity.[20]

Uri's primary goals were to become very famous and make lots of money. He was an entertainer, and show business was where he liked it best. Scientific tests and experiments of his psychic powers had to be endured, but he was often impatient about the scrutiny. During the early 1970s, Geller's abilities were extensively examined at no less than a half-dozen laboratories throughout the United States, as well as in several foreign countries. The large number of tests he underwent were well detailed in *The Geller Papers*, written by Charles Panati in 1976.[21]

Uri Geller recognized when it was time to present his own version of his life and career, at least in part to temper some of Puharich's wilder claims. In 1975, he wrote the autobiographical *My Story*.[22] It was around that time that Joel Martin first met Geller and personally watched him demonstrate his professed psychic abilities, recording an interview with Geller for his late-night radio show, which dealt with paranormal phenomena and UFOs.

Joel's background as a schoolteacher in some of New York City's toughest schools and his years going to college at night and having to walk through crime-ridden neighborhoods is relevant to his appreciation and understanding of Geller's abilities, especially in light of what James Randi said about the intellectual attributes of scientists in comprehending Geller. According to Randi, and other magicians and debunkers, Geller had duped even some of the brightest scientists with his alleged sleight of hand. By this reasoning, only a magician would be clever enough to catch what Randi described as Geller's illusionist's tricks. To a degree, Randi might have been correct. A scientist may not be looking for signs of deception. However, one magician is likely to recognize another, according to Randi. Of course, he was only referring to conjurers who, like himself, discredited Geller. But Randi and other debunkers were never certain how to react to those magicians who closely observed Geller and concluded he was demonstrating a paranormal power.

Although neither a scientist nor a magician, Joel's experiences as a teacher and an all too frequent late-night subway rider attuned him to an environment where to survive required street smarts, the instinct to be aware of danger by watching very carefully anything and everything one could. This meant drawing quick conclusions from the way a stranger makes—or doesn't make—eye contact; how someone is dressed, right down to whether a young man is wearing a wedding band or bling jewelry, also matters. Knowing which subway car looked relatively safe became instinctive after a while for Joel, who on more than one occasion saw a fellow whose nervous fumbling with something in his coat pocket mentally tipped him off that he was carrying a gun.

Joel's street smarts taught him to be careful when buying into any story calling itself paranormal just because it called itself that. When he interviewed those who purported to have psychic ability, he was deeply skeptical, even cynical, as he watched and listened for anything that might be a visual or verbal clue to a person's deception. For example, he'd keep a close eye on the manner of dress, body language, and facial expressions of a subject of a psychic reading to determine if a psychic or medium was picking up on any inflection in the way a person answered, or even winced at a question or comment from the psychic.

When Joel met Uri Geller for the first time to witness him demonstrate his alleged psychic powers, he didn't leave his city upbringing, or radio and TV news reporting skills, parked at the curb. He watched Uri's every move carefully and, ultimately, thought it quite arrogant that Randi made the assumption that only he could detect Geller's fraud, if in fact there was any. The implication that we're all ill-prepared and delusional if we experience something paranormal is insulting and condescending. It's not unlike some of the debunking crowd who for years argued that airline pilots in flight were as prone to error as the rest of us terrestrial simpletons when they glimpsed UFOs whisking through the sky, therefore they were no better UFO witnesses than anyone else. Candidly, airline pilots had better be more observant. That is what they are trained and paid for. Having said all that, here's what happened when Joel observed Uri Geller demonstrate his abilities.

Joel was invited into Geller's apartment by his assistant. Moments later, Uri walked from another room and greeted him warmly. He was personable, trim, and good-looking, not yet thirty years old. While producer Chris Moleta[23] set up the recording equipment for the interview, Joel explained to Geller what he hoped to do. Asked if he would demonstrate his abilities while Joel narrated what he was doing, Uri readily agreed.

Joel explained that he'd brought along from home his own objects for Uri to bend, which included a metal ring of sturdy keys. They were personal keys to several offices, radio and TV studios, and a house key. A couple of others opened classroom doors where Joel had taught when he wasn't broadcasting. In all, there were no less than a dozen keys on the bulky ring. Joel admitted later that he didn't expect Geller to bend them, or if he did, Joel would surely spot how he was doing it and reveal his trick right there during the interview. Joel fantasized the headline in his mind: NY TALK-SHOW HOST EXPOSES FAMED PSYCHIC AS FAKE.

Joel and Uri sat at a dining room table, diagonally facing one other across microphones. For several minutes they talked about Uri's upbringing and abilities. Then the demonstration began. Joel pulled the ring of keys from his jacket pocket. The listeners would hear them rattle when the show aired. "You brought all those keys?" Geller asked, his voice rising.

He asked Joel to pass them over, which he did. Uri held them in the palm of one hand while he lightly ran the other hand over the keys, barely touching them. At first the sturdy keys just sat there, and then, in a matter of seconds, they began to bend, as if something had melted them. All of them curled in the same direction. One didn't need to be a physicist to realize that it would take a tremendous amount of heat to soften twelve pieces of unyielding metal as if they'd been liquefied. No sooner had they seemed to move themselves than they stopped, and Geller handed the key ring back to Joel.

"They bent! All of them bent. Did you see that?" Geller exclaimed excitedly, describing the action perfectly. Joel acknowledged for the listening audience that, yes, they'd bent. The keys were inexplicably contorted. They were now also useless as keys. Then Joel realized that they were cold. In other words, if Geller had somehow applied a hidden chemical or device, those keys should have warmed up at least a little. But they hadn't.

There was no possible way Uri Geller could have instantly curled or bent the keys all at once by barely touching them without Chris and Joel seeing him do it. Chris, by the way, was far more street-savvy than Joel, and equally skeptical about the paranormal.

Geller resumed the interview, and Joel peppered him with questions about every conjuring trick that might explain what we'd just witnessed. Geller remained calm, although the questioning style sounded like a courtroom interrogation. Next, the questions turned to his purported ESP abilities. Several minutes later, Uri asked if he could perhaps demonstrate his supposed telepathic powers that people had heard about through news reports and stories about him.

"Now, it's better for me if you believe I can do this. If you don't believe that I have this [ESP] ability, I can't promise it will work," he said. His caveat was surprising. Joel answered by saying only that he would remain open-minded, no more or less, until the results were clear. From behind the recording equipment, Chris watched him, but from where Uri was seated he could not see her. Uri asked Joel to draw something relatively simple, and not show it to him. He would try to tell Joel what he'd drawn. This is a well-known magician's trick. The skilled conjurer needs only to follow the movement of the pen or pencil to decipher, more or less, what the subject has sketched. Perhaps this was how he'd pretend he was endowed with some supernatural or ESP power.

As the taping of the show continued, Joel took a pad and pencil and placed them in a way on his lap so that Geller could not see the top of the pencil moving, thus preventing Geller from seeing the direction of the sketching. Joel purposely did not tell Uri that he'd spent years in art school, majoring in cartooning. It took Joel only a few moments to draw a scene, not quite one as simple as Uri had requested. It was Joel's intent not to draw a stick figure, on the chance that many people did, and Uri might guess Joel had done the same. Joel hurriedly sketched a log cabin with a window and a smoking chimney, included several pine trees, some bushes, a bird flying, clouds in the sky, and a boy walking toward a small pond to the right of the cabin. Joel drew the child carrying a pail. Then he quickly turned the pad upside down so Geller had no way to see what he'd drawn, during or after the process.

"Okay. You've drawn the picture," Geller said, seeming to momentarily stare in space. Perhaps he was concentrating. Then he took a piece of paper and a pen to sketch what he telepathically thought Joel had drawn. After a few moments, when he'd finished, they showed each other their respective drawings. Uri Geller had drawn nearly the identical picture Joel had: a house, a tree, a pond, and a boy carrying a rectangular box with a handle. He'd even reproduced the bird correctly. There had been no one else in the room to communicate to him what Joel had drawn. Unless Geller had a complicated system of mirrors or a hidden confederate watching through a secret camera or a hole in the wall or ceiling, who whispered to him through a hidden earpiece, he could not have known what Joel had sketched unless he somehow discerned it telepathically.

There was one more Geller demonstration to come during the program. Joel had asked around the radio station the previous week for anyone who could lend or give him a broken watch or small clock. Geller's claims in his book and TV appearances included his ability to apply his PK or psychokinetic power to repair nonworking timepieces. Joel had borrowed a wristwatch from the president of the radio station that aired his talk show for many years. It was a small, inexpensive white plastic watch that had belonged to the station president's son. The hands on the watch had been overwound so they could no longer turn. Nor could the watch be reset, since the stem couldn't be moved. Joel had no expectation that Geller could possibly do anything with it, and he anticipated that Uri would do what many psychics did, offer some mumbo jumbo about why his psychic vibes were fading or that Venus was no longer aligned with Mars.

Joel handed Geller the broken watch. Uri took it in one hand, turned it back and forth, and moved it from side to side, then returned it to Joel. He had held it for less than a minute and never even touched it with his other hand. To Joel's shock, the watch was working! The stem now turned, and the minute and second hands moved. Most incredibly, the watch was somehow set to the correct time. If Joel had just witnessed tricks, they were among the best he'd ever seen, and this from a person who'd interviewed magicians before. Yet, those experiences had an entirely different feeling about them than Geller's demonstration. After giving that day's events a great deal of thought, Joel admitted that despite his skepticism going in, he had no answer.

Though an eyewitness to Uri Geller's abilities, Joel faced another problem when he returned to the radio station. No one believed Geller had bent the dozen keys, repaired a kid's broken watch, or read his mind. His colleagues reacted to his description of the Geller interview and demonstration with looks that ranged from rolling eyes to condescending smirks. A station engineer told Joel flatly that it was impossible for Geller to use the power of his mind to bend metal or to repair watches and clocks, implying that Joel was either a liar or that he'd hallucinated and failed to see how Geller performed his clever trickery. The worst skeptic was the radio station's president, a sometime cantankerous attorney in his mid-sixties. Although Joel and his boss had always gotten along well, and he'd been at the station since he was a teenager, this time there was no persuading him. He told Joel there was no such thing as psychic powers that could mentally affect a watch. Nor did he believe that Joel had seen the keys behave like molten wax and then freeze into the bent position he was looking at. When asked how the wristwatch was repaired, the president said that Joel must have taken it to "someone" to fix it. What about the keys? Those, Geller or Joel bent themselves. Why? It was to benefit the show. Then he asked for his son's watch back—it was still keeping time—and he walked away without another word. Although Joel was angry at the implication that he'd been dishonest or deceived, he decided to reserve his decision until after he'd seen a magician or two who could explain or duplicate what Geller had done.

Joel's chance came only a few months later, in November 1975. Using his professional name, The Amazing Randi, the Canadian magician had earlier that year written *The Magic of Uri Geller*, a blanket denunciation of Geller. Randi left no doubt about his opinion: Geller was not a psychic. He was a fraud, and anything Uri could demonstrate, so could Randi. He was promoting his exposé, and so Joel and Randi arranged an interview. To accommodate Randi's busy schedule of appearances, they met at his publisher's office in Manhattan. Now Joel would have an opportunity to compare Geller and Randi. Both had made news debating the question of whether Geller was a gifted psychic or a skilled conjurer, and separately, they'd appeared on many major TV talk shows at the time, including the shows of Johnny Carson, Merv Griffin, Mike Douglas, Tom Snyder, and Barbara Walters, to name a few.

Randi was small and bald, with a full beard and a mustache that was quickly turning white. His eyes burned with intensity, and he was obviously enthusiastic about his role as America's premier paranormal debunker. He was cordial and seemed likable as they took their seats behind microphones, facing one another in a quiet room where they would tape the one-hour radio interview. Once underway, they devoted a segment to Randi's book and the reasons he thought Geller was a magician, not a psychic. Randi was a compelling and articulate speaker—he'd once hosted a New York radio talk show. He warmed quickly to his subject, passionately dissecting Uri Geller's career as the "psychic wonder" of the decade. Randi proclaimed he was defending the honor of magicians whose good name Geller had "sullied." Why, even the eminent scientists at SRI had been "hoodwinked" by the "Israeli nightclub magician."

Then came the time when Joel requested of Randi, as he had of Geller, to demonstrate his abilities. That was Randi's major argument: Geller's metal bending and mind reading were magician's tricks that Randi could easily duplicate. His friend Leon Jaroff, then a senior editor at *Time* magazine, wrote that Randi had been able to "duplicate all of Geller's feats, demonstrating that only fast hands and clever psychology were necessary."[24]

Joel had brought kitchen utensils, a man's broken watch he'd found buried in a dresser drawer at home, and a few spare keys he no longer used. Geller had irreparably bent Joel's first set of keys, and since he'd had difficulty replacing some of them, he didn't want a repeat performance. Joel passed a spoon and fork to Randi. He took each in turn, and he rubbed his fingers back and forth at the part where both curved. Joel could see he was exerting pressure on them to bend. Then with his other hand he quickly forced each to a noticeable angle, and announced that he'd bent the silverware just as Geller did. Joel, who had witnessed Uri do something entirely different, suggested to Randi that he had not. But he let the incident pass, hoping to return to it momentarily, while Randi persisted that he accomplished by sleight of hand exactly what Geller had.

What about the keys? Randi explained that he'd have no problem replicating Geller's key bending "trick." All the while Randi was quite animated and talked rapidly in his clipped Canadian accent. Then what Joel saw nearly left him speechless. Perhaps Randi didn't realize how closely Joel was watching him when he took each key and quickly slipped it into a small space in his belt buckle until it bent. Then, without missing a beat, he proclaimed he'd done exactly what Geller did. Was he serious? Joel had no partiality to either Randi or Geller. But in all honesty, Randi had bent the keys by obvious trickery. Joel was almost embarrassed for him, and pointed out that is not what Geller did when he curled Joel's ring of keys while barely touching them. Randi insisted he'd performed the same "trick."

The two went back and forth a few times, and Joel realized to go any further would make him seem rude and overbearing. So he let Randi have the last word, and they moved on to the broken watch portion of the show.

Randi took the thoroughly nonworking watch. He looked at it studiously for a few moments, then turned it up, down, and around, just as Uri Geller had done. Randi resumed his on-air conversation, enthusiastically denouncing Geller, and while he apparently thought Joel was distracted by their interview, Joel saw him move hurriedly to pull the stem on the watch so the hour and second hands appeared to turn. But that only moved the two hands on the watch in unison. It did not restart the timepiece. When he reluctantly returned it to Joel, it was as dead as when he first held it in his hand. Nonetheless, Randi pronounced that he'd successfully repaired the watch and that it was again running. Joel told him, as graciously as he could, that the watch remained broken. Again, that wasn't what Geller had demonstrated. Randi remained adamant that he'd demonstrated exactly what Geller had. He had not, but Joel allowed him the final word in the interview. Incidentally, Randi never offered to duplicate Geller's feat of being able to reproduce an unseen drawing.

Randi had been true to his word when he said that what he demonstrated were the tricks stage magicians employ. The problem was he hadn't been a very good magician. Perhaps he'd just had an off day, despite his boasts. Joel realized that just because he'd seen the way Randi performed each demonstration, that did not lead automatically to the conclusion that while Randi was a magician, Geller was a phenomenal psychic. It was possible that Geller was a far better magician than Randi. However, Randi had not told the truth. He had not replicated Geller's feats as he promised, no matter how loudly he insisted otherwise. Joel's experience with The Amazing Randi had been a disappointment.

But it was obvious that James Randi was bright, glib, quick, and obsessed to win to his side anyone he could, in order to steamroll over Uri Geller who'd ironically made Randi a lot better known than he was. Randi had no intention of slowing his crusade. Debunkers can be mighty determined fellows, convinced of the righteousness of their cause that paranormal and religious beliefs must be eradicated. If Randi had to bend metal—or the truth—on his self-appointed mission to explode the paranormal into tiny little pieces, so be it. He'd openly bragged that he was a trickster and illusionist, and he meant it.

A couple of words in Randi's book, *The Magic of Uri Geller*, were disturbing, and neither had to do with his opinions of Geller as a psychic fraud. Perhaps they were more a reflection of Randi's biases then any arguments about the paranormal. Throughout his book, Randi reminds readers often that Geller is Israeli, raising the question for some about whether Randi was revealing unconscious anti-Semitism with using such derisive expressions as the "Israeli Wonder," although it is unclear what relevance Geller's nationality would have to claims of the supernatural. Another frequently used word was "miracle," implying that Geller's PK and telepathy somehow sprung from a religious experience. The word *miracle* is verboten in the language of debunkers who consider themselves rationalists. A miracle falls within the realm of the supernatural, and, therefore, as with any religious belief, it cannot be tolerated. It must be discredited.

Curiously, debunkers have dealt far more harshly with Geller than have many scientists. One of those who commented on his experience with Geller was the late, noted rocket scientist Dr. Wernher von Braun, long ago dubbed "the father of the U.S. space program," who had worked for NASA, and during World War II played a major role in the development of the German V-1 and V-2 rockets when he worked at a missile facility on the Baltic coast that was also a concentration camp. His scientific credentials were extraordinary, and author Jonathan Margolis included the following quote from Braun in his biography of Uri Geller: "Geller has bent my ring in the palm of my hand without touching it personally. I have no scientific explanation for the phenomena."[25]

Margolis also told about another scientist, Dr. Wilbur Franklin, physicist at Kent State University in Ohio, who, after testing Geller, commented, "The evidence based on metallurgical analysis of fractured surfaces produced by Geller indicates that a paranormal influence must have been operative in the formation of fractures."

Then there were various members of the media who'd each watched Geller only lightly touch silverware, and saw their metal utensils weaken and droop, as if they'd melted. For others, Geller caused their keys to bend or curve. But magicians and debunkers were ready to refute any and all eyewitness accounts: those who believed that Geller had paranormal powers were gullible, naïve, ignorant; they'd fallen for Geller's tricks. How could anyone possibly trust the observations of rocket scientist Wernher von Braun when The Amazing Randi assured the public he knew so much more? But, not even all magicians shared Randi's negative opinion of Geller. One frequently told incident concerned well-known Danish magician Leo Leslie who'd tested Geller in Denmark, and concluded he was a legitimate psychic.[26]

John Taylor was a noted British mathematician and author of *Superminds*. In that 1978 book, Taylor said he believed Uri Geller was genuine. He theorized that when "metal is 'paranormally' bent," it could be the result of a "redistribution of 'strain energy,' and most probably, a lowering of the energy in the area of bending." Later, for reasons that were unclear, Taylor reversed his opinion about Geller's abilities.[27]

Few of us were raised to believe psychic powers are genuine. Therefore, when they occur, we are psychologically and intellectually unprepared, and we seek explanations that fit more comfortably within the limits of our respective belief systems. Often, that becomes a search for some "rational" explanation, assuming we've been duped or somehow deluded by a paranormal incident. Perhaps we were hallucinating or imagining a so-called psychic experience. That is what we've been taught and, in turn, we teach our children. Debunkers have long worked to reinforce our doubts about the paranormal, doing their best to trample it, on the way to their larger goal: humanism, their nonreligious philosophy. In other words, marginalizing religion, if not erasing it completely, is the ultimate intent. A secular society would have no need for traditional religious or spiritual beliefs that many skeptics and debunkers regard as nothing more than magical thinking or medieval superstition.

Author Jonathan Margolis, who candidly admitted his skepticism, attempted his own test of Uri Geller's telepathic abilities when they met for a demonstration. Margolis was accompanied by his fourteen-year-old son, David. Geller asked the youngster to draw a picture of his choice, and then place it "face down" so Uri could not see it. Next, Geller instructed David, "Try to transmit the picture to me mentally." It was very similar to the mind-reading demonstration Geller had done for many others.

However, Margolis thought of a novel way of satisfying himself that Geller was psychic by attempting to "sabotage the supposed ESP demonstration by thinking of spurious images and beaming them in Geller's direction," he said. If Geller were truly telepathic, would "signals" from Jonathan interfere with those from his son? Whose mind would Geller read, the son or the skeptical father—if either of them? The elder Margolis thought intently about "hippopotamuses, dollar signs, and Stars of David," apparently the first random objects that came to him.

To Jonathan Margolis's surprise, Geller unexpectedly told him to stop "all that junk" because it was interfering with him reading young David's mind. Then Uri proceeded to tell the boy what he'd drawn: a stick figure. It seemed to Margolis that Geller had read the minds of both him and his son. Incidentally, when Margolis looked at Uri's drawing, it was so identical to the one his son had sketched that when they were measured, the two drawings were exactly the same size. Geller's next demonstration was not unlike so many others, a spoon Margolis brought curled. He and his son were stunned as they watched the silverware bend after Uri held it lightly between two fingers. When Margolis took back the spoon, there was no evidence that any corrosive chemical had been applied, nor was it warm or hot to the touch.

There is an interesting story Margolis told about Geller's apparent precognitive abilities. He predicted an earthquake on the Pacific Coast, just a day before there was a sizable one on Mexico's west coast. Geller also foresaw a plane crash and explosion only a couple of days before the TWA Flight 800 crash off Long Island that killed all aboard in July 1996.

Debunkers summarily dismiss reports in which a psychic or medium successfully demonstrates a genuine paranormal ability, even when it is for someone both skeptical and observant. To combat such credible eyewitness accounts, debunkers have developed their own pat response that serves a two-fold purpose. One is to convince people who've had paranormal experiences that they are victims of self-deception or chicanery on the part of a psychic or medium. The second objective is to prevent or discourage serious consideration of parapsychology by maligning and ridiculing all psi events as irrational and anecdotal, saying they were based on superstition, pseudoscience, trickery, or hoax, and that they should be vehemently challenged and opposed by any means necessary.[28]

A prime example of this were Randi's many appearances as Johnny Carson's guest on *The Tonight Show*. There are several versions of how James Randi met the late TV personality Johnny Carson (1925–2005). What's most important is that they took a liking to each other, and the famed *Tonight Show* host offered Randi an incredible platform to reach millions as the "Grand Inquisitor" against the heresy of all paranormal claims. Randi made more than thirty *Tonight Show* appearances, a remarkable number. He'd obviously impressed Carson, who was once a magician himself.

Johnny Carson, as a boy growing up in Nebraska, had a fascination with magic. He became an accomplished amateur magician in his teens, and the interest remained all his life. Randi ingratiated himself with Carson, and that led to the national celebrity Carson afforded Randi, not as a magician but as a psychic debunker.

Without question, Randi's proudest achievement was the night in 1973 when Uri Geller was Carson's guest, and Randi, although he wasn't present, arranged to unsettle Geller so that in his appearance on *The Tonight Show*, which ran more than twenty minutes, Geller was unable to perform so much as one psychic feat. It seems curious in retrospect that Geller did not realize he would be facing hostility from Carson, a self-professed skeptic. Uri had been warned in advance by friends about Carson's predisposition against the paranormal. But it's likely the idea of appearing on the immensely popular *Tonight Show* was irresistible. The occasion proved to be a major embarrassment for Geller, and although he bravely moved ahead, his lack of success that night impacted him negatively, somewhat diminishing the public's belief in him. It didn't help that

Carson, a master of comedic facial expressions, rolled his eyes in ridicule as Geller failed.

How Randi was able to bring about Geller's failure on *The Tonight Show* is not certain, since we have only Randi's explanation. But making a giant leap of faith and assuming Randi was truthful, he'd arranged with Carson's staff to exert the tightest controls possible. One demand that Randi issued concerned Geller confidant Shipi Shtrang. Randi had long alleged that Shipi was Uri's confederate—although it was never clear how—and without Shipi nearby, Geller failed to perform. Randi constantly harped about some secret code or tricks the two had concocted. Take Shipi away, he said, and Geller became professionally impotent. But that wasn't true. Many people who'd witnessed or tested Geller swore he demonstrated successfully without Shipi anywhere in sight. But Randi was adamant, and Shipi was not allowed on the set of the Carson show.

Curiously, some of the abilities that Geller was unable to demonstrate on *The Tonight Show* were ones he'd been successful with at SRI. What would explain his achievement there, and his failure with Carson? During Joel's interview with Geller, he asked him that question. Uri answered that he sensed Carson's hostility from the outset, and perhaps that contributed to his discomfort. He also suggested that if he had accomplished PK and telepathic feats through trickery or deception, they would have worked during the Carson show. For example, one Randi allegation was that Geller had small but powerful magnets and other "micro devices" hidden on his person that aided in creating the PK effect on metal objects. The fact that he was unsuccessful in such an important venue, Geller said, proved he was genuinely psychic, and sometimes his ability foundered.

This also suggests something that has long frustrated parapsychologists: the unpredictability of psi. Debunkers have repeatedly seized on that to attack psychic phenomena, contending that if it were truly of a scientific nature, it would be consistent and repeatable, a fallacious argument. There are innumerable scientific phenomena that do not respond on command, as quantum physics reveals, and many that are still inexplicable.[29]

Randi said he'd controlled every aspect of Geller's *Tonight Show* appearance, and since the magician was not present at the Carson show, his directions were conveyed long distance. Uri's failure was sufficient for Randi to boast that it was because he'd prevented Geller's trickery. The implication was that he'd "exposed" Geller, another falsehood.[30] Ironically, while Randi constantly alleged collusion between Geller and Shipi, he conveniently overlooked whether he and Carson had conspired to discredit Geller in the context of discrediting the paranormal. In fact, Carson, through his own charitable foundation, later donated one hundred thousand dollars to Randi's debunking efforts.

While his fellow debunkers were ecstatic about Geller's failure and heaped praise on Randi, the *Tonight Show* debacle left Geller understandably depressed. But despite Randi's exaggerations that the episode ended Geller's celebrity and credibility in the United States, Uri did not cut and run. He continued making appearances, and while it is true that he later kept a lower profile as a psychic, he remained in the United States until the mid-1980s. He said he stepped back from the grind of constant psychic work because he'd grown tired of the pressure, pace, and travel, as well as the frequent and unfair attacks against him. By then, however, Geller had the satisfaction of achieving "super-celebrity" status—a rare accomplishment for any psychic.

Left unanswered were questions about the extent to which Geller's powers were employed by the CIA or the Israeli top-secret intelligence agency, Mossad. Whether either or both governments were simply curious about Geller's abilities, or were sufficiently impressed to employ him is not certain; he has never said. However, over the years, Geller and others have hinted at some connection between him and intelligence work. At the very least, the U.S. government had funded the tests he underwent at SRI. But it is probable that his involvement with the CIA went beyond that, and interest by the Mossad would not be a surprise.

In addition to the SRI, Geller was also tested at the Lawrence Livermore Laboratory in northern California, one of the nation's top-secret nuclear weapons research installations. According to the book *Remote Viewers: The Secret History of America's Psychic Spies*, by Jim Schnabel, Geller had once been secretly tested there. Livermore scientists and engineers, working on their own time, were especially attentive to his purported PK powers. According to Schnabel, there was some uneasiness that Geller might pose a threat to national security. How? What if his psychokinetic energy was genuine, and capable of moving or dislocating even a small amount of nuclear substance by only a few inches? That could be enough to trigger off, or sabotage a nuclear weapon. Remember, at SRI, Geller's metal-bending tests were inconclusive. At Livermore, the outcome was decidedly better. Uri not only curled metal, he also erased computer disks by merely touching or holding them.

In his book, Schnabel also told of several Livermore personnel who experienced strange psychological phenomena, including "hallucinations and visions" they felt were a result of Geller's visit. The most bizarre incident concerned an audiotape recording found to contain a "metallic" sounding voice that could not be identified or deciphered. One of the few discernible words apparently mentioned a secret code for a classified project. Was it the result of some psychic manifestation—or something more mundane? Perhaps it was a hoax—someone's idea of a joke or a trick. But who was responsible?

When Geller moved permanently, it was to London, where he

settled comfortably with Hannah and their two children, Daniel and Natalie. He now had the wealth that afforded him the freedom to delve into other projects and interests. Once he'd given up the spoon-bending business, debunkers were quick to proclaim, "Geller is through." That was wishful thinking on their part. To the contrary, Geller remained busy writing books and columns, among myriad other projects, including TV specials and a popular Web site.

One new enterprise Uri engaged in was dowsing, the ancient practice of psychically detecting underground deposits of water and other substances. He was employed by a number of companies that sought subterranean accumulations of oil and minerals, work that was largely kept confidential because of the concern that using a dowser might not sit well with many conservative corporate types. However, there were several published articles, throughout the 1980s and 1990s that supported Uri's claims of success. "I use my dowsing skills to locate mineral and oil deposits, and have become a multimillionaire as a result," Geller told *Psychic World* magazine in 1997.

In 1997, a British TV documentary titled *Secrets of the Psychics* dealt with Uri's abilities. As is typical when network TV approaches anything about the paranormal, for purposes of what is considered "balance," skeptics and debunkers are included. In the case of a TV show about Uri Geller, it was no surprise that the opposition included appearances by several of Britain's top skeptics—and America's premier Geller debunker, The Amazing Randi. They said what they always did, that Geller was a fraud.[31] It should be noted that despite the constant barrage of accusations, Uri Geller was never "debunked." His ability to bend metal remains a mystery. In that way his story is similar to the nineteenth-century medium D. D. Home, against whom there were always accusations of trickery, although no deception was ever proven.

Sometimes, The Amazing Randi displayed a tendency to carry his zealotry too far, and one adventure backfired on him. Still flushed with national recognition that he debunked Geller, Randi created something he called "Project Alpha." His idea was to take two young magicians and train them to pretend they were psychics, capable of psychokinesis, the ability that had put Geller on the map. Randi's hope was to embarrass the entire field of psychical research, once it was revealed that a couple of youthful conjurers had hoaxed supposedly trained parapsychologists. The two Randi cohorts cultivated a relationship with inexperienced staffers at the McDonnell Laboratory for Psychical Research at Washington University in St. Louis. Then they spent the next two years continuing their charade, by design, deceiving the researchers in every way they could.

When the results of testing the two hoaxers were presented to a national convention of parapsychologists, the group, like worthy bloodhounds, overwhelmingly detected the fraud. The parapsychologists were furious at the deception, and the waste of time and resources the magician had cost. Randi had not fooled them. Even *The New York Times,* no friend of the paranormal, questioned the ethics of Randi's attempted hoax. But instead of acknowledging that some of America's best parapsychologists, many of them scientists and professors, had recognized psychic chicanery, Randi doubled down. He actually held a press conference, sponsored by *Discover* magazine, to claim he'd bamboozled the parapsychologists. It apparently did not bother him one bit that he had not. In actuality, he'd failed to show that psi researchers would buy any psychic claim thrown at them. The parapsychologists had displayed their integrity, much to the dismay of Randi and his fellow debunkers.

Randi wasn't exactly banished to a remote island for his bungled hoax. He had plenty of support within the ranks of skeptics, and many applauded him, calling Project Alpha, "a daring but important exposé." Some reinvigorated debunkers boldly stated that parapsychology must be "stopped at any cost."[32]

Uri Geller moved to England, but his story didn't end once he left the United States. Nor did Randi disappear off Joel Martin's map. Joel was destined to speak to both Randi and Uri again in that curious, synchronistic way lives cross when it's least expected. In 1983, Randi's publisher called to ask that he be a guest on Joel's then nightly radio show to promote something he'd recently written. However, when Randi was told that nationally recognized parapsychologist Stephen Kaplan (1940–1995) would be on the same program, he canceled his appearance. Randi and Kaplan had a long-running feud, not unlike the verbal battle Kaplan had throughout the 1970s with anyone who supported the *Amityville Horror* alleged haunted-house claims. So instead, Joel invited Randi to appear alone but to no avail. Perhaps Randi expected a Kaplan ambush at the last minute, but Joel would never have allowed that.

Prior to the aborted appearance, Kaplan said that he and Randi had had an unpleasant incident on a boat ride, a publicity event arranged by a then popular network TV series both had appeared on. As the two spoke, the physically imposing Kaplan pressed in against the much smaller Randi until Randi was leaning backward over the boat's railing. Kaplan asked the magician why he refused to admit that any psychic phenomenon was genuine. Randi's answer was abrupt but revealing, "Kaplan, you do your shtick, and I'll do mine!" Randi then pushed past Kaplan and angrily walked away.

One evening, Randi found himself at a social function, where among the guests was a psychic who'd demonstrated remarkable ability. Randi did not know or recognize the young man, who attempted to introduce himself to the bearded magician, and then made the mistake of offering Randi several pieces of information of a deeply personal nature that he said he'd obtained through ESP. Randi stared and told him, "Go to hell," then turned and hurried off.

In retrospect and in all fairness, James Randi did perform a valuable service when he called out several self-described faith healers, especially such "televangelists" as Peter Popoff, Oral Roberts, and Pat Robertson. Psychic and faith healers have long been a controversial subject, and Randi moved to reveal what he believed was "deception and chicanery" on their part. In pursuing faith healers, Randi was positioned to hit two home runs. Psychic healing and faith healing are not identical, but are certainly sufficiently similar, so that at the same time psychic fraud was being uncovered, a mighty swipe was taken at Christian fundamentalism, where most faith healers are ensconced.

The exposé of the Reverend Peter Popoff arguably earned Randi his most well-deserved attention during the 1980s. Popoff, a California-based televangelist, professed to be a faith healer, and his success was no doubt aided by his stunning ability to call out in advance the names of people in his audience and exactly what ailment each suffered. Then, with a great display of emotion, he would pray, exhort out illnesses, bless, and miraculously heal those he called before him—and raise millions of dollars in donations for what he said was his ministry in the process.

Popoff contended that the information came to him directly from God. But Randi suspected fakery was responsible for the reverend's seemingly supernatural gift, and this time he was correct. Randi discovered that Popoff wore a small hidden earpiece secretly connected to his wife, who fed him the data based on cards that audience members filled out before taking their seats at Popoff's claimed "healing crusades," which drew as many as several thousand people at a time. Thus, by knowing beforehand a person's first name, based on where they sat, and what their specific malady was, thousands came to believe that Popoff had a remarkable divinely-inspired ability.

When Johnny Carson gave Randi the opportunity to show a videotape of Popoff's activities on *The Tonight Show*, it meant millions of viewers were able to see the deceit on network television. Popoff rode out the storm of criticism; in fact, he claimed the publicity was helpful. He may have been correct; two decades later Reverend Popoff's ministry—and its "miraculous healings"—were still going strong.

However, as he often did, some said Randi went too far. No serious parapsychologist or clergy with an ounce of ethics would defend Popoff's charade. But Randi used the Popoff revelations to claim that all faith and psychic healers were fraudulent; that is not what the evidence has shown.

Likely because of the dishonesty he uncovered about some faith healers, in 1986, Randi was a winner of a prestigious MacArthur Foundation grant, often given to scientists and scholars. The award amounted to $272,000 tax free, no questions asked. Randi, who lived in New Jersey for many years, relocated to Fort Lauderdale, Florida, to continue his debunking work, under the auspice of his own educational foundation.

By the 1990s, Uri Geller had become more aggressive against those who'd made careers by attacking him. Geller called the psychic debunkers "miserable people."

The conflict between Geller and Randi had dragged on for two decades into the mid-1990s. In many respects, this conflict mirrored the larger conflict taking place between debunkers and spiritual believers as well as UFO researchers since the 1950s—inspired, we believe, by national security organizations looking to discredit anything that smacked of personal empowerment. In 1980, Randi himself published a book called *Flim-Flam!*, reprinted by Prometheus in paperback in 1982 with an introduction by famed science fiction writer Isaac Asimov, about his opinion on all psychic claims, in which he predictably again attacked Geller and the scientists who dared test him. The Asimov connection, as well as the Carl Sagan connection in *The Faith Healers* (Prometheus, 1989), is very interesting when looked at through the prism of ufology. Some UFO researchers argue that Carl Sagan was inside the loop of highly classified Special Access Projects regarding the UFO phenomenon, but could stay inside only by debunking UFO claims to the public at large.

Isaac Asimov is another story. There are those UFO researchers who believe that extraterrestrials (ETs) are not just out there, but down here among us, unseen because they operate to control our society completely beneath the radar. Taking positions of key influence, these extraterrestrials, some UFO researchers say, are able to manipulate events on a macro scale, maneuvering human society to a point of their own choosing. This is exactly the plot of Asimov's seminal and brilliant original trilogy, *Foundation* (Doubleday, 1963). Although Asimov later wrote additional novels to the story, the original three books detail how the Foundationers worked to bring mathematician Hari Selden's plan of psychohistory to fruition. It's also funny that Asimov's two major fictional theories, robotics and psychohistory, actually turned into academic pursuits. Yet, if Asimov was not writing fiction at all, but reality because he had been brought into the inner circle, perhaps by the ETs themselves, then what better cover than to fictionalize it. This is all speculation, of course, but it would make sense that a national security organization or a nongovernmental organization (NGO) tasked to deal with ETs here on Earth would use scientists and popular writers like Carl Sagan—who also wrote the intriguing novel *Contact* (Pocket, 1997), later a feature film starring Jodie Foster—and J. Allen Hynek and Isaac Asimov to marginalize the truth by fictionalizing it or straight-out debunking it by calling a

1966 UFO sighting in Hillsdale, Michigan, nothing more than "swamp gas."

Curiously, neither in *Flim-Flam!* nor in any of his other books, did Randi ever satisfactorily or specifically explain how—if it was a trick—Geller bent metal. Nor could Randi ever duplicate Geller's feats in exactly the same way he did. In fact, as author and army remote viewer Paul H. Smith explains in his book, *Reading the Enemy's Mind* (Tom Doherty Associates, 2005), when Army Major General Albert N. Stubblebine III, was first introduced to the concept of psychic-driven spoon bending, he delighted party guests by demonstrating the feat with his mind and teaching others to do it. These were not tricks, Paul Smith wrote, but a skill. If Randi truly believed that Geller had tricked the world into thinking he could bend spoons with his mind, Randi never was able to demonstrate it in the same way that Geller did. Subsequently, there was a reasoned answer to Randi in a book by the late D. Scott Rogo, a prolific writer and thoughtful parapsychologist, in *Psychic Breakthroughs Today,* in 1987, that was supportive of Geller's PK and telepathic abilities. Rogo also explained in a radio interview that there was continuing animosity between Geller and Randi.

Back in 1995, an old friend in Hollywood had become engaged to Ben Webster, the man who introduced Velcro to North America and who was one of Canada's wealthiest and most successful venture capitalists. He always had extensive involvement in paranormal research, largely behind the scenes. At this time Geller was still in an ongoing battle against the debunkers. By then, Randi had resigned from CSICOP because his ongoing litigation made it more prudent to separate himself from the debunkers group. Both Randi and Paul Kurtz agreed that this would prevent CSICOP from being drawn into Randi's legal issues.

Ben Webster had a quiet, but persistent, involvement in the paranormal. More than a passing interest, psychic phenomena had long been a personal passion and intellectual journey for him. He was a visionary, a man who saw the potential of Velcro, an original investor in everything from the Internet and dot-com businesses that mushroomed in California's Silicon Valley to several pharmaceutical companies, and held financial interests in valuable real estate, vineyards, mountain bikes, nuclear energy, a textile museum, and media, including the creation of a major Canadian TV station and an American video company. He'd also been involved in the initial planning of the Toronto Blue Jays, Canada's major league baseball team.

Tall, handsome, and patrician, as befit a multimillionaire—or billionaire, no one could say how much Ben Webster was actually worth—he could be aloof and distant. But when he relaxed and opened up to share his incredible life and accomplishments, the paranormal was at the top of the list. Because of Ben's involvement with mainstream financial companies and his dealings with investors and investment bankers, he purposely kept a low profile as a paranormal researcher to avoid the inevitable criticism and ridicule from the staid business world that he was "weird" for his interests in the occult and supernatural. For example, few knew that he often utilized such ancient divination tools as the *I Ching* for employment decisions in his enormously successful venture capitalist business. His wife, Margaret Wendt, herself highly sensitive and intuitive, brought her psychic skills to the corporate table, advising on everything from investments to personnel.

A Princeton University graduate in engineering and a convert to Buddhism, Ben Webster, with no publicity attached to it, had for years been one of the major private benefactors of monies for serious psychic research. The impressive list of those he endowed is too long to name, but it included investigation of mediumship, healing, psychokinesis, divination, ESP, and ancient mysteries, among many other disciplines. He had long friendships with such famed twentieth-century mediums as Arthur Ford and Eileen Garrett, and personally knew the Dalai Lama, among other world leaders, and famed literary figures such as Aldous Huxley. He was also the founder of the Toronto Society for Psychical Research (TSPR) and the New Horizons Foundation, which quickly became among the most prestigious and respected organizations of its kind in North America, attracting major scientific and academic figures to convene for the serious study of psi for more than twenty years, from the 1960s through the 1980s.[33]

In addition to his personal involvement with major figures in the world of the paranormal, Webster also had a long and close friendship with Uri Geller. Apparently Ben had supported Uri's efforts to sue James Randi. As part of his efforts, Ben had arranged for an investigation into James Randi's past in an attempt to impugn his credibility as an objective expert about paranormal claims. The investigation found leftwing links and evidence of at least one arrest in Randi's past. Was it possible that Randi's crusade against the paranormal was motivated, at least in part, and perhaps even unconsciously, by a desire to appease government interest at a time when charges of leftwing associations could destroy careers? Although this was unproven and perhaps unprovable, it is clear that the government would also have had an interest in debunking the paranormal, seeing a threat if the abilities Geller claimed to possess were present, or were widely believed to be achievable (to one degree or another) in all citizens.

Indeed, there is wide latitude for rampant speculation about political conspiracies to debunk the paranormal, especially the question of UFOs. First of all, apart from the military and political paranoia about the threat of Soviet or Maoist Communism that threatened the United States around the world during the Cold War, a paranoia corroborated by the release of the KGB documents after the fall of the Soviet Union, there was another paranoia that spiritualists were a sect of "one worlders," people who were so naïve politically they would have rolled over for self-proclaimed egalitarian worker states in the interests of world peace. Paradoxically, Communists were hardly spiritualists. Religion is an opiate, Karl Marx, wrote, and in China, Mao Zedong was often referred to as "the living God." Accordingly, atheism had become a firmly held tenet of Communism by the 1950s, and a ripe field for any government agency to plow when it came to enlisting debunkers in the cause of fighting Communism by also fighting spiritualism because in their minds Communism and spiritualism were anti-Christian. For American debunkers, as we mentioned earlier, the paranormal and religion are virtually one and the same. For many, neither has a place in their vision of a secular society, the dream of humanists and atheists.

Secularization is the "process by which sectors of society and culture are removed from the domination of religious institutions and symbols," wrote Peter Berger in *The Sacred Canopy* (Doubleday, 1967). What philosophers and writers have called "secular theology has deep roots in the great intellectual and social forces that forged twentieth-century experience: Sigmund Freud and Karl Marx," noted author Robert Elwood. "Religion is an illusion," Freud had said. Obviously a stubborn one, since repeated surveys and polls reveal that nine out of ten Americans believe in God, and three of every four believe in the paranormal, according to a Gallup poll.[34] Since no one is forced to have a particular religious belief in America, you are as free, under the First Amendment to the Constitution, to be an atheist as you are to practice Christian fundamentalism, Orthodox Judaism, Buddhism, or Islam. The First Amendment, under its Establishment Clause, expressly prohibits the federal government from imposing any religion upon U.S. citizens.

However, for some reason, American debunkers have been unable or unwilling to separate parapsychology from theology, unlike the former Soviet Union where psychic research continued for decades, and was never confused with religion or God, since both were officially banned. That does not suggest support for totalitarian, state-sponsored paranormal inquiry. It simply suggests that Paul Kurtz never intended for CSICOP to objectively examine psychic phenomena. He'd headed the American Humanist Association prior to founding CSICOP. His practice was to use the paranormal as a whipping boy, a subterfuge to preach the creation of a rationalist secular humanist society that scorns the belief in any otherworldly devotional exercise. He was free to do so, of course, but his demonizing of those who wanted to consider the "normal" in the "paranormal" was more irrational than rational.

Debunkers have repeatedly referred to psi as "pseudoscience." But they have purposely obfuscated the definition of science. Not all branches of science can fit the narrow confines assigned by debunkers. If the paranormal is "junk science," because it is difficult to replicate and measure, what is to be said about psychology? That is defined as the "scientific study of the human mind." Yet we cannot predict specific behaviors on a daily basis, nor do courts routinely allow the citing of prior bad behaviors to influence a jury regarding a current behavior.

Chemistry, for example, allows for rigid experiments with repeatable results. Can one say the same for meteorology? Weather forecasting is hardly as precise a science as we would all like. What about seismology, the study of earthquakes? That also is a science that wrestles constantly with the difficulty of predictions. Not even the seismologists were able to predict the earthquake that struck the Northeast from Washington, D.C., through New England on August 23, 2011. And the engineers building the nuclear facility at Fukishima in Japan never took seriously enough the prospect of an earthquake and resulting tsunami that not only closed the plant down but also caused a meltdown and the resulting release of deadly radiation. Obviously, every branch of science cannot be identically defined or subjected to the same test conditions.

The posturing by debunkers against psi as "junk science" or "pseudoscience" is disingenuous. Worse, it has often become an obstruction to serious scientific research into the nature of psychic phenomena. Equally frustrating is the considerable amount of time wasted answering and justifying psi to a group that will never be satisfied with any evidence because they have prejudged the outcome. Why look at the scientific evidence, the physical trace and photographic evidence substantiating claims of UFO encounters when you have already said the UFOs do not exist and therefore there can be no evidence?

For no matter how strict the conditions are for any test or experiment of the paranormal, debunkers will immediately deride the results and insist that "tighter scientific controls" were needed. Thus, no matter how far parapsychologists go, the debunkers will demand it is not far enough. They move the goalposts at their convenience. Their repeated criticism of test conditions as never sufficiently rigorous implies that positive results for psi can only be achieved by some deception or fraud, a charge that modern debunkers rarely support with actual evidence. In taking that rather dark and cynical approach, debunkers who march to the tune of CSICOP have raised as many questions about their own integrity as they have about paranormal claims. It is no stretch to argue that if an obdurate skeptic or debunker has a psychic experience, he will not hesitate to deny it.

Dennis Rawlins, an astrophysicist and one of the founders of CSICOP in 1976, who later exposed the "Starbaby scandal," came to the same sorry conclusion. Rawlins became disenchanted with CSICOP's eagerness to debunk all paranormal claims, regardless of the evidence. When statistics meant to debunk astrology instead seemed to favor it, something Paul Kurtz never anticipated, he falsified the data about the so-called Mars Effect. That prompted Rawlins to reveal the CSICOP disgrace in a *Fate* magazine article in October 1981. He wrote: "I now believe that if a flying saucer landed in the backyard of a leading anti-UFO spokesman, he might hide the incident from the public."

Another misleading technique frequently employed by debunkers is to blur past and recent history. Because spiritualism was rife with fraud during the nineteenth century, debunkers say we can assume the same is true today. But there are vast differences between séances during the Victorian era and the readings or consultations given by psychics and mediums in the past several decades.

For example, in the séance parlors of the 1800s, lighting, at its best, was poor. Neither oil lamps nor gaslight could illuminate a room to anywhere near the brightness that electricity later provided. A disreputable psychic or medium in, say, the 1870s had a far better chance of fooling paying customers with such wondrous physical phenomena as flying bugles, bouquets, tipping tables, and even alleged spirit materializations. Clever trickery in dimly lighted rooms persuaded many gullible people that they'd witnessed genuine psychic or spirit phenomena. But, even in that simpler era, countless charlatans were exposed.

Compare that with Uri Geller, or one of several mediums in recent years who have demonstrated their paranormal abilities to millions of people watching them on TV or in personal appearances. It's difficult to fathom how Geller, for example, could have repeatedly fooled both live and TV audiences over a period of many years. The same is true for mediums such as George Anderson, whose accuracy in countless thousands of predictions has been seen by millions on TV, and repeatedly tested and scrutinized.

When Anderson was on a Boston TV program in 1988 promoting

Joel Martin's book about Anderson's life and career, *We Don't Die*, Dr. Ray Hyman, a psychologist, a frequent CSICOP spokesman, and a founding member, challenged him. Hyman insisted he could imitate Anderson's so-called cold reading, an expression used by debunkers to explain away mediums' abilities as little more than clever guesswork. There on live TV, Hyman gave it his best effort but failed, in stark contrast to Anderson's remarkable accuracy with anonymous subjects. That's the same Ray Hyman who in the mid-1990s, at the government's behest, evaluated many years of CIA-funded psychic research, and found the CIA's efforts a failure. Whether or not his conclusions were colored by preconceived notions, they advanced two government objectives. First, it would get the government out of the psi business. Second, even if the CIA did remain in the psi business, debunking it and publicly shutting it down was the best way to confuse the Soviets into thinking we were no longer practicing psychic spying.

It's also not hard to understand why most traditional psychologists, especially those in clinical practice, reject claims of the paranormal out of hand. If one looks in the psychologist's diagnostic handbook, the *Diagnostic and Statistical Manual of Mental Disorders* (DSM), one will see there are no itemized billing codes for anything having to do with the paranormal. Medicine, psychology and psychiatry are medical practices, about diagnosing pathological conditions. No pathogen, no cause for medical treatment. Consequently, those seeking medical help for paranormal or otherworldly experiences either have to fit into a medically defined condition or be accused of faking, and that, too, could be a medical condition. See a ghost? Either you're suffering under some delusion or have eaten a piece of underdone potato, as Ebenezer Scrooge once described it to the ghost of Jacob Marley on Christmas Eve. Experience an alien abduction? Probably sleep paralysis, many academics will tell you.

As for Kurtz, he was once asked by *Omni* magazine to comment on Anderson's startling psychic gift. The magazine's reporter said Kurtz was "evasive," apparently not eager to confront the mountain of evidence in the medium's favor. Finally, the persistent reporter forced a reply from Kurtz to the effect that Anderson likely employed "mass hypnosis" to convince subjects he was accurate. That explanation was as ludicrous as it was untrue. The reporter said she had the distinct feeling that CSICOP really did not want to answer. Was it because the Kurtz group couldn't bring itself to admit that Anderson was repeatedly tested and genuinely psychic?

Another CSICOP founding member, Martin Gardner, was a columnist for *Scientific American* for many years, and long an outspoken critic of psychic research. In their book *The Mind Race*, authors Russell Targ and Keith Harary told how Gardner "was invited to discuss his accusations in a public debate with a psi researcher." But Gardner turned down the invitation, saying he "did not know enough about psi experiments, was not up to date on the subject, and therefore would certainly lose the debate."

With respect to what paranormal researchers call eyewitness evidence, debunkers dismiss all psychic experiences as "anecdotal," belittling its scientific value even though eyewitness evidence, if deemed credible by a finder of fact, can send an accused party to prison. But statistics tell us there are millions of paranormal incidents of many types taking place. It's hard to fathom that hundreds of millions of Americans have all lied, hallucinated, or fabricated such psi episodes as apparitions, spirit phenomena, telepathy, clairvoyance, premonitions, precognition, near-death experiences, UFO encounters, and even photographic evidence, among others. Equally curious is why innumerable psi incidents bear striking similarities to each other, regardless of where they take place or to whom. The commonalities suggest that something more than imagination is at work. Many millions of so-called psi anecdotes form a substantial body of evidence that something is occurring that should not be ignored.

Curiously, while debunkers and skeptics insist that hundreds of millions of paranormal experiences are worthless as evidence, in the criminal justice system, one witness is sometimes sufficient to convict someone of a crime. So, we are willing to take the word of a single individual in a court of law, while at the same time, ignoring multitudes of witnesses to the paranormal.

Admittedly, parapsychology has long suffered a serious problem with language, much of which is stigmatized. For skeptics and debunkers this has provided a convenient opportunity to reinforce blatant negativity by lumping vocabulary together, until there is utter confusion on the part of the public and many in the media. For example, most debunkers continue to employ the pejorative word *occult,* knowing that is rarely if ever used anymore by serious parapsychologists. The use of such words as *miracle* and *supernatural* to describe paranormal events is meant to blur the line with religious experiences. Neither is to be tolerated, according to the skeptical worldview. On the subject of confusion, professional debunkers have purposely made a hodgepodge of the paranormal so that "fortune teller," "medium," "monsters," "UFOs," "astrology," "alternative medicine," "near-death experiences," "ESP," and "extraterrestrials," all become part of one mixed-up mess. Serious paranormal researchers are usually ignored, lumped together with supermarket tabloid fiction, or passed off as "spooky" Halloween ghost hunters.

The term *supernatural* can be particularly onerous when applied to psi. The word implies some force that operates above the laws of nature, suggesting the occult, or magical forces, a stigma the paranormal has long endured. It is more accurate to suggest that rather than supernatural, psi is natural and normal, but not yet well understood by science. Even the well-intentioned word *paranormal* can be misleading. The prefix *para* means "beyond," suggesting that psi is beyond or outside that which is normal, a negative connotation.

Some have taken issue with the word *parapsychology,* since it also does not accurately describe the subject. It is a word that dates back to the late nineteenth century, and was popularized by J. B. Rhine as a way to define the serious study of and experimentation with ESP and PK, so they would be more academically and scientifically acceptable. Most people, unsure of what to call psi, still use the expression "psychic phenomena," for lack of a better term. Not only is the subject elusive, so is its terminology.

Often, topics that have little or no connection are stirred together, like mismatched ingredients in a bad recipe, to the delight of debunkers. In fact, parapsychology, ufology, and cryptozoology are distinct and separate fields of study. By bunching them together, debunkers hope to sink all unexplained and anomalous phenomena at one time, while they often add ridicule and sarcasm to further befuddle and discourage the public, suggesting that to entertain anything psychic is to mark oneself as a delusional misfit or unscientific rube. Never mind that the history of parapsychology, as well as its contemporary research, includes a long list of bona fide scientists, physicians, psychologists, and other professionals with substantial and impressive credentials. Rarely do books and articles by skeptics and debunkers mention the serious and distinguished individuals who've long devoted time and energy to exploring the paranormal, often in the face of wilting criticism.

A belief suggests an element of faith, such as a religious conviction. To reinforce the premise that psychic phenomena are the equivalent of "junk" science, superstition, or so-called magical thinking, debunkers nearly always bolster their arguments against the paranormal by referring to it as a "belief." For example, how many times have you heard—or asked someone—"Do you believe in ghosts, mind reading, UFOs, or life after death?" But the paranormal is more than a belief. When the late psychoanalyst Dr. Carl Jung, an unwavering proponent of psychic phenomena, was asked whether he believed in such experiences, Jung typically answered, "No. I don't believe; I know."

Still it is common to hear people talk about the paranormal in terms of a belief, rather than as fact. It is understandable, to an extent, since we are dealing with the "invisible world." However, once a person has had a psychic encounter, he or she often has a change in thinking, and considers the experience as more than imaginary. Paranormal incidents are experienced by thousands of people, unknown to each other, every day, whether they "believe" in them, or not; and regardless of what debunkers and skeptics say.

A well-regarded psychic, with a national reputation, made the mistake of appearing on a talk show on a major Midwest radio station. The host, an admitted skeptic, had secretly arranged before the program with a CSICOP debunker to cause the psychic to appear to be a fraud. The plan was to have the debunker phone in, pretending to be an anonymous listener, and no matter what information the psychic's telephone reading provided, the debunker would vehemently disavow its accuracy.

The devious setup worked. The disguised debunker adamantly denied any of the psychic's information was correct. That was a lie; but it was more important that the well-known clairvoyant be discredited, even if he did not deserve to be. The next day, a major newspaper in that city carried the story about how inaccurate and inept the highly touted psychic was, a blow to his credibility. But what purpose was served? Deception by a debunker should be no more acceptable than when chicanery is committed by a fraudulent psychic or medium.

How do professional debunkers, such as the founder of CSI-COP, Paul Kurtz, rationalize and explain their animosity toward the paranormal? Consider some of his remarks that appeared in an article he wrote in 1997. Kurtz was a longtime professor of philosophy at the State University of New York at Buffalo, an author and publisher, and an atheist. Bear in mind he was never a scientist per se, although he long led the fight against psi under the pretense that "the huge increase in paranormal beliefs is symptomatic of a profound antiscience attitude."

Debunkers have noted correctly that the American attitude toward science has changed. Even as science and technology have grown by "leaps and bounds," and profoundly altered society in ways our ancestors could never have dreamed, to quote Kurtz, "a strong antiscience counterculture has emerged." But others reply that we have not become "antiscience" as much as we've become more discerning about what science can—and cannot—do.

The CSICOP argument that attention to psi lowers our scientific IQ is utterly without merit. In fact, even debunkers' groups have had to admit that interest in the paranormal and ufology in recent years has grown most significantly among the best educated. *The X-Files*, a highly popular TV series during the 1990s and early 2000s, featured storylines about the paranormal and conspiracy theories, and drew a large viewing audience that included many college students and graduates, a substantial number of them with a scientific or technological bent. In fact, by 2006, several studies found that "children as young as seven are using technology—computers, digital cameras, cell phones, and video games," and most of these youngsters had a profound interest in such things as UFOs, evidenced by the high viewership among school-aged children for History Channel's reality series *UFO Hunters*.

Debunkers have impeded serious paranormal research by presenting it as an "either-or question." In other words, by that reasoning, either you are scientific and rational or, if you "believe" in the paranormal, you are "antiscience" and presumably irrational. That black or white choice is both unfair and inaccurate. There is more than enough evidence that psi phenomena are both scientific and genuine; interest in it does not require us to surrender "critical thinking" or toss test tubes, computers, and other scientific tools to the winds. Melissa Pollack, for example, an admitted skeptic, was a researcher with the National Science Foundation in 2001 when she wrote an article for the CSICOP magazine *Skeptical Inquirer*. According to Pollack, there is a correlation between "paranormal beliefs" and "a decline in critical thinking skills among Americans." There is absolutely no empirical evidence that proves a connection between psi and a decrease in "critical thinking," an impressive sounding but ill-defined phrase.

In the late nineteenth and early twentieth centuries, many Americans were positively giddy with wonder and optimism that science and technology could provide answers and opportunities the world had never before known in medicine, transportation, and communications, and that they held the promise of longer and healthier lives. It was the age of electricity and the invention of the automobile and airplane. The spellbinding science-fiction stories of Jules Verne and H. G. Wells promised to become science fact. And the discoveries of Nikola Tesla are still coming to fruition today with such things as the wireless transmission of information, robotically controlled devices, and even messages beamed as well as launched into space. One might well ask, why beam or send messages into space aboard craft if no one is there to receive them? Are NASA scientists believing in the paranormal?

Once the euphoria inevitably settled in the middle of the twentieth century, science and technology were viewed from a slightly more sober perspective. There was more than one way to consider scientific achievements, and they were not the answer to every problem. In fact, we became painfully aware that the wonders of science and technology also had their downsides and raised ethical questions. Einstein, a pacifist, was appalled that his theories in physics became the basis for the atomic bombs that instantly killed tens of thousands in Hiroshima and Nagasaki, ending World War II. The same chemicals that have made modern life easier and more convenient have also been the subjects of great concern about their potential dangers to the environment. The ominous threat of nuclear and biological weapons in the wrong hands is perhaps science's darkest side. Ancient prophecies of cataclysmic climactic changes, often scoffed at as superstitious nonsense, have suddenly become a serious concern worldwide. Glaciers melting in locations such as Greenland and elsewhere are a result, scientists say, of human-created global warming. Many claim that we are at least partially responsible due to the use of chemicals and emissions that have released an overabundance of carbon dioxide into the atmosphere.

The idea that any thinking person seeks a return to the pestilence and drudgery of past centuries is ridiculous. But, exploring, experiencing, or testing the paranormal will not send us on a backward slide to the Middle Ages, as some debunkers have actually alleged. Few people reject the marvels of modern medical care, or want to revert to a time when remedies were crude, often barbaric, and sometimes more dangerous than the ailments being treated. Laser surgery, DNA testing, cloning, and organ transplants are only a few of the medical wonders that would have been science fiction a century ago. But today we are also conscious of potential—and sometimes lethal—side effects and medical mistakes, just as most of us are aware of such contentious issues as stem-cell research, artificial life support, and the agonizing question: When does life itself begin and end?

Debunkers have also attacked the surge of interest in alternative medicine in recent decades, alarmed at the prospect that they might replace traditional physicians and treatment modalities. However, some unorthodox medical approaches and herbal remedies have provided patients with added choices, "last resorts," and certainly more attention from practitioners than many doctors who hurriedly dart in and out of examining rooms, spending too little time with their patients. Whatever their worth, alternative methods have become a multimillion-dollar business annually.

One example of an alternative medical practice based on non-Western science is the long-standing debate about acupuncture. When the ancient Chinese technique of inserting very thin needles into a patient's body as an analgesic or pain reliever was first introduced in the United States in the early 1970s, many skeptics railed against it as quackery, perhaps psychosomatic in nature, and at odds with conventional Western medical treatments.

Especially noxious to debunkers is the centuries-old Asian belief in the chi, an energy or "life force" that is said to flow through every human and members of other animal species, and that acupuncture is believed to influence. It was not a concept consistent with Western science, and was criticized by skeptics as more New Age silliness. However, science now suggests that the tiny needles, no wider than a hair, inserted correctly in a patient release endorphins, neurotransmitters occurring in the brain that act as the body's own pain relievers.

Debunkers still attack other alternative techniques such as chiropractic, homeopathy, and vitamin therapy, and certainly there are pro and con arguments for each. Perhaps the one that grates at them most is prayer as a healing method. Prayer, of course, is a component of religious belief, and mediums often suggest it is a means to communicate with deceased loved ones. Suffice it to say here, that for debunkers and skeptics who hold to humanist or atheistic beliefs, prayer is nonsense. Science, in recent years, has found otherwise.

As debunkers argue, do American students need more science education? Probably. But they also could use a good dose more of history and geography. Neither, however, has any relationship to the large numbers of people who report psychic or paranormal experiences. There is a need for healthy skepticism about many situations in our lives, from phony fortune-telling to disreputable home contracting, political promises, and even fraudulent charities. There are quacks and fakers in every field, science included, unfortunately. That doesn't mean a wide range of paranormal experiences need to be discarded on the word of self-anointed debunkers who, with evangelical fervor, are dedicated to the destruction of everything psychic, mystical, or spiritual.

It's been a bit tricky for the CSICOPers to appear on network television with their true agenda. After all, nine out of ten Americans believe in God. So, by posing as protectors against psychic fraud, and proponents of so-called scientific and rational thinking, they are usually able to dance around their secular humanist agenda, avoiding discussion in the media about their abhorrence to religion.

Once, in a debate on an Ohio radio talk show, parapsychologist Stephen Kaplan confronted The Amazing Randi about religion, specifically, whether the magician believed there was a God. Randi was incensed by the question, and protested it had nothing to do with his crusade against the paranormal. However, he adamantly refused to answer. It was likely one of the few times that he'd had been publicly confronted on the question of religious belief as it related to the paranormal.

Randi is skilled in promoting himself as a celebrity, as are most performers. He is responsible for one of the cleverest and most enduring public relations stunts ever in the history of psychic debunking.

For years, Randi claimed he carried a ten-thousand-dollar check to give to anyone who could demonstrate "genuine paranormal ability." That sounded fair, his fellow debunkers and many others said. But there were few takers.[35] Then, in the 1990s, Randi raised the amount to one million dollars. There were still no winners. That gave Randi bragging rights—since no psychic successfully met his challenge, it proved they were all frauds.

Actually, most psychics and mediums had caught on to the catch-22 in Randi's criteria for the demonstration of a true psychic experience. And if Randi actually had a check for that huge sum of money, he seemed convinced that he would never have to part with it. But the offer attracted immense public and media attention over the years. It sounded quite straightforward. If one claimed to be a genuine psychic or medium, why not simply demonstrate the ability, and walk away a million dollars richer? The truth was that Randi's test conditions were designed so that no psychic, medium, or healer could ever satisfy them. As the sole arbiter or judge, how could Randi—and his cohorts—possibly admit they'd been wrong for decades? Unfortunately, many people have been fooled into believing it was a genuine offer—which it never was.

Among the recent crop of debunkers is Michael Shermer, a California-based college professor and editor of *Skeptic* magazine. In 1997, he wrote the book *Why People Believe Weird Things: Pseudoscience, Superstition, and Other Confusions of Our Time*. That title should tell you everything you need to know about his objectivity in examining paranormal claims. Shermer has never had a problem stepping up to the podium, smirking, and proclaiming, "The existence of psychic ability has not been proven." That, as he well knows, is not true, although by his criteria, nothing paranormal is ever permitted to pass the debunkers' test.

For example, Shermer, who has become something of a media

personality, dismissed some fourteen thousand psychic readings given by Edgar Cayce. The testimony of anyone who received a Cayce reading does not count, he said, because it "does not represent a controlled experiment." What's more, Cayce's unorthodox remedies, "read like prescriptions from a medieval herbalist." Herbalist, indeed. When one considers that Cayce was the principal means of communicating with President Woodrow Wilson, who had been debilitated by a stroke, in his second term, it is anecdotal evidence with a great credibility.

Similarly, the great number of ESP tests performed at Duke University by pioneer parapsychologists J. B. and Louisa Rhine were equally debunked by Shermer. What appears to be statistically significant evidence of ESP received this explanation, "Statistics tell us that given a large enough group, there should be someone who will score fairly high." Synchronicity is coincidence, not "psychic communication," according to Shermer, apparently no fan of Dr. Carl Jung or the idea that "God signals us through coincidences," as was put forth in a 2006 book, *When God Winks,* by Squire Rushnell. For instance, if the phone rings and it's a person you were about to call, "it's an example of statistical coincidence," Shermer concluded. And so it goes. For every psychic or paranormal event or test there must be a nonpsychic explanation; no evidence of psi is ever sufficient. For the record, Shermer is not a scientist.

Today there are no less than eight around-the-clock all-news and talk cable TV networks. That does not include the broadcast networks, public television, virtually unlimited sources of news and information on the Internet, supersize bookstores, libraries, newspapers, magazines, and all-news and talk radio stations. America is hardly suffering an information drought. It's more of a glut. Combined, there are more sources for learning than the world has ever known. Whatever percentage is devoted to the paranormal could not possibly be responsible for any deficit in "critical thinking" or alleged "scientific illiteracy." Perhaps other factors are responsible for why more people can name the most popular TV reality shows than the three branches of the federal government and what they do? Might CSICOP and other debunkers' groups be oversimplifying their insistence on a lack of critical thinking—just a bit?

One more point about the media. If films and TV shows about the paranormal and occult are such a pervasive and negative influence, why don't reports of psychic experiences reflect the sensationalized plots of movies about the subject? The fact is that thousands of dream visions, apparitions, premonitions, synchronicities, and a multitude of other psi incidents are typically brief and considerably less spectacular than what we see on motion picture and TV screens. If debunkers were correct about the mass media's negative impact, what accounts for centuries of supernatural events occurring long before there were any allegedly mind-polluting electronic media?

Incidentally, it's highly unlikely that psi will ooze through the doors of America's secularized public schools, like some crawling, otherworldly entity. The paranormal is a no-no in official school curriculums; it is never taught. You will never find it in a textbook. The only exception is at Halloween when ghosts, goblins, and witches are treated as "creepy and spooky" fun in some communities. Even at the college level, there are few courses and programs about parapsychology, with only a handful of universities treating it seriously, if at all.

Another clichéd argument against psi concerns those who read horoscopes. While overdependence on psi or astrology is as unwise as any other excess, it's difficult to picture students bolting from the classroom, throwing their hands in the air, and forgoing careers in science or technology simply because they peeked at a horoscope in a newspaper, magazine, or on the Internet.

Debunkers and skeptics often bemoan the amounts of money they say is needlessly spent on psychics, mediums, and astrologers. While it is true that there are people who've been unfairly bilked by bogus fortune-tellers and "1-900" phone-line psychics, there are many others, especially the bereaved, who consider that paying for a reading by a medium brings a measure of comfort, in the belief that they've made contact with departed loved ones. Rightly or wrongly, some say a medium is more immediate and affordable than months or years of psychotherapy, and while some seek pastoral or grief counseling, many do not.

Nowhere have skeptics shown more insensitivity and cruelty than in their mockery of bereaved people who seek help from mediums. Debunkers tip off their true agenda when they condemn mediums for providing "false hope." The phrase is virtually meaningless, but hurtful to those grieving for deceased family and friends. Dismissing all mediums during the past several decades because Houdini supposedly debunked them in the early twentieth century is both callous and preposterous. What the debunkers really mean is that they do not believe in an afterlife; it's a religious concept, so it's useless to "hope" that we survive physical death in any form.

Also denied by groups like CSICOP is the fact that countless paranormal incidents occur directly to people; there is no expense involved when someone experiences a premonition, has a precognitive dream, or witnesses an apparition, and so on. Many psychic healers charge modestly; rarely does a medium or psychic ask for payment to work with law enforcement, and a handful of adult education courses about divination or developing psychic ability, among others, require only a nominal fee. No person should ever be intimidated or manipulated into paying an exorbitant price to any psychic practitioner, or be subjected to frightening or dire predictions.

Incidentally, for those so inclined, prayer is free, and so are practicing meditation and yoga.

Americans have not exactly been forced to embrace psychic phenomena, let alone pay what they cannot afford. New Age types do not go door to door, in the manner of Jehovah's Witnesses, seeking converts. Why have surveys in recent years shown a steady increase in paranormal beliefs? Perhaps more people are confident in acknowledging their psi experiences, with less fear of ridicule: Books and media can certainly take some credit. Network television was long reluctant to treat psi seriously; it was the public's interest that pushed TV toward more programming about the subject in recent years. Polls that repeatedly revealed that better educated people are more open to psi than people with less education were contrary to the debunkers' arguments that psychic phenomena have contributed to a nation of fuzzy thinkers, desperately in need of skeptics to straighten out their gullible minds.

Of course, psi should be held to a scientific standard, but one that is fair, even-handed, and without bias. The late astronomer Carl Sagan wrote, "The best antidote for pseudoscience, I believe, is science." He was correct; however it is not clear where the line between the two is drawn. In 1979, in his bestselling book, *Broca's Brain,* Sagan referred to "understanding human limitations," an ability he said "skeptical magicians" grasp since they are "able to perform similar effects by sleight of hand." But, who can say with certainty what the limits of perception and ability are?

Sagan recognized as much when he said, "The history of science is full of cases where previously accepted theories and hypotheses have been entirely overthrown, to be replaced by new ideas that more adequately explain the data."

Sagan had nothing but praise for Randi's efforts to debunk Uri

Geller, although he'd never actually seen a Geller demonstration. Imagine how he stunned some hard-core debunkers, when he later wrote the bestselling book *Contact* in 1985, which was made into a successful motion picture in 1997. In it, Sagan's opinion about such taboo subjects as faith, intuition, and even the question of a God seemed to have changed, to the disappointment of many skeptics for whom Sagan was an icon. He even suggested that scientists might want to investigate paranormal claims before they summarily dismiss them all. He also questioned why so many disparate people have had similar psi experiences—something he thought was worth considering. Most surprising was his willingness to seek explanations for why some very young children seem to have uncanny and detailed knowledge of past lives. Sagan remained a skeptic, but he became more open-minded about psi in the last decade of his life, to the chagrin of the debunkers.

Another skeptic who became disenchanted with CSICOP hardliners was the late sociologist Marcello Truzzi, an expert on parapsychology and the occult. He departed the group when he realized it had veered from its original promise to examine psi claims, and instead became an organization dedicated only to debunking the paranormal. Truzzi preferred the term "anomalous phenomena" to describe psychic events.[36]

Perhaps of all the criticisms of the paranormal, one of the strangest, raised in the *Skeptical Inquirer,* is that the paranormal can cause "harm." Exactly how and what substantiates the blanket accusation is unclear. But when there are instances of psychic fraud or psychological or physical harm as a result of the paranormal, skeptics would do well to expose and warn people of the specific danger, rather than attacking all of psi as unsafe or impossible. "Parapsychologists have nothing to fear from responsible criticism," noted Richard Broughton in *Parapsychology: The Controversial Science*.

Debunkers are fond of insisting the paranormal cannot be scientific since it is unreliable; it is elusive; it cannot be measured, repeated, or tested under "strict" controls; and witness accounts of psi experiences are anecdotal, and therefore, potentially undependable or inaccurate. Coauthor Joel Martin once asked CSICOP founder Paul Kurtz, "How do we explain dreams?" No rational person denies that we all experience them—dreams are universal— and many of us attempt to analyze and interpret their meaning. However, there is no possible way that one person can "show" another the pictures or events in his or her mind during sleep. Why, then, do we believe other people also dream, since no one can ever see someone else's dreams? Kurtz did not appreciate Joel's curiosity; he told him it was a "trick question," but had no answer beyond that. However, he did promise that he'd never talk to Joel again; and he never did.

If there was ever a rematch, we might ask psychic debunkers about "love," one of the most important and powerful emotions humans have. Do we know what arouses the feelings that attract one person to another? Science can neither measure love, nor predict the longevity or outcome of a relationship. Yet there are biological and hormonal factors involved, such as pheromones, which are chemicals that, when secreted, release a scent that contributes to the attraction. What we know is that "falling in love" is not a very rational process, and sadly, it sometimes proves to be dangerous. It seems the paranormal isn't the only human experience that can't be submitted to so-called strict test conditions.

John Stossel, best known for his long association as a reporter and anchor for the ABC-TV newsmagazine *20/20*—he's the fellow with the dark, curly hair and mustache—is proud of his skepticism. Stossel once raged so vehemently against a *20/20* appearance by George Anderson, one of the most successfully tested mediums in the country, that the proposed segment was canceled. In 2006, Stossel wrote a book titled *Myths, Lies, and Downright Stupidity*— even though he'd done no research about psi. Nonetheless, Stossel offered his opinions as fact, telling readers that psychics and astrologers are bunk. What about police who use psychics for crime solving? "Police get suckered too," Stossel concluded. A quote by *Skeptic* magazine editor Michael Shermer described psychic powers as "magical." Homeopathy was branded as "absurd," and chiropractors offered "dubious treatments." Finally, with a straight face, Stossel dredged up The Amazing Randi's tired million-dollar offer to anyone who could demonstrate that paranormal ability is genuine. Incidentally, Stossel identified Jim Randi as a "skeptic," overlooking or purposely ignoring that Randi is a debunker.

There's also a suggestion of gender bias in the debunkers' thinking. It's acknowledged by both sides of the acrimonious psi debate that women have more psychic experiences than men. Therefore, the constant hammering against anything paranormal suggests that those who are psychic are naïve, irrational, unscientific, and perhaps deluded; an implication that is obviously sexist. Nowhere is there a reference by debunkers that perhaps women are more sensitive to and aware of psi phenomena. Incidentally, CSICOP and its affiliated groups and "fellows" throughout the country include very few women among its leadership and members.

By the 1980s, it was apparent that professional debunkers were losing the fight against the paranormal, as polls and surveys showed the enormous growth of interest in the subject. Perhaps that is why many debunkers seemed so strident, even belligerent. The CSICOPers had every reason to feel defensive as the rising tide of the New Age seemed poised to overwhelm them. In the past several years the number of TV programs about the paranormal has grown immensely, from *Unsolved Mysteries* and *Sighting* in the 1980s and 1990s, to the more recent *Medium* and *Ghost Whisperer*. That's not including reality shows starring mediums, and a slew of documentaries featuring every imaginable aspect of psi experience from haunted houses, to the psychic experiences of U.S. presidents, UFOs, crime-fighting psychics, life after death, and the prophecies of Nostradamus, among others. If they were not drawing large audiences, they would not be on the air.

Besides Randi's rants, of all the self-proclaimed psychic debunkers who've gained a measure of recognition in recent years, one deserves special mention for lowering the standard of decency in public discourse on the question of psi. No psychic debunker has made the issue so bitterly personal as Penn Jillette, one half of the team of gifted stage magicians, Penn and Teller. They had their own TV series on the Showtime network for several seasons, titled *Bullshit!* If you've ever seen them, Penn is the large one with glasses and a ponytail, who does all the talking for the pair. His partner, Teller, smaller in stature, never speaks.

Penn has very definite opinions about the paranormal, religion, alternative healing, and New Age ideas. They're all, well, bullshit. About Uri Geller's metal bending, Penn has described it as "a lousy trick for lousy people." On condition of anonymity, a friend of Penn's told Joel Martin recently that the magician's anger and frustration is quite genuine. Whether Penn was bellowing about the Bermuda Triangle or the Bible, a psychic medium or a weeping icon of the Virgin Mary, obscenities were generously sprinkled throughout his diatribes; his favorite was the word "fuck." How mean-spirited tirades and insults will bring converts rushing to the side of skeptics is more of a mystery than the origin of the Shroud of Turin or whether there really was an Atlantis. It's an odd approach to take for someone claiming the high road to so-called rational thinking in the United States where three out of four people believe in the paranormal, and nine out of ten believe in God.[37]

To sum up, as the history of the paranormal has shown, there is a need for honest and open-minded skepticism, but debunkers have not always acted in the best interests of the public or science. As we've said throughout this chapter, their ultimate goal is a secular society, as has already occurred in some parts of Europe. However, it is possible to separate paranormal events from religious belief. It must have been terrible news for skeptics and debunkers in recent years when physicists posed quantum theories consistent with the possibility that psi exists. Worse, probably, was the discovery by neuroscientists of the "God spot," a specific part of the human brain, in the right temporal lobe, that appears hardwired for psychic, religious, and mystical experiences.

In a typically disingenuous comment, CSICOP founder Paul Kurtz said, "The emergence of a paranormal worldview competes with the scientific worldview." Actually neither side is a threat to the other; they are two spokes of the same wheel. Similarly, religious belief need not be at odds with paranormal phenomena, although there is a certain irony in the fact that fundamentalist Christians, conservative scientists, and atheistic debunkers are all on the same side in opposing psi.

The authors of this book, as have millions of others, each witnessed events and incidents that cannot be explained, but leave no doubt that something more than the limits of our five senses exists.[38] The amount of research and evidence supporting the existence of psi since the late nineteenth century is staggering, despite what debunkers would have us believe. Pulitzer Prize–winning science writer and author Deborah Blum, who has also written about the subject, pointed to a number of psi tests that reveal statistical evidence for telepathy and after-death communications far beyond chance. A century ago, parapsychologists did not have the advantage of the technology that exists today to examine psi, including highly sensitive devices to detect evidence of apparitions, brain imaging, and even voices from the beyond. Science has an opportunity to prove debunkers have made errors, some deliberately. The fear, as Deborah Blum wrote, is that if science continues to ignore what millions have experienced, "there is the risk of failing to investigate the world in all its dimensions."[39]

2

Candy Jones, Long John Nebel, and MK-ULTRA

The CIA claims that secrecy is necessary to hide what it's doing from enemies of the United States . . . the real reason for secrecy is to hide what the CIA is doing from the American people.

—PHILIP AGEE, field officer, Central Intelligence Agency, 1975

Candy Jones was a devastatingly stunning young woman in 1943—not quite eighteen years old and already one of America's best-known models. Her face with its exquisitely chiseled features and long wavy blond hair, a style made popular during the forties by movie stars like Lauren Bacall and Veronica Lake, conveyed a natural beauty that her perfectly applied makeup only accentuated. She was tall, lithe, and slender. Her looks were so striking that in just one month during 1943, she appeared on eleven magazine covers and was named "Model of the Year," noted author Donald Bain in *The Control of Candy Jones*.[1]

In an era of pinup girls, she was a knockout, and her photos in her signature polka-dotted white bathing suit adorned many a soldier's or sailor's quarters during the war in the South Pacific. The pinup girls were supposed to be a morale booster for war-weary fighting men, a reminder of home, and their waiting wives and sweethearts. The most famous was the beautiful blond movie star Betty Grable; her pinup seemed to be everywhere American servicemen were fighting. Candy Jones also ranked in that rarified stratosphere of wartime beauties. So popular and in-demand was Candy Jones, that she signed on with the United Service Organization (USO) to entertain the troops, and traveled widely throughout the South Pacific until 1945. When the war ended, she was not yet twenty years old.

She'd had the looks and tenacity that helped her escape a lonely childhood, growing up in Wilkes-Barre, Pennsylvania, where she was born Jessica Wilcox in December 1925 to a domineering mother, who remained an intimidating presence throughout her life. Her father left when she was just three years old, and the only person she could count on was her beloved grandmother, who died when Jessica was eleven. It was a devastating loss for the young girl.

Candy's first modeling job happened by chance in 1941, when, on a visit to New York with her mother, she caught the eye of one of the nation's top modeling agents, Harry Conover. He signed her to his agency when she was only sixteen, after she'd strongly resisted her mother's wishes that she attend secretarial school. It was also Conover who changed her name from Jessica Wilcox to the more glitzy-sounding "Candy Jones." By 1945, Conover could boast that his was the most respected modeling agency in the entire country. The next year, twenty-one-year-old Candy Jones married Harry Conover in a lavish wedding.

But, if her modeling career was a success, her marital life was an emotional disaster. Consumed by business and other concerns, Conover was neither attentive nor affectionate. Although the couple had three sons, Harry rarely showed any sexual interest in his attractive wife. Soon it became a nonissue for both. They'd been married twelve years, Candy swore, before she discovered her husband was bisexual. She eventually opened her own charm school to teach aspiring actresses and models, and she was approaching her thirty-third birthday, with three young sons, when Harry Conover simply walked out one day in 1958. Unbeknownst to Candy, when Conover abandoned her, he also cleaned out their joint bank account worth $125,000. She filed for divorce, and what followed were lengthy and acrimonious proceedings that provided plenty of fodder for the gossip columnists and tabloids. Finally, in 1959, Candy was granted a divorce from Conover. However, that did nothing to solve her money woes. She found herself facing a mountain of debt, both hers and his. Her only source of income was her school, which she barely kept afloat.

One day around that time, as Candy walked toward her office in a midtown Manhattan building, she ran into an army general, an acquaintance from her USO days during World War II, and they exchanged pleasantries. It was not long after, that a young man came by her office, identified himself as an FBI agent, and asked for a favor. Would she be willing to lend him the microphone to the audiotape recorder she used to train student actresses? He claimed he needed that specific piece of equipment for an FBI surveillance he was working on, but hadn't been able to find one. It was an odd request, but Candy willingly gave him the microphone.

About a month later, the same youthful federal agent came by to return it, as he'd promised. And he had another favor to ask. Would Candy permit "some mail" to be delivered to her office for an FBI operation? He explained someone would come by on a regular basis to pick up the letters. With little hesitation, she agreed to help. Remember, the late fifties and early sixties were a time when most Americans harbored far less suspicion about government intent and intrigue. In fact, Candy might have been flattered that she'd been asked to help, and felt no reason to seek any further information.

For the next year, Candy's office became a "mail drop," also called a "dead drop," for the government, according to author Donald Bain in his compelling book about this stranger-than-fiction story. It's certain that Candy had no idea about the specifics of the FBI's plans. But the general she ran into in front of her office building the year before surprisingly stayed in touch with her during this period, seemingly knowledgeable about the FBI's surreptitious goings-on.

Toward the end of the summer of 1960, the young FBI agent who'd first approached Candy about using her office to receive mail unexpectedly wrote her at home to advise that she'd receive a telephone call within the next several days. The promised call came two days later. It was from her friend, the general. He asked Candy if she'd hand-deliver a confidential letter to someone in San Francisco since he knew she'd be traveling there for a public appearance at a fashion show in November. The general explained that the letter was intended for someone in government, and Candy would be contacted at her hotel as to where it should be delivered. Good patriot that she was—or from the perspective of time and distance, a naïve one—Candy agreed without question.

She was staying at the St. Francis Hotel in San Francisco when she received the expected call. To her surprise, it was someone she'd also known during the war years, a medic identified in Bain's book by a pseudonym, "Dr. Gilbert Jensen." He was now a physician practicing in nearby Oakland. At Jensen's suggestion, Candy met him for dinner. In answer to her queries about the letter she expected to carry, Jensen replied that he'd talk to her about it the next day, and urged her to visit him at his office. He also said that he wanted to discuss some work she might be qualified for involving the government. He added this incentive: "It could be lucrative," quoting from Donald Bain's writing of the events. Candy agreed to drop by Jensen's office the following day.

"That," Bain explained, "was the beginning." Unbeknownst to her, Candy Jones was on her way to becoming a "covert operative" for the Central Intelligence Agency, an assignment that would go on for the next twelve years. She was likely never meant to be a major player in secret intelligence activity. Actually she would be, at most, a glorified messenger. But that was sufficient for her to face some genuinely dangerous and even physically painful experiences. In fairness, however, it should be pointed out that Candy had initially agreed to take the position for financial reasons because she needed the money. No one forced her to accede to requests every step of the way. She was to be paid and certain risks were implicit in her assignment.

However, what she did not know—and was never told—was that she would become a "human guinea pig" in a CIA mind-control experiment, according to Donald Bain. She was never told that part of her job was to submit to a psychological operation to create for her a secret personality turning her into a version of a "Manchurian candidate" who would follow the suggestions of her CIA handlers. And the end point of this experiment, implanted in her mind to cover up the CIA's tracks, was a plan to set into motion her own suicide, a cold-blooded way of dispatching the evidence. And it would have all come to pass had it not been for her marriage to the celebrated nighttime radio talk show host Long John Nebel. Her own suicide was to have been choreographed by her friend, Dr. Gilbert Jensen.

In 1972, Candy remarried, still an attractive woman, but in her late forties and past the age for modeling to be a professional option. Her name remained quite well known, and she turned to broadcasting, working at NBC for a time. Her new husband was one of New York's most popular radio personalities, Long John Nebel, host of a wildly successful late-night talk show since 1956 that dealt with every imaginable supernatural, psychic, and occult topic one's mind could conjure. He'd lead six hours of talk show conversation, six nights a week, with panels and guests that included psychics, UFO abductees, flying saucer experts, people who claimed to have lived innumerable past lives, mind readers, mediums, scientists, psychologists, and experts and eccentrics from virtually every field of endeavor.[2] It was an eclectic mix probably unmatched anywhere else on the radio dial at the time and a format that led to today's successful late-night radio talk show hosts such as George Noory, George Knapp, and Art Bell, all of Premiere Radio's *Coast to Coast AM*. But despite having created a fascinating world for night people, Nebel was proud to tell you that he believed virtually none of it. "I don't buy it," was one of his pet expressions about psychic claims, and his questions to guests with unusual stories could be sarcastic and biting. He wore his skepticism as though it were a badge of honor, and was proud that one of his closest friends was the magician none other than the equally skeptical The Amazing Randi.

When Nebel married Candy Jones in 1972, he was sixty-one, fourteen years her senior. He was tall—six feet four inches—and elegant with close-cropped gray hair, a neatly trimmed mustache, and wore studious-looking horn-rimmed glasses, belying a curious background. Born in Chicago in 1911, he'd quit school after eighth grade, ran away, and joined a carnival. He was an excellent tent pitchman, and an extraordinary salesman. But Nebel found his true calling in his mid-forties when he turned to broadcasting in 1956. Endowed with a sharp mind, a quick wit, an insatiable curiosity, and an appetite for learning, he created a unique show that would air for more than two decades, and earned a legendary place in New York broadcasting history.

Ironically, Nebel had once met Candy, back in 1941 when he did

a stint as a photographer, and she was already a model. His assignment was to take her picture for a major magazine. Each then went
their separate ways. When they met again, some thirty years later,
both were divorced, and they wasted no time. After a courtship
of only a month, they married on New Year's Eve, December 31,
1972. By then, Nebel had already been diagnosed with prostate
cancer, and had been hospitalized for it the year before. But that
did not slow down his busy career, or his new marriage. However,
he had no idea about Candy's secret past connection to the CIA
because she had not told him anything about that part of her life.

It was during their brief honeymoon at a Manhattan hotel that
the usually unflappable Nebel was startled when Candy's behavior
and demeanor inexplicably changed. On one occasion, she suddenly emerged from the bathroom in their hotel suite, speaking in a
voice that was lower and with an ominous quality that he'd never
heard before. Nebel admitted he was momentarily shaken. It wasn't
what she said, which was indiscernible. It was the way she spoke that
unnerved him. A little while later, she was back to herself, "warm
and sweet and lovable," Bain quoted him as saying, and Nebel dismissed the incident as inconsequential.

But the next day, Nebel again saw an abrupt difference in Candy's
demeanor and personality. Her eyes became cold, and she seemed
quite angry. When Nebel asked what might be the matter, she snapped
that nothing was wrong. But her voice again grew distant and strange.
However, in a short while, she returned to the loving Candy Jones
that Nebel had married. That night, before he began his radio show,
Nebel phoned her to be certain that she was all right. Candy replied
that everything was fine. Then, abruptly, there was the icy tone
again. But this time, Nebel told her so. She apologized, denied anything was amiss, and then grew silent.

When Nebel returned home in the early morning hours, Candy
was still awake, and he gently asked her what was causing the

sudden flashes of anger and coldness. She seemed genuinely baffled by the question and did not recall the abrupt changes in her mood or voice. However, Nebel pressed the issue. He knew something was seriously amiss, and he wanted an explanation. Eventually, Candy revealed that following her divorce from Harry Conover in 1959, she'd been asked by someone from the FBI to deliver some messages for the agency, and allowed it to use her office as a "mail drop." But she added that she no longer was doing any favors for the FBI.

Nebel said that he found Candy's disclosure "interesting," but did not recognize its importance or relevance to her odd behavior and mood swings. However, after he'd thought about his wife's peculiar admission for some time, Nebel wondered if there was more to her story than he was aware of.

In May 1973, Nebel asked Candy to join him as cohost of his popular talk show, and she happily agreed. The hours, however, played havoc with her schedule as she worked all night, then spent the days attempting to solve myriad personal financial problems that had accumulated from the operation of her money-losing modeling school that she'd since closed. Not surprisingly, Candy was having a very difficult time falling asleep. Nebel noticed that her insomnia had worsened. She wasn't able to find time for more than irregular naps. The lack of sleep was taking its toll. Candy was exhausted, and she looked more tired than she ever had.

Nebel, concerned for his new wife, suggested that he might be able to help her relax through hypnosis, so she could get the rest her mind and body badly needed. At first, Candy objected, claiming she was one of those people who couldn't be hypnotized. Actually, Nebel had never hypnotized anyone before, but he'd read a good deal about the subject, and he knew several doctors who understood and utilized it for medical purposes. Finally, in desperation, she acquiesced, and Nebel induced a trance state. Candy finally had a full night of restful sleep.

Nebel had no hidden agenda when he hypnotized Candy. It was only to sedate her without medication; it was just a matter of helping her find a much needed repose. However, what he inadvertently discovered when she was in a trance took him in a completely unexpected direction, with a sinister undercurrent that he never could have imagined. Nebel continued to relax Candy through hypnosis, and the process was working well; each time she fell comfortably asleep.

But another element emerged when Nebel placed Candy in a trance state. She began to regress to earlier times and places in her life. Such "age regressions," as they are called, are not unusual, and have long been utilized in medical and psychiatric cases. Bain said that Nebel eventually accumulated more than two hundred hours of audiotaped sessions of his wife's regressions. Nebel had not thought to record the first two times he hypnotized her, but he recorded the third and most subsequent sessions on a small cassette machine that he discreetly placed within the headboard of their bed.

In June 1973, Nebel was still hypnotizing Candy so that she'd be able to sleep, when she began speaking in a young girl's voice. She had regressed to childhood, and for several minutes, recalled memories long buried in her subconscious. When she later awakened, Nebel told Candy that she'd gone back to an early age. At first, she did not believe him. She thought she'd been dreaming. During June 1973, Nebel made more than a dozen audiotape recordings of Candy, and in July, thirteen more tapes. He also noticed that she was slipping into what is called "spontaneous trance." In other words, it did not require Nebel to induce the hypnotic state because Candy was entering it on her own. All Nebel had to do was ask her, "Where are we now?" At some points she cried, recalling early experiences, such as the time when her beloved grandmother was ailing.

Then something began happening during June 1973, which Nebel had neither considered nor expected. Bain explained that "another distinct personality" began to emerge through Candy. At first, Nebel did not realize what was occurring. He'd been focused only on helping her find sleep. He mistakenly thought that her second personality with its cold and hostile voice was simply Candy in a momentary mood swing. But through further questioning while she was in the trance state, Nebel learned that Candy had another identity. She said her name was "Arlene Grant." It was as if Nebel were talking to two different people. There were clearly differences in their voices and personalities. Candy was calm and pleasant, while Arlene was angry and coarse. Candy had stopped smoking several years before she married John Nebel, but Arlene showed no inclination to give up the habit.

As the hypnotic regressions continued, Nebel now had another reason to probe Candy's life, beyond helping her to sleep. There was obviously something hidden that Candy recalled very little of when she was awake. Who was "Arlene Grant," and why did her personality manifest itself through Candy Jones?

Although age regressions, in which hypnotized subjects recall earlier times in their lives, are widely accepted as a valid and useful tool, there are cautions. Hypnotists and medical professionals have noted the twists and pitfalls of age regressions. One of them is a phenomenon called confabulation. The hypnotized subject is not purposely lying. "However, in the absence of actual memories, the person is very likely to create fake 'memories' unconsciously that they cannot distinguish from real memories," parapsychologist and author Richard Broughton explained.[3] That's one reason given by skeptics and debunkers who dismiss past-life regressive hypnosis. But Broughton also noted that, "hypnotism has been shown to facilitate the accurate recall of old memories, when such memories exist."[4]

For Nebel, always cautious and skeptical, there were, understandably, some initial doubts and confusion when he first heard his hypnotized wife reveal some of her experiences with Dr. Jensen. Nebel was a fairly conservative fellow. Offbeat topics were fodder for his talk show, and not meant to be taken home in real life. But now the woman he'd recently married had confronted him with one of the strangest tales he'd ever heard, and it touched upon such sensitive concerns as the military and national security. He concluded this was not some supernatural yarn spun by one of his eccentric guests that he could simply brush aside.

Nebel now had a purpose far beyond helping Candy overcome her apparent bouts of insomnia. What had occurred in her life before she met him? There was a certain irony. Here was John Nebel, the ultimate skeptic, stumbling into the outrageous discovery that his lovely, soft-spoken wife had been a CIA operative, hypnotized as part of a secret U.S. government mind-control program. Had someone proposed it as a subject for his radio show, Nebel might well have scoffed at the allegation as preposterous—even unpatriotic.

Candy's story sounded just as incredible as those told by people who claimed they'd witnessed flying saucers. Hadn't the military officially denied them? Prior to the assassination of President Kennedy in 1963, few Americans pictured their government officials involved in wild conspiracies. The Vietnam War, the turbulent sixties, and the Watergate scandals eventually shattered the country's innocence, and replaced it with suspicion and cynicism toward the nation's leaders. But that painful disillusionment was not yet etched into the American psyche when Candy Jones—and thousands of others—was unwittingly co-opted into CIA experiments that began in the 1950s.

In late 1975, a *New York Times* editorial noted the change in America's collective thinking when it said that before president John F. Kennedy was murdered, "Few Americans were prepared to believe in official cover-ups and murder plotting." Although the newspaper's reference was to the wave of public skepticism at the time about the Warren Commission's controversial conclusion that Lee Harvey Oswald was the lone presidential assassin, *The Times* had assessed the nation's mood correctly. Nebel made the presumption that Candy's revelations while in the trance were truthful, no matter how far-fetched they sounded, and despite not understanding why certain incidents occurred to her under Gilbert Jensen's control.

Remember that what Nebel learned about his wife's secret past from 1960 to 1972 was mainly gleaned from their regressive hypnosis sessions. Candy revealed that her first meeting with Dr. Jensen was actually a job interview for what was essentially a messenger position for some unspecified government agency, and they also talked about providing her with a false passport to go along with her bogus identity as "Arlene Grant" since some travel would be involved. She was given a dark wig and a dark shade of makeup to disguise her appearance. Jensen had been particularly interested in Candy's revelations about "imaginary playmates" when she was a child. That was how Jensen and Candy arrived at her pseudonym, "Arlene Grant." It was a combination of one of those childhood imaginary friends and her middle name.

According to Donald Bain, Candy had raised to Jensen the suggestion that his job proposal "sound[ed] awfully cloak and dagger." Jensen denied that it was, and Candy subsequently agreed to complete some routine paperwork for him. On the surface, it seemed to be an innocuous conversation between an employer and a prospective employee. However, Candy had unknowingly signed on to carry out duties in a unit, established and operated by the CIA.

The CIA was—and still is—referred to as "The Company." Candy Jones, and other part-time personnel, who served The Company were known only as "control agents." For Candy, that meant her sole connection was Gilbert Jensen. Recordkeeping for such contracted part-timers was also maintained secretly and separately from the rosters of thousands of full-time CIA employees.

Candy—and many others—had unwittingly become a part of a shadowy and insidious government undertaking that operated stealthily, far from the eyes and ears of the public. It was the world of military and intelligence agencies that involved spies and top-secret activities, and was well beyond the gathering of information to protect America from its foreign enemies. Some startling and harebrained schemes that involved mind-control and drug experiments of questionable ethics and legality, many under a covert CIA program known as MK-ULTRA, were largely immune from government supervision.[5]

Candy, too trusting, was not told that her involvement went beyond simply delivering messages. Between November 1960 and the beginning of 1961, she'd had three meetings with Jensen. What she did not know was that, from the first meetings with Jensen and her agreement to work for him, she became part of a top-secret operation in which she was totally under Jensen's control, a personality she manifested not even known to herself.

As Nebel continued with the regressive hypnosis sessions, he often played the role of Dr. Jensen as a means of coaxing more information from Candy. For example, while she was in a trance, Candy revealed that Jensen had shown great interest in her health. When he noticed that she smoked, he suggested she stop. Remember, during the 1960s, smoking was far more sociably accepted than in recent years. Therefore, Jensen's advice was less typical than it would be today. But Jensen pressed the issue, and suggested that hypnosis could help her quit cigarettes. Candy protested that she was not susceptible to hypnosis, a claim many people mistakenly make. Actually, Candy proved to be an excellent participant. She had the qualities that made her highly suggestible, including an ability to concentrate, a good memory, and a willingness to trust. She was not critical or judgmental, and was able to roll her eyes back and upward, an indicator found in good hypnotic subjects.

Once Nebel brought his wife out of the trance state, she recalled very little of what she'd said while hypnotized. Her scant memory in the waking state may have been the result of the hypnotic suggestion given to her by Jensen. But Nebel initially could not understand the reason Jensen had hypnotized Candy in the first place, and then why she'd been given posthypnotic suggestions that resulted in her inability to remember events that happened prior to, throughout, and following the trance state.

Learning about Candy's secret life before she married Nebel was somewhat like assembling a jigsaw puzzle. There were pieces, but until they were joined together, the entire picture was unclear. For example, while in a trance, Candy told Nebel that Jensen regularly gave her intravenous injections of what he told her were vitamins. But were they actually vitamins or might they have been hypnosis-inducing drugs? Nebel immediately became suspicious, since vitamin injections are administered intramuscularly, not into the veins. He wondered if it was more likely she'd been injected with some drug that hastened a trance state. But that still did not answer why Candy was subjected to such manipulations.

Another question concerned the significance of the second distinct identity, "Arlene Grant," that emerged through Candy, which Nebel had first erroneously blamed on mood swings. When Candy was regressively hypnotized, that other personality emerged, one that he could communicate with. Unlike Candy, Arlene was abrasive and aggressive. She disliked Candy, calling her "weak." Jensen bore the responsibility for having created that second persona which was also programmed to hate others. As a result, the hostile Arlene often spewed anti-Semitic and racist remarks when she spoke through Candy. Jensen's apparent purpose had been to isolate her from social contact and interaction with others. The fewer people she talked to, the safer was her secret identity. Arlene would emerge upon Jensen's command, even via telephone, by use of a code, a technique the Soviet KGB had also conditioned its deep-cover agents to respond to when they lived out their lives in America as agents provocateurs. When Candy heard some of the tapes made of her while in a trance, she was both surprised and upset, particularly about the combative Arlene.

Although she had no idea whom she worked for, and reported only to Jensen, Candy was sufficiently concerned about her physical safety that she contacted her attorney. Since her duties included travel to such faraway locations as Taiwan and to other potentially dangerous places, she worried what would happen to monies due her if she met her demise. Since compensation was paid to her circuitously, she wanted to be certain any salary owed went to her children in the event she was incapacitated—or worse.

When Candy wrote to her lawyer, it was the first time she'd given anyone a hint that she was engaged in secret work for the government. However, she provided few details, possibly because she'd been given a posthypnotic suggestion, and did not consciously recall specifics. She seemed most concerned that any unpaid monies be forwarded to her children. In the correspondence to her attorney, Candy never referred to the CIA by name, only that she "worked for a secret government agency." But, when hypnotized, she admitted to Nebel that her job was "sometimes scary," in her own words, and she blamed Jensen for the circumstances she found herself mired in.

Without her conscious knowledge, Candy had a relationship

with her secret personality, reacting with her to help keep it secret. It was as if Candy and the Arlene personality actually spoke to each other below the level of Candy's awareness. She was so successful at keeping the secret, having been so programmed and conditioned by Jensen, that not even Candy's own mother could sense the presence of another personality. In fact, Candy's mother knew nothing about her daughter's secret life and work, but twice heard a second and deeper voice coming from Candy's bedroom at home in New York, that she attributed to a male visitor.

During the hypnotic trance sessions with Nebel, Candy provided enough information to surmise that what she thought were "vitamin shots," were actually drugs administered by Jensen to enhance her suggestibility to hypnosis. She possibly was given a barbiturate known to produce a "trancelike reaction." Candy revealed that she'd complained to Jensen that her arm was sore because of all of the intravenous injections she was subjected to. She'd also suffered adverse reactions, including headaches and dizziness. But when she'd asked Jensen what he gave her, he was evasive.

In fact, it was likely that Jensen had dosed her with several drugs. One of the drugs might have been a powerful tranquilizer, Thorazine, well known to psychiatrists, who sometimes called it a "hypnotic drug." Too often, mentally ill people who were administered Thorazine gave the appearance of being dulled or in a stupor. Thorazine was also popular in the 1960s on college campuses as a drug administered to counter the effects of LSD when users were reporting a bad trip.[6]

It was also possible that Candy was slipped LSD in beverages such as orange juice. LSD was promoted by the CIA to experiment with programming or disorienting enemy agents and was also tested in members of the army general staff by the head of Army Research and Development, General Arthur Trudeau. The mix could have also included other hypnotics such as sodium pentothal or "truth serum," administered to lower a subject's resistance by inducing a twilight sleep. These drugs, Candy revealed during her hypnosis sessions with her husband, were administered to her against her will.

Nebel also discovered that Candy had been warned by Jensen not to visit any medical doctors or dentists unless he approved them. The reason? The CIA was concerned that if Candy, or any other hypnotized subjects, received anesthesia or Novocaine, they might begin to talk and reveal details of their secret government work. In fact, Bain said, Jensen never placed any complete trust in Candy, raising the question of whether a CIA operative could be controlled by such means as drugs or hypnosis or both. How long would a hypnotic suggestion remain effective? Would it wear off, and under what circumstances?

Finally, in 1972—after twelve years—Candy told Jensen she was quitting her position with the government, something the CIA did not like. The abrupt or sudden resignation by an operative posed a potential risk that the person might talk. Thus, "loose cannons" were a danger to covert CIA operations. Jensen was fully aware of that when he reacted the only way he knew to keep Candy under control. He threatened her life.

Had it not been for Nebel's hypnosis of his wife, she might never have revealed details of a story that read more like a spy thriller than real life events. The trance sessions became a routine part of the Nebels' lives, eventually amounting to more than two hundred hours of audiotapes. But one incident bears special note: the night that Candy attacked Nebel.

As Nebel slept, the "Arlene Grant" personality unexpectedly emerged, grabbed his neck, and tried to choke the life out of him. Nebel quickly awoke and fought off the angry and aggressive persona, until she calmed down, and Candy was, again, asleep. When she awakened several hours later, Candy had no recollection of her outburst.

Nebel knew that Arlene had to be erased from Candy's mind. That personality, controlling and bitter, also proved to be potentially dangerous, and she was damaging Nebel's relationship with his wife. Arlene had become an interference and meddler in their lives. Perhaps she was a manifestation of Candy's own controlling side? Or was the second persona an example of what some—but not all—psychologists termed "multiple personality disorder"? It was as if the two identities were fighting within the same body, and it became apparent that Arlene wanted to dominate Candy. She'd even expressed jealousy of Candy's new career as a talk show host with Nebel. Psychological theories and speculations aside, the hostile second persona had been created through hypnotic suggestion. Now, Nebel reasoned, hypnosis could be the tool that would eventually "weaken" and eliminate Arlene Grant, lest she become the dominant personality.

Nebel recognized that Candy had tried to suppress Arlene, to keep the angry identity from taking control. But she also needed help to thwart Jensen's ultimate plan, the hypnotic suggestion given to Candy that was to result in her taking her own life. So the Nebels' regressive hypnosis sessions continued. It was a difficult process, but eventually, Arlene came forth less and less, until she was weakened to the point where, for all practical purposes, she was gone. Hypnosis had been used to erase what it had created. Of course, Nebel still worried that perhaps the CIA would try to reconnect with Candy, and Arlene might someday resurface. Fortunately, however, she had not returned by the time Nebel told his story to author and friend Donald Bain.

There really was no ending, in the traditional sense, to the story of Candy Jones, even when her ordeal seemed over. Bain had witnessed one of the regressive hypnosis sessions at the Nebel home, and he'd heard the tapes. With Nebel's consent, when *The Control of Candy Jones* was published in 1976, the *Joel Martin Show* aired excerpts of the tapes on the radio, with Bain as the guest. By then, the American public had learned about the CIA's years of mind-control experiments on untold numbers of subjects who never knew that they'd been used as something akin to laboratory rats.[7]

Long John Nebel and Candy Jones continued hosting their late-night talk show on New York radio station WMCA until 1978 when Nebel finally succumbed to the prostate cancer that he'd long and valiantly fought. After his death, Candy continued hosting the show herself. She died of cancer in 1990, at the age of sixty-four. Curiously, in many obituaries about her life and career, her involvement with the CIA received no mention.

No doubt, only a few years before Candy Jones's story was made public, many people would have questioned that so bizarre a tale could be true. But after President Kennedy was murdered, America's mood changed; increasingly it was the government that was the object of skepticism and suspicion. The post–World War II years, through the 1950s and early 1960s, were a watershed. The blind trust Americans placed in government institutions and leaders, especially after the Vietnam War and Watergate, were over. The 1975 Church hearings in the United States Senate, revealing that the Kennedy assassination of 1963, was indeed a conspiracy, was in itself shocking. And by the time the 1980s rolled around, most Americans, having slogged through the turbulent 1960s, with its social upheavals, riots and protests, and traumatic political assassinations, and then the cynical 1970s, were ready to turn to a more spiritual explanation for a definition of reality. But there were more surprises in store.

3

The Weaponization of Mind Control and LSD

In the late 1960s and into the 1970s, a new brand of popular self-help psychology began to appear in the consumer marketplace. The premise of this approach to self-analysis was that inside the human mind was a kind of biological tape recorder that started with our earliest memories, and kept on recording. Its practical applications for readers of such books as *The Games People Play* by Eric Berne (1964) and *I'm OK, You're OK* by former Navy psychiatrist Thomas A. Harris (1967), told readers that memory recordings generate scripts that people play out unwittingly throughout their lives. Recognizing what's in those scripts by going back to what roles people play in their relationships is a key, these authors argue, to forming and maintaining healthy relationships.

All well and good, but what does this have to do with the

paranormal and why is it a conspiracy? In *I'm OK, You're OK*, Harris gives credit to research conducted in Canada by Dr. Wilder Penfield, who was experimenting with tapping into memories stored along the cerebral cortex.[1] Penfield applied a low-voltage current to a subject's cortex and asked his subject what he was experiencing when the current was applied. The subjects replied that they were reliving memories when certain parts of their brains were stimulated. Different areas of the cortex returned different memories, memories that the subjects weren't even aware they had.

More than one subject remarked that the eerie thing about the emergence of the memories was that the experience didn't even seem like conscious recall. It was almost like a strange dream state in which the subject was actually hearing and seeing what was happening in memory while at the same time being perfectly aware of where he was, in a hospital, and talking to Dr. Penfield. It was a very strange experience, reminiscent of a scene out of the Marcel Proust novel *Swann's Way*, in which the narrator bites into a small cake and is immediately transported in his mind back to a childhood memory. It's an example of how a sensory experience stimulates a memory. In Penfield's experiment, the sensory experience was an electric current.

To readers of *I'm OK, You're OK* and *The Games People Play*, the discussions of Wilder Penfield and hidden memories were certainly a fun piece of scientific fact. But the real facts behind Penfield's experiments weren't known to the general public and still aren't. However, medical students who worked with him and with his associate, Dr. Donald Cameron at McGill Medical School, described experiments involving altering the perceptions and memories of test subjects.[2] These experiments, ostensibly sponsored by the CIA, were part of a program to peel away the layers of conditioning that the KGB used to create identities for their undercover agents planted in the United States. We knew about the KGB and

Communist Chinese identity playback programs at the end of the Korean War. According to the late Lieutenant Colonel Philip J. Corso,[3] who was on the negotiating team to repatriate American prisoners of wars (POWs) at the end of the war before he was posted to Army Psychological Warfare, the U.S. government was very worried about the extent to which undercover Soviet saboteurs had penetrated American society. The experiments, part of the CIA's program known as MK-ULTRA, the program under which Dr. Jensen had manipulated Candy Jones, were the agency's strategy to uncover this spy network. MK-ULTRA was one of the CIA's early attempts to experiment with something as ephemeral as the human psyche, but it was only part of a grand scheme of psychological warfare techniques.[4]

By the end of the twentieth century, many Americans learned that long before the counterculture and hippies began experimenting with LSD, the U.S. government had. Since the 1950s, the CIA was engaged in LSD research on untold numbers of unsuspecting subjects. The numbers may have reached the thousands, including members of our own armed services. In Lieutenant General Arthur Trudeau's own memoirs, for example, he describes an experiment that took place in the Pentagon in which, at a morning meeting of the Army general staff, experimenters doped their coffee with LSD 25. The resulting confusion and disorientation indicated that using LSD on the enemy might work to make him more vulnerable.[5]

The exact number of people experimented on with LSD would never be known. The records were ordered destroyed by the CIA, and the agency claimed its mind-control tests ended in 1967. But did they? Candy Jones said she was still being subjected to them after that year. That meant one of two possibilities: government researchers and agents, such as Dr. Gilbert Jensen, were rogues who were operating on their own in defiance of the CIA's announced ban, or the agency was not telling the truth, and its covert programs involving drugs and hypnosis had continued, perhaps under a name other than MK-ULTRA. That named program would earn a reputation as "one of the most disturbing instances of intelligence community abuse on record," according to writer Jon Elliston, voicing an opinion many eventually held.

In telling the Candy Jones story, author Donald Bain suggested Jensen's purpose was to make Candy Jones "the perfect spy." That brings us to an important book Bain referred to, *Hypnotism* by G. H. Estabrooks, written in 1943 and revised in 1957. It is nearly certain that Jensen and his colleagues studied or were influenced by it. The late G. H. Estabrooks was a psychologist and professor at Colgate University, recognized for groundbreaking research about hypnosis, and a strong advocate of hypnotism for military purposes.[6] Yet, during World War II, the Office of Strategic Services rejected Estabrooks's ideas. Perhaps he was ahead of his time. However, Estabrooks's ideas were eventually said to have influenced the CIA in its own experiments with mind control.

What was especially relevant to the Candy Jones saga was Estabrooks's chapter titled "Hypnotism in Warfare," which provided specifics about how hypnotism could be employed in wartime to create messengers to deliver secret or classified data. "The use of hypnotism in warfare represents the cloak and dagger idea at best—or worst," Estabrooks wrote.[7] "We don't need the subject's consent when we wish to hypnotize him [and] some will have no memory whatsoever when they awaken." Since a hypnotized messenger carried no documents, the data was memorized when the subject was entranced. The courier would also be unquestionably loyal because consciously he or she knew nothing about the materials being carried, and thus would not be capable of betrayal. The hypnotized messenger could also be made "insensitive to pain," so enemy torture to extract information would serve no purpose. If you think back to the 1960s, you might remember that what Estabrooks was saying was also the basis for both the John Frankenheimer motion picture *Manchurian Candidate* as well as the Charles Bronson action feature *Telefon*, about deep-cover Soviet agents provocateurs.

Jensen might have actually been more interested in the techniques that would convert Candy into a "superspy" than in the supposedly secret messages she carried. There's no evidence that anything she delivered was of great significance; it was likely more important to Jensen that Candy unwittingly became his "guinea pig," as Bain termed it.

In his book, Estabrooks offered a scenario of how hypnosis could be used to program the "superspy" or "perfect messenger."[8] It involved the so-called multiple personality theory that we mentioned before, and you may recall from the 1957 motion picture based on the Corbett Thigpen and Harvey Cleckley book about the true story of Chris Costner Sizemore, who was portrayed by Joanne Woodward in the movie *The Three Faces of Eve*, where a psychiatrist, played by Lee J. Cobb, reached into the mind of his subject, Eve White, to communicate with her alter personality, Eve Black. Through the use of hypnosis, two separate personalities were created within one person.

For his part, Estabrooks gave the following Cold War example that someone such as Dr. Jensen could have used as a virtual road map. Estabrooks designated someone in their normal waking state as "personality A or PA." That person will become a "rabid communist." Then, a second personality, "B or PB" is developed; it is the "unconscious personality," Estabrooks explained. "PB has all the information possessed by PA. But PB is a loyal American and has all the memories of PA, whereas PA does not have this advantage.[9]

"My superspy plays his communist role in his waking state, aggressively, consistently, fearlessly. But [his] actual loyalty [remains] with the United States," Estabrooks wrote. It is impossible "to detect [those] who have been prepared for espionage work by this method," he added.[10]

If such CIA intrigues as creating "superspies" sounded too fantastic for Americans of earlier generations to believe, consider what an incredulous public learned in late 1974 when *The New York Times* revealed that the CIA had engaged in "illegal domestic activities," that included experiments on American citizens throughout the 1960s. For Nebel, the published report confirmed what he'd already personally discovered by hypnotizing his wife.[11] In the next year, 1975, spurred by the *Times* report, there were two well-publicized investigations of the CIA's domestic operations, both a congressional committee, chaired by Senator Frank Church, and a separate presidential panel, called the Rockefeller Commission. To say the least, some of what was divulged about the CIA, FBI, and military intelligence agencies was disconcerting. Church called the CIA "a rogue elephant." The Church hearings also officially classified the Kennedy assassination as a conspiracy.

One especially disturbing story that became widely reported concerned a CIA employee named Frank Olson. In 1953, he was researching biological warfare. However, he was never told that surreptitiously he'd been given LSD. Olson later committed suicide when he jumped from a tenth-story hotel window in New York. But his family did not know that he'd taken a powerful hallucinogenic drug, a contributing factor to his death, until twenty-two years later, in 1975. He was only one of many Americans upon whom the CIA experimented during the 1950s and 1960s, amid rumors of other suicides.[12]

Another CIA tactic was its practice of subcontracting certain experimental programs to independent research facilities. Thus, the government could technically state that it was not engaged in tests it preferred to distance itself from. You'll recall that when Uri Geller's psychic abilities were studied at SRI in California in the early 1970s, it was the CIA who covertly funded those experiments. Jensen had tested Candy Jones at the same laboratories in California where a number of psychics claimed they had been examined. For the CIA, mind control and the paranormal held promise as weapons and the use of psychics for military and intelligence purposes would be secretly tested for many years, beginning with MK-ULTRA. The CIA was able to experiment with little or no accountability beyond the agency since MK-ULTRA was classified as "exempt from the usual oversight procedures," explained author Mark Zepezauer.[13]

When the Central Intelligence Agency was created under the National Security Act in 1947, its mission was to gather intelligence from around the world, wherever America's enemies lurked, and Congress forbid the new agency from acting in any domestic capacity. In other words, the CIA was meant to function in foreign countries. It was given no authority to conduct domestic policy or security operations, and that included developing new projects and domestic surveillance or other intelligence activities within the United States. CIA officials promptly ignored the instructions and, under a mantle of secrecy, proceeded to create their own tests and programs.[14]

The CIA was not America's first intelligence agency. Its predecessor in the field was the Office of Strategic Services (OSS) that functioned during World War II. By 1943, the OSS was experimenting to find a so-called truth drug. After a group within the OSS eliminated barbiturates and mescaline, they turned to cannabis, that is, marijuana, although it had already been made illegal in the United States in 1938 under legislation supported by the nation's first drug czar, former Prohibition official Harry Anslinger. Dubbed "TD" for truth drug, at first the OSS thought that cannabis held some promise. By relaxing blood vessels and lowering a subject's blood pressure, it "appears to relax all inhibitions," scientists suggested. But marijuana failed because it was not only essentially nonhallucinogenic, it also didn't deprive a subject of his or her sense of reality. No one given the drug offered up any confidential or classified data. What's more, several subjects became quite ill from overdoses that sedated them. At the same time, the Nazis were also similarly experimenting with drugs, using concentration camp prisoners as subjects, and presumably finding as little success as the OSS had. At the war's end, the United States confiscated Nazi documents, but they were never made public. The extent to which the Third Reich had any success with their version of mind-control experiments remains a mystery.

But the quest had begun. "Since World War II, the United States government, led by the Central Intelligence Agency, has searched actively but secretly for techniques to manipulate human behavior," wrote John Marks in *The Search for the Manchurian Candidate*.[15] These mind-control experiments continued when the CIA followed the OSS.

By the early 1950s, the CIA had become increasingly fascinated with the hallucinogenic drug LSD, and began giving it to subjects without their knowledge. The CIA invested large sums of money and dosed many people, including President John F. Kennedy, to see if LSD could be a brainwashing tool, only to conclude that it was unreliable and the government ultimately abandoned its experiments. This was after an enthusiastic CIA reportedly tried unsuccessfully to purchase the entire world supply of LSD. The next time most Americans heard about the hallucinogenic drug was when it flashed across the 1960s counterculture, accompanied by colorful psychedelic art, and untold numbers of acid-tripping hippies throughout the country made LSD virtually a household word. You may recall that in the early 1960s, it was the CIA that surreptitiously funded Dr. Timothy Leary's controversial LSD research. Timothy Leary (1920–1996), by the way, had also worked for the CIA and, according to the late Dr. Max Jacobson (1900–1979), President Kennedy's unofficial doctor, had given Dr. Jacobson LSD to deliver to the White House for Kennedy and his friends.

Dr. Jacobson, who had come to the United States in the 1930s, fleeing Nazi Germany, had been trained in Vienna by the Soviet Union, according to Jacobson's FBI file, and by the time he was administering liquid meth by injection to President Kennedy, had been identified by both the FBI and the CIA as a Soviet operative. Yet the CIA was using Jacobson to dope the United States president via Timothy Leary.

When the United States government became involved in exploring psychic phenomena in the early 1950s, it had no interest whatsoever in the spiritual dimensions of the paranormal. There were some people who were uncomfortable with psychic abilities being applied to warfare. But psi represented another potential secret weapon in the arsenals of the military and intelligence agencies during the Cold War, a time when America faced a genuine threat of nuclear annihilation from the Soviet Union.

At the heart of the government's interest in psychic ability was "remote viewing," best described as a form of clairvoyance and telepathy, and once known as "second sight." One notable example from history was Emanuel Swedenborg (1688–1772), the Swedish mystic, who in 1759 clairvoyantly saw and described a terrible fire in Stockholm, three hundred miles from where he was at the exact moment of the conflagration. We'll come back shortly to examine the history of remote viewing and the making of "psychic spies" in the United States in the years after World War II, and continuing right up to the present.

Given human nature, it's no surprise that governments, the military, and psychics crossed paths and then joined forces as far back as the ancient world in what has correctly been termed a "symbiotic" or mutually advantageous relationship. When a king, emperor, or pharaoh faced a battle or the threat of war from an opposing army, in addition to prayers and sacrifices to the gods of war, it made sense to call upon people with "special powers," the ones we've come to know as psychics and mediums. In ancient civilizations they might have been better known as shamans, priests, oracles, or soothsayers. Perhaps they had obtained information supernaturally through dreams, trances, rituals, or potions. What if their "occult" or "magical" abilities, to use the language of centuries ago, allowed them to glimpse the future, and provide important predictions that were otherwise impossible to obtain? Perhaps prophets and oracles could determine an enemy's location or strategy, foretell what an adversary was thinking or planning, or predict the outcome of a battle or war.

Even kings and conquerors did not always hear what they hoped to. You'll recall the Old Testament account of King Saul who, in disguise, secretly sought advice from the medium at Endor. Her prediction from the spirit of the late King Samuel warned Saul that he would be killed in battle against the Philistines. The medium's peek into the future proved to be chillingly correct.[16]

The Old Testament contains a number of references to the prophets, including Moses, Daniel, and Joseph, who communicated the Lord's commands to the Israelites, and even what He had to say about war, which God deemed sometimes necessary to "smite the enemies" of the Israelites.

In ancient Egypt, "prophetic dreams" were valued as a means to predict the results of battles and wars. In order to access that knowledge, the Egyptians employed magical incantations or "spells" that were supposed to encourage psychic dreams of the future.

In *Mind Wars,* author Ron McRae recounts one of the earliest written records of "second sight" that dates back to ancient Greece in the time of King Croesus of Lydia. As did many other leaders, Croesus consulted one of the oracles for which Greece was famed. His question concerned "whether to cross a certain river in order to attack the Persians." Unfortunately, in a scenario that would be repeated often throughout the history of the paranormal, some oracles were inept; others were vague in their responses, or were simply frauds. But, there were those considered genuine, especially the famed oracle at Delphi. It was not unusual for her, the most celebrated medium in ancient Greece, to be asked many important questions, on "matters of state," by some of the most influential figures of the time.

The Delphic oracle informed King Croesus that war with Persia "would destroy a great empire." In the king's hasty interpretation he assumed the oracle meant the destruction of his enemy, Persia. Actually, the military assault Croesus undertook proved to be cataclysmic, but not to Persia; it was Croesus's empire that was conquered and destroyed.[17]

In ancient Rome, augurs or soothsayers carried considerable influence, and by law, they were to be consulted prior to making major decisions, such as carrying out war. The augurs were to the Romans what the oracles were to the Greeks, and the biblical prophets had been to the Israelites. Omens or portends were taken seriously by the Romans, and among the more popular forms of divination was "reading entrails or intestines" of an animal to determine "good and bad omens." You'll likely recall the emperor Julius Caesar ignored the soothsayer's warning that danger would befall him in March 44 BCE. That prediction proved to be accurate when Caesar was stabbed to death; among the assailants was his friend Brutus.

At about the same time as the ancient Greeks and Romans, there were the mysterious Druids who dwelled in Britain and other parts of Western Europe before the birth of Jesus. Dressed in long white robes, the Druids were the "high priests" of the ancient Celts, and were regarded as the "psychic soldiers" of their time for their "magical powers" to vanquish their enemies. Their religious ceremonies, held in the utmost secrecy, added to the mystery surrounding them, but we know the Druids regarded the head as the seat of the soul, and believed it continued to live on separately after the death of the body. Thus, following successful battles, human heads became trophies, and supposedly helped those who possessed them.

As Christianity grew and became powerful in the Roman Empire, divination was discouraged, as were other occult beliefs. Once the Roman Catholic Church dominated life and thinking across Europe during the Middle Ages, every form of occult and magical practice was forbidden, and punishable by fiery execution.

The inspiring and true story of the remarkable Joan of Arc, patron saint of France, is an example of how psychic powers were employed to predict the course of battle. Acting on visions and voices she heard psychically, the young maiden led the French army to victory over the British, only to be betrayed, tried, and burned at the stake in 1431. By every definition Jeanne d'Arc was a "psychic soldier."[18]

McRae also told of the real-life psychic who was the basis for the signature of one of the most known fictional spies ever created: James Bond, Agent 007. Author Ian Fleming based that now famous number for the dashing character, a motion picture icon since the 1960s, on Dr. John Dee, alchemist, and astrologer to the court of Queen Elizabeth I in the sixteenth century, who actually signed his name with the numerals *007*. Each *0* represented an eye. The *7* was the sum of two eyes, the four other senses, and one for the mystical knowledge from spirits who Dee said spoke through his crystal ball.[19]

In America, the Founding Fathers, many of them Freemasons,

were steeped in ancient occult and mystical beliefs. Their arcane knowledge was an influence in guiding them through the Revolutionary War and the founding of the United States. The American Revolution is "an example of the most successful social experiment ever attempted by secret societies in human history," according to Michael Howard in *The Occult Conspiracy* (1979).

During the Civil War, President Abraham Lincoln sought advice about the course of battle from psychic mediums, notably Nettie Colburn, whose story we told in an earlier book. Lincoln, himself psychic, apparently was not reticent about consulting spiritualist mediums, even regarding some critical political and military decisions. Nettie Colburn's clairvoyance, or second sight, allowed her to glimpse distant battles, and even future events, so that she was able to secretly provide Lincoln with military information during the War Between the States.[20]

Lincoln had also been impressed by a young magician named Horatio Cooke, only eighteen, but remarkably gifted at freeing himself from tied ropes. As a result, the president designated Cooke to be a "scout," a term used during the Civil War to denote a spy whose very dangerous job was to penetrate Confederate lines. Cooke once employed his abilities as an "escape artist" to help free a group of captured Union scouts that the Confederates had intended to put to death. Cooke was at Ford's Theatre on April 14, 1865, the night the president was assassinated, and he was also among the small group of people gathered at Lincoln's bedside the next morning when he died. Once the war ended, Cooke made his career as a stage magician, and for more than forty years also uncovered deceptive spiritualist mediums. Late in his life, Cooke was on good terms with world-famous escape artist Harry Houdini, no friend of spiritualism.[21]

Historical records show that Cooke was not the only conjurer to serve the U.S. government, as far back as the late nineteenth century the Secret Service recruited magicians. Their "sleight of hand" proved extremely useful for picking locks, doors, and safes to then secret out information about current or potential enemy action.

In 1898, the same year that H. G. Wells wrote *The War of the Worlds,* and William McKinley occupied the White House, tensions were mounting between the United States and Spain over Cuba. In February, the battleship *Maine* sank in Havana Harbor after being hit by a mysterious but powerful explosion. Two hundred and sixty Navy officers and sailors were killed. Outraged Americans blamed Spain, and the so-called yellow or tabloid press fueled public anger, although the official cause of the *Maine* tragedy was never determined. However, it was the spark that moved President McKinley to declare war to free Cuba from Spain's dictatorial rule and in April, the Spanish-American War officially began.

Shortly after the *Maine* tragedy, John E. Wilkie, a skilled veteran of government law enforcement work, was appointed head of the U.S. Secret Service. One of Wilkie's immediate goals was to ferret out Spanish spies in the United States. This was twenty-five years before there was an FBI and fifty years before the CIA. The Secret Service was the nation's only agency charged with intelligence and counterintelligence work.

According to the authors of *The Secret Life of Houdini*, William Kalush and Larry Sloman, the search for the enemy took the Secret Service to Montreal, Canada, and right to the door of the Spanish attaché, the spy ring's leader. To infiltrate their clandestine operation, Wilkie ingeniously employed two professional actors to work with one of his agents. By pretending they wanted to rent an apartment, the trio managed to slip inside the attaché's residence where they surreptitiously removed a letter intended for delivery to Spain. It was a synopsis of that country's continuing espionage efforts against the United States. Once the story became news, public indignation forced the Canadian government to oust the Spanish, thus smashing their spy ring.

As Kalush and Sloman noted, it was rather innovative that as far back as 1898, a top American intelligence official employed performers to gather secret information. The actors, incidentally, came from a theater group headed by a man named Bob Fitzsimmons, who was also a prize-fighting champion and a magician.

If you've arrived at the conclusion that political and military leaders were willing to secretly employ unconventional means, such as the skills of magicians, mediums, and psychic spies, in the pursuit of intelligence, you are absolutely correct. Traditionalists and skeptics might debate the value of conjurers and clairvoyants as spies—however, the more urgent goal was to protect their nation's security and win whatever war was being fought. If psychics and mediums were able to summon their extrasensory powers to accurately locate or identify enemy plans and positions, the military advantage would be immense. If magicians and escape artists had the ingenuity to slip through enemy lines to retrieve secret data or save the lives of captured soldiers, why not press them into service? If someone could read minds, what valuable information might he or she discern that was otherwise known only to the enemy?

4

Harry Houdini

This is the story of the world-famous magician and escapologist, Harry Houdini, who, according to an intriguing book, *The Secret Life of Houdini,* was a spy for both the United States and England before and during World War I. At first, the conclusion may sound startling or sensational, but the authors provide strong suppositions to make their case. As a master of deception, Houdini understood the skills required for espionage work. He became renowned for his extraordinary feats of escape and—as twentieth-century America's first and most vociferous psychic debunker—a mission that may have cost him his life.[1]

Early in his career, on the vaudeville stage, Houdini and his wife, Bess, performed a successful spiritualist act in which she pretended to be a medium. While Houdini did not profess any serious interest in spiritualism, the movement that had swept the country since the mid-nineteenth century, Bess was of another mind; she'd been raised in a family that believed in the supernatural, ghosts, and the spirit world.

By 1898, Houdini was on his way to fame and fortune as a master of escape tricks. He was able to free himself from locked handcuffs and other restraints so amazingly that he was billed as "The Wizard of Shackles," and audiences flocked to see him wherever he appeared. Police officials who tested Houdini's ability to escape from various handcuffs, leg irons, jail cells, even straitjackets, were astonished at his skill.

Typically, as audiences watched, he was bound in hardware used to restrain prisoners, tied tightly with ropes for good measure, and placed in a cabinet on stage. Moments later, out he'd come, free from the bonds and shackles, to the cheers and amazement of all. Harry Houdini's star was rapidly ascending; he was fast becoming a huge celebrity, and that fact had not gone unnoticed by the chief of the United States Secret Service, John Wilkie, who also happened to be an accomplished amateur magician, and reportedly could read minds.

The Spanish-American War lasted only two years, and ended with Spain's defeat. Wilkie turned his attention to other pressing problems, such as hundreds of "suspected threats to national security," wrote Kalush and Sloman. He also had the responsibility of tracking down a growing epidemic of counterfeiters turning out well-made but bogus coins in denominations from one to twenty dollars, especially in the western United States.

Kalush and Sloman in *The Secret Life of Houdini* surmised that the magician's "first mission for the U.S. Secret Service" occurred during the summer of 1899, as part of the effort to break the counterfeiting operation. Houdini received police instruction in the ways of the counterfeiters. Then he went to work. He was able to aid government agents by employing sleight of hand to switch a real coin with a bogus one back into the slippery fingers or pockets of known or suspected counterfeiters as they tried to pass off the fake money. Once the imitation coin was seen in the criminal's hand, it was considered sufficient evidence for an arrest.

In 1908, in a newspaper interview, Wilkie acknowledged that, "sleight of hand is figuring more and more in the operations of the Secret Service," and he disclosed that the government was employing "several" skilled magicians.[2]

A great advantage of having Houdini serve as a spy was the ease with which he was able to travel from one country to another, without arousing foreign suspicions. Kalush and Sloman found evidence that not only was Houdini an American spy, he also served our ally, British intelligence. He'd become a world-famous celebrity, and that entailed performing in England and around the European continent, as well as in the United States. It was the perfect cover for him to gather information useful to the Secret Service, as well as the American military.

At the same time John Wilkie was heading the U.S. Secret Service, the responsibility for gathering intelligence in England rested with a veteran of law enforcement, William Melville, who headed Scotland Yard's Special Branch and was widely known as "England's most celebrated spymaster," Kalush and Sloman explained. Melville had built a superb network of both contacts and informants so that he could keep tabs on the whereabouts and activities of those who needed watching. Melville worked in an era when the electronic surveillance that we take for granted today was unknown, and he became so familiar to his countrymen that he was an inspiration for author Ian Fleming's fictional spy, James Bond.[3]

Before 1899 had ended, American newspapers reported that Houdini and his wife, Bess, were sailing to England where the magician would be tested at famed Scotland Yard. Prior to the voyage, according to Kalush and Sloman, an uneasy Houdini visited Paul Alexander Johnstone, a New York magician who was also a "palm reader" of some note, for reassurance about the future.[4]

The couple arrived in London in June 1900, and Houdini was soon introduced to William Melville at Scotland Yard. Accompanying Houdini was C. Douglas Slater, London's most highly regarded theater manager. Supposedly, Houdini was taken to Melville so that the famed magician could be handcuffed as a favor to Slater, who said that if Houdini could free himself from the strong metal restraints, he had a contract to perform at Slater's prestigious theater. But Melville cautioned Houdini that Scotland Yard's shackles were "scientific manacles; not stage handcuffs." In other words, Melville did not think Houdini would be able to release himself.

Houdini placed his arms around a post, and Scotland Yard's state-of-the-art handcuffs were locked securely onto his wrists. Once that was done, Melville told Houdini that he and Slater would return within a couple of hours, and expected to see him where they'd left him cuffed. Perhaps the famed magician and escapologist had finally met his match. But, before either could reach the door, Houdini was right behind them, free as a bird, while the cuffs had been tossed on the floor. According to Kalush and Sloman, Melville and Slater were stunned, the latter so greatly impressed he immediately signed Houdini to play at his highly acclaimed Alhambra Theatre in London.[5]

That's the story most often told about how Houdini was introduced to Scotland Yard, and England's most famous spymaster. But Kalush and Sloman are among those who do not think that's what happened. Also making a case against that version of events was a top expert and author on British spy matters, Andrew Cook. He thought it most improbable that Harry Houdini was permitted to audition for a theatrical appearance in the office of someone of Melville's stature. In *The Secret Life of Houdini,* Kalush and Sloman said that Cook reached the conclusion after studying "the only copy of one of Melville's diaries." In Cook's judgment, there was an audition, all right—however, it was not for a theater owner. Houdini's demonstration of his remarkable escape skills was for the benefit of Britain's top spymaster, William Melville.

Someone able to open locks with Houdini's alacrity was a potentially invaluable resource for Britain's law enforcement establishment, especially in its intelligence activity. The American magician's talents could be used to gather secret information in countries he traveled to, which then could be sent back to Scotland Yard. Harry Houdini had been recruited as a spy for Britain, just as he was in the United States.

Houdini's skills often took him to foreign jails to demonstrate his astounding escapes for officials. That placed him in the rare position of being able to evaluate the security and prison systems of different countries. It was knowledge that translated into important intelligence for Scotland Yard that was otherwise very difficult to obtain. But Houdini the famed magician aroused no suspicions; he simply reported back to Melville what jail conditions and prisoner treatment were like in the countries he traveled to.

Kalush and Sloman also revealed that Houdini's service to England included performing espionage duties in Germany, the country that Melville feared most as a potential enemy. By 1900, Melville had a strong hunch that Germany posed a threat to England. Having Houdini bring back potentially useful intelligence material from Germany was of inestimable value to Melville. There is also the curious matter of Melville's foreboding. Probably the result of great political acumen and foresight, it bordered on clairvoyance that fourteen years before England fought Germany in World War I, Melville had sensed the danger to come.[6]

One place Houdini was able to visit in Germany in the early 1900s was its largest and top-secret munitions factory, Krupp. Rarely did an American ever witness the Krupp foundry. However, for Houdini, the pretext of performing his magic and escape act for Krupp's many employees was his ticket in and no suspicions were aroused. Thus was Harry Houdini the perfect intelligence gatherer, in the guise of a stage performer bowing to the applause of an audience of enemies.

On May 4, 1886, a worker protest in Chicago's Haymarket Square turned ugly and violent. The demonstration had been spurred by anger over the shooting deaths of four strikers by Chicago police at the McCormick Reaper Works factory a day earlier. Hundreds of workers faced off against some 180 armed Chicago policemen. Then suddenly, there was an explosion. Someone had thrown a bomb into the line of cops, killing one officer immediately. Seven more died later, and many others were injured. When the bomb blast shook the police ranks, they fired back indiscriminately into the crowd of strikers. Once the mayhem calmed, seven demonstrators lay lifeless, fifty more were wounded, and police counted fifty injured officers.[7]

The deadly violent incident came to be known as the Haymarket Square Riot, and it made headlines throughout the country, frightening many Americans not yet used to the sight of worker protests. Who was to blame? Politicians quickly joined with business leaders in accusing "anarchists" for the disorder. What's more, they said, the protesters were not Americans—they were "foreigners," a buzzword that touched a nerve, especially among the xenophobic.

The idea "of an international anarchist conspiracy to create disorder and topple the established world order gained strength among all sectors of society as the 1880s progressed," wrote Kalush and Sloman. Actually, there was genuine reason for concern about anarchists. The time from 1892 to 1901 was a period when leaders of countries fell victim to assassins in greater numbers than at any other time before. Among the victims were the czar of Russia, the German kaiser, and the king of Italy. The wave of assassinations even reached the United States when President William McKinley was shot and killed by an anarchist in September 1901.

As head of the Secret Service, it was Chief Wilkie's job to penetrate the anarchist conspiracy in order to protect the public and, of course, the president. By the summer of 1901, Wilkie stepped up Secret Service surveillance of anarchists in a number of U.S. cities. But when President McKinley was assassinated on September 6, 1901, Wilkie was shocked and grief-stricken by the news, although he'd had no way to prevent the murder. The assassination understandably increased concerns about the danger that anarchists posed to America. Upon McKinley's death, Vice President Theodore Roosevelt assumed the presidency. Among his first remarks, he said, "Anarchy is a crime against the whole human race, and all mankind should band against the anarchists."[8]

Harry Houdini was again enlisted in the cause; of particular interest was Houdini's ability in gathering information from Russia, considered "the epicenter of the anarchist movement." Once again, his access was based on his world fame as a magician.

While performing in Russia, Houdini demonstrated his remarkable escapes from Russia's infamous and draconian jails. For anyone else, they would have been impenetrable; Houdini, the escape artist, managed to free himself from even Russian shackles, to the surprise of officials, while no one was aware that Houdini the spy was gathering intelligence that was being sent back to the United States. Sometimes Houdini used codes or ciphers to transmit secret communications. He also invented chemical ink with which he could write invisible messages. As well, he took ads in magicians' magazines in which he embedded secret messages, and invented a tiny hidden camera that was able to take a single picture, Kalush and Sloman explained.[9]

Unlike other countries, many of them monarchies and dictatorships, the United States did not have a national police force. It had not been easy for Wilke to track the anarchist movement to Europe where it had its roots. You can imagine his anticipation of the better intelligence that Houdini was secretly able to gather and return with in the course of his travels throughout the European capitals, and especially Russia.

Kalush and Sloman backed up their theory of Houdini's ties to government intelligence by noting that the magician was issued a new passport stating that he was born in the United States in 1873. In fact, he'd been born Erich Weiss in Budapest, Hungary, and was a naturalized citizen. One reason the government may have provided him with a new passport was as protection if he was ever arrested in Germany, a close ally of Hungary where Houdini still had relatives who could be pressured or used as "pawns" to coerce Houdini to cooperate if he was arrested.[10]

The idea of the government employing skilled magicians did not end with Houdini or World War I. Some thirty years later, when the CIA was created, magicians were still considered a useful tool for the agency's mind-control projects. Perhaps Houdini's years as a spy was an influence. In 1953, the CIA, in the throes of its MK-ULTRA project, commissioned a "manual on trickery," that was to be written by an accomplished magician in order to "describe ways to conduct 'tricks with pills' and other substances," specifically, how "mind- and behavior-altering substances could be" surreptitiously administered, according to writer Jon Elliston. As well, "tricks [could be devised] by which small objects may be obtained."[11]

Because the government has never been very forthcoming about exactly how much was accomplished during the years of MK-

ULTRA, dating back to the 1950s, it is difficult, if not impossible, to conclude with certainty what the relationship was between the CIA and magicians, or for that matter, with psychics and mediums, although we know that the CIA considered the use of ESP within MK-ULTRA.[12]

World War II was in its waning months by early 1945. It was just a matter of time before the Allies defeated Germany and Japan. An ailing President Franklin D. Roosevelt had been elected to an unprecedented fourth term in November 1944, serving in the Oval Office to see the war to its conclusion against the strenuous advice of his physicians, who said the job was killing him. One of FDR's major concerns was the postwar world and dealing with Russian dictator Joseph Stalin. Russia had been a U.S. ally during the war, an ally the United States supported with shipments of war matériel but did not support with an early invasion of Europe to assist the Soviets in repelling the Wermacht. Stalin was left to bear the brunt of the German invasion, something he would not forget. Now that a powerful Communist Soviet Union had emerged after the war, the question was, what role would it play? FDR had guided the nation through the traumatic years of the Great Depression, followed by the war. Now what lay ahead?

In November 1944, FDR turned to a psychic for advice, although he preferred never to use that word. She was a young woman named Jeane Dixon, and she'd quickly attracted attention for her psychic abilities and predictions. Now she'd been summoned to the White House, in strictest confidence, to meet the president and to answer his questions. Roosevelt wanted to know how much longer he had to live. Dixon told him truthfully, "Six months or less." Then the questioning turned to FDR's concern about Russia's postwar role. Dixon said the United States and Russia would not be allies after the war but would be again someday far in the future.

Dixon, who lived in Washington, D.C., with her husband, was called again to the White House, at FDR's request, in January 1945. Haggard and pale, he appeared to be in worsening health. When he asked how much time he had left to finish his work, Dixon told him honestly, only a very short while. But the president seemed more concerned with America's postwar policy and ways to handle Russian demands for carving up Nazi-occupied Europe. Dixon advised FDR not to give anything to Russia that the United States had a right to.

In February 1945, a gaunt and visibly ill Roosevelt attended a secret conference at Yalta, in the Crimea, with British prime minister Winston Churchill and Soviet dictator Joseph Stalin. Against Churchill's advice, FDR agreed to give the Soviets control over the eastern half of Germany. Worse, the weakened president, no longer capable of conducting difficult negotiations, allowed Eastern European and Balkan nations to be carved up and handed over to the Communist puppet governments the Soviets were putting into place, thus singularly determining their future for the next forty years.

Roosevelt did not listen to Dixon's warning. And as she predicted, FDR's time was, indeed, very short. He died suddenly of a cerebral hemorrhage at his home in Warm Springs, Georgia, on April 12, 1945, at the age of sixty-three. Jeane Dixon's predictions had come true; her warnings had been neglected.[13] When Vice President Harry Truman became president upon FDR's death, the grave responsibility fell to him to end the war decisively against Japan—with nuclear weapons—and to lead the country in the difficult postwar era.

What followed the end of World War II was a forty-year period known as the Cold War, an ideological struggle between capitalism and Communism that many Americans feared could escalate into a full-scale nuclear war, capable of destroying the United

States, and in American retaliation, decimating the Soviet Union. It was in this environment that U.S. intelligence and the military sought to gain the upper hand, and stave off that terrifying and cataclysmic ultimate confrontation.

Then, in June 1950, barely five years after the Allied victory in World War II, Americans were once again fighting on foreign soil. This time in divided Korea, where U.S. troops were sent to repel North Korea, backed by Communist China, from overtaking and controlling South Korea. The American forces were joined by troops from fifteen other nations under the auspices of the United Nations (UN). Ultimately, the North Koreans and Chinese were forced from the south, and an uneasy cease-fire was reached that continues to this day. The Korean War ended in July 1953, not with "total victory," but rather with a truce or armistice. The "limited war," as it was called, halted further Communist incursions into South Korea. But it was a concept that did not sit well with many Americans who expected a full defeat of the enemy, and were dissatisfied with a truce, an indecisive outcome in a conflict that cost more than 22,000 American lives, and nearly 120,000 more wounded, at a price to the United States of 22 billion dollars.

That impasse figured into presidential politics in 1952 when the Republican candidate, Dwight Eisenhower, was elected, garnering public support for pledging to visit Korea if he won the office. Among the Korean War's more contentious issues were the use of biological warfare, and the question of Communist treatment of prisoners of war. There was also an allegation that many American POWs were subjected to something called "brainwashing" or Communist indoctrination.

According to the late Philip J. Corso, who, as an army officer working under Eisenhower, oversaw the prisoner exchanges known as "Little Switch/Big Switch," some American service personnel were being held back by the Communists. Their identities would be taken by Communist spies to be deployed, in Corso's words, as "playbacks." These spies, whose existence was publicly revealed in the publication of the KGB's VENONA files, would launch terrorist attacks against civilian industrial targets and infrastructure targets in the event of a war between the Soviets and the United States. Corso said that the American POWs were subjected to intense psychological torture and that the Soviet agents were psychologically programmed to live their lives in the United States under such deep cover that not even they knew they were spies.[14] This was one of the reasons the CIA began the MK-ULTRA program so as to penetrate this deep psychological cover.

Some of the CIA experiments, carried out under the guise of national security, seem, in hindsight, bizarre, of questionable ethics, and almost certainly illegal. Nonetheless, the top-secret projects went on, fueling rumors and speculation about what they were.

One theory deserves a moment of conjecture, for it brought together covert intelligence activity, psychic powers, and the use of magicians. We know from several declassified CIA documents that the use of magicians and trickery was being considered by the spy agency during the 1950s. That fact lends more credibility to the supposition that the magician Harry Houdini had served as a spy years earlier. At the same time, the U.S. government in the fifties had begun secret research of psychic abilities for possible military and intelligence use.[15]

What if, given the CIA's penchant for secrecy, it turned to magicians, not only to write "manuals on trickery," but also to provide a distraction for its tests with psychics? For example, when a certain skilled magician was arrested in the 1950s on charges of violating immigration laws, then weapons possession, and years later accused of fomenting communist sympathies, might the cases have been adjudicated because the magician not only taught CIA and other intelligence agents sleight of hand, but, borrowing a page from Houdini, also vigorously debunked psychics, mediums, and astrologers, so as to discourage public curiosity while the government went about secretly testing ESP for its weapons arsenal against the Soviet threat? There was a second individual with alleged communist leanings who went on to national notoriety in a brash secular movement to debunk all psychics.

During the long Cold War that dragged on from the end of World War II until the collapse of the Soviet Union in 1989, a time when the U.S. and the Soviets were each building huge stockpiles of nuclear weapons, the admission of communist associations was a chancy revelation in many fields of endeavor. For example, in the early 1950s, the era of the McCarthy hearings and communist "witch hunts," well-known Hollywood figures—actors, writers, and directors—were caught in a web of accusations of "communist ties," and many saw their careers turn to ashes when they were "blacklisted."

Yet, at least two individuals with alleged communist sympathies turned up among the national leadership of psychic debunkers, years before the end of the Cold War. Is the parallel to Houdini an interesting coincidence—or something more? Separated by over a half century, magicians at the turn of the twentieth century, as those of later generations, were recruited by the government to engage in covert operations tied to national security. Houdini, as have several of his more recent counterparts, also waged a scathing campaign against psychics and mediums.

Houdini, in his dogged pursuit of spiritualism, dismissed all mediums as frauds, and spiritualism as a "swindle." The heated debate became public when Houdini argued vociferously with Sir Arthur Conan Doyle, author of the popular *Sherlock Holmes* stories, and a devout spiritualist, as mentioned in an earlier book.[16]

But there was another aspect to Houdini's campaign as America's first publicly acclaimed psychic debunker, for which he attracted wide attention. The mediums, psychics, and astrologers who made a living from séances, sittings, and readings watched the famed magician with both dread and anger. The entire spiritualist movement was under attack and, if Houdini was successful, they could be put out of business. Houdini sensed that his life was in danger as a result. He confided to a friend in the publishing business that "fraudulent spiritualist mediums" would kill him, aware that mediums all over the country—indeed, all over the world—despised him that much. Houdini could imagine spiritualists celebrating wildly at news of his death. Yet, he made no effort to abandon his self-financed debunking campaign, even in the face of open hostility and threats against his life.[17]

When Houdini pressed for a law against mediums in Washington, D.C., it caused alarm in the spiritualist movement. A number of mediums plying their trade in the nation's capital had become rather influential; they counted political figures among their clients, including senators and congressmen. It was strangely similar to the statesmen who sought help from the Delphic oracle centuries earlier in ancient Greece. Spirit communications often secretly influenced legislative decisions, and Washington, a city with no law against fortune-tellers, had an abundance of psychics and mediums. Houdini pronounced himself deeply disappointed that even those in the White House attended séances and consulted with mediums, including First Lady Florence Harding, and later, the wife of President Calvin Coolidge. Outraged, the famed magician called for Coolidge to investigate, and demanded a law to ban the practice of mediumship.

At Houdini's insistence, a New York congressman introduced legislation that would prohibit fortune-telling in Washington. The proposed law called for a $250 fine and/or six months in jail for anyone claiming he or she was a professional medium offering services to the public. In February 1926, the bill was the subject of a House committee hearing, and Houdini was right there urging its passage. But, also present were hundreds of outraged mediums and other psychic practitioners who made their voices heard—and loudly; the hearing became a raucous affair. Although the legislation failed to pass, Houdini maintained that he'd performed a public service by exposing fraudulent mediums who "preyed on the vulnerable, gullible, and bereaved."[18]

There was no question that Houdini's antispiritualist crusade made an impact. By claiming that all mediums were frauds, and that he could duplicate their performances by legerdemain, Houdini had contributed mightily to discrediting the movement. He'd even offered a "challenge": ten thousand dollars to anyone who could demonstrate a psychic feat that he could not duplicate by conjuring. No one ever claimed the money, but Houdini, not surprisingly, had made powerful enemies in the spiritualist camp. Knowing he would never cease his holy war against them, how far would spiritualists go to stop him? Might some of them have plotted to carry through with their threats against his life?

In October 1926, Houdini was in Montreal, when two McGill University students who'd heard him speak a couple of days earlier were permitted to visit him in his dressing room. One of the boys asked Houdini whether he had the strength to "withstand blows" to his body. The magician answered, yes, he could, if he readied himself in advance by tensing his muscles.[19] Moments later, as Houdini reclined on a couch, one of the youths "leaned over and struck him several times sharply in the abdomen with his clenched fist," explained Beryl Williams and Samuel Epstein in *The Great Houdini*.[20] But Houdini had not readied himself, and the swift punches left him in terrible pain, although he assumed the blows hadn't been meant to inflict such serious injury.

Houdini performed his magic act that night, but it was apparent after the show that he was in pain. The following day, still not feeling well, he gave another performance, and then boarded a train for Detroit, the next city he was to appear in. And it is here that the story becomes murky. The most frequently told version of events is that Houdini was diagnosed with appendicitis and immediate surgery was ordered, but it was too late. He was already running a high fever and had suffered peritonitis. In other words, his appendix had ruptured. Although surgery was performed, Houdini died soon after on October 31, 1926, at the age of fifty-two.

But authors Kalush and Sloman in their book, *The Secret Life of Houdini*, suggest another scenario. They wrote that there was not one, but two incidents that resulted in Houdini's fatal injuries. After being struck in the abdomen by the college student in Montreal, there was a second assault that was strangely similar to the first. Houdini was in the lobby of a Detroit hotel when, unexpectedly, a trio of young men approached him. One in particular was large and menacing, and with no warning whatsoever, he punched Houdini violently in his stomach, so that he "doubled over in pain," according to the version suggested by Kalush and Sloman. Houdini suffered a ruptured appendix or peritonitis as a result, and surgery could not save him. He died in a Detroit hospital several days later on Halloween, October 31.

Whether Houdini suffered one crippling blow—or two—to his abdomen, the outcome was the same. However, the traditional version that there was only a single incident in which Houdini was punched forcefully has fostered the impression that his assailant's action was foolish and thoughtless, but not malicious. If there were two separate assaults on Houdini, one coming not long after the other in different cities, then the theory that the attacks were premeditated becomes more plausible. Who would have been responsible? Kalush and Sloman contend the villains were angry and vengeful spiritualists who knew that Houdini's crusade against them would never end as long as he lived.

He had damaged mediums financially, and contributed to a substantial loss of public confidence in spiritualism. Death threats had been made against him ever since his antispiritualist campaign escalated to an unrelenting tirade. Is it possible that a conspiracy of disgruntled spiritualists murdered Houdini? The supposition presented by Kalush and Sloman in 2006 is quite plausible, although why it took eighty years for the allegation to surface is difficult to understand.

Prior to his death, several mediums had "predicted" that Houdini's life was in danger. A skeptic might well conclude that perhaps the prognostications were not psychic. Did one or more of those mediums have information they knew would come true, because they were privy to the plot to murder Houdini?

The mythical Houdini has lived on, and his drive against spiritualism continues even today among debunkers and skeptics who still regard his exposure of fraudulent mediums as the ultimate word on the subject. Had Houdini lived in recent years, he'd likely have been shocked that mediums made mighty strides forward, and gained hugely in popularity. No doubt, he'd still be in relentless pursuit of them. The theories offered in *The Secret Life of Houdini,* while at first surprising, are not far-fetched. Houdini, a man of enormous ego, may have felt invincible, even in the face of powerful enemies. If he did, he underestimated his foes, and obviously made a serious miscalculation that cost him his life.[21]

Houdini's legacy to the paranormal is a controversial one. On the one hand, he performed a valuable service by exposing fraudulent mediums. On the other hand, as many debunkers did, he went too far in trying to discredit the entire spiritualist movement, and was just as guilty of fraud as any bogus medium when he resorted to trickery to discredit those that he could not otherwise expose, as in the case of Margery, the Boston medium (see Notes). As many authors and researchers have pointed out, his "aura of invincibility" was a huge part of his appeal. But any way you consider Houdini's life and death, he was a controversial, influential, and complex figure in the history of America—and the paranormal.

5

Hitler, the Paranormal, and the CIA

Although the use of both conventional and psychic spies runs through the course of humankind, in virtually every society, it is not unusual for traditional American historians to ignore or minimize the role of psychics, mediums, and astrologers in the business of espionage. The truth is that many rulers and military leaders here, as in other countries, were not averse to making use of information from psychics and psychic spies, as well as through more conventional espionage channels.

How exactly did the paranormal and attempts at mind control fit into the top-secret world of intelligence gathering? Before the CIA was created in 1947, there was the Office of Strategic Services (OSS), begun in 1942, during World War II, by President Roosevelt.[1] "The secret derring-do of the OSS was new to the United

States, and the ways of the OSS would grow into the ways of the CIA," John Marks wrote in *The Search for the "Manchurian Candidate."*[2] The first to command the OSS was General William "Wild Bill" Donovan, a World War I hero, former intelligence adviser, and attorney. His goal, as he saw it, was "to mobilize science for defense," Marks explained.[3] But Donovan was open to a wide range of secret "tricks and devices" toward the ultimate goal of destroying America's enemies, Germany and Japan. For example, the OSS had begun a covert operation in hopes of creating a drug that would prompt captured enemy agents and spies to talk more readily under questioning.[4]

Another OSS idea was to somehow poison Adolf Hitler, something that neither the American spy agency nor the British military intelligence organization's special branches unfortunately ever accomplished. It would have been a fitting end to Hitler. But Hitler said he was protected by the force of destiny. Indeed, for someone so psychotically evil, it seemed that for much of his life, Hitler was protected by the same occult powers he claimed to have unleashed on millions of others. The late historian and author John Toland (1912–2004) said that Hitler was involved in the "black arts," the same conclusion several other historians arrived at.[5] The late research psychologist Dr. Joel Norris also said that Hitler belonged to, or at least adhered to the teachings of, an ancient secret society, akin to Lucifer worship, that promised occult powers to its followers.

Toland gave as examples the number of times Hitler's premonitions saved him from death. One amazing incident occurred during World War I when Hitler was a soldier, and one night dreamed that enemy fire killed him. When a shaken Hitler awoke, he quickly fled to another area. A short while later, the soldier who took his place was blown up by an allied artillery shell. There was also the time in a latrine when Hitler had an uneasy premonition of danger. He quickly moved. Moments later the plumbing fixture was shattered by an explosive device. Hitler was leading a line of Nazi followers in Munich in 1923 when police opened fire. At least sixteen of Hitler's thugs were killed, others injured. Miraculously, Hitler escaped unscathed. Also in Munich, several years later, Hitler stepped into the street, and right into the path of a speeding car. Amazingly, he was unhurt.

One of the most infamous of incidents took place on July 20, 1944. It was the result of a plot called Operation Valkyrie. That day, a bomb had been planted under the conference table, on the side where Hitler always stood. But, inexplicably, the Führer's sixth sense compelled him to stand elsewhere, just as the device that was supposed to kill him detonated. Hitler, although wounded, miraculously survived the assassination attempt. It had been a plot hatched by Colonel Berthold von Stauffenberg and other frustrated and dissatisfied Nazi officers, including Field Marshal Rommel. The conspirators were quickly arrested and 150 of them were executed.

The symbolism of Hitler's National Socialist Party was also calculated to inspire fear. For example, the choice of the swastika as the emblem of the Third Reich was no accident. The swastika or "twisted cross" represented a demonic evil. Although versions of the symbol were revered by the Hopi tribe as a good luck sign, the Nazis used it to instill terror not only among Germans but primarily among the populations conquered by the Germans during World War II. Today, the swastika is banned in Germany and is a hated symbol in those countries who fought World War II.[6]

Hitler's background and his ascent to head of the German state still intrigue historians. It is easy to dismiss him as demented, but that only misses the truth. It was as if he became the personification of evil, whose pure hatred triggered bloodlust in an entire population. The question still remains, however, how was Hitler able to rise quickly from poverty, a vagabond who painted post-card pictures, to the pinnacle of world power? Might Hitler have been the tool of an evil force on earth? The German occultist Walter Johannes Stein, who personally knew Hitler, acknowledged that Hitler had an immense knowledge of black magic.[7] Did he also practice the black arts?

Hitler was known to suffer from nightmares. But beyond that, several credible historians have claimed that Hitler often saw a demon in the dark of night. The origin of the word "nightmare" actually means "night incubus" or "night demon." The shadowy specter never failed to frighten Hitler, although no one else could see it lurking in a corner of the Führer's bedroom. Had Hitler long before given himself to the Devil? Was the Nazi dictator a tool of Satan on earth? Many occultists believed that one or the other accounted for the monster Hitler became on the world stage, which was why, in the aftermath of the Treaty of Versailles, which ended World War I and the Great Depression in Europe, Hitler became the political spokesman and a tool of a cabal of ultra-rightist generals to preach a clarion call for nationalist Germans to arise and overthrow the Weimar Republic. However, Hitler quickly turned this message of nationalism to his hatred of the Jews and thus began what would become the Shoah that swept across Europe and still survives among the most fanatical elements of populations in the Middle East.

Finally, what explained Hitler's ban on books about the occult and mysticism? It may seem a contradiction for someone as open to the occult as he was to order thousands of books on the subject confiscated in 1934, only a year after he came to power in Germany. The answer Toland offered was quite simple. Hitler dreaded competition, and made it clear that in Nazi Germany he and his cohorts would be the only ones empowered with occult knowledge. If the conjecture about Hitler being a tool of the Devil is true, the United States and its allies fought World War II not only against the evil of flesh and blood enemies, but also against supernatural forces that were heinous and depraved.

It was the menacing effectiveness of Hitler's secret police and Nazi intelligence apparatus that confronted the United States military intelligence agencies in World War II. The U.S. also marveled at the effectiveness of British military and civilian intelligence agencies as well as the work of the NKVD, the Soviet military intelligence. Allen Dulles and John Foster Dulles, founders of the U.S. intelligence community in the wake of World War II, claimed to have been inspired by both allied intelligence agencies as well as the concept of a central intelligence analytical mechanism and data clearing house for the development of defense policy. As a result, they pushed postwar president Harry Truman to sign the National Security Act of 1947, thus creating what would become an ultraconstitutional fourth branch of government that continues to exercise jurisdiction today, not just around the world, but in America as well, as we have seen from recent revelations about NSA domestic spying and searches of all phone and Internet data. In his retirement, President Truman once said that one of his biggest mistakes was signing the National Security Act. President Eisenhower also regretted the fact that the Central Intelligence Agency had been brought into existence.

The CIA was created in 1947, during peacetime, unlike the OSS, which was born during war and had been privately funded as well by the Rockefeller family. Actually, other modern nations had built covert intelligence and spy operations before the U.S. Arguably, British intelligence was the best at the time. It also was believed to employ psychic spies. For the CIA, "influencing human behavior was a deadly serious business," Marks noted. He added, "The CIA's interest in controlling the human mind had to remain absolutely secret."[8]

When the agency began its clandestine MK-ULTRA program, it was supposedly in response to Chinese and North Korean brainwashing of American POWs during the Korean War. Actually the

U.S. had experimented with brainwashing before there was a CIA. However, by 1953, the agency had stepped up its behavior- or mind-control research under MK-ULTRA and specifically for the US Navy when it tested the psychological resiliency of test subjects to stress during World War II. Among the methods tested were "radiation, electric shocks, electrode implants, microwaves, ultrasound, and a wide range of drugs," wrote author Mark Zepezauer.[9] The CIA had some imaginative goals that included creating "torture-proof couriers" and "programmed assassins," Zepezauer explained.[10] There was also interest in whether LSD could be used to disorient the general staff of an adversarial army. The U.S. Army itself had a psychological warfare branch called "Psychological operations (Psyops)," which is where *The Day After Roswell* author Philip J. Corso was posted before he joined President Eisenhower's staff as a military liaison officer.

By the early 1950s, U.S. officials realized that if psychic ability was genuine, it could play a useful role in military and intelligence activities. Soon, under the auspices of the CIA, secret ESP research was being funded, as would any other weapons development program. John Marks explained that the spy agency sought to determine whether psychics were able to read minds or control them from a distance, as in mental telepathy; if they could access information about faraway places or people, the ability we know as clairvoyance, or, in more recent parlance, remote viewing; whether psychics could predict the future, a facility called precognition; or if they could influence the movement of physical objects or even the human mind, known to parapsychologists as psychokinesis or PK.[11] You'll recall that PK was the power claimed by Uri Geller. If, in fact, PK worked, "it could have incredibly destructive applications," Marks said.

An added impetus for CIA psychic research was the fear that the Soviet Union was not only engaged in such experimentation but was possibly far ahead of the United States, a situation deemed perilous by American intelligence and military officials. The general American public, for the most part skeptical about the paranormal, was alarmed in 1970 with the publication of Sheila Ostrander and Lynn Schroeder's book, *Psychic Discoveries Behind the Iron Curtain*. That book presupposed a "psi race" as a Cold War contest between the Communist bloc and the U.S.[12] Any advantage the Soviets had during the tense Cold War era needed to be met by the United States, if not exceeded. That included the use of the paranormal, even though there were many government officials skeptical of the subject that had long been relegated to the "fuzzy fringe" of science, and had been branded superstitious, bogus, or just plain weird.

Whether the CIA should have engaged in mind-control and psychic experiments has long been argued. Once American intelligence discovered that the Soviets were involved in research of both mind control and the paranormal, the argument went, we had no choice but to maintain parity, if not superiority over them. There was also concern that U.S. military personnel captured during the Korean War, and held as POWs, were susceptible to Communist Chinese and Soviet torture and brainwashing. If hypnosis could make our military less vulnerable to enemy punishment, then using it as a mind-control technique was worth developing went the rationale.

The counterargument was that the CIA's function was to gather foreign intelligence, not to develop surreptitious and sometimes bizarre domestic schemes that played with people's physical and mental health. There were also serious ethical questions about why it was necessary for the CIA to engage unwitting subjects who did not know they were being tested, in some cases exposing them to substantial risks and danger, such as with LSD and other drugs that they never knew were being administered. Many of the legal and moral questions raised by CIA intrigues will likely never be resolved.

When eventually parapsychologists learned about CIA machinations involving the paranormal, some were disheartened. Much as Einstein, a pacifist, had disliked that his famed theories of relativity eventually contributed to the development of the atom bomb, there were those who detested the use of psychic abilities for espionage and military purposes, contending that psi should be reserved for more peaceful and positive pursuits, such as mediums who comfort the bereaved through spirit communications, and psychic healing, to give but two examples. However, from day one, it was apparent that the CIA and other intelligence agencies had not given an iota of thought to whether or not a spiritual component was imbued within psychic abilities and the supernatural. And so drugs—some of them dangerous—hypnosis, convulsive electric shock treatments, and psychic experiments pushed forward under the top-secret MK-ULTRA project with neither public scrutiny nor congressional oversight. The CIA was seeking to control the human mind, according to John Marks.[13] Senator Frank Church chaired congressional hearings in the mid-1970s to investigate the CIA's covert operations, and concluded the agency was a "rogue elephant." The Church hearings were among the first Congressional attempts to exercise any oversight over black projects and in so doing pointed at various government covert conspiracies.

Ultimately, the CIA deemed LSD and other mind-altering drugs unreliable, ineffective, and unstable, and experiments involving them were abandoned, or so intelligence officials claimed. What spy agencies did—and when—was not always easy to determine. A covert project might technically be abandoned, then renamed and continued under a different title. Stealth and obfuscation were deemed necessary for intelligence agencies to function successfully, and information officially released for public consumption had to be regarded with a certain amount of skepticism. Where the question of the public's right to know collided head-on with the government's wall of secrecy, it was reasonable to assume that surreptitiousness would prevail.

Where the issue became particularly thorny was when intelligence officials moved into the murky waters of what was neither legal nor ethical. When Richard Helms left his position as CIA director in 1973, most records that pertained to MK-ULTRA and possibly other secret projects, were ordered destroyed. Thus, the full extent of CIA mind-control experiments will likely never be known. Not coincidentally, it had been Helms who was in charge of "clandestine services" for the CIA in its early years. However, even the relatively small number of files and documents that survived provided a sufficiently troubling picture of the government's efforts to penetrate and control the human mind.

Considering that psychics, spies, and soldiers joined forces many centuries ago, dating back to ancient times, the CIA was hardly original when it turned its eye toward the paranormal. The question was, how could or should ESP best be harnessed for intelligence work? The CIA considered psychic phenomena to be of, at least, some worth, throughout the 1950s and 1960s, although how much was accomplished with the use of psychics is difficult to determine since the research was classified as secret.

For the military, as far back as 1952, the army had provided money to Dr. J. B. Rhine for ESP tests at Duke University. By the 1960s, the Air Force was quietly performing it own ESP experiments, and the navy was funding remote viewing tests at SRI in California, where ultimately Dr. Harold Puthoff would experiment with the ESP abilities of renowned psychic Ingo Swann. As Cold War fever raged on, American intelligence took increasing notice of the Soviet interest in the paranormal for military and spying purposes. That was sufficient motivation for the CIA and the U.S. military to step up their efforts, fearing a "psychic arms race" between the world's two superpowers was inevitable.

By 1970, new fuel was added to the fiery debate when two young women, one American and the other Canadian, traveled to the Soviet Union and returned to report what they'd discovered there about paranormal research. The book by Shelia Ostrander and Lynn Schroeder titled *Psychic Discoveries Behind the Iron Curtain* quickly caught the attention of Americans, and remained a best-seller through the seventies, and by 1979 it had gone through an impressive thirteen printings and is still in print today.[14]

Of course, for Soviet scientists and researchers it was easier to tackle the elusive paranormal than it was for their U.S. counterparts. The Soviet Union, after all, was a tightly controlled dictatorship that could do pretty much whatever it wanted with little or no public input or accountability. In addition, ESP did not create a storm of religious controversy behind the Iron Curtain as it did here, since the USSR was officially an atheist state, and by reliable accounts Soviet scientists had been experimenting with psi since the 1920s. But, if the Soviet Union was successfully testing psychic abilities, so would the United States. Such was the Cold War mentality.

To what extent the book *Psychic Discoveries Behind the Iron Curtain* influenced U.S. intelligence and military officials is difficult to determine even though it was popular with the reading public. However, by the early 1970s the CIA quietly began funding "psi research" at SRI International in California where the Israeli psychic Uri Geller's paranormal abilities had been famously tested. SRI physicist Russell Targ later wrote that the CIA's financial support continued for more than a decade, and amounted to a "multimillion-dollar program." Targ explained the monies were for "exploring techniques to increase the accuracy and reliability of a human perceptual ability known as remote viewing."

So, in 1972, "remote viewing" was introduced as a new term applied to some very old psychic abilities, namely clairvoyance and telepathy. Ingo Swann, an American psychic, is credited with originating the phrase *remote viewing,* for which he was tested at Stanford Research Institute (SRI) in Menlo Park, California. The terminology was critical because of the deeply rooted stigmas associated with psychic and paranormal events; many still misidentified them as "occult." Scientists, such as Dr. Harold Puthoff and Russell Targ, and their colleagues at SRI, understood the need for a "neutral" word or phrase, and "remote viewing" seemed to fit their requirements. No Ouija boards, crystal balls, tarot cards, spooky noises, séances, or other stereotypes were involved. The psi research at SRI was serious business, developing objective metrics for determining levels of psychic ability.

Targ and Keith Harary in their book *The Mind Race* explained that, "In remote viewing, individuals are able to experience and describe locations, events, and objects that cannot be perceived by the known senses, usually because of distance."[15] The size of a target does not matter; it can be as large as a building, or "as small as a pin."

"The principal finding of remote viewing research is that most participants in these experiments learn to accurately describe buildings, geography, objects, events, and activities from which they are separated by both time and space."[16] Locations, even thousands of miles away, have been correctly detailed, and in at least two documented instances, as reported in *UFO Magazine,* events that had not yet occurred were accurately predicted. The implications of the results of remote viewers' experiences, inasmuch as they seemed to defy the statistics of chance, were potentially earthshaking. They indicated that human beings seemed to be able to gather information about things, including things in the future, from a different reality.

Here's how remote viewing worked, according to the remote viewers themselves.[17] In testing, there was a remote viewer and a tasker, a partner who held in his or her mind a set of coordinates. The tasker did not know what the coordinates meant, where they were, or even what the target site was supposed to be. The tasker and the viewer were not in visual contact with each other, nor did they speak to one another during the process. Hence, this was a double-blind test because neither the tasker nor the viewer knew what was the actual target of the session. Remote viewers were asked to close their eyes and describe, as the images formed up in their minds, whatever mental pictures they had regarding the target they were supposed to discern. They wrote down their descriptions in stages as the images became clearer, but without imposing any judgment upon what they were seeing. They were asked to write down raw data only, pure data without any categorization or explanation. Then the viewer was asked to sketch or draw what he or she psychically perceived of the target site.

Typically, in test situations, viewers were given immediate feedback. Incidentally, the tests were designed so that the person guiding them had no advance knowledge of the target site, and didn't find out until after the viewer had described it. The purpose was to rule out the chance of telepathy. In fact, several possible channels of psychic communication: clairvoyance, precognition, as well as telepathy, may have all been involved at once.

Targ and Harary told of a remote viewer named Hella Hammid, tested at SRI in 1978. She described a target site she chose randomly as a "square tower, some technical installation," and then drew what she psychically saw. The sketch of the target site was accurate, matching the actual location: a nearby regional airport. The downside was that Hammid's description, although accurate, was vague and could have applied to any number of structures.[18] But other remote viewers, such as army major Paul H. Smith, now a PhD and director of his own remote viewing training institute, were far more accurate, both in time and place.

In one long-distance experiment, a remote viewer at SRI in California sketched the intended target: a "large white building [with an] arched look about it."[19] It psychically looked like a "ticket booth." The target? It was Grant's Tomb in New York City, a distance of three thousand miles away. But, critics could argue, there was nothing about the sketch of the target that was specific to Grant's Tomb beyond the general shape. Was that enough to say the test was a success?

On the other hand, some remote viewing tests were so complex that the person being tested was asked to psychically "see" and sketch a target site that turned out to be an entire small city, thousands of miles from where the test was being conducted. Viewers seemed to be able to identify Soviet missile sites and other enemy installations.

Another long-distance target was the Superdome in New Orleans. The remote viewer, in California, was accurate in describing and drawing the circular building with "its large white dome," Targ and Harary explained in *The Mind Race*, adding that the remote viewers' drawings were often "more accurate than the verbal descriptions of target sites."[20]

As you might have guessed, like competing athletes, the Soviets also took a serious interest in remote viewing, apparently believing in ESP to a greater degree than their American counterparts. Celebrated British novelist Ian Fleming, the creator of James Bond, once wrote that because of what the Russians learned from Pavlov's experiments with conditioning dogs to salivate at the sound of a bell, Russians came to believe in the power of the mind to sense things that were beyond the range of the other five senses. Thus, the American researchers in military and intelligence-gathering aspects of the paranormal believed that the Soviets knew more than they did and were more advanced in the weaponization of the paranormal than the Americans. Some parapsychologists and psychics wondered what the results of tests between the United States and the then Soviet Union would have produced? It never happened, to the best of anyone's knowledge, but it would have been fascinating if such remote viewing experiments could have been implemented.

Compared to experiments involving precognition, clairvoyance and telepathy were relatively straightforward. Theories to explain psychic functioning often fell back on conjecture taken from theoretical physics. Perhaps psi could be explained by some theory of "extremely low-frequency radio waves," or ELF, as it was called. But what explained precognition, the ability of some remote viewers to see events in the future? It raised the long-asked question about free will versus destiny.

Did precognition negate free will? And, where did "precognitive information" come from? Some theories suggested that the past, present, and future were all one. Einstein had considered "the distinction between past, present, and future only an illusion and not a physical reality.[21] For his part, Russell Targ pondered the dilemma, and answered this way: "Our customary view of linear time in which information is only carried forward along the time line, may not be the correct picture of our world."[22]

In his book, *Reading the Enemy's Mind,* and in interviews with *UFO Magazine,* with *Coast to Coast AM* with George Noory, and on *Future Theater* radio, remote viewer Dr. Paul H. Smith said that because the process of getting funding from the U.S. government required Dr. Harold Puthoff, Russell Targ, and other pioneers of the remote viewing research to come up with a scientific explanation underlying the phenomenon of remote viewing, they ultimately determined that there was real science behind theories of physics that presupposed an almost Platonic universe of "things," external data that superseded what human beings perceived with their five senses. In fact, what human beings relied on to construct their reality, common sensory data, actually interfered with the perception of a reality inside this external world of things or the Platonic reality. It was a theory that seemed to satisfy agencies such as the CIA, who provided the initial funding before the army moved the operation to Fort Meade. As Smith explained on *Coast to Coast AM* with George Noory, the government did not want to invest any money in the paranormal. Therefore, Hal Puthoff, Russell Targ, and psychic Ingo Swann had to come up with a completely bulletproof scientific rationale for the mechanism of remote viewing. The interpretation of quantum theory and nonlocality as ultimately set forth by David Bohm in his later book *The Undivided Universe* provided the basis for the science of remote viewing as perception not altered by the viewer himself or herself. This theory became the key that unlocked the door to government funding of a project involving a psychic teaching others to use their paranormal abilities.

The fascinating part of remote viewing, according to Paul H. Smith, was that this wasn't necessarily a skill that people had to have been born with. As Smith told his interviewers, anyone could learn how to remote view just by practicing the methodology of not allowing what he called the "analytical overlay" to interfere with what was being perceived. In other words, remote viewing was an exercise in going with the flow of whatever perceptions came into the viewer's mind. A simple analogy, Smith explained, was learning how to play "Chopsticks" on the piano. Anybody could be taught to play it in a single lesson. However, only once in a generation or two was born a Mozart, who could become a true maestro of music composition and performance. So it was with the difference between workmanlike and masterful remote viewers.

One example of an excellent remote viewer who could seemingly go into the future was a former Burbank, California, police commissioner named Pat Price who defied time and space as we have conceived them.[23] There is "something seriously inadequate about our current model of the space and time in which we live," Targ and Harary concluded, adding, the human concept of its "relationship" with time is actually more of a mystery than the straightforward single line that stretches from birth to death. Both Pat Price and Paul H. Smith demonstrated that human beings could transcend the straight-line concept of time and psychically enter into a realm where time was not a simple continuum but a constant presence viewable from any perspective. Smith demonstrated that he could view twenty years into the future when he saw the Huygens flying disk separate from the Cassini robot satellite to descend into the atmosphere of the Saturn moon Cassini. Smith might well have also remote viewed the Iraqi missile attack on the USS *Stark* in the Persian Gulf a full forty-eight hours before the attack took place. The philosophical implications of these possibilities, Smith explained to George Noory in *UFO Magazine*, were truly staggering.

The remote viewing ability could be enhanced by practice, Russell Targ explained. Even previously inexperienced people could be taught to improve their abilities with practice. In addition to the tests at SRI, remote viewing was being studied in laboratories throughout the country. If Targ's theory of remote viewing was correct, it led to the conclusion that our entire layman's concept of space and time was simply incomplete. Reality was far more fascinating and complex, and Targ looked toward theoretical physicists—those whom author David Kaiser referred to as "hippies," such as Fred Alan Wolf and Jack Sarfatti—to save modern physics and eventually decipher the mysteries of remote viewing.

Targ acknowledged that even though the psi tests at SRI had amassed a large amount of credible data concerning the reality of human psychic abilities, gaining a common acceptance of that data was more of a challenge in the United States than it would have been in the Soviet Union, where psi research was familiar for decades. Apparently thinking about revelations from Ostrander and Schroeder of Soviet paranormal tests, as well as later reports from nationally syndicated columnist Jack Anderson that both the U.S. and the Soviets were using "psychic spies," Targ bemoaned that news of Soviet psi research had come to public attention through writers who lacked the scientific background needed to assess paranormal research. However true that was, the media's mention of Soviet psi research did help Americans gain some awareness of parapsychology behind the, often impenetrable, Iron Curtain.

Targ and Harary were also frustrated by persistent American media distortions and misrepresentations of psi as "strange" or "unconventional." They considered, the concept of a psychic awareness to be a completely natural human ability. In fact, as Targ cautioned, human paranormal abilities were so manifest and so important, they should not become so weaponized as to become the sole domain of governments. Nevertheless, as intelligence agencies on both sides of the Iron Curtain realized, the enormous promise of using psychic spying techniques to gather secret data made it a natural asset fought over by the military of both the U.S. and the Soviets. Targ would have been one to know. SRI ultimately received millions of dollars from the CIA. Military and intelligence applications constituted the major reason both superpowers had reached for psi.

But the physicists' concerns about faulty news coverage were not exaggerated or misplaced. "Few in the media understood psi from a depth at which it could be reported fairly and accurately," observed Margaret Wendt, producer of network TV documentaries about the paranormal, Ben Webster's widow, and a former anchorwoman for the CBS television affiliate in Cleveland.

When columnist Jack Anderson wrote an introduction to a book titled *Mind Wars* by Ron McRae in 1984, Anderson compared psychic weapons to "voodoo dolls" and branded the subject "voodoo warfare." At another point, Anderson confused psychics and swamis. He dubbed psi the "black arts," and those interested were labeled "New Age loonies."[24] So much for Anderson's well-researched, objective investigative reporting.

Regardless of the success of the experiments at Stanford Research Institute and the army's investment in psychic spying, among the media and the general public, the so-called snicker factor dominated all discussions of the paranormal. When the major newspapers reported about parapsychology, the stories nearly always had a touch of sarcasm, if not outright derision. For instance, Targ noted, in 1977 the *Chicago Tribune* reported that, "The CIA [had] financed a project in 1975 to develop a new kind of agent who could truly be called a 'spook,' CIA Director Stansfield Turner has disclosed."[25]

U.S. Navy admiral Stansfield Turner, as rumor has it, was one of the few people in the loop about the existence of UFOs. A former United States naval officer, George Hoover, also Walt Disney's adviser on the *Man in Space* series back in the 1950s, once explained in a private interview that the military believed that human beings had the same types of psychic or paranormal abilities as extraterrestrials. Hoover went on to say that much of the very early thinking about ETs and the paranormal, even encounters between ET humanoids and human beings, took place within the military, especially the Navy and Army. Hence, it would be no surprise if Admiral Turner, who became CIA director, might have been the source of information allegedly reported to astronaut and former naval officer Dr. Edgar Mitchell about the U.S. government's knowledge and interaction with UFOs and the entities that piloted them.

Admiral Turner, despite what he might have known about UFOs, was nevertheless a rational person and evidenced his frustration that the paranormal "projects," as the CIA chief defined them, were often extremely difficult to replicate under controlled laboratory conditions, thus resulting in a major criticism by American skeptics of psi functioning.

The repeatability factor did not pose the same roadblock to Soviet parapsychologists that it did for their American counterparts. Soviet researchers agreed psi ability was genuine. Their goal was to determine how it worked, and what its practical applications were.

Targ and his colleagues at SRI acknowledged that remote viewing was at an early stage and not perfected or 100 percent reliable. For example, he said, viewers sometimes failed to describe their targets accurately. Nevertheless, approximately two-thirds of the experiments in remote viewing conducted at SRI resulted in matches with their targets. This was an impressive number, which caused Targ to conclude that, "This 66 percent reliability of remote viewing is statistically significant." For a psychic or medium's accuracy to be considered statistically significant, the experiment's result must be better than what would be "expected by chance by odds of at least twenty to one," Targ explained. In the remote viewing trials, he said, "The odds were roughly one hundred to one against chance."[26]

Targ and Puthoff discovered what nearly all paranormal researchers have, that psychics and mediums often connect better to genuine places and events, rather than to guessing what picture or shape was on a card or some other printed material. The latter was the method used by J. B. Rhine at Duke University as far back as the late 1920s. Charles Tart, a respected psychic researcher and writer worded it this way: "It is as though card guessing were a highly refined technique for unlearning or extinguishing psi in the laboratory!" Targ and Puthoff also found that remote viewers performed better when they were more enthusiastic about the task than not.[27]

Too often in the more recent history of the paranormal in America, researchers and scientists have been stymied by their own experimental designs that were constructed with unnecessary complexities. One example is something called the Ganzfeld method, best described as a "sensory deprivation approach" to psi testing. Remote viewers have their eyes covered with halves of Ping-Pong balls. Then, surrounded by red light, they also wear earphones that play nothing but static, which is called "white noise." The Ganzfeld approach, created by Charles Honorton and William Brand, is simply a combination of two German words for the "whole" or "entire field." There are claims that the Ganzfeld method has had considerable statistically significant success. However, it necessitates an altered state of consciousness (ASC) that turns out not to be required to demonstrate psychic ability. To an outside observer, the Ganzfeld method seems complicated, or at least gimmicky, as if it were accomplishing something. In fact, all it does is add an unnecessary complication to the testing procedure. It has not improved psi powers one iota.[28]

If there is a moral to the Ganzfeld story, it is that testing for psychic ability can often be simpler than many scientists purport. Bells, whistles, and lights become unneeded overcompensation. What about those well-intentioned paranormal researchers who wince every time a psychic debunker alleges that scientific controls were not strict enough any time a test of psychic functioning shows positive results? Psi investigators—many of them also scientists—have fallen repeatedly for the same tired sleight of mouth. Professional debunkers have no finish line in the race to validate psi. In other words, no matter how high a psychic jumps, the debunker will reply that it hasn't been high enough. There is no way any paranormal event will ever be accepted as genuine by debunkers. The reason is simple, and the history of the paranormal bears it out. The single-minded goal of professional debunkers is to promote secularism. In this country, psi and religion are inseparable and "irrational" in the minds of obdurate skeptics, as we explained earlier.

If you're not familiar with the name Ingo Swann, who died in 2013, the author of the book *Penetration* (1998), his autobiography, he was a Colorado native, born in Telluride in 1933, and he turned to a career as a psychic in 1969 when he was thirty-six. Prior to that, Swann was employed at the United Nations for a dozen years, and had also studied art. But it is his contributions to the paranormal that are our focus here.[29]

When Swann had the original idea for a project, he submitted a proposal to Dr. Harold Puthoff at the Stanford Research Institute (SRI), in which he described the value and applications of a "government-funded psychic program." Swann suggested calling it "remote viewing," and was of the opinion that all people were capable of developing some degree of telepathy and intuition. He also had several theories about the "mental processes involved in producing evidence of psychic phenomena," such as ESP and PK, noted the *Encyclopedia of Occultism and Parapsychology*.

Swann, unlike other psychics, never publicly demonstrated his abilities. Hence, there was none of the public adulation many psychics attracted, even craved. However, he wrote about the subject, and most significantly, he willingly participated in literally thousands of psychic trials. Swann made himself available to scientists for an unprecedented number of paranormal experiments, including remote viewing, for more than twenty years. He was the subject of so many examinations of his psychic abilities that author Martin Ebon called Swann "parapsychology's most tested guinea pig." In the early 1970s, Swann participated with Cleve Backster in an effort to affect plants by using mental power. He was also the subject of PK experiments that demonstrated temperature changes in a "controlled" setting, and scored well in out-of-body experiments at the American Society for Psychical Research (ASPR). Swann's contributions had been central to the development of the government's remote viewing operations.

The scientists at SRI considered remote viewing to be "the capacity of people to describe remote locations and events accurately through channels of perception whose very existence was being denied by the scientific community at large when the SRI project began," explained Willis Harman, senior social scientist at SRI. "Remote viewing is primarily an ability to process pictorial, non-analytic information," Russell Targ added.[30]

Over the course of human history, remote viewing went by other names. The definition has been as elusive as the ability itself. Some said it was likely similar to what Native Americans long ago called "spirit walking." That is the phenomenon by which the spirit is released from the physical body. At one time in history, it was described as "traveling clairvoyance." "The controlled process of leaving one's body, often called out-of-body projection, enables a person to travel from one location to another, in order to observe distant events," according to *The UFO Magazine UFO Encyclopedia* (W. Birnes, Simon & Schuster, 2003). It also notes, "According to those who have practiced this skill [remote viewing], one can discern what others are thinking and feeling, and understand their thoughts and motivations while in this mode." You can imagine how promising such potential was to intelligence and military officials.

As in any other field of endeavor, certain individuals emerged through the years of remote viewing tests to become known as highly accomplished at the ability to travel out of their bodies in order to access information about distant places. One highly successful remote viewer was Joe McMoneagle, a pleasant-looking man with a neatly trimmed beard and mustache, and a military background that included service during the Vietnam War. He'd been recruited for the "psychic spy unit" known eventually as Project Stargate, and came to be regarded as perhaps the most knowledgeable person there was on the subject of remote viewing.

McMoneagle's accuracy rate was statistically far beyond chance in psychically sensing and describing distant "targets" or locations for "intelligence purposes." It's estimated that he performed at least four thousand remote viewings, and was described by a number of writers as the program's "superstar." He remained in the government's employ as a remote viewer for some eighteen years. Later, McMoneagle became a well-regarded lecturer and author of several books on the subject, including *Mind Trek, The Ultimate Time Machine, Remote Viewing Secrets,* and *The Stargate Chronicles.* McMoneagle was also a guest expert on the History Channel's *UFO Hunters,* explaining to the hosts in an interview on Andros Island in the Bahamas that he had personally viewed extraterrestrials in their craft lurking underwater near the top-secret U.S. base on a remote part of the island.

There are simply too many remote viewers or "psychic spies" to be able to include all of them and their achievements here. However, should you wish to look further into the subject, there were other noted viewers over the years; in addition to Joe McMoneagle, some were Lyn Buchanan, Russell Targ, Harold Puthoff, Keith Harary, Pat Price, Ed Dames, Mel Riley, Paul H. Smith, and David Morehouse.

Then there was Major General Albert Stubblebine, not a remote viewer himself, but at one time in charge of the program during the early 1980s. He was a high-ranking official supportive of studying "human performance enhancement," including remote viewing, and Uri Geller's psychokinetic (PK) abilities. Stubblebine was of the opinion that PK held the potential to be used as a "military weapon," and for tasks such as disabling enemy computer systems.

He was also an unabashed UFO believer, another unusual position for someone high up in the military.

In addition to tests at SRI, there were other laboratories throughout the country working on remote viewing, as subcontractors for the CIA and the military. Puthoff and Targ guided SRI's remote viewing program from its inception in 1972 until 1986. Both scientists left when they accepted positions elsewhere. From 1986 until 1995, when Stargate ended, the work continued under the direction of Dr. Edwin May.

Although remote viewers were tested at SRI in California, the so-called operational unit was maintained at Fort Meade, Maryland, where the majority of records and research materials were stored; since they remained classified, they were not available to the public, although some material had been reported in journals and professional articles.

Some people have demonstrated more remote viewing ability than others, not unlike those who seem to possess a greater natural or inborn talent for art, music, or athletics. Those without the innate skills can be taught—but only to a point. That is why one of McMoneagle's books is specifically about developing remote viewing abilities. Remote viewers point out that they are not searchlights wandering about the sky seeking to "produce a location." It is generally more successful when a remote viewer is asked to target a place or event. McMoneagle said that remote viewing has not been shown effective in detecting UFOs, or such "mythical or hypothetical events" as the elusive monster of the Pacific Northwest woods that was known as Sasquatch or Bigfoot.

Generally, the remote viewers' accuracy rates hovered at 60 to 65 percent, and in the case of McMoneagle, a statistically significant percent of his drawings were near-perfect matches with his targets. As we mentioned a bit earlier, some remote viewers seemed to transcend time and place, and go into the future to detect events that have not yet occurred. McMoneagle gave as an example the futility in trying to "remote view" a UFO landing station on another planet, since such a base is hypothetical. However, a skilled remote viewer could likely "see" the planet itself. Russell Targ pointed out that remote viewers were also capable of assisting law enforcement in locating missing persons.

Seriously researching and testing the paranormal is far more complex than one might think at first. Psychology, neurobiology, Eastern philosophies, mysticism, and altered states of consciousness all factor into studying and testing psi. For example, parapsychologists can now confirm with brain imaging technology that psychic ability is a right-brain function.

There were procedures and protocols for remote viewers to follow. The best psychics and mediums are people who allow psychically obtained information to flow through them, while they act only as a conduit for the messages. Having preconceived notions about what psi is—or is not—can quickly become a negative attribute. The several people working together on a remote viewing experiment need to cooperate with each other, from the person being tested; to the one who acts as a "beacon" or target who actually has gone to the test site; to the monitor who gathers the information, and keeps the project focused; to the person who acts as the independent analyst or evaluator of the test, and who has had no contact with the viewer. However, the remote viewer was given immediate feedback on his or her accuracy.[31]

Unlike the insidious nature of the CIA's bizarre mind-control experiments, carried out on countless unsuspecting subjects such as Candy Jones and Frank Olson, the government's remote viewing program did not involve the same "web of deceit." Presumably, MK-ULTRA had concluded, albeit mired in controversy and uncertainty, without the CIA having created the so-called Manchurian candidate. Around the same time, the government began its remote viewing tests, and those who were recruited or volunteered came from various backgrounds and were aware of what was expected of them, although the details of the experiments were to remain secret, supposedly for reasons of national security.[32]

Referred to earlier, among the first remote viewers to be tested at SRI was Pat Price, a former Burbank, California, police commissioner. Parapsychologist and author Richard Broughton explained that Price had contacted Dr. Harold Puthoff at SRI volunteering to be tested for what Price thought might be his psychic ability. During his years in law enforcement, Price realized that his keen intuition had often helped lead him to suspects.[33]

Puthoff agreed to test Price, and gave the former police official "a set of map coordinates" as a remote viewing experiment. It would be Price's task to psychically describe the location in as much detail as he could. The coordinates indicated an area that was more than 130 miles southwest of Washington, D.C. Price could have done some research of the location, but that was highly unlikely. For what Puthoff received from Price was no vague description of a place. It was several pages containing a detailed depiction of a "complex of buildings and underground storage areas," Broughton said. Price also reported "communication and computer equipment manned by Army Signal Corps personnel, and even the names on desks in the buildings," according to Broughton.[34] Other information he revealed psychically was from "labels on file folders in a locked file cabinet in one of the rooms."

Until his death in 1975, Price would be a valuable remote viewer in SRI experiments. He became part of a project Puthoff created, called SCANATE, an abbreviation for "scanning by coordinate." The remote viewing targets had been prepared by the CIA, and chosen at random from a number of possible targets all over the world, including some in the Soviet Union and China. Only CIA personnel involved knew the top-secret coordinates, they'd been kept encrypted, that is, converted into code to prevent unauthorized access, and then given to intelligence officials in the supersecret National Security Agency (NSA).

The CIA acknowledged that Price's remote viewing was accurate. What's more, "there was no way Price could have obtained his information by normal means," Broughton wrote. Project SCANATE was in operation from 1973 to 1975, and hundreds of tests followed, including the whereabouts of Soviet submarines. Also participating in SCANATE was the psychic Ingo Swann. As Broughton explained the testing procedure, Swann was given "map coordinates for locations on the globe, and then asked for a virtually instantaneous description of the locale." In one instance, Swann proved accurate in describing a "French-Soviet meteorological research installation," and even sketched the island it was on.

SCANATE proved to be a successful experiment in intelligence gathering by ESP, specifically remote viewing. However, that alone was not considered sufficient; conventional intelligence gathering was still necessary. Psychic ability's role was to augment traditional methods, not to supplant them. The "official reports" about SCANATE remained top secret, and were not made available for outside or independent evaluation.

Just as it was *The New York Times* in late 1974 that first revealed the CIA's mind-control experiments, in 1977, *The Washington Post* broke the story of "psychic spying."[35] Following SCANATE, the CIA continued to covertly fund remote viewing at SRI for the next several years, until Targ and Puthoff left to take positions elsewhere. After that, parapsychology research at SRI continued under new leadership, focusing mainly on precognition and psychokinesis experiments.

In February 1984, *The New York Times* headlined an article,

"Sorcery at the Pentagon," in which the government denied its participation in "psychic spying." But several books around that same time contradicted the official denials. Then, only weeks later in March, *The Times* reported, "Pentagon Is Said to Focus on ESP for Wartime Use." The government response was to lie; it "[denied] spending money on psychic research."

Political controversy was the inevitable fallout from news of the government's paying for psychic research. It was the rare congressman or senator who risked speaking in favor of the persistently ridiculed and reviled paranormal, which in some parts of the country was considered "the work of the devil." One notable exception was U.S. senator Claiborne Pell of Rhode Island, who supported psi research and for years had the courage to say so publicly, apparently with no serious damage to his career other than occasional snide remarks in the press about the politician who believed in the "weird," "far-out," and "occult."

In December 1987, the National Research Council (NRC) reviewed the use of parapsychology by the U.S. Army, and concluded it had not found "scientific justification from research about psychic phenomena conducted over 130 years." The NRC was part of the National Academy of Sciences whose responsibilities included reviewing and evaluating various methods and programs for the army, including parapsychology. Here the story becomes a bit confusing, beyond the usual bureaucratic snafus. The NRC had received a subcontract from the U.S. Army Research Institute for Behavioral and Social Sciences, a mouthful that was easier to remember as the ARI.

The army, of course, had every right to an unbiased assessment of psychic functioning, but supervising the NRC contract was an army psychologist, Dr. George Lawrence, who opposed using any paranormal methods. In fact, Lawrence once collaborated with Dr. Ray Hyman, a University of Oregon psychologist, who became a nationally known psychic debunker as a founding member of CSICOP in 1976, the skeptics' group dedicated to the overthrow of all things paranormal and spiritual.

Curiously, the NRC never consulted any parapsychologists in its supposed quest for objectivity, and not surprisingly, the NRC rejected the paranormal. But then, in something of a contradiction, the same NRC advised the Army to "monitor" Soviet psychic research, and keep an eye on some of the better psi experimentation in the United States including SRI; Princeton Engineering Anomalies Research (PEAR); random generator (RNG) studies; and the Ganzfeld approach we mentioned a little earlier.

The NRC even suggested that skeptics and parapsychologists cooperate in order to seek practical applications for psi. If you read the above carefully, the NRC conclusions actually gave tacit recognition to Soviet psi research. That brings us to the question, what exactly was going on in the Soviet Union concerning parapsychology?

There was no question that the two superpowers considered the "development of psychic abilities" to be important. Some critics of paranormal research argued that the U.S. would never have delved into the subject had it not been for signs of strong Soviet interest, and our fear that we were being outpaced in applying psychic functioning to military and intelligence purposes.

By 1984, when Russell Targ and Keith Harary wrote a popular book titled *The Mind Race: Understanding and Using Psychic Abilities,* tensions between the United States and the Soviet Union had eased somewhat. However, it would still be another five years before the official demise of the Soviet empire. In early 1945, when psychic Jeane Dixon warned FDR not to concede Eastern Europe to Stalin, she also predicted that someday, far in the future, the U.S. and the Soviets would end their animosities toward each other. Dixon's prophecy would prove correct, but not until 1989 when the Soviet state collapsed under the weight of its faulty Communist ideology and economic priorities that were top-heavy with military spending.

To what extent the bestselling book, *Psychic Discoveries Behind the Iron Curtain*, first published in 1970, was an influence on U.S. policy about the paranormal is difficult to determine. But it's apparent that American political, intelligence, and military officials were aware of the buzz created by the claims of psychic advances in the Soviet Union. The authors were two well-educated young women, both professional writers, who'd been invited to an international ESP conference in Russia in 1968. Sheila Ostrander was a Canadian and Lynn Schroeder was an American, from New Jersey.[36] One criticism they faced from skeptics was that both were journalists; neither was a scientist able to properly evaluate what they'd witnessed.

When Joel Martin interviewed author Lynn Schroeder, she explained that the collaboration began with their attendance at the First Annual Parapsychology Conference in Moscow in 1968. There they had the opportunity to meet and interview Soviet scientists engaged in psychic research throughout the "Soviet Union, Central Europe, and the Balkans." It was apparent that in a closed society such as the Soviet Union, the two writers were observing and learning only what officials wanted them to regarding psi. Perhaps it was psychological warfare on the part of the Soviets to both alarm and intimidate America. Was the Soviet involvement in the paranormal genuine, or had it purposely been fabricated to confuse and frighten the United States? Some skeptics and debunkers insisted that the Soviet leadership had cleverly concocted an extravagant propaganda ploy by falsely claiming it was deep into successful psychic research, and far ahead of the United States.

Whether they were leading in up-to-date paranormal investigations or not, the Russians had a long and bona fide tradition in mystical subjects, such as healing, and there were a substantial number of psychic healers in the USSR. It was from Russia that Madame Helena Blavatsky of Theosophy fame emerged in the last half of the nineteenth century. Then there was Rasputin, the "mad monk" with his hypnotic eyes, who was actually a trained shaman and psychic healer to Czar Nicholas's young hemophiliac son in the early twentieth century. Behind the dark legend of Rasputin was a man expert at hypnosis, who possessed genuine "psychic powers." After Rasputin was murdered, his reputation lived on, and may have served as an impetus for Russian scientists to more deeply explore the mind-body connection. Indisputably, Blavatsky and Rasputin were "the two most powerful and most famous occultists of modern times," Lynn Schroeder said.

There was also the famed Russian dancer Nijinsky, whose amazing moves raised questions about whether he could levitate. The late psychiatrist and author Dr. Nandor Fodor wrote about Nijinsky in the 1964 book *Between Two Worlds,* speculating whether his leaps through the air were supernatural, as if he were defying gravity. Nijinsky explained that he could watch himself while dancing, suggesting he was out of his body at the time he glided through the air and descending more slowly than he had ascended, as if gravity was something he could control. In fact, Nijinsky had privately explored both yoga and spiritualism. Fodor compared him to the Hindu yogis who seemed as if they were "walking on air."[37]

There was no question that mysticism was deeply rooted in Russian history and culture. In the 1920s, even under Stalin's brutal rule, experiments with psychic powers were underway. The long Russian interest went beyond mere disinformation on the part of the Soviet leadership, and paranormal demonstrations were not just contrived events when Ostrander and Schroeder reported what they saw behind the Iron Curtain, including "psychic research laboratories" in Soviet Russia, Bulgaria, and Czechoslovakia that were paid for and operated by the government.[38]

Shortly before the breakup of the USSR in 1989, Joel Martin learned that a book he'd coauthored about a much tested and highly gifted psychic-medium somehow found its way behind the Iron Curtain. For the Soviet researchers, there was serious interest in the American medium, and he was invited to the Bekhterev Institute in Leningrad, a respected parapsychological facility where his psychic ability would be examined.

The laboratory was named for famed Soviet neurologist Vladimir Bekhterev who, in the early part of the last century, became interested in the paranormal, especially mental telepathy. One of his most intriguing experiments had been "ESP tests" with dogs; the idea was to determine whether canines would respond to telepathic commands from humans. "Mental suggestion can directly affect the behavior of trained dogs," Bekhterev concluded in 1920. Later, he studied telepathy between people, reporting considerable success.

The American medium accepted the invite to Leningrad, only to have the offer unexpectedly put on permanent hold as a result of the Soviet political upheavals at the time. However, after the collapse of the Soviet Union in 1989, several former Kremlin officials traveled to the United States, and one of their stops in New York was to see the medium for private psychic readings. What made this visit especially interesting was the fact that the Russians declared themselves atheists. There was no pretense that parapsychology had a spiritual or "God" component. They had no belief in religion, or an afterlife, but did express a sincere curiosity about what a medium, purporting to be in contact with the spirit world, might tell them—if anything.

The outcome was surprising, although perhaps it should not have been. In one of the readings the medium gave to a once top

Soviet official, names and details poured forth, almost effortlessly. There were departed loved ones, who identified themselves by name, and communicated their greetings, and there were reminiscences of the subject's childhood in Moscow as well as comments about the sweeping changes underway in the USSR. When the nearly one-hour session ended, the Russian was impressed with the accuracy, and a bit shaken to "hear from" the late relatives who'd raised him, even what caused their deaths. He admitted to feeling emotionally moved by the experience, his first with a medium. However, he protested, nonetheless, since, as a good atheist, he had no belief in the hereafter.

For his part, the medium was at first amazed that messages came through so easily, until the spirit communications from the departed Russians explained that the transition to an afterlife surprised them as well. However, with no preconceived notions or religious expectations of a "heaven," "hell," or survival beyond the grave, they said, the passage from here to hereafter was actually smoother than one would think.

The same medium had once given a reading to the distraught mother of a young Air Force pilot, missing in action in Southeast Asia. When the U.S. government insisted the pilot had been shot down and killed by enemy fire over Vietnam, his mother held out the tenuous hope—the slim chance—that perhaps he'd been captured as a POW and was alive. The medium gently but firmly disagreed. He psychically "saw" an area where the pilot's plane had crashed—in neighboring Laos. Was this an example of remote viewing? At the least, it was clairvoyance. Telepathy was ruled out, since the downed pilot's mother had no idea that her son was killed in Laos because according to the official version of his disappearance, he was not supposed to be in Laos. Some time later, however, after a protracted dispute with the military, the mother confirmed that what the medium told her was substantially accurate.[39]

In the Soviet Union, since there were no theological obstacles and little public opposition, psychic phenomena were more closely aligned with science than in America, and that influenced the vocabulary of parapsychology. The Soviets had invented terminology such as "bio-energy," "bio-plasma," and "psychotronic energy" to replace the more spiritual concepts the West connected with psychic events. For example, what we in the West for centuries called astrology, the Soviets referred to as "cosmic biology." Telepathy was also defined as "bio-information," while Kirlian, or supposed aura photography, was dubbed "bio-luminescence."

One of the most renowned psychics in the Soviet Union was Nina Kulagina, especially recognized for her psychokinetic (PK) abilities to move both "metal and nonmetal" objects, demonstrated under "controlled conditions" through the 1960s and 1970s. She could produce a "psychokinetic burn" on a person's skin. It was her "favorite feat," Russell Targ and Keith Harary wrote in *The Mind Race*. She was also able to "suppress [the] vital functions of white mice."[40]

Another curious phenomena that Ostrander and Schroeder learned about behind the Iron Curtain was Kirlian photography, named for its inventors, Semyon and Valentina Kirlian.[41] Many years ago, the couple identified the kaleidoscope of colors that surrounds every living thing as an energy field. In one experiment a leaf displayed a corona of colors around it. But when part of the leaf was cut off, a halo remained as if the entire leaf was intact. The Kirlian photograph helped demonstrate that energy fields are not the stuff of paranormal hype but real, physical entities.

Historically, the concept of an aura enveloping human beings dates back to ancient times. Paintings of Catholic saints typically show auras or halos encircling their heads. If the colors were the result of an "energy body," this held implications for healing. Did physical or emotional illnesses, and even fatigue, emanate as colors? Was there a difference in color or intensity depending on whether one was healthy or ill? If that was true, could Kirlian photography be of value in early diagnose of diseases? In the years before and after World War II, the Kirlians created the special instruments to photograph the color manifestations, and in the 1960s, the Soviet government finally funded their work. After an initial flurry of interest, Western science rejected the concept as having no medical value, arguing that the aura of colors reflected the moisture normally found in living things, rather than the discovery of a new and useful form of energy.

What those in Western parapsychology referred to as an "astral body" or "etheric body," Soviet researchers considered an "energy body." If a limb was amputated, photographs showed a faint outline of the entire intact arm or leg as it had once been. The concept of a second body that perfectly matched the physical body also went back to antiquity. But what was the relationship between the two bodies—one visible, the other invisible? And, could they really be separated from each other as distinct entities?

It seemed from the conclusions drawn by Ostrander and Schroeder that Soviet parapsychologists were less concerned in their examination of psi with "repeatability." In the United States, scientists and parapsychologists had difficulty moving beyond the questions of what psi was and how it could be tested dependably in a laboratory setting. For the Soviets, there was less attention to theoretical and experimental questions, and more emphasis on learning how to use psi specifically to control or "manipulate consciousness, especially through telepathy," even at a distance from the subject.[42]

Soviet scientists sought the means by which psi could be applied to military and intelligence purposes. Could one person "psychically influence the minds of others?" What if psychic or telepathic power could be mentally targeted to an agent or soldier? Could that individual be given a "posthypnotic suggestion" to detonate a bomb? Might he be programmed to surreptitiously pirate important documents? These were among the questions Ostrander and Schroeder saw Soviet parapsychologists wrestle with as they sought to "manipulate consciousness through telepathy."

The two writers realized that "control" was an overriding objective for Soviet leaders, and psi was thought to be a way to control behavior. But control is a double-edged sword. As Ostrander pointed out, to control a disease or epidemic is obviously a positive and worthy goal. However, the Soviet government's penchant for repressing people's thoughts and policing behavior was detestable, consistent with the tyrannical nature of a dictatorship, and hopefully not the way most American parapsychologists wanted ESP to be used.

An area of strong Soviet paranormal interest was mental telepathy. In the late fifties, one experiment concerned "ship to shore telepathy" involving Soviet submarines. Coincidentally or not, at about the same time, the U.S. Navy was allegedly engaged in similar experimentation aboard the nuclear submarine *Nautilus*. However, the navy strongly denied that it had anything to do with ESP, and was adamant that it did no experiments with psi involving any submarine. It remained U.S. policy to publicly distance itself from involvement with the paranormal. While the Soviet government did not have to answer for what it did or did not do, American public opinion had to be factored when the CIA or the military engaged in anything as politically volatile as parapsychology. It appeared that most Americans could deal better with news of a nuclear bomb being tested, than they could with a psychic spy on the government's payroll. But secretly, reports of psi activity by one nation pushed the other to further research, and, based on espionage reports, it seemed the Soviets knew more about American parapsychology than vice versa.

In December 1957, paranormal pioneer J. B. Rhine, at Duke University, wrote an article in *The Journal of Parapsychology* titled "Why National Defense Overlooks Parapsychology." Rhine bemoaned that attitude. "The evidence of psi does not seem to have reached the defense mind," he complained.[43] What's curious about the piece, is that beyond the call by Rhine for psi to be employed against communism in the battle for people's minds, he seemed completely unaware that the CIA and military had already been engaged in ESP research and extensive mind-control experimentation.

Reading that article recently, so many years after it was written, with the benefit of hindsight, raised two intriguing possibilities. Was it possible that Rhine, the acknowledged dean of American parapsychology, had been oblivious to the fact that the U.S. was already researching mind control and ESP by the 1950s? If that was true, it meant U.S. military and intelligence agencies kept top parapsychologists in the dark, just as it did the public.

The other troubling possibility is that Rhine knew what the CIA and army were surreptitiously doing, and not only was forbidden from discussing it publicly, but beyond that, was encouraged to write articles to further create the appearance of distance between the government and its covert psi research. That would have made Rhine's pronouncements exercises in disinformation, since in 1952—five years before the journal article—the army initiated financing Rhine's ESP tests at Duke University. Does it all sound slightly contradictory and paranoid? Unfortunately, that's what excessive and obsessive government secrecy can do, but to whose benefit?

In 1963, the Kremlin issued an order that accorded "top priority" to what the Soviets called "biological sciences," and that included parapsychology. Ostrander and Schroeder revealed in their book that it was the "Soviet military and secret police that had been behind the push to find a way to harness ESP." They also reported that by the late 1960s, the Soviet Union counted "some twenty or more centers for the study of paranormal with an annual budget estimated at between thirteen and twenty-one million dollars." Not every Soviet official was overjoyed about the direction the country was going with the paranormal—or its cost. The USSR had its fair share of skeptics, and some Soviet scientists discredited psi as a genuine ability, not unlike the negative attitude in the United States.

On a more positive note, one of the most notable Soviet scientists who devoted time and effort to parapsychology was Dr. Leonid Leonidovich Vasiliev (1891–1966). He was also a highly regarded physiologist, and held "many Soviet honors." His interest in psi began after World War I. By the 1930s he'd engaged in the testing of "telepathic hypnosis." In 1959, he created a "specialized laboratory" to research telepathy at Leningrad University, described by colleagues as a "unique achievement in East European countries at the time." His writing was credited with encouraging the study of parapsychology throughout the Soviet Union. Vasiliev, by virtue of his reputation and scientific accomplishments, was an influence on opinion about the paranormal among his peers as well as the Soviet citizenry.[44]

By the mid-1960s, colleagues and former students had created a well-respected center for paranormal research in Moscow; their emphasis was on telepathy or, as it was called, "bio-information." Vasiliev's research brought together scientists from several different disciplines: engineers, mathematicians, psychologists, and even philosophers to research and test telepathy. At the time, the tightly controlled Soviet state media pressed for funding of psi, noting its importance. What Soviet spokesmen often omitted was the true purpose of their interest: the application of psi to military and espionage functions, especially against the United States.

Anyone who believed the Kremlin was committed to psi for the betterment of humankind was terribly mistaken. Following the dismantling of the USSR and the end of the lengthy and acrimonious Cold War, huge investments of government money into parapsychology soon dried up, as Russia faced crushing economic problems and changing priorities.

For a long time, psychic research went on not only in Russia, but also in other Soviet-dominated countries, including East Germany, Poland, Bulgaria, and most notably Czechoslovakia with its long history of Catholicism, prior to its annexation to the Third Reich in 1938, and after its takeover by the Communists after World War II. But the ancient Czech culture was rich in mystical and religious tradition, and that likely contributed to a greater sensitivity regarding the paranormal, said Dr. Vladimir Rus, a Czech-born educator and linguist. "By the thirteenth century, the Czechs were already among the most civilized peoples in Europe," Ostrander and Schroeder observed, adding, "the critical and meditative character" of the Czech people encouraged openness to psychic phenomena. In the beautiful old city of Prague, with its various styles of classically ornate architecture that transport visitors back in time, and its impressive history in music, art, and science, many of the old mystical and magical ideas lived on.[45]

For example, the legend of the golem, an evil avenging spirit, was born in Prague. It was created by a sixteenth-century rabbi, who was learned in Kabbalah or Jewish mysticism, the foundational theology for Hasidism. Physically, the golem was a small wooden or clay figure that was magically brought to life. Once brought to life, the golem would carry out the wishes of its creator and wreak vengeance on the creator's target. However, the golem was really a two-edged sword, which, once brought into existence, also made its creator pay the price for its creation.

Both alchemy and astrology were well known in Czech history, as was religious diversity that posed a challenge to authority, Rus noted, adding that the Czech religious reformer John Hus preceded Martin Luther by a full century. At the University of Prague, psychic research dated back to the early twentieth century, even as Czechoslovakia was on its way to becoming a "leading industrial nation," said Ostrander and Schroeder.

The Czechs changed the term *parapsychology*, renaming it *psychotronics*. Interest in the paranormal was such that the country had several well-known psychics, including Adolf Fencl-Bilovsky, and psi research experts, such as Dr. Zdenek Rejdak and Dr. Vladimir Drozen who declared, "The existence of psi is not contrary to any known law of physics."

Ostrander and Schroeder also introduced readers to the once famed Czech clairvoyant, Erik Hanussen, who was murdered by the Nazis in the 1930s because he psychically "saw" their secret projects, and foolishly repeated them aloud. That was enough to frighten Nazi higher-ups who ordered his death. Prior to the German takeover of Czechoslovakia in 1938, on the eve of World War II, the Czech army had successfully used clairvoyance in battle. It provided accurate warnings and advanced word of enemy strategies. Ostrander and Schroeder noted that by 1925, the Czech military had prepared a "handbook" about the use of ESP in wartime. The Nazis, however, officially prohibited the Czechs from psychic research during World War II, but one noted Czech parapsychologist, Bretislav Kafka, nonetheless, called on "psychics to follow the progress of the war."[46]

There was also the respected Czech doctor Milan Ryzl, who explored how ESP could be taught to people with no recognized prior psychic abilities. At one time, although he remained in Prague, he was a "research associate," cooperating with Dr. Rhine at the Duke University laboratory in North Carolina. Ryzl had a strong interest in precognition, theorizing that psychic ability could not be electromagnetic in nature, as many conjectured, since it was able to access information from the future, events that had not yet happened. "Precognition is key to the mysteries of psi," Ostrander and Schroeder quoted Ryzl as saying.[47]

One idea that sprung from the work of the Czech radio engineer Karl Drbal found its way to the United States during the early 1970s where it became a national fad called pyramid power. Pyramid power captured the imagination of the disco 1970s, satirized in fiction and motion pictures, such as *Semi-Tough* with Burt Reynolds and Kris Kristofferson.

For many millennia, there has been fascination with the mysteries of the great pyramids, built by the ancient Egyptians. They became the tombs of deceased—and mummified—pharaohs. How the pyramids were constructed was still unknown when Drbal had an idea in 1949; he built a small cardboard model of the Great Pyramid of Cheops. It took him a full decade, until 1959, to obtain a Czechoslovakian patent for his little device.

Essentially, Drabl's theory claimed there was something unique about the pyramid shape that produced an energy field that could sharpen razor blades, scissors, and knives; preserve meat, eggs, and flowers; and even relieve headaches and arthritic pain when a pyramid-shaped hat was worn. Some people went so far as to meditate in pyramid-shaped tents, contending it increased their level of relaxation. Advocates suggested that the pyramid shape aided the mummification process. Another claim was that army troops in czarist Russia were given their meat rations in pyramid-shaped containers. If that was so, they asked, was pyramid energy responsible for preserving the food?[48]

In the United States, proponents said their conclusions were based on scientific experimentation. The most influential and successful book on the subject was *Pyramid Power* by Max Toth and Greg Nielsen. Toth's summation was that "there is some inexplicable or unknown energy which is peculiar to the pyramid shape."[49] But scientists, and even many parapsychologists, ultimately debunked pyramid power, arguing that any positive benefits were psychosomatic or psychological in nature, and the fad eventually petered out; but not without leaving some questions about so-called shape energy unanswered.

In the end, however, neither the supernatural nor nuclear weapons could keep the Soviet Union intact. The cost of waging a cold war with NATO and especially the United States was too great, and the Soviet leaders realized that Communism itself was not economically viable. Ironically, much of the credit for contributing to the fall of the Soviet Communist state went to President Ronald Reagan, no stranger to the paranormal, thanks partially to his wife Nancy's long fascination and belief in astrology. Credit also went to Pope John Paul II, a native of Poland, all too familiar with the heavy-handed, atheistic Soviet system that he strongly opposed. Ultimately, it was not the power of psychic warfare, telepathy, or hypnosis, but Soviet leader Mikhail Gorbachev, whose political sense helped topple the totalitarian Soviet empire. As for any stupendous scientific discoveries of paranormal functioning, they seemed to play little if any role in hastening the demise of the Soviet Union—or saving it. The protracted and resource-draining Cold War was officially declared over in 1990.

Finally, in November 1995, the U.S. government got out of the psychic business—we think. At least that's what the American public was told when it was announced that after more than twenty years, Project Stargate was shut down. The government had spent more than twenty million dollars, dating back decades, on psychic research that went for intelligence and military purposes. A panel of experts was consulted to advise the government about whether parapsychology had been worth the investment. Among them was Dr. Ray Hyman, psychologist at the University of Oregon, an avowed debunker and a founding member of the Committee for the Scientific Investigation of Claims of the Paranormal (CSICOP). Hyman's evaluation was predictable; as befits a professional debunker, he concluded the government wasted a great deal of money on Stargate and other similar programs that went by a variety of clever code names over the years, including Bluebird and Artichoke.

"CSICOP had criticized the SRI remote viewing project," wrote author Martin Ebon. As usual, CSICOP reverted to one of its favorite anti-psi ploys: the debunkers "called for tighter monitoring of its research designs, controls, and conclusions," Ebon added. Whether anyone from CSICOP actually studied the results of Stargate was hard to say. Others who offered their evaluations were divided between those who thought Stargate worthwhile, and some who managed to walk a fine line between the extremist positions on both sides.

What was actually accomplished, we'll likely never know. However, there were some startling psi successes and highly accurate predictions revealed. One example was the Iraqi missile attack on the warship USS *Stark* on May 18, 1987. Only two days before, a U.S. remote viewer named Paul H. Smith had predicted such an attack and drew a sketch of it.

"Between 1979 and 1984 Fort Meade's [remote] viewing site conducted roughly 250 projects involving thousands of missiles," noted *U.S. News & World Report*. One critical event occurred in 1987 when a "mole" was being sought within the CIA. Who was the spy working in the agency that had sold out to the Soviets? American remote viewers psychically created a "composite" of him. He was someone living "in the Washington, D.C., area, drove an expensive foreign car, possibly gray, living in a palatial home, and was intimate with a woman from Latin America, possibly Colombia," according to *U.S. News & World Report*.

When the CIA finally got their man in 1994, his name was Aldrich Ames, and remote viewers were correct in their description, including the large home, a Jaguar, and a Colombian wife. Ames was described in the media as one of the "worst traitors in the history of the Cold War." Author David Wise, who wrote about Ames, said, "You can't put a dollar amount on the damage [done]. Ames gave away the CIA's network inside the Soviet Union." It would seem that psi functioning played a role in his arrest.

Psi might have also helped President George W. Bush triumph over Iraqi dictator Saddam Hussein in 2003 when a psychic might have aided in Hussein's capture. A November 2006 Reuters report raised that possibility. According to the Reuters story, Israeli psychic Uri Geller, who said he'd worked for the CIA during the Cold War, claimed U.S. troops had help from a clairvoyant as they sought Hussein, who was on the run. Geller said it was an American "remote viewer" that led U.S. forces to Hussein's underground hideaway.[50]

"You remember when they found Saddam Hussein in Iraq? A soldier walked over to a rock, lifted it, and then found a trap door and found him in there," Geller told Reuters. "Well, I know that soldier walked over to that rock because he got information from a [U.S.] remote viewer." According to Reuters, Geller's information was from a "high level source involved in U.S. paranormal programs." There was no comment about his claims from U.S. officials. But when Hussein was captured, the U.S. military credited a "source" close to the ex-dictator for "giving him up under interrogation," said Reuters.

It was already known by the latter part of the twentieth century that remote viewers had applied their skills toward psychically gathering intelligence in some very important situations affecting national security. Among them, in addition to the Aldrich Ames spy case, was the "Iranian hostage crisis, locating nuclear weapons sites, the kidnapping of Captain James Dozier by the Red Brigade,[51] and the whereabouts of Libyan dictator Muammar Qadhafi during raids on Tripoli in 1986," according to reporters Marianne Szegedy-Maszak and Charles Fenyvesi.

The enormity of Stargate is proven by the fact that, between late 2002 and early 2003, the CIA released more than seventy thousand pages of formerly classified documents with the expectation that a thousand more records would be declassified and made accessible; while tens of thousands of pages remained "too sensitive" and were not made public.[52] When former president Jimmy Carter granted a wide-ranging interview in 2005 to *GQ* magazine, he acknowledged the government had employed psychics, presumably remote viewers, to help locate a downed military plane in a thick jungle area, not in the United States. While that situation was apparently successful, there is a feeling that some presidents might have known less about the CIA's use of psychic spies than we would have thought; this is not unlike the secrecy that has kept many White House occupants from access to classified information about UFOs.

Perhaps as military science and technology become increasingly complex and sophisticated, spy satellites hovering above us, and new gadgetry on terra firma will negate the need for many living, breathing spies. On the other hand, there may always be a place for "cloak and dagger" types, especially those with remote viewing, ESP, and PK abilities, as long as humans choose war and conflict over peace. Of course, there is also the likelihood that given the long tradition of secrecy in the "alphabet soup" of government agencies—CIA, NSA, NSC, FBI, DIA, BATF, and IRS, to name some—as well as the branches of the military, they will not be any more forthcoming when informing the public than they have been in the past.

With the Cold War over, in the world in which we live since the terrorist attacks of September 11, 2001 (now referred to as 9/11), the West faces new threats and dangers from international terrorism, Islamic fundamentalists, suicide bombers, rogue nations arming themselves with nuclear and biological weapons, and who knows what other horrors waiting around the bend. In addition to spy satellites and other high-tech methods, psychic spies may still provide information about enemy strategies and military installations, employ telepathy to learn what an enemy is thinking, hopefully locate soldiers taken prisoner and civilians kidnapped as hostages, and perhaps predict future events. PSI applied to espionage and warfare will never be 100 percent accurate, but can any one method or approach guarantee perfect hits every time?

The CIA was adamant that it no longer delves into psychic spying when it announced Stargate's end. However, when asked about the military's use of remote viewing, ESP, and PK, the answer was more circumspect, and not quite as absolute, some in the media thought. In the age of terrorism, we are fighting a new and deadly form of war, both at home and abroad. Certainly there is a need for spy satellites and other high-tech methods of gathering intelligence data. But, if recent history has taught us anything, it is that there's also a need for the skills psychics and remote viewers offer in the life and death struggle for national security.

Debunkers, few of whom have ever actually researched psi, pose a potential danger when they argue against remote viewing. These are not objective conclusions from impartial evaluators. Whether their zealotry is to rid us of psi, or to proselytize on behalf of the secular world they hope for, their obstruction is not in the best interests of protecting the United States. Fighting to defend a democratic way of life requires openness to ideas and weapons that could save, or at least aid, the country. Psi is no panacea, but it is genuine and its history in wartime shows it can be useful. To discard psychic spying because it offends some atheist fantasy of a secular nation is highly irresponsible, especially in this country where nine out of ten people believe in God, and at least half the population admits to having had psi experiences, according to polls.

Psychic spying is probably no better or worse morally than traditional or nonpsychic intelligence gathering. Likely, the paranormal is neutral. We humans provide it with the energy to be positive or negative. And, in a time of war, if each side believes it alone is righteous, the question of right and wrong often becomes equally subjective.

And, finally, there is one more truly critical and frightening scenario that begs to at least be considered, if not answered. What happens if enemy nations or the terrorist networks we fight in the future have the same ideas about psi? What, in other words, are our options and defense if and when terrorists employ telepathy, clairvoyance, precognition, psychokinesis, hypnosis, mind control, brainwashing, drugs, and remote viewing in their arsenal of weapons? What's to prevent America's adversaries from surreptitiously employing psi to read our minds, and to torture and kill us? Shouldn't we be ready for the potential psychic wars that may yet occur? Given that chilling possibility, isn't it a better strategy for us to remain psychically prepared? And, in the interest of the public's right to know, shouldn't our intelligence agencies and military leaders, without compromising national security, at least acknowledge truthfully whether psi is or ever will be on the "battlefield"?

6

Remote Influencing and Paranormal Warfare

South Vietnam, 1967.

An army helicopter descended onto the jungle floor, its wheels barely touching the dirt, and a squad of airborne infantry piled out and formed up. The helicopter ascended, getting out of that hot zone before enemy fire disabled it. A young lieutenant named James Channon organized his squad into a formation, assigning point positions to some of his men, and moved them out. It didn't take long for the enemy to open fire on them as they fanned out into the dense foliage, and Channon's men began taking casualties. This scene repeated itself more than once until, Channon said in a 2008 interview with *UFO Magazine*, he learned from members of his unit that some of them said they were able to sense the enemy's presence in the nearby jungle even when they were well hidden.

Channon came to realize that some of his men had what he called "second sense."

"I had some troops who seemed to have a second sense about the presence of danger. I decided to use that to put them on point where their skills would be most activated and could protect us," he revealed.

As a result, Channon found, his troops who could sense danger had honed their psychic skills to the point where they could sense the enemy's presence before an ambush. Channon said that it not only saved lives, but opened him up personally to a realization that there are more than five senses. When he only relied on conventional thinking, Channon said, his leadership of his squad was confined to what he could hear and see. But when he accepted the reality that some of his troops had the ability to perceive beyond their five senses, his casualty rate dropped to zero even though he and his squad were still in the line of fire. It was a personal revelation. From those experiences in Vietnam, Channon realized that if there were people truly sensitive and they could be put in positions where their levels of awareness could be utilized in combat situations, regardless of how much that challenged conventional belief systems, it could save lives just as it did with Channon's squad.

By the middle of the 1970s, Channon explained, the army was going through a reexamination of what had happened in Vietnam. We deployed overwhelming firepower on the ground and air power in the skies, but we were still forced to negotiate our way out of a difficult situation. What had gone wrong? There were lots of opinions, but Channon said that in his opinion, the army was looking at the wrong things. Channon had personally observed the power of psychic phenomena, and he believed that if the army would allow him to explore the background of what he had personally experienced, he could bring to the army an entirely new set of skills that might forever change the nature of warfare. Channon also said that he believed that warfare itself, as it had been fought in Vietnam, was outmoded.

"Right around 1975, the Army was trying to put together what it had learned in the Vietnam War," Channon told *UFO Magazine*. "It was trying to find itself in terms of what kinds of wars it would be fighting. They decided to look at what worked in Vietnam and what didn't, and concluded that it was time for a rethink, an out-of-the-box analysis."

Channon, whose character in the movie *The Men Who Stare at Goats*, was portrayed by Academy Award–winning actor Jeff Bridges, also explained that at the same time the army was re-thinking its model of warfare, he was also going through his own catharsis in which he sought to explore the nature of human poten-tial as well as the human potential movement of the 1970s. It was a time when many people who had come out of large bureaucracies were looking at ways to examine the effects of creative individual thinking on these bureaucracies. It was the time of the *new* New Age, the age after Vietnam and after the be-ins and love-ins of the 1960s. This was putting New Age to work, and one of its by-products was James Channon's new type of army.

While visiting places like Esalen and coming to grips with the meaning of the counterculture, Channon also wrestled with what had happened to the army in the Vietnam War. Here was the most powerful army on the face of the Earth that had to retreat from a third-world country in which the U.S. was fighting a counterinsur-gency. The military learned the same lessons that the French learned fighting in Vietnam a decade earlier and that the British learned fight-ing in the American colonies two hundred years earlier. As he studied all of this, Channon realized that one solution, especially in small engagements such as Vietnam, and now in Afghanistan, was to teach troops to rely on their innate instincts to sense the enemy, just as he had done with his own squad. In other words, Channon suggested to

UFO Magazine, he was coming to the conclusion that reliance on the paranormal might be an effective defense.

Channon explained that his challenge was to tap into what he described as a natural human psychic potential so as to utilize it for defense, just as he'd done in Vietnam. But how to teach that to a bureaucracy such as the U.S. military? That was his biggest challenge. It was a two-pronged challenge. First, Channon had to prove, scientifically with evidence, that the natural human psychic potential existed. He had to prove it in a way that Puthoff and Targ had to prove to the government that there was a real scientific basis for remote viewing. And second, Channon had to show the military that if such a natural human psychic potential existed, it could be deployed for a military purpose.

What Channon said he needed was something akin to a "toolbox," a selection of psychic approaches to tactical situations, which, taken as a whole, could transform the strategy of the military. Channon's argument was that the U.S. military, in particular, the army, had to adapt to conditions on a battlefield in which, like the British during the Revolutionary War, they were fighting an indigenous insurgency on the insurgents' home ground, which, incidentally, the U.S. is currently fighting in Afghanistan.

For starters, Channon used Stewart Brand's *Whole Earth Catalog* (1969) as a toolbox blueprint. Brand's approach was to create a toolbox to effect an earth-changing lifestyle. Channon saw that as the rationale for creating a catalog of human potential tools for effecting a change in military approaches to battlefield deployment so as to increase the survival rate of troops. His list of tools were sets of tactics from which combat planners could pick and choose. The list of tactics presupposed that the U.S. Army was fighting on a battlefield on which they were outnumbered by Warsaw Bloc forces or by insurgent forces operating within their own country, which is what happened in Vietnam.

Channon's toolbox drew from ancient—heretofore called psychic—skills, used by Asian martial arts skill-masters, as Buddhist beliefs, and for paranormal insights. This, Channon said, is what Jon Ronson parodied in his book *The Men Who Stare at Goats* when he wrote about army officers soaking in steaming hot tubs overlooking the Pacific and dreaming up New Age strategies for the military. In part, that was true.

However, this was neither the spiritual New Age of Madame Helena Blavatsky nor the so-called psychic projection of the falsely accused Salem witches. It was far more utilitarian. It was a way for the individual foot-soldier to use psychic potential to fight against overwhelming odds in a hostile environment by relying on senses, instinct, and messages that most rational linear-thinking individuals would reject as woo-woo. It was an application of psychic awareness to life-and-death combat situations. And it was in this way that Channon saw himself as a human potential change agent for the army, a change agent who took what he had gleaned from the human psychic potential movement of the 1970s and 1980s and applied it to the battlefield of the new millennium.

Channon's toolbox of tactics so impressed his senior officers that at a meeting at the officers' club, they embraced his ideas and named him the commander of what came to be called the First Earth Battalion. It was a mission in which Channon was tasked to develop these human potential skills into strategies, basic psychic strategies, for asymmetric warfare and to then incorporate them into a battlefield manual. Far from witchcraft or sorcery, Channon's approach was to accept a human psychic potential as a reality, not to reject insights from the core of that potential, but to utilize them practically for survival. After all, he said to *UFO Magazine,* for a thousand years before Western modern warfare, the Chinese martial arts philosophers used them as everyday tools. We had much to learn from ancient Chinese thinkers and masters of human spiritual thinking.

Here's how Channon's ideas worked. He suggested that if a soldier believed—truly believed—that he could make himself invisible in such a way that he blended into the background environment and was able to simply walk right past the enemy, then the army should encourage that type of thinking. If a soldier believed he could walk through walls, maybe by attempting to match his own physiological vibrations to that of the wall, then the army should encourage that as well, a scenario parodied in the movie *The Men Who Stare at Goats.*

But there were other approaches. For example, Channon said that there was an ancient Chinese martial practice called "dim mak," a way of incapacitating or killing an opponent simply with a touch. Also called the "death touch," the mastery of dim mak became a holy grail for practitioners of ancient Chinese martial arts. Dim mak mastery also became linked to the "death stare," in which simply by looking at an opponent, in this case a laboratory rat or even a goat, hence the title *The Men Who Stare at Goats,* the force of one's will could knock the animal over or kill it. Martial arts master Guy Savelli, who was credited with bringing this type of combat approach to the West, said that the technique of dim mak was to transfer energy from the practitioner to the target so as to incapacitate or kill it. Guy Savelli called this art "kun tao," and said that a well-trained master could project his energy from a distance at a target in such as a way as to interfere with the target's life force, or chi.

Imagine, Savelli explained, a martial arts technique in which a combatant utilizes his volitional intent to strike an enemy from a distance, using only his mind, but with an intent coupled with emotion and prayer. In his own successful application of kun tao, in which he killed an animal by staring at it, Savelli said that he envisioned the archangel Michael standing above the target with his sword and severing the target's circuitry of life force. The animal died.

Retired army colonel Dr. John Alexander, in his book *The Warrior's Edge* (1992) and in a paper entitled "Staring at Goats: The Rest of the Story," as well as his own article in *UFO Magazine*, describes the dim mak blow as something that "defies conventional physiology because it is a relatively light blow not administered to a vital organ." How can it be that just a simple touch, albeit directed by intense and focused mental energy, can incapacitate? Is it magic or is it wizardry? The answer is decidedly no.

Dr. Alexander explains that he worked with Jimmy Channon on the U.S. Army's Task Force Delta, a unit designed to investigate the application of what might be called paranormal tactics into army tactics, which operated out of the army's chief of staff office. That in itself indicates just how important the army saw this research. The unit was then moved to the Army War College. It was during these sessions of research and investigation that things, in Dr. Alexander's words, "got pretty wild." The whole idea of using a martial arts tactic to project energy to interrupt the chi of one's target or to make oneself undetectable to the enemy was a concept that Dr. Alexander referred to as "remote influencing" as distinct from, but tangentially related to, remote viewing.

Dr. Alexander recalled how dim mak master Guy Savelli had been sought after by Lieutenant James Rowe, a former U.S. Army Special Forces officer who had been taken prisoner by the Vietcong in 1963 in An Xuyen province, because Rowe wanted to learn techniques to resist the enemy even if his own physical strength was declining. Rowe had been assigned by the Army to teach survival techniques to Special Forces troops and other personnel who were headed to high-risk assignments in which survival and evasion were essential. One of those techniques was the army's adoption of dim mak and the skills that Savelli could teach.

John Alexander said that he was an evidence-based analyst. In reviewing the claims of Guy Savelli, Dr. Alexander explained that after Savelli killed a goat by the dim mak technique, the colonel personally reviewed photos of the necropsy of the animal and was amazed to see that the path of destruction was directly through the goat's chest. It was as if a bullet had passed through the chest, but there was no entry or exit wound. What had caused that fatal wound? It was, Dr. Alexander concluded, simply the path of energy directed by Guy Savelli that seared through the goat.

For his part, Jimmy Channon explained that he also tried to develop a technique in which he used specific tones in his voice to influence others. This technique is also based on ancient techniques of directing sound and was even used in Jungian forms of exerting influence over otherwise suggestible people. Stage hypnotists often use vocal techniques and changes in tone to induce a light trance state rapidly so as to get the subject to perform feats on stage such as bodily paralysis or behave as if they were statues. Paul Smith explains that one of the differences he noted between remote viewing and remote influencing is that remote viewing is passive while remote influencing is active. Remote viewers literally view a target while remote influencers intervene in the behavior of the target so as to influence it.

Over the years, there were senior army officers at the general staff level who sought to kill the remote viewing program. But, according to Paul H. Smith, because of the success that Jim Channon enjoyed in opening up the minds of senior army officers to out-of-the-box thinking, even when the remote viewing program was on the chopping block, the army saved it.

In his *UFO Magazine* article, "The Rest of the Story," Dr. Alexander writes that imprisoned Special Forces officer Lieutenant James Rowe was rescued by an army air cavalry raid in the U Minh forest in 1968. Rowe subsequently revealed that he had tried to escape his Vietcong prison on numerous occasions and that the VC punished him severely after each attempt, often with torture and with threats of execution. For over five years in captivity, Rowe had played mental games with his Vietcong captors, convincing them that he was only an engineer working on civilian projects. However, Dr. Alexander writes, when a group of American peace activists visited North Vietnam and provided the Vietnamese government with a list of names of American operatives, including Special Operations Forces personnel, the Vietcong came to realize who they had in captivity. Rowe was interrogated, tortured, and physically abused, but he convinced the Vietcong that any information he had about the disposition of Special Forces was too dated to be of any actionable use. Finally, Lieutenant Rowe managed to escape, this time evading capture, just days before his scheduled execution.

Rowe suffered physically after he was rescued in the jungle by American forces, but was recalled to active duty in 1981, posted to Fort Bragg, and assigned the task of teaching his skills at evasion and survival to Army Special Forces. Rowe drew upon the remote influencing techniques he had developed as a POW. One of his research directives was to track down any information on dim mak, and he learned through a noncommissioned officer (NCO) who visited West Point, about Guy Savelli and his martial arts skills. Dim mak seemed to be the perfect solution for POWs who, because of hardships and physical deprivation, would lose strength. However, by keeping mentally alert and focused, they could use remote influencing techniques to deceive and evade their guards and even to incapacitate their guards. Rowe arranged for Savelli to visit Fort Bragg, where he taught his techniques to the students.

As Dr. Alexander wrote, Rowe did not confine his training to physical activities. He also researched mentally influencing others. In his experience as a POW, he had managed to deceive his guards on several occasions and believed he could develop the ability to appear to be invisible to his captors, at first by simply making them look the other way. Savelli himself described a technique called "mind stops." As explained by Dr. Alexander, Savelli said that he could confront an enemy and then, using only his mental ability, maneuver himself behind that enemy without the enemy's knowing.

Savelli's mind stops technique was not unique to him. In his article, Alexander tells the story of a German Jew named Wolf Messing, who fled from the USSR at the outset of World War II. His mental abilities so intrigued Soviet party chairman Joseph Stalin that Stalin demanded a demonstration of them. Messing managed to walk into Stalin's residence, right past Stalin's bodyguards, who had been somehow convinced that the person entering the compound was not Wolf Messing but Lavrenti Beria, the head of the NKVD, precursor to the KGB. Other experiments in psychic weaponry that Dr. Alexander talked about were tests in which pure mental energy was exerted to fracture the spines of subjects. This was the kind of intelligence that Rowe was made privy to when he took over the training of Special Operations Forces personnel at Fort Bragg.

When we take the amount of research and energy the government expended on remote viewing and the serious training protocols the army developed for remote influencing, we can see that despite the catcalls and derision of debunkers, the army and the CIA—as well as our Soviet adversaries during the Cold War— took the paranormal very seriously. In his radio interview on *Future Theater,* Dr. Alexander repeated more than once that, although a pragmatic military officer, his exposure to Rowe's training and his knowledge of the army remote viewing programs proved conclusively to him that the paranormal was real, not fiction or a delusion in the minds of true believers, and that it could be weaponized as part of combat tactics.

7

The Light Beckons:
Near-Death Experiences

Amchu, **One of Us: The Story of Sam Goldberg**[1]
You can see Sam Goldberg tell his story on video at the National
Holocaust Museum in Washington. With tears in his voice and in
his eyes, he tells of an encounter with a young girl selling food-
stuffs in Nazi-occupied Poland. The old woman he's working for
suspects the young girl who sells her fresh eggs is a Jew. She needs
to find out before telling the German soldiers. Sam, posing as a
Catholic and serving as a partisan fighter with the Polish Resistance, warns the girl about the old woman's suspicions. In his conversation with the girl, he inserts the Hebrew word, *amchu,*
meaning "one of us." It is a code. If the girl answers with the word
amchu, it means she, too, is Jewish and so identifies herself. It will
be safe to speak.

Sam speaks the code and the young girl responds. A broken-hearted Sam tells the camera that the young girl is indeed Jewish and it's his job to tell her she's in serious danger and to get away. He does. She does. And that's the story Sam Goldberg, a Holocaust survivor, tells the camera. But it is only a small, small part of Sam's story, which, like all the other stories coming out of the Holocaust, is remarkable.

Born in the small village of Piotrków and descended on his father's side from the legendary Hasidic rabbi Chaim David Bernard, Sam Goldberg grew up seeking his fortune as a nightclub performer, dancer, comic, and actor. As the descendant of a great rabbi, Sam was destined, by his father, to become a rabbi himself. But Sam had other ideas and, with the encouragement of his mother, he set off for the garment center in the city of Lodz, Poland, to take a job as a manager in a garment factory. By night, Sam performed in clubs and on stage, becoming a locally famous stand-up nightclub comic. But all of this took place just a few years before the Nazi invasion and the world of Polish Jewry was forever changed.

As the Luftwaffe's Stuka dive bombers almost wiped out the ranks of refugees fleeing the cities for the forest, Sam pulled favors and obtained Catholic identity cards. Then he joined the Polish resistance, a guerrilla band of fighters harassing the German patrols, until one day, one of his fellow resistance fighters saw him urinating in the woods, saw that he was circumcised, and began screaming, "Jew."

Sam fled for his life, his career as a resistance fighter over. He fled first to the Warsaw Ghetto, then to his home village of Piotrków as the Germans closed in. There he reconciled with his father, who had opposed his going to Lodz and his going on stage, but Sam contracted deadly typhoid fever, which did not abate. For weeks, Sam lay in a delirium, until finally, he was near the point of death and the doctors, themselves under siege and without any medicines at their disposal, could do nothing to save him. His parents and his sister sat at his makeshift bedside as the Germans closed in, and waited for him to stop breathing.

Sam remembered very little about being sick. But until the end of his days he remembered an experience in which he was no longer in his body. He was in a court, a court inside a small synagogue. But it wasn't a government or a civil court, it was a *beth din*, the traditional Jewish court where parties pled their cases before three rabbis, who would decide the case based on the law of the Torah and Jewish teachings. Three rabbis appeared to Sam, two of whom he could not recognize. The third rabbi, the one who spoke for the tribunal, was Sam's own ancestor, the one in whose footsteps his father demanded he follow. It was Rabbi Chaim David Bernard.

Rabbi Chaim David Bernard spoke to Sam. They had decided, he said, but Sam actually didn't hear the words. He only knew somehow what they were saying, whether in Hebrew or Yiddish, it wasn't apparent. Sam heard from his ancestor that the rabbis of the *beth din* had decided he would live through the fever and recover. They decided that he would live through the terrible times around them, the Shoah, even though he would undergo unbearable hardship. He would live even though he would be at the point of death more times than he could imagine. But he would live to tell the story. And, they said, after all of the terrible times were over, when Sam looked into the face of pure evil, that's when he would die.

And Sam found himself lying in his bed again, looking up at his sister while he heard the prayers of his father giving thanks that he was alive. Sam had made it through, his experience at the point of death still resonating in his mind.

Sam got well very quickly. As the German troops occupied the town, going through the Jewish neighborhood to round up the prisoners bound for Treblinka, Sam made plans to flee. His father said that the rest of the family wasn't strong enough to flee or to escape, and at their final good-bye, he exacted a promise from his son. Extending his hand in what Jewish tradition calls the *tsaitz-kopf,* the promise that once given can't be broken, he asked his son to agree that whatever he did, wherever he went, he would never again appear on the show business stage for any reason.

The sound of artillery could be heard nearby as could the sounds of German troops barking orders to the frightened inhabitants of the village. They would be marched off to the boxcars. Sam still had time to disappear. He took his father's hand, made the agreement, and fled into the woods. It would be the last time he ever saw his father and his sister, both victims at Treblinka.

Sam's journey took him to the Jewish enclaves in Warsaw again and from there, following a young woman he liked, to a work camp where Jewish prisoners sewed uniforms for German soldiers. Sam was imprisoned in the camp, but he was working and eating and staying alive. His situation changed, however, when the work camp was, in Sam's words, "liquidated," and all of the prisoners were shipped to Auschwitz, a death camp.

Once at Auschwitz, as a young and robust-looking man, Sam was not marched off to the gas chambers. That immediate fate awaited the elderly, the children, and the infirm. Sam was assigned to work details. But he noticed that a group of prisoners seemed to have cleaner clothes, looked better fed, and wore shoes that were in better condition than inmates in other barracks. He approached one of them, asking to be assigned to whatever detail they worked, but the man told him to go away and find another way to stay alive. This detail was worse than hell. But Sam persisted and finally one of the men said, "What does it matter? We're all going to die anyway." And Sam found himself reassigned to the infamous

Canada barracks at Auschwitz, where the prisoners, transport-kommandos, worked the rail platform for the even more infamous monster Dr. Josef Mengele.

If Sam believed his life had been arduous before, it became unbearable once in the Canada barracks. Each morning, Sam was positioned on the train platform, forming the arriving prisoners into two lines. At signals from Mengele and those soldiers under his direct command, the transport-kommandos directed individual lines to the right or to the left. One line went directly to the work barracks. Those chosen to die immediately went directly to the gas chambers. Once in the chambers the inmates, told that they were being deloused, were made to take off all their clothing and walk into what the guards said were showers. There the crystals of Zyklon B were dropped into the heating units and the inmates choked to death, poisoned by the gas.

After the first groups of inmates were sent to the chambers and ordered to undress for the showers, Sam Goldberg had another task. As a garment worker, he knew where people sewed their valuables into seams and under collars. He would go to the clothing stockpile and cut open the stitches of the garments where he would find rings, jewels, sometimes even gold teeth, and other items that he could use to barter with the guards for sausages and potatoes. Ultimately, after he had been told by partisan fighters inside the camp that one of the Czech resistance groups was planning a raid on the camp to liberate the prisoners, Sam began bargaining with the guards for rifles, which he buried in the fertilizer fields or *scheiss felder*. The raid, however, was unsuccessful in liberating the prisoners even though it resulted in the destruction of one of the crematoria. The executions did not stop and the bodies of prisoners kept on being incinerated in the remaining crematoria.

The days wore on, morning trains, disposition of the arriving prisoners, inspections conducted by Dr. Mengele. By this time,

Sam had developed the ability to make himself almost invisible to Mengele's unwavering eye by not looking directly at him so as to avoid staring into the face of evil. Mengele, Sam remembered, had a penchant for selecting siblings for experiments—gruesome experiments, the results of which ultimately made their way to the CIA, and British and Soviet intelligence agencies—as well as individuals with sores or blemishes on their body. Sam, during the barracks inspections, would position himself among taller prisoners, covering his body with a towel, as if he had just cleaned himself, and Mengele, walking by the line of inmates and selecting those for visits to his infirmary, would simply pass him by. Sam had learned the ability to make himself blend into the background, looking away from Mengele just to stay alive each succeeding day.

On one particular night, as Sam Goldberg smelled an all-too familiar smell of burning flesh, he fought with his conscience. He wrestled with the idea that some of the incoming prisoners were selected for death and others selected for work. What did it mean? Who shall die and who shall live? Even in the camp, prisoners died from exposure, from hunger, and from illness every day. Stories ran through the camp of people from certain villages that Sam knew, who had died during the cold night. Who, Sam asked, shall die by gas or who by starvation, or who from illness? These were the questions posed in one of the holiest of prayers uttered on one of the holiest days in the Hebrew calendar, Yom Kippur. The prayer was called *Unetanneh Tokef*, composed by the famous rabbi Amnon, who was at the point of death after having had his arms and legs cut off by a monarch who was angry the rabbi would not convert to Christianity. The prayer, chanted during the Days of Awe, the ten days starting on Rosh Hashanah, the Jewish New Year and culminating with the Ne'ilah service ending at sundown on the Day of Atonement, Yom Kippur, asks not only who will live or who will die, but casts it into the image of whose name shall be inscribed in the Book of Life for the coming year and whose name will not, and if inscribed during the Days of Awe, whose name will be sealed in the Book of Life as the gates to heaven close at the end of the Ne'ilah service. It is a very moving prayer, repeating over and over again, "On Rosh Hashanah it is written and on Yom Kippur it is sealed. But prayer, return to holiness, and just deeds avert the severity of the decree."

These were the images on Sam Goldberg's mind as he contemplated not just the horror he was going through but his involvement in it as he met the inmates coming off the trains at the Auschwitz platform. His thoughts so disturbed him, he decided he could not live for another day and attempted suicide. Having no weapons, Sam's only method was to hurl himself against the electrified fence that surrounded the camp, attempting to kill himself. And this is exactly what he tried to do, knowing all the while that the three rabbis at the *beth din* had foreseen his survival through the Holocaust.

In the darkness, Sam ran toward the gate, hoping in a final leap to end it all. But, his foot caught on something, a branch or a root, and he fell forward into the mud. He decided to try again, this time running even harder and from a different angle. He ran, but suddenly the ground gave way under him before he reached the gate. He found himself in something like a foxhole or a pit. Odd, he thought, for all the time he was in the Canada barracks he had come to know the perimeter well and never saw the root he tripped over or the pit he fell into. He went back to the barracks just in time to hear the snarling and barking of dogs and the voices of the guards screaming in shrill voices, *"Raus, mach schell. Raus mitt ihnen."* The guards were ordering the inmates out of their barracks, quickly. There was a night train arriving at the camp.

There were very few night trains that ever arrived at Auschwitz, but this one was special. As Sam waited on the platform, the train lights playing harshly across the muddy fields, it looked like snow was falling in fine white flakes. It wasn't snow.

When they returned to the barracks, Sam carefully checked the perimeter of the building. No pit. No root. What had he fallen over? And once inside the barracks, in the latrine, Sam discovered a young child cowering in a corner. This child, who spoke Czech, would have been sent directly to the gas chamber had he been discovered. But somehow he eluded the guards and made it into the Canada barracks. Sam would shelter him through his stay at Auschwitz and leave him with a Czech-speaking farmer as the death train, the train that carried the Auschwitz survivors from the camp west into Germany as the war was ending, stopped at the German border while Allied bombers tried to destroy the tracks.

Sam survived the death train, even though he himself was at the point of starvation and critical dehydration. He was saved again when the Wehrmacht soldiers guarding the train tried to machine-gun the prisoners, but were stopped by a U.S. Army Ranger advance recon patrol. The year was 1945 and Auschwitz had been liquidated of inmates so that the bodies of German soldiers could be incinerated in the crematoria instead of going back to Germany, proof that the Eastern front had collapsed and the Soviets were advancing through Poland to Germany itself.

Sam was saved by American doctors and intelligence officers who, seeing the tattooed serial number on his arm, knew that he had been in the Canada barracks and that someday he would be a living witness against those who had imprisoned and killed the six million Jews. The American intelligence officers told the German doctors whom they ordered to care for the inmates that if Sam Goldberg died in their custody, they would be executed. Sam was that valuable a witness.

At war's end, because Sam had had military training in the Polish resistance, he was made the police chief of the displaced person and refugee camp in Wahlheim, Germany. But he quickly established links to Menachem Begin's Stern Gang, sending Allied money and even smuggling young Holocaust survivors into Palestine to bolster the Jewish resistance there. Sam had become either a terrorist or a Zionist resistance fighter depending upon which side you take. After the UN vote on partition of what had been designated as Trans Jordan into the Jewish state Israel and the Arab state of Palestine, Sam was given a visa to the United States of America where he and his new wife, also a Holocaust survivor, saved from the gas chamber because a German officer took a fancy to her and saved her life, even as the Zyklon B crystals were being dropped into the heating unit. The married couple immigrated to the United States where they started their new life together.

In the following decades, Sam, just like many other Holocaust survivors in the "golden land" of the United States, not only planted his roots but achieved enormous financial success. Sam moved to Los Angeles. He raised a family, grew old, and settled into retirement and grandparenthood when he received a strange call from someone identifying himself as an officer at the United States Department of Justice. Was this a knock on the door? A frightened Sam Goldberg—after all, he had been through the Holocaust—called the FBI, asking for help. They told him that Nazi Hunters from the Justice Department believed they had identified the remains of Josef Mengele in South America. Could Sam, who had been identified at the end of the war as one of the kommandos working for Mengele, meet with the Nazi hunters to describe Mengele to them? Sam was fearful, of course. He'd heard stories about the Odessa group, modern Nazi terrorists seeking to eliminate all witnesses to the horrors of the concentration camps. But Sam agreed to meet an FBI agent, who would accompany him to the meeting, assuring him of complete protection.

They met at the Airport Hilton adjacent to Los Angeles International Airport. Sam wore a yellow tie, a code to the FBI agent looking for him in the coffee shop. From there they took the elevator to one of the upper floors, knocked on the door of one of the rooms, and met the Nazi hunters, who had laid out a series of photos on the bed.

The federal officers from the Justice Department began by asking Sam rudimentary questions. "What was the color of Mengele's uniform? Black like the SS, yes?"

"No," Sam answered. "In his infirmary he wore a green field uniform."

"Mengele had no limp, correct?"

"No, he had a limp on his left side," Sam answered. And he told the story of how Mengele told all of the younger men in the Canada barracks to parade past him. Sam had grown a skin blemish on his shoulder and at the last minute had thrown a ragged towel over it as if he'd just cleaned himself and was able to avoid Mengele's attention.

"Dr. Mengele was a harsh master, was he not?" they asked.

Again Sam answered, "No. He was menacingly charming and solicitous."

"Please look at the photos," the federal officers asked him. "Can you identify any of them?"

"No," Sam answered. "I don't know any of them. None of them is Mengele, if that's what you're asking."

Then one of the officers opened a small attaché case and flipped a photo onto the bed.

"Recognize that?" he asked.

Sam Goldberg stared into the face of pure evil and answered, "That's Dr. Mengele."

It would not be long after Sam Goldberg had told his story, recording it on tape, that he suffered a heart attack and died. The prophecy in his near-death experience finally came true. Sam Goldberg of blessed memory had closed the book on Josef Mengele.

Elise's Story[2]

Although Elise was only eighteen years old, she suffered with lupus, an incurable autoimmune disease that was first diagnosed when she was twelve. Lupus is a complex disorder in which the body's immune system turns against itself, attacking virtually every organ, including the skin and joints. Although it is a debilitating disease that can strike anyone, lupus targets mainly young women, and its cause is uncertain, possibly genetic. Treatments are limited. Often steroidal or other antiinflammatory drugs are administered to ease pain and inflammation. The name *lupus* is derived from the Latin word for wolf, and the disease is so named because it can ravage the bodies of those with it. Even sunlight can trigger what are called lupus "flare-ups."

Thin and petite, with shoulder-length dark hair and warm eyes, Elise was pretty, and looked surprisingly well, in spite of her interminable pain and suffering. Her positive attitude was certainly helpful, but lupus complications can occur unexpectedly. One warm summer night, as she readied herself for sleep, Elise suddenly felt pressure in her chest, pressure as if an elephant were standing on her. And then, as she lay down, her heart and breathing both ceased. She was, as medical doctors would define it, clinically dead.

To the world, she might have appeared completely lifeless. But, almost miraculously, she was fully conscious. She felt herself rise out of her body, and float upward toward the ceiling of her bedroom, all the while, what looked to her like "a cord of bright white light," kept her attached to her physical body, which remained in bed. She peered down and saw herself lying there. At the same

time she experienced a feeling of weightlessness. Then a lumines-
cent figure caught her attention and soon identified itself. "I am
your guardian angel," it communicated telepathically. Elise sensed
that it was a female being, and the light it emitted was "beautiful,
warm, and comforting," she thought. "It was as if I'd been bathed
in love."

As Elise's experience continued, the guardian angel guided her
through what she described as a "tunnel of light," and she had the
sensation of moving forward. Soon she felt she'd gone beyond the
tunnel and became aware of other beings of light surrounding her.
Some appeared angelic. However, several others telepathically
identified themselves to Elise as her deceased uncles, aunts, and
great-grandparents, family members she had not known on Earth
since they'd passed over before she was born. "I could feel and
sense them to my right. They were also behind me and I was hovering slightly above them. I was most aware of the brilliant light,
though. I was sure I was in heaven, what some people call the
'other side,'" Elise later recalled.

"I sensed the spirits of the departed were there, and each had a
guardian angel. The beings of light were flying toward the center
of an incredibly powerful white light," she continued. "What was
strange about the light, in spite of its radiance, was that somehow
it was not blinding. I looked right at the light as my guardian angel
guided me toward it. When I was in that light, it felt like I was
bathed in pure love, and I was totally at peace. The other wonderful thing is that the pain and pressure in my heart and lungs were
gone. I wasn't aware of any of the earthly suffering I had so much
of," Elise explained.

"Then it was as if the next voice I sensed came from within the
light itself," she continued. "The light seemed to be talking to me!
It was saying that I had a purpose to fulfill on Earth. It was a male
voice this time that said I would help many people on Earth, and in

order to help them I had to return to my body. When the voice spoke, I just listened. I felt humility and awe in its presence, and I wanted badly to stay in the light. But the voice and my guardian angel were communicating the same message: that I had to return to earth to do work that would be of service to God. It was as if those were His instructions to me."

Next, the guardian angel telepathically told Elise, "I have one more place to show you. Hell." The next sight she faced was a "lower level," as her guardian angel called it. Elise thought a better description of hell, if that's what she was seeing, was a "pit." She saw spirit beings; however, she thought they were in a "very sad place." These were not souls bathed in the "loving light" she'd described earlier. Here "they were twisting and turning, and all pressed together." It was a horrible scene of "people screaming in pain," Elise said. "Their faces were contorted." She was shocked by the "writhing mass of beings," that she described as "dark and gray," nothing like the spirits enveloped in light she'd seen earlier in what she thought was "heaven."

Her guardian angel pulled one of the tormented spirits closer so that Elise could see its raw and unrelenting agony, and the suffering of those who had been condemned to this shadowy abyss, the result of their misdeeds and wrongful behavior when they were on Earth. Elise began to cry for what she called "these lost souls."

"Can I help them?" she implored her guardian angel.

"No, the only one who can help them is God or Jesus," answered the angel. "Do not worry. You are being guided. You have a job to do. You must go back now!"

The next sensation Elise had was of floating in her bedroom, near the ceiling, and struggling to return to her physical body. Finally, she did, and gasped for air, as she had before. The pressure and pain in her chest were back, and her heart was beating abnormally. It felt as if the heartbeats were irregular, and she discovered some blood in her mouth. The experience awakened her, and she cried in fright.

When morning came, Elise told other family members what she'd encountered. There was one more aspect to her near-death experience, or NDE, that deserves mention. "My guardian angel told me my mother owned a medal of Joan of Arc. I never knew that," Elise said. "The being of light insisted that would prove my experience was genuine." When she asked, she found out that such a silver medal had been in the family for generations. Elise's visit to her cardiologist revealed she suffered from aortic insufficiency and mitral valve prolapse that caused a heart murmur, damage that persists to this day.

Did Elise have what is known as a near-death experience? Had she actually gone out of her body, for a glimpse of the afterlife, or heaven, if one prefers a religious appellation? Or had she suffered a significant lack of oxygen to the brain that produced the sensation or a hallucination of traveling beyond her body? Depending upon whether one believes the conventional medical explanation of oxygen deprivation generating a hallucinogenic dreamlike state that produces images from deep in one's subconscious, or other interpretations claiming that one's soul actually transits out of the body at the moment of death, one can form either opinion. However, popular culture indicates a belief in near-death experiences.

By 1982, a Gallup poll found that some eight million Americans reported having near-death experiences, and many were convinced that they'd actually died and gone on to briefly see the afterlife. Most—but not all—found the event surprisingly comforting, and admitted they would have preferred to remain on the other side. However, invariably, those who saw deceased loved ones also reported that they'd been instructed to return to their physical or earthly body. "It wasn't my time," many said they were told. A majority described the experience as "life-changing." Often that included less fear of death, and once that had been achieved, many said, they could more fully devote themselves to living.

Even former president Bill Clinton was said to have reported that when he was having his heart-bypass operation after his heart attack, he experienced a floating sensation and actually saw himself on the operating table with surgeons performing the procedure over him. Certainly, now on a vegan diet to restore his health, President Clinton did undergo a life change. But the question remains, and only President Clinton can answer it, what really happened to him and what does he believe?

When clinical death occurs, the heart stops and breathing ceases. Not everyone who is revived claims they've been drawn to a brilliant light as they advanced through a tunnel, to emerge in an idyllic setting where their deceased loved ones wait. Many people who are resuscitated from unconsciousness or the brink of death make no claim of having seen anything. But for millions of others who've reported having NDEs, there is an overwhelming sense of peace associated with the experience.

What is going on? Arguments about the reality of NDEs have raged for as long as people have had out-of-body experiences, and that dates back to ancient times. Even poets from the ancient Greeks through Shakespeare have written about what they call "dream visions," sometimes prophetic visions that those who have fallen into an unconscious deathlike or trancelike state describe. The dream vision is actually a meme in medieval literature, particularly in Chaucer's *The Book of the Duchess*. However, the question persists: do near-death experiences represent the best evidence we have that life continues after death? Or are those who've claimed they'd had NDEs mistakenly reporting a hallucination or a brain anomaly, caused by either drugs or oxygen deprivation? It is not an insignificant debate because the importance of the NDE, if it is genuine, provides science with an entirely new paradigm of what life and death are. On the one hand, for skeptics and debunkers, the NDE must be imaginary or the product of wishful thinking, since for secularists, there is no afterlife. Regarding out-of-body experiences (OBE), though, author and retired army colonel John Alexander, in an interview on *Future Theater*, said unequivocally that he believes the government knows the paranormal is actually very normal and the supernatural is quite real.

On the other hand, another argument against the near-death experience is that no one returns from the finality of death. If we accept the conclusion that NDEs are genuine, we've opened the door to an entirely new way of positing what happens at the moment of physical death and beyond. The NDE, therefore, becomes potential evidence of an immortal spirit body separating from the earthly or corporal body. It also opens up questions about the reality of the soul, and suggests that death is not a termination, but rather a transition from one dimension to another, the next stage of life.

Over the course of humankind's history, the argument has been approached from many perspectives: scientifically, medically, psychologically, theologically, and metaphysically. In other words, the NDE potentially goes to the heart of the centuries-old debate about the possibility of an afterlife. It is one of the most frustrating and persistent, yet fascinating, questions in the annals of not only the paranormal, but of all human history. Skeptics and debunkers abhor the issue. For them, there is no discussion necessary, since death is the cessation of life. "Survival" is a religious and philosophical belief, not meant for scientists and physicians to seriously consider, insist debunkers and atheists. And they may find evidence for their theories of conventional shutdown of brain function due to loss of oxygen based on recent research into the role of the hippocampus region of the brain, which can survive loss of oxygen for short periods. The hippocampus is where core memories are stored, and thus may involve memories of loved ones appearing in visions at the point of brain death, giving the illusion of an NDE.

Even Dr. J. B. Rhine, the eminent parapsychologist whose life's work was the study of ESP at Duke University, admitted that the issue of survival was elusive. Despite its obvious importance, Rhine felt the difficulty in testing was more than he and his wife could manage. Would one deliberately put a subject into a death-like state, flatlining a volunteer and then resuscitating him so that the volunteer could report on what he saw on the other side? The illegality of that experiment notwithstanding, playing with death is not something even Dr. Frankenstein was successful in doing.

Rhine acknowledged that finding evidence for ESP was difficult enough without tackling questions about the Great Beyond. Fortunately, there were—and are—others willing to delve into the ultimate mystery about whether there is life after death, and what constitutes evidence, albeit without flatlining subjects. The use of modern statistics does allow for anecdotal evidence to be categorized and cross-evaluated.

Dr. Raymond Moody received a PhD, then went on to earn his degree as a medical doctor, completing his residence and specialty in psychiatry. He applied those impressive credentials to teaching the philosophy of medicine. As a psychiatrist, his intense interest in and curiosity about the human mind led him to research a phenomenon that he named the near-death experience. It was not that out-of-body incidents were new, because those dated back to the beginning of recorded history. However, those experiences, when they described a postmortem (now we'd consider them perimortem) had never been given a term of their own when they occurred at the moment of death, until Moody's bestselling book *Life After Life* was first published in 1975. Before that, most doctors regarded such experiences as the domain of parapsychologists or the clergy—if they regarded them at all—but not within the perimeters of medical science.

Moody first heard details of a near-death experience about a decade earlier when he was studying at the University of Virginia. It was there that Dr. George Ritchie, a psychiatrist, described an experience he'd had. Ritchie, who was a scientist and a skeptical medical doctor, said he'd nearly succumbed to pneumonia, and doctors had pronounced him dead. However, Ritchie remembered traveling out of his body, then returning to it, in a Texas hospital. Moody was intrigued by what he heard, and unlike many colleagues, later courageously pursued the subject. Moody had apparently decided that if one of his colleagues in the medical profession could give some personal and anecdotal credence to a phenomenon that had been relegated to medieval sorcery or the hallucinogenic experiences of indigenous peoples, then it was worth a medical exploration of Ritchie's story.

The 1960s were an important decade for near-death experiences for that was when medical technology made significant leaps forward in the ability to resuscitate patients who'd been declared clinically dead. That was the key. Medical science and associated technologies were the mechanism for discovering witnesses who'd been to the other side and came back, bringing with them their stories of what they'd seen. Many more individuals were being brought back to life, following automobile accidents, heart attacks, and other sudden death events, thanks to cardiopulmonary resuscitation, electroshock cardiac defibrillation, and drugs. Therefore, both the suddenness of the onset of death, almost as though chance had intervened in human destiny, and the immediacy and effectiveness of medical treatment had made trips possible back from the Beyond. Yes, it inspired a cultural belief in the phenomena of near-death experiences even as it also inspired scientific skeptics and debunkers to hoo-hoo those in the medical profession who gave credence to it.

Moody was persistent, however. His research spelled out several characteristics of the NDE that helped define the phenomenon more precisely. Here are the criteria Moody developed:[3]

The person is aware he or she is dead.

The person experiences peace, release, and freedom from the physical body and earthly pain.

There is the sensation of floating out of one's body, often accompanied by the spirit's ability to look down at its own body, even watching medical personnel at work.

There is also the sensation of quickly traveling up or through a tunnel, where waiting are "beings of light"; some are the spirits of deceased loved ones. One being of light may appear and act as a "spirit guide" for the individual experiencing the near-death encounter.

A so-called life review may take place of both a person's positive and negative experiences.

The individual having the NDE indicates an unwillingness to return to their physical body and has to be urged by the light beings, often being told that his or her time and purpose on Earth has not yet been fulfilled.

Finally, when the spirit returns to its physical body, following the NDE, the person frequently undergoes a dramatic change, recognizing that he or she has been through a life-altering experience, that is more often than not, positive in nature.

Unbeknownst to Moody, there was other similar research going on at the time. One of those at the forefront was Dr. Elisabeth

Kübler-Ross (1926–2004), a Swiss-born American psychiatrist, teaching at the University of Chicago, who'd written a landmark book, *On Death and Dying,* in 1969. Shortly after World War II ended, Kübler-Ross was a young woman, still in Europe, when she had the opportunity to visit Majdanek, an infamous Nazi concentration camp. It was there that Kübler-Ross saw for herself the actual crematoria—the ovens—where the bodies of murdered Jews had been incinerated. The shock and horror stirred her to question life and death, and when she later devoted herself to the study of "death and dying," it was with such commitment that she ultimately earned a reputation as one of the world's leading authorities on the subject.

Kübler-Ross's impact on America's consciousness was extraordinary. As a society, but also because of individual fear, we'd increasingly distanced ourselves from death as the twentieth century wore on, preferring instead to celebrate the culture of youth. It was easier to live in denial about death when most loved ones expired in hospitals, rather than at home as was common before the advances of modern medicine and surgery required special facilities. It became increasingly rare for the "death bed" to be at home, with loved ones gathered around. And as the twentieth century wore on, the hospice industry emerged, corralling the dying in terminal care facilities so as to provide an environment that most families in private residences could not. As a result when it came to the rituals surrounding death, the parlor at home gave way to the commercial funeral parlor.

We tended to make the concept of death more amenable during the twentieth century even as we distanced ourselves from it as best we could. Euphemisms such as "memorial parks" often took the place of "cemeteries" and "graveyards." The word "marker" replaced such stark words as "gravestone" or "tombstone." People didn't "die." They "went to their eternal sleep," or "were laid to rest." They weren't "dead"; they were "in their final repose." "Funeral directors" replaced "undertakers." "Graves" became "interments," and "wakes" became "viewings." And what was embalming, if not an effort to pretend the dead still looked alive, through the magic of a mortician's makeup? Avoiding frank discussions about death and dying became an unfortunate fact of contemporary life from the post–World War II years on as American society unloaded its dying population upon the medical profession, their hospitals, and the hospice community.[4]

The growing psychological and physical separation between life and death left most Americans by the mid-twentieth century uncertain about how to face death honestly, and, thanks to medical progress, people were living longer. Today, according to current popular thinking, if you can make it through your sixties and seventies without any debilitating medical conditions, such as cardiovascular disease or cancer, you stand a good chance to join America's largest growing segment of the population, centenarians.

In addition to people living longer, infant mortality rates had fallen dramatically, as did the number of women who died in childbirth. Vaccinations meant that far fewer children succumbed to illnesses than had earlier generations, particularly polio as a result of the Salk vaccine and research supported by the Mothers March of Dimes. With the disappearance of childhood epidemics, the twentieth century also saw antibiotics become readily available and as a result, many infectious diseases, plagues, and epidemics were largely eradicated. HIV (human immunodeficiency virus), of course, remains an incurable disease, which thirty years ago had threatened to become a serious pandemic. However, AIDS drugs, although not curing the disease, nevertheless reduce symptoms to the point where HIV-infected individuals are able to live their lives without the immediate worry of succumbing to AIDS (aquired immune deficiency syndrome).

As discoveries in medical research and technology promised longer and debilitation-free lives and as advertising and marketing, increasingly aimed at youth, promised a kind of Utopia, older people became nearly invisible in the mass media. By the 1970s, talking about death and dying had become the great American taboo. It was out of sight, out of mind.

But death is inevitable despite our best efforts to ignore or mask it. At some point in life, usually as we grow older, we face the fact that our physical being is neither immortal nor indestructible. Immortality, once the quiet belief system of the young, disappears with an all too frightening suddenness at the onset of the first heart attack, the flat-mouthed delivery of a painful diagnosis from your heretofore friendly doctor, the black and white printout results on your iPhone display of a deadly prophetic hemoglobin count, the weathered Medicare card that now sits very accessibly in your wallet. Our vision fails, our grip grows weak, dizziness overtakes us in the morning, and we begin to look at what we once took for granted as a blessing. The proximity of death becomes very real. Like Edmond Rostand's character Cyrano de Bergerac, we may face death bravely with our white plumes flying and rapiers drawn, but it is still death. We watch our friends fall. As a result, like our ancestors, we harbor fear, uncertainty, and many questions about the end of life, and, with an almost blind faith, what might lie beyond it.

Somewhere, most of us have heard references to death from a priest, minister, or rabbi. However, when there was mention of the soul or heaven, the concepts were often impersonal or abstract. Ironically, most primitive peoples had elaborate rituals and definite explanations concerning the afterlife. In that sense they were likely better prepared for death than we were by the mid-twentieth century.

Living in denial about death could only go so far, even in a world of medical miracles and increased longevity. There were still wars, natural disasters, accidents, and diseases that ultimately took us, sometimes sooner rather than later. When a British author, Jessica Mitford, wrote *The American Way of Death* in 1963, it was an unsettling exposé "of the cynicism and greed" in the funeral business, and meant as a wake-up call that we were attempting to cope with the deaths of loved ones by spending more money on rituals than perhaps we needed to; many of the grief-stricken were motivated by guilt and fear, and were frequently taken advantage of by the funeral home industry. Their not-so-subtle message was that the more one spent on the final going away, the greater was the love for the person who'd departed. Mitford's answer, though it flew in the face of traditional religious practices, was cremation, if it was kept affordable. Repeatedly, messages communicated through mediums told grieving loved ones that funerals and other death rituals were for the living while the souls of the deceased had moved on to what psychics and mediums call the other side.

Cremation in the Old Testament was regarded as a pagan practice. The Patriarch Abraham negotiated with the Hittites for a cave in Malpeth in which to bury his beloved Sarah. It was indeed the first modern real estate deal and the basis of contract law in the West—no contract is valid absent consideration, particularly contracts for the conveyance of property—but it also made the point that the dead were to be buried below ground and not incinerated. Internment amid the leaping flames of burning ships were for the Vikings and the Anglo-Saxons, and funeral pyres were for Eastern polytheistic religions. But for the Old Testament Patriarchs, it was burial, a tradition that remains with us today particularly after the Nazis demonstrated to the world the horror of mass cremation in the death camps.

We'd certainly gained immeasurably in scientific knowledge

and inventive genius since the time of the ancient Egyptians. But spiritually and psychologically, had we evolved as far, despite the passage of thousands of years? The Egyptians built elaborate pyramids in which they entombed their dead rulers, the pharaohs, believing they journeyed on to an afterlife. Many millennia later, we were still spending great sums of money on rituals to bury the dead, and, strangely, had as many questions about the process of dying as our ancestors did. But, supposedly being modern and therefore supposedly more rational, the idea of life after death was left for philosophers and theologians to debate, while paranormal explanations about the afterlife remained anathema to Western religions, although every major denomination had some version of a soul and hereafter in its teachings. To traditional scientists and skeptics, such ideas were irrational flights of fancy, hallucinations, or superstitions; the dead neither lived on, nor did they return to earth. The result was that just as relatively few people talked openly about dying, so too were many inhibited and confused about approaching questions of life after death, fearing ridicule or criticism.

Elisabeth Kübler-Ross was one of those rare scientists with the courage to break free from the restraints of conventional thinking. In her book, *On Death and Dying*, first published in 1969, she boldly confronted the fear of death, and made clear "the greater need for understanding of and coping with the problems of death and dying." Writing as a psychiatrist, she said, "It is inconceivable for our unconscious to imagine an actual ending of our own life here on earth."[5]

Just writing candidly about that very human and understandable fear was a healthy beginning in chipping away at the taboo. For many it was as if Kübler-Ross had granted them permission to talk openly about the universal mystery—and dread—that is death. There was another issue that we'd long ignored in our attitude towards death, which was the dying person. Ironically, when life spans were shorter, and more people died at home surrounded by family and friends, we were closer to accepting death. As death became the responsibility of hospitals and vastly improved medical technology, the dying person was left very much alone, and in a setting that Kübler-Ross rightly called "impersonal."

For example, there is the story of famed nineteenth-century author Louisa May Alcott who, with her mother, remained at the bedside of her dying younger sister Beth, only in her twenties. At the moment Beth "drew her last breath," the Alcotts later told their family physician, they'd seen a wisp rise from Beth that they presumed was her soul departing her body. The doctor was not surprised. He said he'd heard such reports many times.[6]

Regardless of your opinions about the existence and nature of the human soul, and the possibility of an afterlife, Alcott's experience raises other interesting questions. How likely would it be that we'd sit patiently at the deathbed of a loved one—at home—for many hours or days? Many of us, in a home hospice situation, certainly do. Would we share with our family doctor an experience that suggested we'd seen the soul leave the body? Have people changed? Kübler-Ross did not think so. "What has changed is our way of coping and dealing with death and dying and our dying patients," she wrote.[7] And, "many of the old customs and rituals which have lasted over the centuries," she said, were ways of coping with the "grief, shame, and guilt," and were "not very far removed from feelings of anger and rage."

At the time Kübler-Ross wrote her breakthrough book, it was relatively rare for discussions to take place in which terminally ill or dying people were encouraged to express their feelings and thoughts regarding impending death. It was to the dying patients that Kübler-Ross devoted a great portion of her writing. She made it clear that the dying have much to teach those who are yet alive and well. True to her word, she interviewed hundreds of dying patients in the preparation of her books.

Kübler-Ross concluded that there were five stages which dying people go through as they face their own mortality: (1) Denial and isolation. (2) Anger. (3) Bargaining. (4) Depression. (5) Acceptance. For each phase she offered substantial advice in her books and public appearances for both patients and their family members.[8] Somehow, even in the most dire and tragic of circumstances, Kübler-Ross found there was often a spark in terminally ill people that clung to hope, even when the odds were overwhelmingly against them. Possibly a miracle cure would be discovered in time or perhaps the medical diagnosis or prognosis was in error.

How badly Kübler-Ross's advice was needed was evidenced by the numerous printings her book went through, and the book earned its place as a classic on the subject of death and dying. In later books, she dealt at length with the difficult questions surrounding children who are dying, advice for loved ones of those who "die suddenly and unexpectedly," and offered help for patients with AIDS. "Dying can be painful," she acknowledged, but "death it-self is peaceful." Not surprisingly, Kübler-Ross favored home hospice care, a trend that has grown in recent years.

The reactions from her colleagues were, at first, overwhelmingly positive, even effusive, that is, until Kübler-Ross veered from the narrow path of scientific orthodoxy. For, you see, she held strong opinions regarding the paranormal, and believed there was evidence for psychical events, including life after death. One particular circumstance she considered was the out-of-body experience at the moment of clinical death, when physiological functions ceased. She included in her research examples of such near-death encounters that had been reported by her patients. Many of her peers responded by distancing themselves; their accolades soon dwindled. The idea of life after death, in any form, remained taboo within the strictures of conventional science and medicine.

However, Dr. Raymond Moody was inspired by Kübler-Ross, and credited her with further stirring his curiosity into near-death experiences. She gave her last major interview to TV producer and reporter Margaret Wendt, one of the few broadcast journalists with a vast knowledge of the paranormal. By then, Kübler-Ross was quite ill, but no less opinionated, and in her last years, living in Arizona where Wendt visited her.

When Joel Martin interviewed Dr. Moody some years ago, he explained that when he wrote *Life After Life*, he hoped medical science would be spurred to further investigate near-death experiences.[9] In fact, that's exactly what happened in the years since *Life After Life* was first published. Other researchers, including a number of physicians, have enlisted in the search for answers to explain near-death experiences.

Unlike other paranormal phenomena, NDEs did not face the insurmountable resistance that other psychic events seemed to have endured. Why? One possible reason may be because in naming them "near-death experiences," Moody, a respected psychiatrist and philosopher, had been careful to avoid characterizing NDEs as something occult or supernatural. It is also likely that most people found it much easier to identify personally with a near-death or out-of-body experience than they did with PK phenomena, such as the metal bending Uri Geller demonstrated, or the skills of those who purported to be professional psychics. NDEs seemed beneficial and meaningful to nearly all the people who'd had them and possible for anyone; it didn't matter who you were.

When other researchers followed Moody, they, too, had substantial credentials. There was Dr. George Ritchie, psychiatrist; Dr. Kenneth Ring, psychologist at the University of Connecticut;

Dr. Melvin Morse, Seattle pediatrician; Dr. Michael Sabom, cardiologist; Dr. Maurice Rawlings, cardiovascular specialist; Dr. Bruce Greyson; Dr. Bruce Goldberg; Dr. Phyllis M. H. Atwater; and Susan Blackmore, author of *Beyond the Body*, among others.

Some of the NDE research became quite sophisticated, at least in theory. Dr. Sabom, for example, studied near-death experiences with an eye toward the field of vision the experience provides. He suggested that NDEs provided a "multiple angle perspective." In other words, during near-death encounters, people reported they could look up, and at the same time, peer straight ahead. Sabom explained that seeing in two different directions simultaneously was something not possible in the physical world. But during an NDE or OBE, the sensation of "seeing around corners" was achievable. In addition to professional journal articles, in 1982, Sabom wrote a book titled *Recollections of Death*, based on interviews with 116 survivors of near-death experiences.

Why emphasize the medical and psychology degrees held by many NDE researchers? The answer is that debunkers have persistently employed the argument that "science" does not support evidence that the near-death experience is a genuine phenomenon, as if all of "science" speaks with one voice. It does not. The truth is that many physicians and psychologists have lent their names and knowledge to the exploration of NDEs, a fact that has been conveniently ignored by debunkers and skeptics for as long as we can remember.

In 1981, a number of scientists and medical doctors came together to form the nonprofit International Association for Near-Death Studies (IANDS) with the intent of better understanding the "nature and scope of human consciousness in its relationship to life and death, through empirical observation and through near-death experiences," explained author James R. Lewis in the *Encyclopedia of Afterlife Beliefs and Phenomena*.[10] Among the IANDS founders were Dr. Kenneth Ring, psychologist, and John White, a highly regarded paranormal researcher and writer, who'd worked with Apollo 14 astronaut Edgar Mitchell, a pioneer in ESP, mind-body, and human consciousness research. White had an NDE when he was just fourteen years old, an event he shared in *Children of the Light* by Brad Steiger and Sherry Hansen Steiger.[11] IANDS studies established that near-death experiences were largely considered "spiritual or psychological," rather than something "physical." One IANDS finding that bears repeating here was the discovery that there are unmistakable common characteristics in NDEs no matter where or to whom they occur.[12]

That same observation has been made elsewhere throughout history both in the paranormal and in other aspects of life. Why, for example, did ancient civilizations that could not have had contact with each other often develop similar vocabularies, inventions, and belief systems? It may remind you of Dr. Carl Jung's theory of archetypes and the "collective unconscious." Incidentally, Jung once had a near-death experience, although in his time, the term *NDE* had not yet been coined. His out-of-body episode occurred during clinical death following a heart attack. "It was not a product of imagination. The visions and experiences were utterly real. There was nothing subjective about them," Jung wrote emphatically in *Memories, Dreams, Reflections.*[13]

Another well-known figure who put pen to paper about his near-death encounter was the famed American novelist Ernest Hemingway. His near-death OBE occurred in Italy during World War I when a "mortar shell exploded near him," Herbert Greenhouse wrote in *The Astral Journey.*[14] "I felt my soul or something coming right out of my body! It flew around and then came back and went in again, and I wasn't dead anymore," Hemingway explained. And he built his experience into *A Farewell to Arms.*

In addition to Moody's breakthrough book, *Life After Life,* several others devoted to NDEs became huge bestsellers, notably *Embraced by the Light*, a personal memoir by Betty Eadie detailing a near-death encounter she had, and its deep impact on her life. Eadie was thirty-one when she had an NDE following surgery in a Seattle hospital in 1973. During her NDE, Eadie claimed she saw and spoke with Jesus, and learned from him "the meaning of life and suffering." Although the NDE occurred in 1973, Eadie initially told few people other than close friends and family members.

Later, Eadie shared her story with others, and eventually she wrote *Embraced by the Light* in 1992, which remained on *The New York Times* Best Seller list for over two years. In addition to her personal travails, including "unhappy times" at an Indian school on a Sioux reservation in South Dakota, Eadie provided details about her near-death encounter, specifically the moment she left her body. "I felt a surge of energy. It was almost as if I felt a pop or release inside me, and my spirit was suddenly drawn out through my chest and pulled upward, as if by a giant magnet. My first impression was that I was free," she wrote.

It was obvious after reading Eadie's book and interviewing her (on the *Joel Martin Show*, in 1993) that she had touched a nerve as much for the way she told her story as for what she wrote about. Her near-death experience was not exceptional; however, her Christian message sounded the right note for millions. "I have simply been impressed to live within the light of Jesus Christ and to continue to accept His love in my life," she said. However, there were some Christian writers and theologians who were less than ecstatic about Eadie's mix of "religion and New Age beliefs." Nonetheless, it would be foolish and disingenuous to deny Eadie's impact on the public consciousness. In 1996, she penned a sequel, *The Awakening Heart*.[15]

Eadie described her near-death experience in terms of a Christian perspective. Did that mean, some people asked, that if Eadie saw Jesus Christ it meant that the New Testament gospels were true and every other religious testament had to be discarded? Harry Houdini became incensed when Lady Doyle, Sir Arthur Conan Doyle's wife, explained that Houdini's recently deceased mother was in the arms of Jesus. Houdini was Jewish, born of a Jewish mother, and felt, therefore, that Lady Doyle's description of his mother in the afterlife was patently false. That sent him on a quest to debunk every self-proclaimed paranormal event that he could.

Another book that approached near-death experiences from a Christian perspective was *90 Minutes in Heaven,* written by the Reverend Don Piper in 2004, and described as "a true story of death and life." Piper, a Baptist minister, related the details of a near-death encounter that occurred when he was pronounced dead at the scene of an automobile accident, and then "experienced the glories of heaven for ninety minutes," before he "miraculously came back to life" to face a lengthy recuperation.[16]

In September 1975, a young South Carolina man named Dannion Brinkley had a profound near-death experience after he was struck in the head by lightning and electrocuted as he spoke on the telephone. As a result, Brinkley suffered cardiac arrest that left him barely alive. His chances of survival were slight, despite having been "miraculously resuscitated," Dr. Raymond Moody explained. What happened during the twenty-eight minutes that Brinkley hovered at the edge of death became the story he told in *Saved by the Light,* first published in 1994. The book went on to become a national bestseller. In a second book, *At Peace in the Light,* published the next year, Brinkley continued his story.

Brinkley explained that during his NDE he traveled to a "spiritual realm" where he was shown a "review" of his entire life— the good and the bad—or as Brinkley called them, the "successes and failures." He claimed he next traveled to a "beautiful city of crystal and light" where he found himself before thirteen "Beings of Light" who shared with him "revelations about the future." Brinkley said the Beings told him "how to create Centers where people could find their spiritual selves through stress reduction." That was to be his "mission" on Earth.

In 1976, Brinkley shared his newfound knowledge with Dr. Moody. Among his predictions was the terrible Chernobyl nuclear plant accident in the then Soviet Union in 1986. Brinkley told Moody that the Soviet Union would break apart in 1989, which it did. He also foresaw conflict in the Middle East in 1990 that matched events during the Gulf War. At first Moody said he was skeptical of Brinkley's predictions until, one by one, they came true. Since Brinkley's book *Saved by the Light* was published several years before the terrorist attacks of 9/11, and the subsequent U.S. invasions of Afghanistan and Iraq, it was interesting to find references to future terrorism and turmoil in the Middle East among Brinkley's peeks into the future, although cynics might answer that the region is always rife with conflict and bloodshed. One of his most chillingly accurate revelations was that he saw "Iran in possession of nuclear weapons." He also predicted the immigration controversy that has grown in recent years as large numbers of refugees and undocumented aliens have flooded into the United States from Mexico and Central America.

Accepting him at his word, for the sake of discussion, Brinkley's assertion of enhanced psychic abilities, including mental telepathy, following his NDE was not unusual. A significant number of people who've had NDEs have made similar claims that near-death experiences appear to have awakened or enhanced their psi abilities, possibly due to the power of the NDE. Another frequent change reported by those who've had NDEs is a positive transformation in personality and values, a new way of looking at life.

When, several years ago, Brinkley appeared as a guest on a

popular radio talk program, the *Allan Handelman Show,* he admitted that prior to his NDE he was not the most pleasant person to be around. He acknowledged he drank, and could be "mean and self-centered." Brinkley later suffered heart failure that resulted in a second NDE. Again, he said, "he saw his own dead body."

What changed his outlook on life, he said, were his NDEs. This is the response of many people who've gone through the experience of going to the edge of death, or crossing over, peering into the afterlife, and coming back with a revelation about the meaning of life. For Brinkley the transformation was dramatic. Following his NDEs, he decided to devote as much time as he could to working with AIDS patients, and the terminally ill in hospices, as well as speaking about his near-death experiences around the world through television and public appearances. Brinkley also became a critic of what he termed "unnecessary life support [that] builds false hopes and prevents people from making a smooth and spiritual transition."[17]

Although not directly related to near-death experiences, questions about death and dying have taken some controversial, even agonizing, twists and turns in this age of modern medical technology. Yes, patients can frequently be resuscitated and kept alive by artificial means, but for what purpose? And, who decides when such life support should be withdrawn? In our age of medical wonders, we sometimes turn to the courts for those agonizing life and death decisions, which is exactly what happened in the Terri Schiavo case in Florida over a seven-year period from 1998 to 2005.

In this case, Schiavo's parents battled with Terri's husband over the custody and care of the young woman who had lapsed into a vegetative state after suffering from an interruption in blood flow to her brain. The case gained national notoriety because medical technology had kept Terri alive, but, according to doctors, completely unresponsive on her own, for years while her husband argued that she should be allowed to die with dignity because that was her verbally expressed wish. She had left no written living will duly recorded or filed. Her parents sought custody of their daughter, arguing that if she were kept alive by any means possible, she might some day regain consciousness. Both parties turned to the courts for a ruling. The courts held that Terri Schiavo's husband had custody and believed that he was in conformance with his wife's wishes. But the argument over whether to allow Terri to live—she was breathing on her own—or to pull the feeding tubes that would starve her to death, became so vitriolic that even Florida governor Jeb Bush said he wanted to send in state police to take her into custody so that she could be delivered to her parents. The U.S. Congress intervened, pushed to step over the courts by Pennsylvania senator and future candidate for the Republican presidential nomination Rick Santorum, but the U.S. Supreme Court refused to intervene. The radical right exploded over the Schiavo case. The Florida county sheriff, who said he was obeying the order of the state court, said he would have resisted, with force, any attempt by Governor Bush to violate the court's order. Jeb's brother, President George W. Bush, although expressing his support for the efforts to keep Terri Schiavo alive, stayed out of directly intervening in the case. This is an example of what happens when medical technology sometimes cheats death and, in the process, even manages to advance beyond our own moral capacity to make appropriate judgments. In a private interview concerning the Schiavo case, radio personality Glenn Beck said that the American public unfortunately showed more concern for a dying puppy that he talked about on the air than for the vegetative, but fully alive, Terri Schiavo.

"Having died twice, I know that the world that awaits us when we leave here has a lot to offer a terminally ill person," Brinkley wrote. That brings us to one of the most important issues concerning near-death experiences: their value. While many in the scientific community wring their hands trying to find evidence that NDEs are genuine, rather than the result of wishful thinking, a medicine reaction, or oxygen deprivation to the brain, and while skeptics scoff at the very idea of NDEs, few critics have bothered to take into account the usefulness of the experiences to those who've gone through them. Speak with those people—they are everywhere—and most will tell you about the comfort and inspiration their NDE provided them, and how for some it was a life-affirming and life-changing occurrence.

Ask those who have gone through one or more NDEs what they think of skeptics who've worked feverishly to discredit the idea that the soul can move about independently from the physical body, and most near-death travelers will shake their heads. They'd rather share details of their experience at the time they were declared clinically dead. They would prefer to tell you how their NDE altered their thinking about life after death, and especially how it lessened their fear of death. While there is value in seeking scientific and medical explanations for NDEs, it seems the spiritual importance is largely overlooked, with debunkers far more determined to discredit a phenomenon that strongly implies an afterlife, therefore a God and heaven, concepts that are the antithesis of the rationalist and secularist agenda.

Another NDE living witness is Phyllis M. H. Atwater, an Idaho native, a professional writer, a researcher, an astrologer, and a woman who had three near-death experiences in the space of just one year. Atwater had been through a divorce in 1976, and the next year her health declined precipitously to the point where, at the age of forty, she experienced three NDEs, all in 1977, each after a separate illness. By the early 1980s, she began serious research by questioning people who'd had NDEs. The result was a book, *Coming Back to Life: The After-Effects of the Near-Death Experience* in

1988. In a later book, *Beyond the Light*, Atwater described herself as an "experiencer." She said, "I have lived my research, it has been my life."

Because she had a background in metaphysics and divination, Atwater's perspective brought together elements of religion and science, as well as the philosophy of the mind. Her conclusions about NDEs matched closely the sequence of events other researchers found: clinical death, dark tunnel, being drawn to a light, seeing and being greeted by departed loved ones, glimpsing a warm and loving place, seeing a review of one's entire life, unwillingness to return to the physical body, but realizing they had to, and sometimes being disappointed at being resuscitated. Although no two NDEs are identical in nature, they share certain common characteristics, especially the feeling of being lifted from the physical body and movement toward a brilliant light. But where out-of-body experiences (OBEs) are concerned with events in this physical world, NDEs take us to another dimension, presumed to be an afterlife or heaven. Atwater's research of NDE survivors found that 80 to 90 percent of them revealed both "psychological and physiological changes" that included "a more positive outlook, changes in energy, greater sensitivity to light, and better handling of stress."

The success of Moody's *Life After Life* opened the floodgates for accounts of near-death experiences in countless books, articles, and TV programs; suddenly, "death, dying, and life after death" became immensely popular topics, even in the major media and academia, two areas notorious for lagging behind the public's interest in the paranormal. But near-death experiences seemed to have gained acceptance somewhat more readily, although not entirely. Slowly, death education grew in interest, even among those of college-age.

In 1978, Dr. Maurice Rawlings, a Tennessee-based cardiologist, intrigued by the phenomenon that was sweeping the nation, wrote a bestselling book, *Beyond Death's Door*, based on his research. Rawlings said that at first he regarded the NDE as "fantasy or conjecture or imagination," and attributed most NDEs to anoxia, the deprivation of oxygen to the brain. But Rawlings said that one day in 1977, he resuscitated a badly frightened patient who told the doctor he'd been to hell. Recognizing that the belief in an afterlife was virtually universal, Rawlings had uncovered another side to NDEs. Unlike most books that depicted a rosy and warm afterlife bathed in light and love, Rawlings concluded there is "life after death and not all of it is good."

Having discovered that not everyone who claimed to have an NDE went to heaven, Rawlings began to "collect unpleasant cases." He found some people returned from their near-death encounters to report "frightening, horrible, and painful experiences" that fit the description of hell. Rawlings was a medical doctor and a Christian, and his religious beliefs were infused in his exploration of the NDE phenomenon.[18] There was biblical support for "the hope of immortality" or "eternal life": Romans 2:7, I Corinthians 15:53, and II Timothy 1:10.

At the time he wrote his book, Rawlings noted that "only about 20 percent of resuscitated individuals described an experience outside of the body after death." At the time of Rawlings's research during the 1970s, it's likely that most people who had NDEs, as well as other paranormal experiences, were reluctant to admit them for fear of ridicule. There was also the likelihood that people who'd experienced negative near-death encounters were hesitant to openly discuss them. In recent years, NDEs haven't drawn the skeptical reactions they once did. It's more probable that by now nearly everyone knows or has met someone who has had an NDE. At the very least, "near-death experiences" has become a term familiar to most Americans, a change that can be traced directly to the success of Moody's *Life After Life*.

Still, debunkers felt it incumbent to give near-death experiences their best shot. Even if they couldn't deliver a knockout punch, if they kept on kicking and screaming at every opportunity, someone might hear them. The best that professional skeptics could muster was more unnecessary confusion. It was true, however, that Moody's book had received some criticism for presenting "anecdotal" cases. But Moody made it clear from the outset that *Life After Life* was not a "scientific study," and he'd said so publicly many times. Dr. Moody opened the door. Now others had to carry forth with further explorations.

One of those who picked up the challenge of investigating NDEs was a University of Connecticut psychology professor, Dr. Kenneth Ring. To him went the credit for the first scientific investigation of NDEs in which he used statistical and content-based metrics to compare and contrast the experiences of those who claimed visions during a perimortem or clinically dead physical state. In *Life at Death: A Scientific Investigation of the Near-Death Experience*, published in 1980, Ring based his findings on more than a hundred interviews with "near-death survivors." He compared various causes of the near-death phenomenon, seeking similarities and differences. Apparently whatever brought a person to the brink of death—accident, illness, or suicide attempt—had no bearing on the nature of NDEs. Essentially, Ring assessed Moody's conclusions through "statistical analysis." According to Ring there are five stages to the NDE: (1) a feeling of peace, (2) bodily separation, (3) entering the darkness, (4) seeing the light, (5) entering the light.

Ring found that about "60 percent reported a feeling of tremendous happiness" and peace, as well as relief from the physical pain they'd suffered on earth. Approximately 40 percent felt released from their bodies, and most were not frightened by this "separation stage." Some 20 percent were at peace as they moved or "floated through a tunnel" and many recognized they were "no longer in this physical world." Ring learned that more than 17 percent experienced a "brilliant golden light" that bathed them in "an envelope of warmth." Approximately 10 percent saw the spirits of departed loved ones. Few of the NDE travelers wanted to return to the physical plane. Ring concluded that "some form of consciousness" appears to survive physical death.

However, when Ring examined the specifics of the phenomenon as Moody reported it, such as the sensation of leaving one's body and traveling through a tunnel, among other elements of the NDE, Ring found less incidence of them than did Moody. But, like Moody, Ring concluded near-death encounters were positive experiences. They eased the fear of death, and boosted a person's belief in life after death and religion or spirituality. Neither Moody nor Ring reported "hell-like" NDEs on the part of those they questioned. To the contrary, most people who returned from near-death experiences described them as life altering, and often accompanied by heightened psychic abilities, suggesting a change or shift in the person's perspective toward life.[19]

Ring went on to become one of the founders of the International Association for Near-Death Studies (IANDS). In 1984, he wrote a second book, *Heading Toward Omega: In Search of the Meaning of the Near-Death Experience,* in which he focused on the ways NDEs altered people's values and their outlooks on life.

The similarities in anecdotal reports of NDEs, however, still kept the question on the table regarding the specific causality of the visions. Were these truly out-of-body journeys, spiritual trips to where all of us go upon death, or were these the hallucinations of a brain dying from oxygen deprivation, which is what the skeptics argued? We know from studies of enzymes or other types of chemicals in the saliva of predatory animals, lions and tigers who catch and devour their prey alive, that the chemicals in saliva act to sedate the prey, to generate something akin to a euphoria so that the struggle is not only brief but that the living animal, soon to become masticated and digested, feels as little pain as possible. Thus, it is nature's way of protecting animals, who sustain other animals along nature's food chain. Do humans have the same type of physiological response upon death?

The sheer number of NDEs—in the millions—had made them difficult to ignore. By 1992, more than twelve million Americans were acknowledging that they'd had near-death encounters. As well, the NDE proved to be both a universal and overwhelmingly positive experience, according to the majority of those who reported going out of their body at the moment of clinical death and glimpsing the other side, or heaven, before returning to their physical body.

The typical objection to paranormal events raised by Christian clergy, specifically, that they were demonic in nature, did not seem to taint all near-death experiences. In 1977, the Reverend Ralph Wilkerson, a prominent evangelical minister from California, received considerable national attention for *Beyond and Back*, his book that examined NDEs from a Christian perspective. It contained examples of people who'd claimed they'd traveled to heaven and, in many cases, reported they'd seen Jesus Christ, and told of seeing or being bathed in a lovingly warm and radiant light.[20]

When Moody gave a name to out-of-body experiences at the moment of clinical death, he had not discovered a new phenomenon. He'd given new terminology and definition to these life-altering events, and spelled out the specific characteristics that marked the differences between an NDE and other forms of out-of-body travel. While they are similar, Moody found, they are not identical events. What is common to both, however, is the critical question of whether the physical being can separate itself from a spirit or ethereal body under certain conditions. If humans are comprised of physical and spirit bodies, there is a powerful implication for survival beyond death. We come back again to the question that has always, pardon the pun, haunted humankind: does some element of our consciousness survive physical death, and in what form? Where does it go, and is communication with it possible?

As with anything that falls within the realm of psychic phenomena, professional debunkers, skeptics, and secularists have a ready—and predictable—answer. They will eagerly tell you that there is no such thing as an "energy body," a "spirit body," or a soul. Therefore astral travel and near-death experiences are dismissed as imaginary or hallucinatory. This is the typical version of UFO researcher Stanton Friedman's argument that, for die-hard, closed-minded skeptics and debunkers, the rule is ABA or "anything but alien" (or anomalous). In other words, Friedman argues, because die-hard skeptics and debunkers have already reached their conclusion and evidence will not change their collective mind-set, they've already rejected any paranormal causality and, therefore, dismiss the evidence without considering it.

For skeptics, the argument comes down to whether or not, as humans, we occupy the physical body or are the physical being. If the latter is true, skeptics argue, when we die, nothing remains, for we are nothing more than the physical being. Even if "something" survives, debunkers insist, it could not be a spirit, astral, or a second body. Therefore, they claim, near-death experiences are not evidence for life after death. Skeptics and debunkers, however, have no real explanation for how and why many patients report seeing people, places, and events during the time that brain activity, breathing, and cardiac functioning have ceased, as is the case during clinical death, or when a person is unconscious. A person should not be able to survive more than about four minutes deprived of oxygen to the brain. How then have some people who've experienced NDEs been clinically dead for much longer? That remains a medical mystery.

To argue against NDEs by concluding they result from wishful thinking or a fear of death does not explain thousands of years that have produced millions of near-death reports in virtually every culture and religion the world has ever known. It is also a position that is contradicted by research. It does seem reasonable that the fear of death would account for NDEs. However, a 1999 *Los Angeles Times* survey found 83 percent said "they were not afraid to die," according to Barbara Wexler. Interestingly, as we grow older, the fear of death declines substantially. A *Time*/CNN poll in 2001 found that 90 percent of people over the age of sixty-five said they had no fear of death. In the eighteen- to forty-four-year-old age group, 79 percent were not afraid of death.

There is also no explanation for the apparitions that are often seen while one is awake and alert, in deathbed visions, or during near-death experiences. Particularly difficult to explain "rationally" are those apparitions children see of deceased loved ones they'd never met in the physical world, and those visionary beings that appear in NDEs or deathbed visions that the patient did not know had died. For example, in one very poignant example, a woman in a home hospice situation, still conscious even though she had been taking morphine for pain, saw visions of her mother in her room. She also saw visions of her departed sister. When the hospice nurse arrived to see how her patient was doing, the dying woman told her nurse of seeing her mother in the room.

"Don't worry," the nurse explained, as family members also in the room were shocked to hear how casually the nurse explained the woman's vision. "Your mother is here to welcome you to the other side."[21]

A Roper poll considered the question of "life after death." Between 1972 and 1982, 70 percent of Americans said they believed in an "afterlife," while 20 percent did not. In 1996, a Roper survey revisited the same question. This time, 73 percent said they believed in an afterlife, while 16 percent said they did not. Then in 1997, a Gallup poll reported that nearly three-quarters of those who believe in an afterlife "also feel they will experience spiritual growth after death."

So much as an inkling of evidence for life after death is infuriating to debunkers and skeptics, for it suggests a hereafter and a God, concepts that are anathema to atheists. Yet, as survey results show, the majority of Americans not only believe in an afterlife, most of them expect it will be a "spiritual" experience. It is that connection between the afterlife and religious beliefs that further rankles debunkers.

A favorite distraction is to ask where the hereafter is. No map to the "other side" is yet available, but it seems reasonable that other dimensions exist, as many scientists have theorized, and they may be closer than we think, if not somewhere in the direction of outer space. One well-known medium, when faced with the question, usually retorts by asking his detractors, where is cyberspace?

To the frustration of debunkers, medical research of NDEs has not supported blanket denials of the phenomenon as simply the result of a medication reaction or oxygen deprivation to the brain. In fact, those who've had NDEs and deathbed visions typically don't report experiences consistent with either lack of oxygen or drug effects.

In January 2007, *Time* magazine devoted a significant portion of one issue to the "mind and body," specifically the human brain. "One of the greatest frontiers of the twenty-first century does not lie far beyond us but deep within us," wrote *Time* managing editor Richard Stengel in his introduction. Who could argue with that? The magazine's probe into "the mystery of consciousness" was quite interesting and informative until *Time*'s science writers ran smack into questions about the nature of near-death experiences and the soul. Then the writers reverted to the knee-jerk reaction that has marked so much traditional science reporting about anything that falls into the category of "mystical" or "paranormal."

"And when the physiological activity of the brain ceases, as far as anyone can tell the person's consciousness goes out of existence," Steven Pinker wrote in *Time*. "Attempts to contact the souls of the dead (a pursuit of serious scientists a century ago) turned up only cheap magic tricks, and near-death experiences are not the eyewitness reports of a soul parting company from the body but symptoms of oxygen starvation in the eyes and the brain. In September [2006], a team of Swiss neuroscientists reported that they could turn out-of-body experiences on and off by stimulating the part of the brain in which vision and bodily sensations converge."

There are a number of errors in the magazine's conclusions about near-death experiences. Whether they are the result of careless research or written with the deliberate intent to mislead or debunk NDEs is impossible to say. Most likely, the magazine's decades-old editorial position was largely unchanged; the paranormal was to be dismissed or discredited with all deliberate speed, citing whatever "evidence" best served that purpose—even if it was a century old.

Without going over the same ground we've already covered, you have to wonder how the approximately twelve million Americans who've had near-death experiences felt about the magazine's conclusion that they owed it all to oxygen deprivation. And, it doesn't require extensive investigative skills to realize that omitted from *Time* magazine was any opinion from the long list of distinguished physicians and scientists whose extensive research made a strong argument for some element of human consciousness surviving physical death. Most significantly, when debunkers attacked NDEs, they ignored the salutary effects of the experiences.

An important article from the prestigious British medical journal, *The Lancet* (December 15, 2001), concluded that not all NDEs could be summarily dismissed with prosaic explanations. Something clearly seems to survive clinical death.[22] What else explains thousands of instances in which unconscious patients, when they were resuscitated, described witnessing activities around them during the time they were comatose or clinically dead? Many said they peered down from an aerial perspective—such as a ceiling— as doctors and other medical personnel worked frantically to resuscitate them, and some repeated comments they'd heard from those at accident scenes or in operating rooms, that they'd have no other way to know.

Since near-death and out-of-body experiences are related, but not exactly the same, what differentiates them? NDEs only occur to those who've been declared clinically dead or unconscious, that is, on the brink of death. In those instances, people typically report the sensation of rising from their physical body, traveling upward through a dark tunnel that draws them toward a brilliant light, often they see departed loved ones, and then they return to their earthly or material being, and frequently see and hear what is transpiring as their spirit reenters their physical bodies.

Out-of-body experiences, by comparison, can take place when the subject is awake, perhaps in an altered state, such as through hypnosis, or while asleep. During an OBE or astral travel, a person's spirit or "second body" witnesses events taking place close by or at great distances, but they never include the elements found in the NDE, such as traveling through a tunnel and glimpsing the afterlife. The following true examples should help clarify the similarities and differences between the NDE and OBE.

Andy was a veteran employee of a major railroad when he

accidentally fell from a work train, struck his head on the track below, and rolled onto a gravel bed where he lay unconscious. Emergency medical aid was quickly summoned, but with no pulse, heartbeat, or breathing functions, Andy was, in fact, clinically dead at the accident scene. Nearly thirty minutes elapsed before Andy regained consciousness. He'd suffered several severe injuries when he fell, but Andy told of seeing himself on the ground as emergency medical personnel worked frantically to revive him. He'd even heard one emergency medical technician (EMT) tell another that they weren't optimistic about his chance for survival. Once he was resuscitated, Andy, bruised and bandaged, was nonetheless eager to describe his near-death experience. He told of feeling himself rise from his body, travel through a tunnel toward a bright light, where he saw several figures who instructed him to return. He next remembered hovering over his body, as medics worked to revive him. He said he felt no pain until he was back in his body. One element of Andy's NDE that has also been discovered in many other near-death encounters is the length of time that a person remains clinically dead. Since an individual can live for only about four minutes without oxygen to the brain, what explains some NDEs that last much longer? That remains a medical mystery.

Andy's experience, similar to President Bill Clinton's, was interesting because it combined the often-described journey through a tunnel with his lucid vision of hovering over his own body and hearing the EMTs' conversation. We know, from reports from anesthesiologists and surgeons, that anesthetized patients on an operating table can still hear and consciously remember conversations taking place around them. However, these patients are not clinically dead. We therefore have a conventional explanation for this phenomenon. But persons who are clinically dead, like Andy, who can remember and confirm what they heard, provide us with real data about out-of-body experiences.[23]

Army remote viewer Paul H. Smith also described what can be called an OBE when he was in New York, working with Ingo Swann. Smith said that he had a particularly remote viewing experience, receiving impressions of a lusciously beautiful setting. It was very green, he remembers, and perhaps it was in Ireland. After the session, Smith was walking in Manhattan's Times Square when he began thinking about the perceptions he'd experienced. Suddenly, in his mind, he said, he was actually there. It was as if he had psychically traveled to this location, and he could feel the space around him. Just as suddenly, Smith had the impression of falling. He roused himself from his vision and found that he was falling over the curb and into the street. He believes that he actually had an out-of-body experience, a remote viewing event so vivid that he left his body to travel to the place he was seeing. In so doing, he left his body "spiritless," and his body, now unanimated, simply began slumping to the pavement. Smith told *Coast to Coast AM* host and author George Noory (*Worker in the Light, Journey to the Light*) in his interview in *UFO Magazine* that he had experienced something that Ingo Swann had warned about. Swann had told the trainees in the U.S. army's coordinate remote viewing program that if they allowed themselves to travel to the targets they were viewing, they might have an out-of-body experience, which, if uncontrolled through the use of a psychic tether, would leave their bodies unanimated. They might not be able to return. Paul H. Smith's experience was different, therefore, from remote viewing as well as very different from a near-death experience.

A more typical NDE involved Nancy, a public librarian in a picturesque New England town, who was approaching her thirtieth birthday during the summer of 1992 when she was suddenly felled by abdominal pains so severe that she was immediately hospitalized. It was there that she lapsed into unconsciousness, and was soon pronounced "clinically dead." Her next sensation, typical of NDEs, was of traveling through a dark tunnel, then being drawn toward, and emerging into, a gloriously brilliant light. There, to her surprise and pleasure, was a close aunt who'd passed on years earlier. But the elderly aunt motioned emphatically that Nancy was not to move forward. She was to return to her physical body. "Stop, it's not your time. You have to go back." Subsequently, Nancy was revived and treated for what doctors diagnosed as a rare virus.[24]

The late Bryce Bond was a parapsychologist and frequent guest on the *Joel Martin Show* for years. Bryce once had an NDE following a severe "allergic reaction" to a type of nut used in baking cookies and cakes. He also described his near-death encounter as marked by traveling through a tunnel toward a radiant light. Then, as so frequently occurred in such experiences, Bryce saw deceased loved ones, and to his delight, there also was his pet dog, barking happily. But as much as Bryce wanted to remain in what he was certain was the "other side," he was told that he must return, and he obeyed—reluctantly. When he was revived, Bryce said he was overwhelmed by a "sense of peace."[25]

By comparison, the out-of-body experience (OBE) need not be preceded by clinical death, nor does a person having an OBE journey to other dimensions. Here's an example of an astral travel experiment performed in the late 1970s. Max Toth, hypnotist and parapsychologist, gave a hypnotic suggestion to a subject named Charlie. The two had never met before when Toth placed Charlie in a trance, then instructed him to go "out of his body" and report what his astral or second body saw when it traveled to his home, several miles from an office where the OBE experiment was being conducted. In the hypnotic trance, Charlie said he felt as if he'd been lifted out of his physical body, then looked down and watched his wife, Rosemarie, "doing a crossword puzzle" in their living room.

The actual OBE took only several minutes. In fact, Charlie said he had the sensation he'd traveled to his house very quickly. In any event, once his second or ethereal body returned to his physical being, and the experiment ended, he phoned his wife. She told him that, at the time of his OBE, she'd been working on her "needle-point." It seemed as if the experiment had failed.

However, the next day, Charlie said he discovered when he went home that, indeed, his wife was working on needlepoint, but the pattern consisted of small black and white squares. It was easy to understand how he mistook that pattern for a crossword puzzle as his spirit or astral body hurriedly journeyed to and from his house. Charlie's judgment that his wife was working on a cross-word puzzle was similar to the analytical overlay that remote viewer trainers say that viewers should avoid.[26]

Alexander Murray is a New York–based medium with a well-deserved national reputation. One afternoon in the early 1980s, he was tested for his astral travel and other psychic abilities. One task was to tell the technician recording the session what her mother was doing at that precise moment, something not known to the young woman technician, the psychic researcher conducting the OBE experiment, and certainly not to Murray. That ruled out mental telepathy. The decision for Murray's assignment was made by the researcher at the last possible moment to omit any chance of collusion. Within moments, Murray looked above him, closed his eyes, than reopened them. "I saw your mother shopping in what looks like a large department store. I think she's buying linens," Murray said.

The technician instantly disagreed. "My mom is at home," she answered.

"Can we call her anyway?" the paranormal researcher requested.

The technician agreed, but no one answered the phone at her

widowed mother's house. So confirming or denying Murray's accuracy was not yet possible. However, that evening, the technician found her mother at home, and learned that during the afternoon she was in one of the city's large department stores. Normally she would have been at home. But it had been a spur-of-the-moment decision to shop for new towels and sheets, among other advertised household items on sale. At the precise moment that Alexander Murray saw her shopping for what he described as "some kind of linens," she was, in fact, buying bath towels and bed sheets.

The test of Murray's ability to travel out-of-body had been highly accurate, the parapsychologist and his colleagues who reviewed the tapes agreed. True to the nature of OBEs, Murray's astral travel occurred in the present, and did not include any elements of an NDE with its tunnel, brilliant light, departed loved ones, and depiction of an afterlife.[27]

OBEs and NDEs, as they are called today, are certainly not recent phenomena. They've only been retitled from the age-old and shamanic description of dream visions. Those who experienced these visions, especially volitionally, were called "dream walkers." In fact, the long history of out-of-body and near-death experiences dates back to the time humans first appeared on earth. Ancient funereal practices and cave drawings suggest that many primitive peoples had an inkling of a second or spirit body that survived the death of the physical body.

If we go back thousands of years to ancient Egypt, we find the first culture to teach the soul is "immortal." The Egyptian *Book of the Dead* has been described as a "remarkable collection of prayer and formulae for guidance in the next world," to quote author Dr. Maurice Rawlings.[28] The book's title was actually *pert em hru*, which translates into "manifested in the light." What makes the reference to "the light" interesting is the consistency with which "light" has always been referred to as a part of near-death experiences. "Light is often associated with the divine," noted author Robert Van de Castle.[29] "Think of halos and the radiant light"[30] in religious art, and then consider the important part they play in the NDE.

Surprisingly, the Bible has relatively little to say about life after death, especially the Old Testament. Two of the better-known references are: "Your dead shall live; the bodies of our dead shall rise" (Isaiah 26:19), and "And many of those who sleep in the dust of the earth shall awake: some to everlasting life" (Daniel 12:2).

The Old Testament refers to the afterlife as a shadow world, known as "She'ol." In the Book of Psalms, the majority of the psalms authored by King David, there is a reference to She'ol, as the "place of the dead" in Psalm 6:5. David described it as "the valley of the shadow of death" in Psalm 23:4. It is both "deep and sunless."

As for the place called the "heavens," it is referred to in the Old Testament as "the Lord's heavens" in Psalm 115:16, and "Thus says the Lord: Heaven is My throne," in Isaiah 66:1. The story of "Jacob's ladder" describes his vision of a "stairway to heaven." There are more than two dozen references to "heaven" in the Bible, but there are fewer than ten references to "hell," all of them in the New Testament.

There are mentions of "death and dying" throughout the books of both testaments of the Bible, from Genesis to Revelation. There is even an account of an out-of-body experience in the New Testament. The apostle Paul described his famed vision of Jesus on the road to Damascus (Acts 26:13–26). Paul recounted having had an "out of the body" experience, using precisely that wording, in II Corinthians 12:1–4. He also told of witnessing a brilliant light at the time of his conversion to Christianity. There are more than sixty references to "light" in the Bible, according to one concordance. For example, in Isaiah 9:2 there is reference to "a great light." Another example, "believe in the light," is found in John

12:36. Jesus said in the New Testament that "He was the light of the world." Moody, in analyzing biblical accounts, thought they bore "some resemblance to the encounters with the beings of light in near-death experiences."

The ancient Greeks believed the soul was immortal, a position articulated by the philosophers Socrates and Plato. Regarded as one of the greatest thinkers in the history of the Western world, Plato (428–348 BCE) wrote a considerable amount about death and the world beyond. While he held "reason and logic" in high regard, he also found value in "mystical experiences." Plato concluded that the physical body and the soul separated at the moment of death. And he conjectured that there were realms other than this terrestrial plane. "We are imprisoned in our bodies like an oyster in a shell," he wrote. The material body held the soul until the moment when death occurred. Then the soul departed, no longer bound by earthly restrictions.

Plato also considered what happened to the soul after it left the physical or corporeal body. Primarily, the vehicles for his ideas were his famed plays or "dialogues," as they were called, notably *Phaedo, Gorgias,* and *The Republic.* In the latter, Plato told the story of a Greek soldier that bears striking similarities to a contemporary near-death experience. The great philosopher suggested that the idea of time as we know it does not exist in the world beyond death, a concept supported by most contemporary parapsychologists.[31]

The ancient Greek writer Plutarch, who lived some five hundred years after Plato, wrote about a soldier who said that while he was unconscious, he wandered through "another dimension."

The *Bardo Thodol* is known in English as *The Tibetan Book of the Dead.* Based on the beliefs of a branch of Buddhism, it was "passed down" orally from generation to generation, and refers to the "bardo state between death and rebirth," explained author John

H. Hick. It was read to dying people for them to "understand and respond rightly to what was about to happen" to them.

The Tibetan Book of the Dead was eventually committed to writing in the eighth century CE, although it was not immediately made available to the public. The book was used within funeral ceremonies, and offered advice on coping with death and dying. The famed tome also contained details and discussions about the "various stages" the soul travels through following the death of the body "and its return to a new body." *The Tibetan Book of the Dead* recognized that the soul or some element of consciousness left the body at the moment of physical death. The book described the sights and sounds, and how a departed person is "enveloped" in a form of "illumination." Once free of the physical body, the soul can "see and hear" deceased loved ones, even as the soul gazes at what was once its earthly body. Sometimes a deceased person does not immediately realize they have passed on.[32]

The Tibetan Book of the Dead explained that if one was crippled, blind, or deaf on earth, the spirit is restored to perfect health in the afterlife, where it meets other souls with whom it is familiar or drawn to. The spirit may also see a "clear or pure light." The dying were urged to "approach the light" when they made the transition to the other side, and were reminded of the feelings of "immense peace and contentment" they'd experience in the hereafter, to quote Dr. Moody. There was also the warning that every soul must honestly face itself. Remarkably, *The Tibetan Book of the Dead* shows us there is a "striking similarity between ancient times and [near-death] encounters today," Moody observed. It's another reminder that there is nothing new about so-called paranormal events; they have always been a part of what it means to be human.

Out-of-body experiences were known throughout the ancient world, from Egypt and Israel, to Persia and India, author Herbert Greenhouse noted.[33] "St. Augustine wrote about OBEs. So did

Aristotle, Plato, Goethe, and [the English poet Percy] Shelley." In North America, native peoples accepted out-of-body travel without question, as did Siberian shamans.

The Roman Catholic Church's long history of saints includes several who were recognized for their ability to travel out-of-body. Most prominent was St. Anthony of Padua, St. Alphonsus Liguori, and more recently, in the twentieth century, Padre Pio.[34]

Finally, in highlighting this brief history, relevant to near-death experiences, we should mention, once more, the eighteenth-century Swedish mystic and clairvoyant Emanuel Swedenborg (1688–1772). Until his books, anything written about the afterlife came with the imprimatur of the church. Christianity had long dominated Western thought and religious belief. Swedenborg's writings about heaven, hell, angels, and the spirit world he claimed to have visited, marked the first time in Western culture that a secular author had tackled the subject. Although he wrote in Latin, the language of scholars, it may also have been his hedge against church retaliation for expressing ideas that were considered the domain of the Vatican for centuries.[35]

Eventually, Swedenborg's descriptions of the spiritual realms attracted wide attention. Few people know that author Helen Keller was a devoted believer in Swedenborgian ideas, and wrote about their effect on her in *My Religion*, a "tribute to Emanuel Swedenborg." World famous as an educator, Helen Keller (1880–1968), whose story has long been popular since the publication of *The Miracle Worker*, the story of how a young Keller was taught to interact with others, was sightless and unable to hear since her childhood. She had written that she was "aware of encouraging voices that murmur from the spirit realm." Then she added, "I am conscious of the splendor that binds all things of earth to all things of heaven—immured by silence and darkness, I possess the light which shall give me vision a thousand-fold when death sets me free."

Swedenborg took readers on a journey of "heaven," which he described in detail as a complex place, structured much like society on earth. In heaven, "angels talk with each other just as men do in the world." The angels also "have writings," Swedenborg said, and "there are in heaven more functions and services and occupations than can be enumerated." Swedenborg explained that upon death, a person sheds their physical body and becomes a spiritual being. "When a man passes from the natural world into the spiritual, as he does when he dies, he carries with him all his possessions, that is, everything that belongs to him as a man, except his physical body," Swedenborg wrote.

When one studies the details of countless near-death experiences, one discovers that there are remarkable similarities between them and some of what Swedenborg reported he saw and experienced as he traveled out-of-body to heaven, the spirit world. He also reminded readers that "all truth is in light." The sum and substance of his writing was that "there are two worlds," the material or physical realm, and the world of the spirits. Swedenborg claimed that the spirit world, or heaven, was organized as "societies are on earth." Hell—where the evil went—also had an organization. In his writings, he carefully did not contradict the Christian concept of hell, perhaps all the wiser at a time when incurring the wrath of the church was not politically prudent.

Swedenborg had demonstrated remarkable clairvoyant abilities, but how he accessed the world of spirits and angels he claimed to see suggests he may have had out-of-body experiences, or engaged in astral travel, as it was once called. What helped keep his ideas alive were their relevance even centuries after they were written. For instance, his book, *Heaven and Hell*, first published in 1758, is surprisingly contemporary in its ideas and tone. The first

English translation appeared in the United States in 1852, perfectly timed to influence, and then ride the wave of popularity in, the spiritualism that was sweeping the country.[36]

You've likely heard the legend that every U.S. president elected in a "zero year" between 1840 and 1960 died or was killed in office. Known as the "zero year presidential curse," it is one of the oldest and longest debated curiosities in America's paranormal history. Few people, however, know the origin of the ominous "curse," or its unlikely connection to a near-death experience.

By the early nineteenth century, Native Americans struggled against an expanding Caucasian society that was increasingly encroaching on their lands. American governors and military representatives would negotiate land treaties only to break them as American settlers sought prime Indian land. Among the Native American tribes on the front lines of this struggle was the Shawnee, whose fiercest enemy was the then territorial governor and military commander William Henry Harrison. In 1811, a ferocious battle took place at Tippecanoe, Indiana, between American forces led by Harrison and the Shawnee, whose leader was the great chief Tecumseh. The American victory—it was more of a slaughter—thwarted Tecumseh's plans for westward expansion, an outcome that especially infuriated Tecumseh's fiery younger brother, Tenskwatawa, who was widely known by the Shawnee as "the Prophet." He was a religious leader and medicine man possessed with a remarkable gift for prophecy.

Tenskwatawa's paranormal abilities intensified after he experienced a glimpse of a beautiful and peaceful heaven—the spirit world—following a serious bout of illness during an epidemic when he sunk into what doctors might today call a delirium, but was probably a near-death event. The emotionally overwhelming out-of-body experience, which enabled him to reach a transcendental state, transformed him into a "holy man." He made a series of accurate prophecies, among them the prediction of a devastating earthquake in December 1811 throughout a vast section of the Midwest along the New Madrid fault that swallowed entire villages and caused the Mississippi River to flow north for a short period of time. The death toll likely reached into the thousands in what was the worst earthquake this country has ever known.

But it was Tenskwatawa's chilling curse that became his best-known and most enduring prophecy. Incensed by the defeat of the Shawnees at Tippecanoe, and seeking retaliation, Tenskwatawa invoked a curse on "white people" and declared that the U.S. president elected every twenty years, beginning with his archenemy William Henry Harrison, in 1840, would die in office. It proved to be no idle threat. Tenskwatawa's zero-year seems to have run straight through the presidency of George W. Bush, elected in 2000, when during the horrific moments of the 9/11 attacks, the president was sequestered at an Air Force base because of a threat on his life. Ronald Reagan, of course, elected in 1980, had been shot and critically wounded by John Hinckley and was, while on the operating table, at death's door. Some paranormal researchers say the "curse" may have been the result, at least in part, of psychic ability enhanced by a near-death experience nearly two hundred years ago.[37]

On a more scientific note, the Society for Psychical Research (SPR), founded in England in 1882, delved into out-of-body research, investigating that phenomenon, among many others related to the question of "survival." One of their preeminent participants was the noted American psychologist and philosopher William James. Later, OBE research was conducted under the auspices of the American Society for Psychical Research (ASPR), the Parapsychology Research Foundation (PRF), and by the 1970s, SRI International in California, the facility where remote viewing was tested under the direction of Dr. Harold Puthoff and Russell Targ.

While the OBE was attributed to clairvoyance, the ability to describe locations or events at far distances bore an unmistakable similarity to out-of-body experiences.

Much is owed to those pioneers of parapsychology, the founders and early researchers who comprised the SPR and ASPR, nearly a century before Dr. Moody defined the near-death experience as a new paradigm. A related phenomenon was the deathbed vision in which a dying person, shortly before death, reported seeing an apparition of a deceased loved one, an experience that dated back to ancient times. The presumption was that spirits materialized to ease the transition of loved ones from here to the hereafter by helping them "cross over" to the other side. The first "systematic study" of deathbed visions was conducted by one of the SPR's steadfast founders, Sir William Barrett (1844–1925), a psychical researcher and physics professor. Barrett's research of deathbed visions was entirely consistent with the SPR's goal of studying the thorny question of survival beyond death.

It was Barrett's wife, a physician, who first drew his attention to deathbed visions. As Barrett told the story in his book *Deathbed Visions*, published in 1926, his wife had delivered a baby born to a woman named Doris. The infant was fine, but the woman was dying. In her last moments, Doris "suddenly looked eagerly toward one part of the room, a radiant smile illuminating her whole countenance," Lady Barrett said. Doris described what she saw as "lovely brightness—wonderful beings." Then Doris said she was overjoyed to see her late father and "he's so glad I'm coming."

What especially interested Sir Barrett was that Doris said she saw an apparition of her sister, Vida, perplexing because she had no knowledge that Vida had died several weeks earlier. That news had purposely been hidden from Doris because of her fragile health. Therefore, Barrett wondered, how could Doris see the apparition of a sister she didn't know had passed on?

There have been thousands of deathbed visions studied, and like near-death experiences, they reveal certain common characteristics. It should be easy to dismiss them as the product of wishful thinking or hallucination on the part of a dying person. What then explains why there are so many, and why they are described so similarly no matter where they take place, and regardless of the age, race, religion, or gender of the patient? And, just when the skeptics and debunkers had made their best arguments against deathbed visions, along came evidence that could not be so casually dismissed, especially when someone saw the vision of a deceased person they did not know had died.[38]

An elderly woman, in her nineties, the mother of five grown children, was on her deathbed. In addition to congestive heart failure, she was suffering the ravages of dementia. One day, unexpectedly, she raised her weak and shaking hand, and determinedly pointed upward. Her only daughter and a private nurse were present as the aged and frail matriarch clearly called out the name of one of her sons. "Charlie's here. Charlie's come for me!" It had actually been the first time she'd spoken in many days. More unusual was that she said she saw her son Charlie. She could not have known that less than two weeks earlier Charlie had died suddenly of a heart attack, news that was kept from his ailing and elderly mother. Why then, of her four sons, had an old and presumably "senile" woman specifically spoken the name of the one son who'd just passed? The woman died only days after her deathbed vision.[39]

While debunkers scoff at such examples as merely "anecdotal," there are literally thousands of such cases, with more occurring every day, which comprise a substantial body of evidence and make a case for deathbed visions as something more than merely imaginary or hallucinatory. On the subject of hallucinations, deathbed visions are described in remarkably lucid terms; they are hardly the strange and surreal images you'd expect from someone close to death and perhaps medicated.

Few things in life seem crueler or more heartbreaking than a young child's death. Grieving parents often seek comfort and solace from psychic mediums, in addition to other forms of bereavement therapy. In one instance, the parents of a seven-year-old boy who died tragically of a rare brain tumor sought whatever communication they might receive from their son's spirit, through a reading with a well-known medium. One message was actually a confirmation of a deathbed vision the young boy had shortly before he died.

"Your son is telling me that when he crossed over he was met by a grandfather. But he said he never met this grandfather. Do you understand what he means?"

"Yes," they answered.

The explanation was that their son, just prior to his tragic death, said he saw a vision of a man he did not recognize but who identified himself as "Grandpa."

After the psychic's reading, the details became clear: the dying child had experienced a deathbed vision of his maternal grandfather who'd predeceased the boy. The two had never met until the visionary experience.[40]

Karlis Osis became a noted name in parapsychology for his many years of research and leadership with the American Society for Psychical Research (ASPR). His best-known contributions included several studies of deathbed visions. Beginning in 1959, Osis conducted a study of several thousand doctors and nurses who were asked about their patients' deathbed visions. The 640 responses were the result of the "observations" of more than 35,000 patients. Osis essentially found the same results as Barrett had decades earlier. Later, Osis conducted two others surveys, between 1961 and 1964, and again in 1972 to 1973. He and his colleague, Erlendur

Haraldsson published their findings in an influential book they coauthored, *At the Hour of Death* (1977).[41]

Did the dead materialize in order to reassure the dying that they would not make the transition alone to the other side? Many deathbed visions included glimpses of what the dying perceived as heaven or the afterlife, suggesting to patients that they would be going to "another world." Osis and Haraldsson carefully looked at a number of variables, such as the cause of patients' illnesses, religious and cultural beliefs, even mental strain or distress. But, as with NDEs, the deathbed visions seemed to occur "independently of such variables," according to James R. Lewis. Therefore, Osis suggested there was a case to be made for life after death.[42]

Sylvan Muldoon (1903–1971) is likely not a familiar name to most people, but for many years he was regarded as an important figure in the investigation of astral projection or out-of-body experiences. Muldoon was only twelve years old when he had his first OBE, after a visit with his mother to a "Spiritualist Camp" in Iowa. He claimed that he was awakened from his sleep to find himself out of his body, but able to gaze down at it. Muldoon also became aware that he was attached to some sort of "cord." His first thought was that he'd died; but then he floated from room to room, until he returned to his "physical body." What followed was a lifetime during which he had hundreds of out-of-body experiences.

As a young man, Muldoon found some books about occult and psychic phenomena by author Hereward Carrington. In one, there was a reference to astral travel, prompting Muldoon to write to Carrington. What developed was a professional relationship between the two that lead to *Projection of the Astral Body,* a book they coauthored in 1929. They went on to write two more books, and Muldoon penned two others on his own. There have been suggestions that Muldoon's chronically poor health may have been the result, in part, of too many separations between his astral and physical bodies.[43]

For many years Robert Monroe (1915–1995) was a successful radio producer and an executive. But it is his contributions to out-of-body research that are our focus. In the mid-1950s he became deeply interested in "occult and mystical" subjects. His Web site describes him as a "noted pioneer in the investigation of human consciousness." By 1958, Monroe was using "himself as a test subject for [his] research." He "began to experiment and research the expanded forms of human consciousness that he was experiencing." In particular, he'd begun having "out-of-body experiences, a state of consciousness separate and apart from the physical body."

Monroe learned to induce his own OBEs by "self-hypnosis" or, in some instances, "inhaling chemical fumes." During the course of his research, he said he had numerous out-of-body experiences, "beyond space, time, and death," and in 1971, he wrote about them in *Journeys Out of the Body*. A groundbreaking book that did much to increase awareness of OBEs at the time. Monroe found a ready audience of readers who'd had similar experiences, and attracted the attention of "academic researchers, medical practitioners, and engineers," among others, noted his Web site.

In 1974, the Monroe Institute was founded in Virginia, "dedicated to conducting seminars in the control and exploration of human consciousness." The following year, Monroe was granted "the first of three patents" for a "method of altering brain states through sound." Under his direction, his organization continued to "explore, research, and teach others about expanded states of human consciousness and practical methods of enhancing human potential," according to the Monroe Institute Web site. There were practical applications to Monroe's "audio exercises." Among them, "to focus attention, reduce stress, improve meditation, enhance sleep, and manage pain."[44]

Because Americans had long been denied ready access to the history of the paranormal, and discouraged from taking it seriously, relatively few understood the out-of-body phenomenon, although it dated back thousands of years. Probably, many familiar with OBEs at the time were those who'd experienced them through the use of hallucinogenic drugs, such as LSD and mescaline, during the tumultuous 1960s counterculture. Of course, that raised the familiar argument about whether people had actually left their physical body, or had only experienced an imaginary sensation or hallucination as a result of drug taking.

Throughout the often-tortured history of the paranormal, as we've noted, terminology and definitions have always been problematic, often contributing to stereotypes and misunderstandings. It only added to the confusion that sometimes it was difficult to determine which psychic or paranormal ability best explained an event.

For example, in the early 1980s, Joel Martin witnessed an experiment conducted with an outstanding American medium, George Anderson. A computer scientist asked Anderson to describe the interior of a residence they were driving to for a series of psychic readings that would be computer analyzed to determine their accuracy beyond chance. None of the people in the car had ever been in the house, but several blocks before arriving, the impromptu test was suggested. Within a matter of moments, Anderson described what he said looked like a "doll museum." He explained that everywhere he psychically gazed, he saw "hundreds and hundreds of children's dolls of every size and kind." It was a surprising depiction; and whether he was accurate or not could only be verified when they went inside the house.

A short time later, the group arrived to discover that Anderson had been remarkably correct. The home contained hundreds of dolls, one of the largest private collections anywhere in the area, which was something Anderson could not have known in advance. Notwithstanding his accuracy, did he employ clairvoyance or had he "traveled" out-of-body to see what was in the house? Anderson wasn't certain himself how to explain what he "psychically saw" in a place where he'd never before been. Perhaps some combination of psychic abilities was the best explanation. Other similar tests were subsequently performed with Anderson, always resulting in a high degree of accuracy, however which paranormal powers were responsible remains an open question. It seems plausible that out-of-body or astral projection played, at least, some part.

In the early part of the twentieth century, the great medium Eileen Garrett participated in a noteworthy astral travel experiment. Mrs. Garrett was in New York City with several other people as witnesses, when she went out-of-body to a doctor's office in far-off Reykjavik, Iceland. The doctor acknowledged that he'd felt her "presence," and asked the unseen Garrett to describe several objects he'd placed on a table. The doctor then read to himself from a book; he'd silently chosen a paragraph about Einstein's theory of relativity. In New York, at the same time, Mrs. Garrett repeated the passage word for word. Then Garrett's second or astral body glanced at the doctor and noticed his head was bandaged. It was a detail that Garrett, in New York, could not possibly have known.

The following day, the doctor confirmed via telegram that, indeed, Mrs. Garrett was correct: shortly before the out-of-body experiment, he'd injured his head, and her description of the items on his table was also accurate. The experiment suggested that some element of Garrett's consciousness was able to separate from her physical being during the OBE, just as occurred to millions during near-death experiences.[45]

Some skeptics of near-death experiences have raised a reasonable question: Was it possible that when people had near-death experiences, what they believed they'd seen and heard was actually a result of "cultural conditioning"? In other words, might their visions be a reflection of religious beliefs, sacred icons, and images they'd grown up with, or what they had at least seen portrayed in the media? It is a fair question, and one that was addressed by a Seattle pediatrician, Dr. Melvin Morse. In the 1980s, Morse began wondering about the experiences some of his young patients told him about, claiming they'd witnessed an afterlife, as happened in the following case.[46]

Katie was only nine years old when she nearly drowned in a swimming pool accident. She'd probably hit her head on the side of the pool, and although the exact cause was difficult to determine, she fell into a coma. An "emergency CAT scan showed massive swelling of the brain," Morse explained, and her chances of survival were very slim. Morse had been the doctor who resuscitated Katie when she was rushed to the emergency room and he quickly connected her to a breathing machine. While her family fervently prayed at her bedside, Morse and other hospital personnel tried their best to save her. However, no one realistically expected the child to live through the ordeal.

But she did. "Three days later [Katie] made a full recovery," Morse said, describing it as a "medical miracle." She showed no signs of brain damage from her injuries or from a lack of oxygen. There was another surprise when Katie visited Dr. Morse for a follow-up examination. He asked her what she recalled about the swimming pool accident that nearly claimed her life. Although she had no memory of nearly drowning, Katie recognized Morse, whom she'd never met before. Remember, she was comatose and her eyes were closed when she was rushed to the emergency room, and therefore could not have seen anyone attending to her. Yet, here was the young girl telling her mother that Morse was the doctor with the beard. But, she said, there was another doctor in the ER. He was tall and did not have a beard. Katie's descriptions were correct. She also recalled details about the ER, and the medical tests she underwent that included X-rays, and a procedure called intubation in which a tube is inserted into the trachea for ventilation. It usually is inserted orally, however Morse had inserted the tube through her nose. Katie should not have known that. She'd been unconscious all the while yet she remembered it, and described it, not in medical jargon, of course, but in a child's vocabulary.

How was it possible that a comatose child recalled and described events taking place around her? It was the question that Melvin Morse asked himself, and it did not end there. Katie described a visit to a place where she said she saw "the Heavenly Father." She went on to detail a "marvelous spiritual journey through 'heaven'" that Morse said left him "spellbound." She told Dr. Morse she'd seen "God," and described him as "a man of bright light who filled her with his love and kindness." The little girl said she'd "met Jesus and the Heavenly Father."

In a later visit to Morse, Katie offered further details of her experience. She told the doctor she remembered "darkness," and felt "so heavy she couldn't move." But then there was a tunnel and she saw someone named "Elizabeth." Katie described her as "tall and nice" and said she had "bright, golden hair." Elizabeth traveled with Katie through the tunnel, and then Katie "saw her late grandfather and met several other people." Two were boys she said were "souls waiting to be born." Katie called them "new friends," and they acquainted her with many others. It was Elizabeth, likely a guardian angel, who'd taken her to see the "Heavenly Father and Jesus," Morse explained.

Then Katie's memory became even more remarkable. She told of going to her house, where she saw her brothers and sisters, and described the toys they were playing with at the time. Katie even named the song she'd heard one of her sisters singing and told

Dr. Morse that she saw her mother cooking chicken and rice. Her father, she said, was sitting on the living room couch, gazing into space and looking worried. Katie described exactly what clothing each family member was wearing at the time. Although she wanted to stay with the "Heavenly Father," she said she also missed her mother.

After she regained consciousness, when she told her family details of what she saw, they were stunned. Dr. Morse was equally surprised when she shared with him what she believed was a visit to "heaven." He said Katie's story was the beginning of his research into near-death experiences.

One of Morse's first questions was whether Katie's recall of "heaven" might be the result of her religious upbringing. He learned that there was nothing in Katie's background or what she'd been taught that would account for details about "tunnels to heaven" or "guardian angels." What then would explain the little girl's vivid descriptions? When Morse began his investigation of NDEs, he especially examined those reported by children. It was far less likely that young children were influenced by religious belief systems or an accumulation of knowledge and information that could account for what they reported seeing during NDEs. If children who had no connection with each other told of similar near-death experiences, what might explain them? Why would their descriptions of "heaven" be remarkably alike? For those who answered that children's imaginations might have been responsible, the facts did not support that conclusion. While there's no question that young boys and girls can be highly imaginative, what would explain how similar their descriptions of "heaven" were—and are—even when they had no contact with each other?

Another unusual characteristic of children's NDEs was that their depiction of heaven frequently did not match traditional Christian portrayals. One particularly inexplicable feature of children's

NDEs was seeing or meeting departed loved ones who they had not known on earth. For example, some youngsters said relatives greeted them. "I met my grandpa. He said that's who he was, but I never knew him, because he died before I was born," a nine-year-old girl told her doctor and parents about her NDE once she regained consciousness. Many youngsters have told of seeing guardian angels, a brilliant light, and the "Heavenly Father," an apparent reference to God or Jesus Christ. If young children were going out of their bodies when they were at the brink of death, and returning with similar near-death reports, did it make a case for the existence of a soul—and an afterlife? It was far-fetched to conjecture that a child in Portland, Oregon, and another in Portland, Maine, were in collusion. Yet their descriptions of NDEs bore remarkable similarities, and factors such as "sleep deprivation," medication reactions, dreams, and nightmares proved as irrelevant to children's NDEs as were their religious and cultural upbringings.

One type of near-death encounter that top researchers have not found among children is the NDE that takes one through a hell-like experience. Dr. Phyllis M. H. Atwater, for example, has paid particular attention to children's NDEs, and neither she nor the highly regarded pediatrician and NDE researcher-author Melvin Morse have suggested there is any indication of a child returning with details of a negative near-death encounter. Is this a reflection of natural innocence in a child, an innocence so pure that visions of a hell-like environment are simply not applicable? This also poses the question about loss of innocence and when that occurs.

There is one very negative setting where near-death experiences have been reported throughout history, which is in a battle during combat. It bears special mention because the idea of soldiers fighting and dying in battle is sufficiently traumatic without paranormal or supernatural embellishments. Yet, it has been soldiers in every war who've told their personal stories about NDEs on the battlefield, long before Dr. Moody popularized the term "near-death experience." Before that, they were generally known as "battlefield OBEs," and "every war produces out-of-body experiences," the late medium Arthur Ford once wrote.[47]

In his book *Unknown But Known,* written in the 1960s, Ford told about a paranormal phenomenon long known as the "double" which is due to the "projection of the spirit body—being seen [in] two places at the same time." It "has been observed in every era from the famous Greek mystic Pythagoras in the sixth century BCE to Padre Pio, the great Italian psychic and Capuchin monk who died in 1968," Ford explained.[48]

One theory that's been advanced for battlefield OBEs probably dates back many centuries. It suggests that badly wounded soldiers, staggered by the slaughter around them, in order to escape their suffering, mentally and physically, willed themselves out of their bodies to be free of excruciating pain, if only briefly, even when limbs had been blown off. In such instances, many weary soldiers reported the sensation of looking down on their battered and bloodied physical bodies as they drifted upward and astral-traveled, but not seeing the other side or afterlife in every instance.

The second theory, which takes into account a better understanding of the near-death phenomenon, regards those battlefield experiences that are NDEs. Thus, if a soldier was seriously wounded and declared clinically dead, he may have had an NDE, and returned from the "dead" to tell about it, as happened in the following case.

Bobby, a West Virginia native, served bravely during the Vietnam War. He'd just turned twenty-two in 1968, seven years before Dr. Moody created the term "near-death experience." He was far from home, the small coal-mining town he'd grown up in. Now he was in a mountainous region of Vietnam, a place he'd barely heard of before he enlisted.

One day, Bobby was with more than two dozen soldiers on patrol when they were ambushed. It all happened so quickly that in a matter of moments, twelve were killed. Except for one officer, all of the others were seriously wounded, and many of them would eventually die. Bobby remembered there was a whirl of confusion and screams were coming from his fellow soldiers, and then he realized the searing pain through his arms, shoulders, and legs was the result of having been hit multiple times by enemy fire. There was blood everywhere he looked.

Before he could come to grips with that horror, several loud explosions rocked the ground close to where he lay. Bobby knew a rocket had struck him. The pain was excruciating, and he fell backward, literally waiting to die. A moment later, amid the carnage and continuing blasts, Bobby felt himself being lifted out of his body. He heard a strange noise that he described as a combination of ringing and vibrating. Then, as he moved up and above himself, most amazing was that all the terrible, terrible pain was gone! Suddenly Bobby was moving through a "tunnel," and felt drawn to a brilliant "golden light." There he discerned standing before him several figures bathed in the light. Two of them were his late parents, the others he did not recognize. The sight was one of complete love and warmth in a way he'd never felt before. Five years earlier, his father had fallen victim to what coal miners had long known as "black lung disease." His mother, grief-stricken, died of a heart attack less than two years later. Now, in this place that Bobby assumed was the afterlife or heaven, his parents looked well and very much at peace.

Bobby wanted to remain with them because going back, he knew, meant a return to the horrific pain of his injuries and the chaos of the battlefield. But he was told telepathically he could not stay. He had to return to his physical body. This was not yet his time to make the transition. Bobby had no choice but to obey, knowing someday he'd be reunited with his family. As he felt himself travel back to the horror of the battle zone, he was able to gaze down as he remained out-of-body. From his aerial perspective, he looked down at the slaughter. Then his spirit or second body returned to his physical being, and instantly the unbearable pain was back.

Bobby lay on the ground, slipping in and out of consciousness until medics arrived and airlifted him out of the area that evening, once enemy fire abated. His injuries were permanent, and some were seriously disabling. But when anyone asked Bobby about his NDE, there was no equivocation. He said the NDE changed his life, and made him more appreciative of what he had here, notwithstanding his lasting injuries and pain, and what awaited him in the afterlife. Did he think the NDE could have been a dream? "No, it was real. I know what I saw. That was no dream, and it wasn't my imagination! I never believed in any of this weird [paranormal] stuff, and I was never Bible readin' religious, but this was real," Bobby answered.[49]

As history measures time, the 1970s were just a blink ago, yet Dannion Brinkley was correct when he said that the years before 1975, when Dr. Moody defined the "near-death experience," were the "dark ages" for NDEs. You have to wonder why, if NDEs are experiences that empower those who have them, encourage new ways of valuing life, and lessen the fear of death, there remains a raging debate between those who are certain NDEs represent some element of consciousness, such as a soul or spirit body, that survives physical death, and those who are equally adamant that NDEs can be explained by oxygen depravation, hallucination, medication, anesthesia, anything, but not a metaphysical or spiritual explanation.

It appears the new paradigm Moody called the "near-death experience" seriously upset the skeptics and secularists, for it suggested a belief in an afterlife, long a mainstay of their archenemy, religious teachings. Is the NDE "proof" of life after death? Of course it is not; but it may hold evidence that something survives our mortal death. Lost in the debate is the question of how someone can describe events taking place at a time when he or she is unconscious? Debunkers have no idea what happens at that moment when "life meets death." That isn't a criticism; what is scientifically dishonest, however, is that debunkers really have no interest in exploring the question. And they're only too happy to obstruct or denigrate any serious effort by those who are willing to investigate NDEs and related phenomena. That does not advance our understanding of science, the nature of human consciousness, or a host of other scientific, medical, psychological, and philosophical questions.

"In the near-death experience people who are physically dead begin the journey to the afterlife but do not complete it," Joel Martin wrote in an earlier book, *Love Beyond Life*.[50] The skeptics answered with one voice, "If there is no soul, then it cannot separate from the physical body."

Yet for every scientist or physician who shirks the responsibility to remain, at least, open-minded to the possibility of what NDEs might mean, there are others willing to step forward. The late Harvard University psychiatry professor Dr. John Mack, who dared tread into the dangerous waters of academic hypocrisy when he wrote a bestselling book about extraterrestrial alien abductions—to the horror of most of his colleagues—also had some thoughts about near-death experiences. Mack wrote that the NDE is one of the "phenomena that have led to challenging the prevailing materialist/dualistic worldview." Dr. Mack was called to account by his Harvard Medical School colleagues, who sought to have his tenure status removed because of his dabbling in the paranormal, in alien abductions, and the like. But at a hearing, his attorney, Harvard Law School graduate Daniel Sheehan, successfully defended Dr. Mack, who was later killed in a tragic, and suspicious, accident when he was run over by a lorry in London.

While all the earthly debating continues, for millions it will largely go unnoticed, because all that will have meaning is that when they are at the brink of death, they will have the transcendent experience of rising from their physical bodies, and being drawn to that brilliant light, the radiance that just might be a glimpse of heaven, the afterlife. Medical miracles, fierce disputes about the right to die, new technologies, all have their place in helping our physical or earthly bodies. But, as history has shown, regardless of race, religious belief, gender, or status in society, we are also spiritual beings drawn to the love and warmth of the beckoning light.[51]

8

The New Age Becomes
Big Business

"The chief business of the American people is business," said the notoriously laconic President Calvin Coolidge in a speech in 1925. It was a message that has not been lost to the ensuing decades and especially not on the entrepreneurs who saw the potential in the New Age movement a half-century later. If there is a new product, physical, natural, or, in the case of New Age beliefs, spiritual, people will find a buck to be made in it. And this is not a new thing.

History bears out the fact that it was during America's first New Age in the mid-nineteenth century that the economic potential in talking to spirits first became apparent. It was a time when belief in spiritualism galloped across the country at breakneck speed following the Fox sisters' claims of ghostly rappings in their Hydesville, New York, home on the night of March 31, 1848. Suddenly

America was in the throes of the great "Age of Spiritualism," attracting the interest of millions from one end of the nation to the other. As a result, communicating with the dead became a modestly paying career, especially for women. Major cities, such as Boston, teemed with spiritualists, mediums, hypnotists, transcendentalists, and an array of offbeat health practitioners, in a mid-nineteenth-century version of what would occur more than a hundred years later when hope for human transformation dawned in the "Age of Aquarius" in the 1960s, and continued to grow in the decades after that.

Séances and clairvoyant sittings conducted in dimly lighted parlors remained popular into the early twentieth century. But by then, many spiritualist mediums had been accused of deceit or were caught in fraudulent acts. That coupled with an angry and determined debunking campaign by the famed illusionist Harry Houdini seemed to seal spiritualism's fate. Its credibility sank, and many critics, and not just debunkers, branded it charlatanism. Yet, not every medium could be summarily dismissed as a fraud. No one had ever debunked the famed medium D. D. Home, and spiritualism's impact on American popular culture, and even politics, all the way to the White House, could not be denied. No less an icon of American history than President Abraham Lincoln had attended séances. Some of America's most powerful and influential figures—among them, Harriet Beecher Stowe, Horace Greeley, and J. P. Morgan—were believers. Eminent scientists on both sides of the Atlantic, such as American psychologist and philosopher William James, searched tirelessly and in vain for an answer to the great mystery of whether there is life after death.[1]

Once spiritualism waned in the early decades of the twentieth century it was due in large measure to its own avarice and deception. Meanwhile, parapsychology fought the good fight for scientific acceptance through the founding of the Society for Psychical

Research in England in 1882, and its American counterpart, the American Society for Psychical Research (ASPR), three years later, the determination of Dr. J. B. Rhine's ESP experiments at Duke University, and then the recognition earned by the clairvoyant Edgar Cayce. By no means was spiritualism over and done with. It assumed a lower profile, as if it were waiting for just the right moment to reemerge. It found that propitious time during one of the most tumultuous decades of the late twentieth century.

The New Age wasn't so much born in the 1960s, as it was reborn. At first, many called it the "Age of Aquarius," an astrological term and the name of a popular song from the hit Broadway musical *Hair*, suggesting that we were, astrologically, moving from the passing Age of Pisces to a new and more enlightened Age of Aquarius. But this New Age went far beyond hippie characters performing onstage. What evolved by the 1970s and 1980s was a genuine and influential movement, although it had no formal organization, leaders, rules, membership requirements, dues, or even mailing address.

By definition, the New Age embodied a "set of beliefs intended to replace traditional Western culture, with alternative approaches to religion, medicine, the environment, [and] music," among other aspects of life. "A major difficulty with understanding New Age is that it does not conform to traditionally understood forms of religious organization," observed Michael York in *New Religions*. "The fluid organization or even nonorganization of New Age makes it actually more of a consumer phenomenon than anything that could be understood as traditionally religious." York described the New Age as a "spiritual consumer supermarket."

The ferment and newfound freedoms of the 1960s had challenged long-established conventions, ushering in unprecedented sexual liberation, widespread drug use; and a dizzying whirl of colorful psychedelic art, long-haired hippies, the peace movement, and flower power. As American society seemed to totter on the brink of full-scale social revolution, youth, particularly disenchanted with what they collectively called "the establishment"—perhaps today's 1 percent—vented their anger and frustration in antiwar demonstrations from coast to coast. Urban riots rocked ghettos, while political assassinations sapped the idealism of young Americans. Indeed, events during the decade often seemed to move at staggering speeds.

Would difficult and complex questions raised in the 1960s find meaningful solutions in the 1970s, and beyond, with the help of New Age or metaphysical thinking? Would anger and frustration incited by the Vietnam War, racial discrimination, and ecological concerns find resolution? That "sixties thing" was all about effecting positive and significant changes in society, wasn't it? Hadn't meditation, yoga, and Zen become widely accepted as means of creating new mental approaches, some at an intuitive level, to cope with life's stresses and problems? Didn't LSD, among others hallucinogenic drugs, promise to open users' minds to new insights and undiscovered dimensions?

For many of the 1960s generation who sought spiritual growth and guidance, the ideas and their anticipated outcomes seemed freshly minted. However, the fact was that nearly every New Age concept had a lengthy history; many were ancient philosophies and practices that had withstood the test of time. In fact, some thought it disrespectful to apply the term "New Age" to long-established principles and beliefs as if the generations of the 1960s and 1970s were the originators of ideas that, in many instances, predated the birth of Jesus, and could be traced back many centuries, even millennia.

Whether the counterculture paid sufficient homage to its ancestors can be debated endlessly, but it's certain that every generation prior to the sixties and seventies also considered their philosophical and spiritual discoveries to be original. Theosophists had even employed the term "New Age" decades before hippies created "flower power" and tripped on acid in Haight-Ashbury.

Much of the nineteenth century was also a metaphysical New Age for those who lived then, discovering the wonders of Walt Whitman's poetry, Thoreauvian ideas, Emersonian transcendental philosophy, and the questions raised by spiritualism about the possibility of communicating with the deceased. In 1875, a Russian immigrant to the United States, Madame Helena Petrovna Blavatsky, founded the Theosophical Society that opened many Americans to the philosophies of India and the East, and became a strong influence on New Age thought a century later.

Another historically significant contributor to New Age thinking was Alice Bailey (1880–1949) whose understanding of Theosophy led her to write many channeled books, some she claimed were from a spirit entity she called the "Tibetan." After an unpleasant break with the Theosophical Society, Bailey eventually founded the Arcane School in New York in 1923 that professed a "theosophical idea of a coming world religion to unite East and West," J. Gordon Melton explained in the *New Age Encyclopedia*.[2]

Go back to virtually any period in history when there were exciting inventions, explorations, or marvelous revelations, and you'll find that many leaders, scientists, artists, and great thinkers of these long-gone eras considered themselves on the cutting edge of society. Every generation regards itself as new, which it is, of course, when compared to the generations that preceded it. The 1970s and 1980s blossomed into a New Age from seeds planted in the 1960s and before.

"By the time the vision of the New Age began to unfold in the early 1970s, the occult/metaphysical community, consisting of the members and constituencies of several hundred alternative metaphysical religions, formed a preexisting potential audience,"

J. Gordon Melton explained.[3] "[They] became the first to become enthused about the movement's vision." Thus, practiced Theosophists and Spiritualists infused the new movement with their accumulated knowledge. With the introduction of transpersonal psychology, a greater interest in Eastern teachings, and a concern for the environment, the stage was set for New Age, as both a "social and religious movement."

The movement was centered on the concept of transformation, Melton explained. Once a personal transformation has taken place, then New Agers can begin to consider the possibility of a transformation for others, as well as for the "culture" or even for humankind. How do transformations occur? Numerous ones are the result of intense "mystical experiences," frequently coming to the forefront because of a "personal crisis" or as the outcome of an extensive spiritual search.

The New Age also gave birth to many entrepreneurs, Melton pointed out, including health-food store proprietors, authors, lecturers, and publishers as well as those who organized everything from New Age expositions, retreats, seminars, and classes to a range of alternative health practitioners. New Age actually became a subject of cultural research, even prompting a number of colleges to consider it advantageous enough to offer courses directed at New Age interests. To some, the idea of "competition seemed to be at odds with the New Age's professed one-world ideal." In fact, even with the passing of the new millennium, a number of former self-described yuppies of the 1980s transformed themselves into New Age gurus.

It was technically a misnomer to label that time the New Age since there were many similar periods over the course of human history, all regarding themselves as unique or unparalleled. But New Age is what the diverse movement became known as, for better or worse, attracting people of every kind who more likely than not favored being known as spiritual rather than religious.[4]

"Spirituality refers to any sense of meaning and significance beyond what can be [comprehended] by the five senses. Religion involves a belief in a higher power and some set of laws or rituals. An artist can be an atheist and still be spiritual. A witch doctor can be a religious figure," according to Rabbi Yaakov Saacks, an Orthodox rabbi in the New York area, quoted in the newspaper *Newsday.*

Even the counterculture had historic predecessors. In early America, John Chapman (1774–1845), a gentle spiritualist who became better known as the legendary Johnny Appleseed, generously planted seeds, working his way westward from New England to Ohio and Indiana, seeds that later blossomed into acres of orchards of bountiful apple trees. Chapman, a free spirit who preferred to wander barefoot through the countryside, was a believer in the mystical writings of Emanuel Swedenborg, and also an avid reader of the Bible. Many hippies, imbued with that same altruistic character, strove to disseminate what they believed were rousing new ideas. Had Chapman lived during the 1960s, he no doubt would have fit in quite comfortably.

"Men wore their long hair, women cut theirs short, and both lived as equals, building houses and tending gardens, and, at times, practicing free love," wrote *Newsday* writer Cynthia Blair. Was it an accurate depiction of hippie communes or cults that were a phenomenon of the counterculture at the dawning of the Age of Aquarius? Actually, it is a description of Modern Times, an experimental utopian community founded on Long Island in 1851. It remained in existence until 1864. Discussion groups passionately tackled the pros and cons of spiritualism, then at its zenith. Just as many held negative attitudes toward cults and communes in the 1960s and 1970s, most people a century earlier considered utopian lifestyles shocking and depraved.[5]

The confluence of explosive events and radical ideologies that marked the decade of the 1960s ignited a firestorm of controversy, as we explained earlier. It also created sharp divides between generations that threatened to polarize and paralyze the nation. The 1960s seemed to turn everything topsy-turvy, including the role of spirituality and religion in American life.[6]

What happened to the dreams of the 1960s and the promise of peace and love, the watchwords of the late 1960s? The 1970s arrived with a harsh dose of hard, cold financial reality. The Vietnam War would expand into Cambodia, students would be shot dead at Kent State University, a Middle Eastern oil embargo would turn off the Christmas lights all across the United States and queue drivers into mile-long lines at gas pumps at five and six in the morning, Vice President Agnew and then President Richard Nixon would be forced to resign in disgrace, there would be no storybook or utopian endings, and we would all have to go back to work. No matter how firmly planted the New Age was, it did not move in the direction many of the more self-sacrificing had hoped.

The Vietnam War had bitterly divided the nation, and those who served did not receive the heroes' welcome that greeted their fathers when they returned from the battlefields of World War II. In the 1972 presidential campaign, many young Americans rallied for the liberal, antiwar George McGovern, the losing Democratic candidate, while President Nixon was forced from office by the Watergate scandals. Violent crime rates soared in nearly every American city during the 1970s and 1980s. Added to the potentially incendiary mix of crime and poverty were dangerous street drugs, such as heroin, and later crack cocaine and PCP, which replaced mind-expanding LSD and other hallucinogens that had been the hallmark of the more socially conscious 1960s.

What happened to the promise of harmony sung about at Woodstock during the summer of 1969 when American astronauts landed on the moon, taking that giant step for all of us to the lunar surface? Had it all been a fantasy? The Manson family killings that last summer of the decade cast its pall over the dream, and by 1970, rock music luminaries Janis Joplin and Jimi Hendrix, both only in their twenties, were dead of drug overdoses. The 1974 kidnapping of heiress Patty Hearst by a small but violently militant radical group called the Symbionese Liberation Army hardly fit the promised vision. During President Jimmy Carter's administration (1977–1981), the U.S. became ensnared in the lengthy Iran hostage crisis. In 1978 in Jonestown, Guyana, some cult members, followers of the Reverend Jim Jones, committed mass suicide by drinking poison-laced Kool-Aid. It was indeed a decade of horrors.

Then, a new decade dawned, and in December 1980, an icon and political force, former Beatle John Lennon, was murdered outside his New York City apartment house. It was another blow to 1960s idealism and bitter irony to the soaring lyrics of his poignant song, "Imagine." It didn't appear the world could or would live as one.

In March 1981, President Ronald Reagan was shot in an attempt on his life, suffered a critical injury, and for a period of time on the operating table was on life support, thus extending the zero-year curse pronounced by Tecumseh's shamanic brother Tenskwatawa to another president (see chapter 7). The Cold War continued into the 1980s, and nuclear annihilation remained a genuine threat. There was the frightening accident at the Chernobyl nuclear power plant, and the space shuttle *Challenger* disaster in space. Then, more tragedy as the 1980s wound down, a terrorist bomb blew up Pan American Flight 103 over Lockerbie, Scotland, killing all aboard, including many Americans.

There were plenty of reminders that the 1970s and 1980s didn't go according to plan and certainly had not lived up to the expectations of the 1960s reverie. Violence, intolerance, greed, deception, man's inhumanity to man: they all remained part of the human condition, all there to read about in your morning newspaper, or as far back as in biblical chapter and verse. "Our scientific power has outrun our spiritual power. We have guided missiles and misguided men," the Reverend Martin Luther King Jr., had once proclaimed, and his words still rang true.

March for peace, banish nuclear weapons and wars, end poverty and racism, and live happily ever after? They were inspiring goals; but it became apparent to nearly all but the most naïve that it might have been a tad unrealistic to expect the world to be magically transformed, and its evils and errors erased. That didn't mean the idealism expressed so forcefully in the 1960s had to be abandoned. It did, however, require some refocusing.

By the 1970s, purveyors of New Age ideas had rethought the approach of believing they could force massive and positive global changes, and realized they first needed to motivate individual aspects of behavior and thinking including religion and spirituality, mental and physical health, politics, ecology, human consciousness, and an array of metaphysical subjects. In fact, the New Age movement was able to incorporate sundry and myriad ideas under a rather generous umbrella. In the process, the New Age movement that evolved in the early 1970s, and continued beyond that, spawned a vast array of books and lectures, consultations with channelers, alternative medical practices, as well as various paraphernalia from herbal remedies to healing crystals.

By the time "New Age" became a full-fledged movement in the 1970s and 1980s it had a "religious or quasi-religious orientation," Michael York wrote in *New Religions: A Guide*.[7] But pinning it down to a precise meaning was easier said than done, since the New Age meant different things to different people. Many historians suggested it was a combination of several diverse belief systems that included elements of Theosophy, New Thought, and spiritualism. The New Age could embrace virtually any aspect of life; yet it was not a "church, sect, cult, or denomination," York explained.[8] There was never any ecclesiastical hierarchy, or one voice that spoke for the New Age movement, or passed judgment, as was the case with most organized religions. The fact was that nearly anything could be labeled New Age.

Another curious element of New Age concerned the accumulation of its own wealth and power. Without a central structure or chain of command, self-aggrandizement was not limited to a particular guru who represented the entire movement. In other words, under the banner of New Age, there were many individuals and smaller groups, but no one supreme, grand, or revered mentor or spiritual teacher who spoke with singular authority for everyone who considered themselves New Age followers. However, if you heard the fury of Christian fundamentalist leaders as they emotionally—and inaccurately—assailed the New Age as another term for the dreaded "occult," and therefore in league with Satan, you might not be certain what to believe.[9]

Disingenuous evangelical ministers from pulpits, and some using TV time they'd purchased, described the New Age menacingly as a well-financed and organized army of thousands, marching in lockstep to the strains of sinister mantras as they trampled over God-fearing Christians. Then, of course, came their pitch to send money to fight these agents of the Devil, the dangerous New Age types, citing biblical admonitions as the source of their cautions. The Roman Catholic Church also published articles in its diocesan newspapers warning the faithful away from anything that showed signs of so-called New Age teachings, from channeling, to divination, psychic healers, and Eastern gurus, to ghost hunters, astrologers, and mediums, and those practicing past life regressive hypnosis. Even yoga was suspect.

There was a certain irony when the august Vatican, one of the oldest, best organized, and wealthiest religious institutions in the world, felt ideologically threatened by widely disparate New Age ideas and entrepreneurs. Perhaps even more paradoxical was the fact that the Catholic Church had been the Western world's first serious psychical investigator, and within the church were numerous paranormal phenomena attributed to the saints that would capture attention for centuries to come.[10] As recently as the 1990s, there was widespread New Age interest in prayer as a healing technique, and multitudes of angels in books, and even stores that specialized in angel art, jewelry, statues, and virtually anything else that could be decorated with a seraph or cherub. In addition, thousands of people claimed personal experiences with "guardian angels" that miraculously intervened on their behalf, often in times of crisis or danger. The New Age was borrowing from, even overlapping with, some long-held religious teachings.

In the last decades of the twentieth century, ancient wisdom was back in vogue as more people sought spiritual answers to life's problems. And it was here that the emerging New Age movement took an unanticipated course. As we said earlier, eager and impatient youth who were in the front lines of political and social ferment in the 1960s had not seen massive societal changes happen as they'd hoped. But they had altered the consciousness of the country on a number of issues; they had made a difference. However, by the 1970s, Americans had grown increasingly disenchanted with raucous demonstrations and protests as a means to achieve social and political change, and instead turned inward to become what many called the "Me Generation."

There were critics who viewed such personal transformation as self-centered and self-absorbed, and even saw it as a form of mass narcissism. But was it? "The New Age is the expectation that spiritual development in sufficient numbers of individuals will eventually coalesce into a planetary quantum leap of collective consciousness," wrote Michael York in *New Religions*.[11] In other words, the New Age grew into a movement that was primarily concerned with helping people look inward, at themselves, for spiritual growth. Only then could they bond or unite to accomplish constructive change in the larger society or even on the world stage.

The New Age for all its openness and diversity held several common beliefs that infused the movement. One was the wide acceptance of channeling, a variation of mediumship, and a throwback to nineteenth-century spiritualism. There was also credibility given to reincarnation or past lives, a direct influence of Eastern religions, and a precept of Theosophy. Another New Age belief declared that a person was capable of his or her own healing, a concept that appears in many forms of alternative medicine, based on nineteenth-century "New Thought" teachings.[12] And fundamental to New Age theory was the objective of finding "higher truths" within oneself.

The New Age developed several major themes, as Mary Olsen Kelly explained in the *Fireside Treasury of Light*: they included "personal and social transformation," "self-improvement," and "leading a quality life." Those who wrote about New Age stressed the significance of the mind-body connection and tackled every aspect of knowledge and understanding, including "mental, physical, emotional, and spiritual," Kelly noted, adding that New Age philosophy has as a central idea that people "have many levels of consciousness." The purpose of each person's life is to achieve a "well-balanced, harmonious, and direct relationship with God, nature, each other and ourselves," she added.[13]

It didn't take long for those who proclaimed themselves "New Age" authors, experts, and gurus to charge forward. The 1970s through the 1990s became decades closely identified with the genre that was known, sometimes derogatorily, as "self-help," in the form of books, tapes, and seminars. Many criticized the value of these self-improvement, self-empowerment, or inspirational approaches, but millions were drawn to them for advice: a combination of psychology, philosophy, metaphysical thinking, religion, and even cutting-edge or exotic science, self-healing, and alternative medicine. Put them all together and you had, as author Michael York described it, an "eclectic mix."[14]

New Age searched beyond the physical world for what York called "divine truth." And when ancient Eastern philosophies and teachings were embraced they were often merged with Western ideas. Psychic development was recognized as a tool to aid individual growth. For example, past lives therapy that utilized regressive hypnosis allowed many to discover how previous incarnations may have impacted their current life even when those past lives were at the suggestion of the hypnotist herself. Some people learned the roots of their fears could be traced back to traumas in earlier lifetimes. Knowing that, past life therapists claimed, might begin someone on the road to coping with and overcoming phobias. Among the best-known New Age authors/therapists touting this controversial approach was Dr. Brian Weiss, a Florida-based psychiatrist, and author of *Many Lives, Many Masters*.[15]

Dick Sutphen earned his reputation during the New Age for his work with "thousands of people" he'd regressed to their former lives. He was both a hypnotist and a psychic researcher who emphasized the connection between love and reincarnation. In one of his most popular books, *You Were Born Again to Be Together* (1976), Sutphen explained that "lovers from the past will reincarnate within the same time frame again and again. In each new incarnation love will deepen until, after many lives, love is perfected. Love is the most powerful force in the universe." Mindful of high divorce rates, Sutphen wrote "in troubled relationships, regressive hypnosis often reveals why people have their particular problems."

Another of his widely read books was *Past Lives, Future Loves*. Sutphen said he was certain that people together in this lifetime were together in previous incarnations. Modern theoretical physicists might have argued that the universe itself throws entangled souls together through the vortices of time, but Sutphen believed that souls themselves were entangled in their former lives.[16]

One can argue whether individuals were actually visualizing their former lives at all, or was it a myth, albeit a useful myth. A form of therapy, many skeptical psychiatrists and psychotherapists argued, which, if it integrated a personality that was troubled and allowed the person to grow from what he or she perceived was a past life, it was certainly good enough even it were a placebo.

Another angle by which love was approached was the case made by author Jess Stearn in *Soulmates*. Who hasn't dreamed of that one special person with whom there is a deeply felt spiritual connection? The concept of "soulmates" represents love and companionship exalted to its highest level. "It's perfect love," and few relationships "seemed touched by [that] special magic." How would one recognize his or her soulmate? Stearn tackled the question to "reveal how love and spirituality can merge beyond the limits of space and time, of life and death to create a perfect union of body and soul." Stearn capitalized on the era by saying that the New Age was "the time for an outpouring of universal love which would ignite a flame that would spread through a stricken world." As did many books during the New Age, *Soulmates* turned to several disciplines for answers: psychics, mystics, counselors, psychologists, and sociologists.[17]

One of the most significant changes in attitude toward paranormal events occurred when many psychotherapists became accepting of patients' psychic experiences, such as visions, apparitions, and synchronicities, and integrated them within bereavement therapy. Mental health professionals had long stubbornly considered visions and apparitions to be delusions. But such "after-death communications" have proven their worth in psychotherapy, a noticeable shift that was a direct result of the transformation in thinking brought about by the New Age.

The New Age also embraced elements of religion, both from the East and West. Zen, meditation, and yogic practices that originated in the East continued to grow in popularity among Americans in the latter decades of the twentieth century. Chinese medicine, including herbal remedies, acupuncture, and the chi or life force, that elusive, invisible energy that courses through the human body, all found acceptance within the alternative medicine movement, a part of the larger New Age. The change in the political landscape also helped bridge Eastern and Western thinking and practice. When President Richard Nixon made his historic visit to Communist China in 1972, doors long closed were opened, and ancient Asian pain relieving and unorthodox healing techniques such as acupuncture and qi gong were introduced to Americans over the opposition of traditionally trained and skeptical physicians. More familiar to those of Judeo-Christian heritage were the age-old concepts of prayer, angels, and the soul. Each made an effortless transition, so that while they remained a part of conventional religion, they also appealed to New Age types.

The increasing sales of books, audio materials, and videos about a range of New Age subjects suggested millions found self-help books provided them with "motivation," "insight," and "encouragement," three popular terms used by New Age marketing specialists. The pro and con debate about the worth of inspirational and so-called self-improvement books and seminars, ongoing for decades, will likely never be fully resolved. Perhaps, as critics charged, much of the advice was simple common sense, cleverly packaged. However, it empowered many to better understand themselves and others, proclaimed authors and motivational speakers.

Meanwhile, millions of Americans continued their search for life's purpose, and that elusive higher self they hoped would provide access to other and wiser dimensions, along with a deeper understanding of the universe and the individual's place in it. Increasingly, there was a combination of religion, psychology, metaphysics, and spirituality; a mingling of disciplines found in many self-help books that proved quite acceptable to multitudes of avant-garde New Age readers, to the chagrin of old school churches.

Critics, naysayers, and most major media at first underestimated the staying power of the New Age, but this was no passing fad or momentary craze. It became apparent that millions of Americans were restless. Many in the "Me Generation" felt alienated and sought resolve to their individual tribulations, as well as the larger crises that faced the nation and planet Earth. Despite the range of ideas the New Age brought together, each person who embarked on a personal journey of self-discovery and transformation was welcome to take a separate road to spiritual fulfillment and greater awareness. According to New Age thinking, "Spirituality is about choice," author Michael York said.[18]

The New Age was the realization of centuries of ideas and discoveries. Unlike the bearded, sweatshirt-wearing, bongo-drum pounders of the 1950s beat generation, and the braided hair, sitar-strumming hippies of the sixties, those who embraced New Age ideas and values from the seventies on came from every walk of life. They wore no insignias or other uniquely identifying characteristics such as long hair or love beads, as the hippies had. For those who disliked New Age concepts, there was no specific individual to blame for the countless ideas that imbued millions, ranging from channeling spirits, to environmental issues, matters of health, and struggles for myriad social and political causes.

New Age became a movement of eclectic ideas and values—some very good, others quite specious—that its supporters hoped would lead to a more open-minded and harmonious future, and perhaps people would be able to make spiritual connections with each other after they'd concluded their personal journeys of discovery. The 1980s grew into what many called the "We Decade." With "new theories about human consciousness," Mary Olsen Kelly wrote, there was now a generation of books and authors that "inspired readers [toward] in-depth programs of self-exploration."[19] Kelly noted that the decade saw celebrities and rock stars join together for charitable events, one massive effort was the late Michael Jackson–inspired "We Are the World," to call attention to the problem of impoverished children dying from hunger and disease around the globe.

One of the most lasting effects of the New Age was a greater openness to unorthodox medical and healing techniques. With it came the proposition that we, the patients, take greater personal responsibility for our own health. If we developed heightened self-awareness, asserted many New Age writers, we'd learn about the capacity to heal ourselves, as Louise Hay argued in her books about the underlying emotional causes of disease.

Doctor/authors such as Larry Dossey, Bernie Siegel, and Carl Simonton contributed to that awareness by writing and speaking about the power of prayer to restore health, the importance of the mind-body connection in healing, and such techniques as visualization to affect disease. Dr. Deepak Chopra emerged as a hugely influential figure, also emphasizing the "clear relationship between the mind, or spirit, and the health of the body," selling millions of books along the way.

And Dr. Bernie Siegel claimed that the most remarkable cures in drug tests weren't from the drugs being tested, but from the placebos administered to test subjects that actually effected remission of symptoms. If a sugar pill, although believed by the test subject to be a pharmaceutical, can have remedial effects, what does that say about the power of the mind, Dr. Siegel asked? Siegel employed the term "placebo effect" to describe it.[20]

Among the early prominent individuals whose ideas were significant in helping the New Age ultimately develop was, in addition to Madame Blavatsky, founder of the Theosophical Society, her energetic and likable successor, Annie Besant. There was Jiddu Krishnamurti, supposedly the "reincarnation of Buddha," Paramahansa Yogananda who wrote the heartfelt *Autobiography of a Yogi*; Meher Baba, the Indian mystic and "enlightened master"; and George I. Gurdjieff, the brilliant Russian-born philosopher and teacher, and an early believer in "nontraditional spirituality." Then, in the years after World War II, as American youth grew increasingly restive and curious about the world around them, Jack Kerouac and the irreverent "beat" poets of the 1950s emerged, as did interest in Zen Buddhism.[21]

New Age was also significantly influenced by "humanistic psychology," shaped by Dr. Abraham Maslow (1908–1970) in the 1940s and 1950s. From that emerged the "human potential movement" in the 1960s, and its varied therapies that included Zen, Transcendental Meditation, yoga, reflexology, tai chi, Reiki, shiatsu, encounter groups, Rolfing, and EST, among others. Maslow also pioneered "self-actualization," the idea that "one can be all that one wants to be," writer Elizabeth Puttick explained, adding, "Maslow believed that mystics were the most likely group to be self-actualized and have 'peak experiences' of ecstasy and union."[22] Dr. Fritz Perls, who joined the Esalen Institute in Big Sur, California, during the 1960s, was important to New Age thinking for his development of Gestalt therapy, and the idea of the mind and body as one holistic being.

The world of psychic phenomena was not ignored during the

New Age. One significant contribution was the bestselling, *The Sleeping Prophet*, by veteran journalist and author Jess Stearn. The book was a biography of America's premier trance clairvoyant and healer Edgar Cayce, who pioneered many ideas and techniques that came into vogue twenty and more years after his death, including alternative or unorthodox medical treatments, the use of crystals for healing, a belief in the ancient lost civilization of Atlantis, and the exploration of past lives.[23]

For those motivated to learn New Age teachings, books continued to be the principal source of information, even as audio books and e-books, in recent years, have been added. While many self-improvement and inspirational books were not directly concerned with the paranormal or psychic development, there was an overlap in the sense that New Age concerned the whole person. When body, mind, and spirit were considered holistically, many books that focused on improving one aspect of life or behavior often touched upon the others.

The New Age gave birth to the genre of pop-psych, self-improvement books that gained strength from such successful titles as *Your Erroneous Zones* by Dr. Wayne Dyer in 1976. He told readers that rethinking their attitudes could alter certain negative behaviors, ones he cleverly called "erroneous zones," a play on the word "erogenous." As an example, one of the ideas Dyer shared with Joel Martin in the first broadcast interview he ever gave was to suggest people "live in the moment." It was simple, even obvious advice, but many welcomed it.

Dyer had been through orphanages as a child, and his ability to identify with his audience by sharing his own "rags to riches" experiences, as well as his training and background as a therapist and college professor, no doubt contributed to his immense success as a self-help author. He was also quite savvy in the self-promotion and marketing of his books through thousands of radio and TV talk show appearances in which his themes included such recognizable human concerns as "taking charge of yourself," "you don't need their approval," "breaking the barrier of convention," "farewell to anger," and "fear of the unknown."

Dyer saw his first book, *Your Erroneous Zones,* climb to the top of the bestseller lists, then during the years that followed he wrote many more—some with a metaphysical twist, all of which, along with his numerous public and TV appearances, made Dyer an important and influential voice for the "self-actualization" genre of books targeted to the so-called Me Generation.

Other classics from this period were *Games People Play* and *I'm OK, You're OK,* both of which were based on the early work of Dr. Wilder Penfield in Canada, who had researched the storage of childhood memories in various regions of the cerebral cortex. The Penfield studies, financed in part by the CIA, opened up an entire area of popular psychology dealing with retrieving hidden scripts within the subject's unconscious memory, scripts written decades earlier by parents, but constantly replaying and influencing conscious behavior. Discover the scripts, some psychologists said, and it would be like discovering the source of a Freudian trauma that resulted in a neurosis, but with much less psychotherapy, lots of self-help, and far less money.

Centuries ago, Buddha said, "When the student is ready, the teacher will appear." So it was from the 1970s on that many claiming expertise came forward to instruct those eager to learn new approaches to life. There are, of course, too many authors of self-help and inspirational books to adequately describe them all or do justice to their efforts. However, we can highlight several who made their name during and because of the New Age movement, most of whom focused their revelations around the concepts of love and growth, love of oneself to enable one to love others.

Dr. Leo Buscaglia (1924–1998) was affectionately dubbed "Dr.

Love." The native Californian's idea was that "love and self-acceptance" were therapy for the confusion many people feel trapped in because of the tumult of modern life. With a background as an educator, Buscaglia turned to writing and also became a popular lecturer on public television. Between 1972 and 1994, he authored more than a dozen books about loving and sharing, one of his best known was *Living, Loving, and Learning*. Some critics took him to task for writing about "commitment" since he never married or had children. That didn't seem to faze the millions who liked what they read and heard in his enthusiastic suggestions about the "healing power of love." Buscaglia's other nickname was "Dr. Hug," for his habit of embracing audience members after his appearances.[24] Buscaglia's hug therapy was satirized by the character Ari Gold, played by Jeremy Piven, in HBO's hit series *Entourage*, with his suggestion for how to resolve all conflicts being the statement to "hug it out."

"Why do we have lives filled with turmoil, desperation, and anxiety? Why are we always pushing ourselves and others?" asked Ken Keyes, Jr., in his influential 1975 *Handbook to Higher Consciousness*. "As conscious beings the only thing we need to find happiness in life is to perceive clearly who we are. But to achieve this clear perception of ourselves and the world around us takes constant inner work," Keyes wrote.[25]

Also optimistic about the future was Shakti Gawain. "We are living in a very exciting and powerful time," she wrote in her well-received book, *Living in the Light*, in 1986. "My observation [is] that a profound transformation is taking place in our world. There is the promise that a higher level of consciousness [will be] available in the new world," she announced confidently.[26]

Alienated American young people were ripe pickings for some clever Eastern gurus. Anyone who lived through the 1970s will never forget the brightly robed, often emaciated, and hollow-eyed young people with their shaved heads and braids, dancing and chanting at airports and on the streets of large cities. They were members of the Hare Krishna movement. Whether it was a religion or an overbearing cult is still disputed. The founder of what was officially known as the International Society for Krishna Consciousness was, take a deep breath, His Divine Grace A. C. Bhaktivedanta Swami Prabhupada.

To recruit new members, he also wrote what could be called an inspirational book, *The Science of Self-Realization,* first published in 1968, it went through sixteen printings by 1997, with millions of copies in print. Essentially, it was intended to boost the credibility of Hare Krishna. "This very important Krishna consciousness movement is meant to save human society from spiritual death. At present human society is being misled by leaders who are blind. The aim and objective of human life [is] self-realization and the reestablishment of our lost relationship with Krishna, or God," he wrote.

Then, in one of the most stunning examples of New Age–era hypocrisy, the Swami noted that since a person is a "rational animal, he is born to make inquiries." Devotees of the sect were permitted virtually none of the freedoms of inquiry espoused by his "Divine Grace," master teacher of the "science of self-realization," who, while encouraging the practice of yoga and meditation, earned a fortune for Hare Krishna.[27]

Within the genre of self-help books, *The Road Less Traveled,* published in 1978, became one of the most successful ever, selling some ten million copies and remaining on *The New York Times* Best Seller list for more than ten years. The author was M. Scott Peck (1936–2005), a psychiatrist who practiced in Connecticut. Ideally written for the New Age era, the extraordinary book combined psychology with advice for "spiritual growth" and also included examples drawn from philosophy and religion; it offered examples and opinions drawn from his personal life and work with patients as well. Peck's down-to-earth, common sense manner of writing no doubt contributed to the book's great success. Peck stressed that people need "discipline," backed by love, to cope with their problems and relationships.

"Discipline is the means of human spiritual evolution," Peck wrote. Love is the "force [that] provides the motive, the energy for discipline." He added, "The desire to love is not itself love. We do not have to love. We choose to love." Pondering death, it "is part of the spiritual journey, and acceptance of death will give life its full meaning," Peck concluded.

In all, Peck had more than twenty publications to his credit. His last, published in 2005, was *Glimpses of the Devil: A Psychiatrist's Personal Accounts of Possession, Exorcism, and Redemption*. This was a contentious subject that drew some criticism. However, Peck is best remembered for the guidance he offered in *The Road Less Traveled*.[28]

Religious critics of New Age, even those books that included spirituality, expressed frustration, even anger. that "self-help" ignored or skimmed over traditional Christian belief for guidance and direction, an argument that played out in the 2012 election by candidates Rick Santorum and former House Speaker Newt Gingrich.

The fact is that long-established religious convictions could be equally useful for those who were devout in a particular faith. Religion, after all, as a number of theologians pointed out, provided a moral structure answerable to God, a sense of community, and a long history to draw from. However, an increasingly large number of Americans had begun to question conventional Judeo-Christian dogma, seeking new and more immediate answers to what many viewed as the increasingly complex dilemmas of modern life.

Tony Robbins, a California native, made his name and wealth as a self-help author and motivational speaker, attracting a large following for his books, seminars, and motivational tapes and CDs, that have earned him over fifty million dollars. An imposing presence at six feet seven and projecting a softly powerful and inspiring voice, Robbins was just twenty-four when his first book, *Unlimited Power: The New Science of Personal Achievement,* became a bestseller in 1986. And his next, *Awaken the Giant Within,* in 1991, also reached bestseller status. In all, he'd written or coauthored eight books by 1997. You may have seen the energetic Robbins appear in successful TV infomercials in years past. As well, he made millions from a "self-improvement Web site," among other businesses and enterprises.

For Robbins, the New Age was a veritable goldmine that made him a millionaire many times over. By one account, his "motivational tapes" sold more than twenty-five million copies. In public appearances he declared to audiences they "deserve" an "abundance of money." His emphasis on "wealth and power"—his idea of achievement—was at the heart of his message to millions of people.

Robbins's ideas for self-improvement didn't get a free pass from critics, some of whom took him to task for what they characterized as his appeal to blatant materialism and ostentatious living. He was not an example of a New Age guru advocating the simple life and spirituality, detractors charged. His "feel good now" message also brought objections from those who branded it a "quick fix." As for the big business New Age had become, Robbins was one of its most successful examples.[29]

Tony Robbins was compared to the Reverend Eikenrotter of an earlier generation, who preached that he could teach his congregants to achieve their "pie in the sky" and achieve it right away. The "Rev Ike," as he was called, became a model for later self-empowerment preachers.

Marianne Williamson's claim to New Age fame came mainly from her teaching and lecturing, although she'd authored a dozen books beginning in the early 1990s, as well as many audiocassettes about love and spirituality. Her first book, *A Return to Love: Reflections on the Principles of "A Course in Miracles,"* garnered her an appearance on the *Oprah Winfrey Show* in 1992, became a bestseller, and earned her celebrity status.

Williamson's combination of New Age spirituality, inspiration, and psychology, tinged with religious allusions, found a large audience. Among her following were a number of celebrities who praised her advice and "spiritual guidance," earning her the label, the "Prophet of Love" in *The New York Times*. As was the case with many New Age authors, her well-intentioned dreams of "love and prayer" were deemed by critics to be unrealistic and simplistic. Nonetheless, Williamson revisited her successful self-help and inspirational ideas in later books.[30]

She, above all, became known for her ability to analyze and explain *A Course in Miracles,* a well-known channeled work, published in 1975, that runs almost twelve hundred pages in length. *A Course in Miracles* purported its text was channeled material that was the "biblical Christ, speaking in the first person," author J. Gordon Melton explained.

The events that led to the discovery of the course came about in 1965 when Helen Schucman, a Columbia University professor of medical psychology, experienced a sequence of visions and vivid dreams. Following that, Schucman heard a psychic voice tell her, "This is a course in Miracles. Please take notes." At first disbelieving, a colleague persuaded her to write down what she heard. Later, Schucman said she received what she called "inner dictation," or telepathic communication. The "voice" told her the purpose of *A Course in Miracles* was to "remove the blocks to the awareness of love's presence, which is your natural inheritance."

Its main idea was that "nothing real can be threatened, and nothing unreal exists," J. Gordon Melton explained in the *New Age Encyclopedia.*

It took from 1965 to 1973 to transcribe the wealth of channeled material that eventually included a text, a workbook, and a manual for teachers. Finally, *A Course in Miracles* was published in 1975, although no author's name appeared. Miracles were "defined as shifts in perception which allow people to relinquish illusions based on guilt," Melton explained. The book's goal was to "heal the misperceptions which have led humanity to choose fear rather than love by encouraging a radical transformation in people's mindsets," and approached its advice from a religious perspective. In fact, the book suggests, "People need God's help."[31]

Among Williamson's explanations of *A Course in Miracles* was that people see miracles before them every day. In fact, life presents all of us with miracles. The point, she taught, was not to dismiss what life brings us. The point was to recognize the miracles before our very eyes, understand the meaning of the miracles, and act on them so as to make our lives better. It was a powerful message that resonated with an audience anxious to be told not to look beyond their lives, but to look within their lives for a truth that could inspire them.

On a larger scale, perhaps there was truth to what some cynical detractors of New Age thinking said. Readers were only interested in serving themselves, not saving the world. Where was the altruism, they asked? All they saw was a narcissistic "me-ism." However, New Age teachers and authors saw their messages as constructive if enough people followed their advice. Self-empowerment, they said, was derived from the basis of "love thyself," and, as such, could heal the world because much violence and destruction actually stemmed from foundational self-hatred.

By the late 1980s, New Age had become well established, and

the cascade of books, tapes, and public appearances by the self-help experts and gurus was in full flower, and still growing. Bookstores were noting the change: their "occult" book sections were being renamed "New Age," helping to relieve some of the stigma attached to the ancient stereotype that associated psychic phenomena with something dark, sinister, or evil. "New Age," while far from perfect, and the object of disdain by skeptics, was a less pejorative description for books that dealt with the paranormal and spirituality; there was no lack of readers ready to purchase from a growing number of hard covers, paperbacks, and audiobooks.

As we approached the millennium, the theoretical physicists weighed in, suggesting that there was a scientific normal to what people had called paranormal. In fact, by the end of the twentieth century, fields such as theoretical physics, microbiology, and nanotechnology looked more like science fiction. Terms such as "quantum entanglement" and "nonlocality" and the principle that the future determined the past and not the other way around, floated from technical papers read at academic conferences into the general consciousness. What had originally been C. P. Snow's *The Two Cultures*, the separation of the world of traditional science and the world of humanities, was blending into a kind of third culture, the synthesis of the two.

In 1989, Gary Zukav wrote *The Seat of the Soul*. In the book, which became a bestseller, Zukav wrote about a "realm" that he said was imperceptible "to the five-sensory human." What was important about that unseen domain? "It is in this invisible realm that the origins of our deepest values are found," Zukav explained.[32] With references to the "compassionate acts of Christ" and "the power of Gandhi," Zukav noted,[33] "All great teachers have been, or are, multisensory."[34] He explained, "We are evolving into multisensory humans." From that awareness "we are never alone [in] the universe." Zukav also emphasized the importance of "intentions," and their influence.[35] In combining psychology with spiritual growth, metaphysics, and religious examples, Zukav had chosen a familiar and popular New Age path.

Caroline Myss (pronounced Mace) became a well-known New Age author and teacher with a twist. Myss was a "medical intuitive," meaning she had the psychic facility to determine an individual's well-being, even at a distance. She needed only a person's name and age to determine their physical and emotional health. One of her first books dealt with "a healing program" she and neurosurgeon C. Norman Shealy created for a young man who was HIV-positive. According to Myss, her approach that combined "psychotherapy and changes in behavior" was successful.

The magazine *Yoga Journal* explained that Myss then turned to giving workshops on the "science of intuition," and also cofounded the Institute for the Science of Medical Intuition. By the early 1990s, she began instructing people about their health. And in 1993, Myss, and her neurosurgeon colleague, coauthored *The Creation of Health: The Emotional, Psychological, and Spiritual Responses That Promote Health and Healing.* Her focus was on the relationship between sickness and "negative emotions" that accumulate in the "body's energy centers" or chakras.

In a later book, *Anatomy of the Spirit* (1996), Myss "linked three traditions": the Hindu chakras, the Christian sacraments, and the Jewish Kabbalah's Tree of Life. The goal was "to help people develop spiritual maturity," according to the Web site, Contemporary Authors Online. Myss also took strong issue with the New Age precept that "awareness" is sufficient to heal. "We've got to realize that feeling healthy includes feeling good about ourselves," she told *Yoga Journal*, more than a nod to self-empowerment. Myss is yet another example of a New Age author and teacher who combined several disciplines.[36]

By the 1990s, America's consciousness had changed so that fusing alternative health, psychotherapy, yoga, traditional medicine, psychic ability, and mysticism raised few eyebrows. In fact, many were quite eager to learn from such unconventional approaches, just as those who turned to unorthodox medical approaches from the 1980s on, right or wrong, were seeking help they felt traditional doctors had failed to provide.

If Carolyn Myss, a medical intuitive, was no longer considered out of bounds for Americans seeking health advice, then Judith Orloff found a way to push the envelope even further. Orloff, a psychiatrist in private practice in Los Angeles, revealed that she was a clairvoyant who employed her psychic gift when working with her patients, a story she detailed in her book *Second Sight*, published in 1996. There was a flurry of controversy about the appropriateness of Orloff's form of psychotherapy merged with extrasensory ability. But Orloff was quoted in Contemporary Authors Online: "I see myself as a bridge between traditional medicine and the psychic world. I use my psychic abilities in my practice every day. This is the new wave of health care to incorporate psychic abilities and spirituality."[37]

Perhaps one of the most celebrated and ongoing New Agers from the twentieth century into the twenty-first century was actress and trailblazer Shirley MacLaine. The Academy Award winner earned a special place in the New Age movement not only for the ideas she set forth, but also for daring to make them public in a string of bestselling books she authored. With the fame garnered from her many film roles, MacLaine had no difficulty attracting massive media and public attention when she embarked on a personal spiritual journey.[38]

She first revealed her story in the autobiographical *Out on a Limb* in 1983. The book was an immediate hit with readers, and an instant target for skeptics, critics, and late-night TV comedians, who eagerly derided MacLaine's mystical and psychic beliefs as far out, strange, and weird, just a few of the indecorous expressions she was branded with by detractors.

Despite a number of withering attacks from the media, *Out on a Limb* remained on *The New York Times* Best Seller list for nearly six months, and by 1987 had sold two million copies and was translated into several foreign languages. In the book, MacLaine detailed how her travels around the world, visiting Africa, India, and the Far East, contributed to her spiritual growth and consciousness. She also encouraged awareness of such controversial New Age beliefs as channeling spirits. Among those who MacLaine said provided her with direction, she was particularly complimentary to JZ Knight, a young woman who earned her reputation along with a goodly sum of money by channeling an ancient entity named "Ramtha."[39] MacLaine also wrote about the psychic abilities of trance channeler Kevin Ryerson, who produced a "spirit guide" that identified itself as "John," the biblical apostle who declared he'd made his presence known in order to help people become conscious of "the Christ within."[40]

While MacLaine was filming *Being There* with Peter Sellers in 1979, the two stars found they had a mutual curiosity about reincarnation. Sellers "was a great believer in spiritualism," a friend is quoted as telling author Roger Lewis in *The Life and Death of Peter Sellers*. After attending a séance, the temperamental Sellers came to believe that in a past life he'd been Dan Leno, a nineteenth-century British stage performer. He also became intrigued by the Kabbalah, the tradition of ancient Jewish mysticism.[41] There was no question that Sellers and MacLaine "shared interest in metaphysics, numerology, past lives, and astrology," according to author Ed Sikov in *Mr. Strangelove: A Biography of Peter Sellers*.

Sellers and MacLaine were at the end of filming *Being There* in April 1979, when the actor visited a numerologist, according to Lewis's book. The next day, Sellers confided in MacLaine that he was very worried when the numerologist said his numbers did not line up with his wife's. Only a year later, Sellers, the troubled star of the famed *Pink Panther* movies as well as the cult masterpiece, *Dr. Strangelove,* died of a heart attack at the age of fifty-four.

MacLaine's acceptance of psychic phenomena included openness to psychic healing, channeling spirit guides, UFOs and extraterrestrial beings, astral travel, and reincarnation. Her outspokenness likely encouraged others with similar beliefs. Whether it was her intention or not, MacLaine became a role model for numerous people who sought empowerment for their New Age approach to life. *Out on a Limb* also became a prime-time network TV miniseries, in which the actress played herself.

The debunkers' barrage of criticism and ridicule against MacLaine had no effect on the success of her books. As her spiritual search persisted, her next book, *Dancing in the Light* (1985), was a *New York Times* Best Seller. "I like to think of *Dancing in the Light* as a celebration of all my 'selves.'" She described herself as a seeker of her spiritual destiny and "a voice calling for peace in the world."

MacLaine's next successful memoir was *It's All in the Playing,* published in 1987. It told the story of her continuing spiritual journey that took her high into the Andes Mountains of Peru. As she searched for her past lives, she sought to understand their meaning, not simply who she might have been in earlier incarnations.

There was an odd side story to MacLaine's Peruvian expedition. Several years earlier, a young man named Charles Silva, while on vacation in Peru, said he met a girl in the Andes. There would be little unusual about the encounter except that Silva claimed she was an extraterrestrial named Rama. According to Silva, the attractive young woman did not look much different from someone you might meet in any city or town. After explaining that she was a "visitor from outer space," Rama and Silva began a friendship, and had intense discussions about everything from science to religion, metaphysics, UFOs, and their respective lives and beliefs. Those alleged conversations became the basis of Silva's 1977 book *Date with the Gods*.

When Silva was a guest on the *Joel Martin Show*, his first radio interview, many listeners phoned in, and challenged Silva vigorously. But none could shake his story that touched upon everything from the ancient pyramids to astral travel, Our Lady of Fatima, Peruvian Incas, "spiritual travel into the Cosmos," the Holy scriptures, politics, and even predictions for Earth's future. Silva's book left out very little that was metaphysical, explaining his experiences had transformed him from an agnostic into a far more "serious" person. He either had a phenomenal imagination or he'd had one of the most extraordinary adventures in the history of the universe. Was it science fiction or fact? That was for readers to decide, Silva declared.[42]

One person Shirley MacLaine wrote about was someone she named "David" who led her through a number of psychic encounters, notably an out-of-body experience in the Peruvian Andes. "David" was actually a "combination of several people," but mainly the fictitious name referred to none other than Charles Silva. Apart from the accounts by Silva and MacLaine, Cuzco and Machu Picchu were locations in Peru where there were frequent reports of UFO sightings. It was at Machu Picchu where MacLaine said she felt or sensed a "strange energy surge through [her]." It was also where she claimed she saw a "giant metallic craft."

In *It's All in the Playing*, MacLaine shared her discovery "that we have the power to design the world in which we live, and the strength to remake ourselves in the images of our dreams. I'm making all of it happen, good and bad, and I have the choice of how I'll relate to it and what I'll do about it." She became consumed with the question of whether each of us can "create our own reality," a major New Age premise.

MacLaine also raised the question of gender in her writings, suggesting that New Age "was addressing itself to leadership by women."[43] Noting the ancient Eastern belief in the energies known as yin and yang, MacLaine believed New Age was the time when yin, the female energy, and yang, the masculine, would finally become balanced, as opposed to the long-established male domination and control of civilization. It is a fact that many ancient cultures worshiped powerful goddesses and feminine deities. However, as female supremacy eroded, women who searched for a mystical path to follow found little support from family or society. The New Age movement was largely female-driven, and, in fact, coincided with the growth of the women's movement.

At MacLaine's height of acting fame, no one seriously suggested that her New Age writings and teachings were motivated by some crass desire for publicity. Few doubted her sincerity, even if they were unconvinced about her claims and beliefs. What critics failed to realize was how many Americans were drawn to MacLaine's metaphysical experiences, although most were reluctant to share their psychic or mystical occurrences with others for fear of ridicule or disapproval. MacLaine had begun to break down some of the resistance people felt when approaching the paranormal. To her goes significant credit for raising public consciousness about New Age ideas, and specifically for calling attention to such practices as channeling spirit guides. She believed people today are more spiritually and mentally ready to appreciate such ideas than they were in earlier generations.

One of the most popular and influential New Age authors to emerge in the latter years of the twentieth century was Ruth Montgomery. She'd been a syndicated columnist based in Washington,

D.C., where she'd reported on six U.S. presidents, before her interest turned to psychic phenomena. Between the 1960s and 1980s, Montgomery wrote a number of books that detailed the spirit world, reincarnation, healing, and soul transference, a concept she dubbed the "walk-ins" in a bestselling book, *Strangers Among Us*.

One of her many books, *A World Beyond*, published in 1972, is an example of the kind of research into the paranormal she pursued. Montgomery had been a close friend of the well-known medium Arthur Ford who'd gained considerable public notoriety conducting a much debated séance to communicate with Houdini's spirit, and then, years later, a controversial televised séance with former Episcopalian bishop James Pike. Montgomery's friendship with Ford remained intact until the day he died in January 1971, and apparently well beyond that. Montgomery claimed Ford continued to communicate with her from the spirit world via automatic writing. Ford's discarnate spirit was the "source of the written messages [that] seemingly [came] without the conscious thought of a living person, by means of a typewriter or a pencil lightly to a piece of paper," Montgomery explained. Remember, this was in an era prior to computer technology.

In recent decades, the same automatic writing phenomenon has been reported by some mediums utilizing a computer. It may seem strange to seek information about the afterlife by traveling into cyberspace. But the joining of ancient beliefs with our most modern technology suggests that when it comes to the need to tap into our deepest, most heartfelt emotions, such as grief, the tools we use are not as important to the bereaved as the messages of comfort offered from the hereafter.

In Montgomery's case, the communications she received from Ford's spirit comprised the essence of what she wrote in *A World Beyond*. She provided "vivid descriptions of [the] afterlife," emphasizing, "this book [is] not the [product] of my imagination or conscious knowledge."

This was not Montgomery's first foray into automatic writing, or automatic typing, to be more precise. She'd already successfully written two earlier books that had been dictated by what she called "a high-minded control" named "Lily." That material became a substantial part of her books *A Search for the Truth* and *Here and Hereafter*.

Later in her career, Montgomery wrote about "walk-ins," a theory she popularized in *Strangers Among Us*, written in 1979. A walk-in, she explained, was a being or entity that took over a body when the original soul had departed it. The concept was an ancient one. Elderly Indian yoga masters were believed to "take over" the physical bodies of young men whose deaths were untimely.

Montgomery gave the idea a New Age spin when she wrote, "A walk-in is a high-minded entity who is permitted to take over the body of another human being who wishes to depart. The motivation of a walk-in is humanitarian." There are "tens of thousands of them." Montgomery continued the story of the walk-ins in *Threshold to Tomorrow* (1982), claiming that throughout history such towering figures as Moses, Jesus, and Muhammad were walk-ins. There were others, she said, including Christopher Columbus, George Washington, Abigail Adams, Benjamin Franklin, Mohandas Gandhi, Thomas Jefferson, and Abraham Lincoln.

In other words, Montgomery was suggesting that "some of the greatest spiritual and political leaders" who ever lived have been walk-ins. Often, walk-ins are people who have gone through an extremely disturbing or distressing experience. "Walk-ins are harbingers of a new order that will bring peace on earth in the twenty-first century," Montgomery wrote. "Our modern walk-ins are intent on teaching us the skills for survival," she explained. "One of their goals is to forestall World War III."

In 1985, Montgomery wrote *Aliens Among Us* in which she expanded on the theory by proposing the idea of "extraterrestrial walk-ins." The suggestion was that souls came to Earth from other planets to occupy human bodies, and she offered examples of such individuals in "case studies." Notwithstanding the inevitable criticism from debunkers and skeptics, walk-ins became an immensely popular subject during the New Age, discussed, debated, and written about. In fact, during the years that Montgomery wrote her many books, from the 1960s to the 1980s, her impact on New Age beliefs was such that it was unlikely one could engage in a conversation about the hereafter or spirit world without raising her name.

Montgomery's books enjoyed vast success and influenced millions of Americans. It's worth mentioning at least one reason why the books met with success, even though so-called serious scientists and parapsychologists ignored virtually all New Age writings. While the scientists tenaciously pursued evidence for psychic events by designing "strictly controlled" experiments to test psi, Montgomery understood that millions were eager to know about life after death, and she answered her readers.

In *A Search for the Truth* she asked, "Why were we born? Did we live before, and is birth, like death, simply another step in a continuous progression of the soul? Do personality and memory survive our passage through the door that man calls death? Do we have a mission in life? Is there a Divine plan?" She answered the questions in clear and uncomplicated writing that never equivocated on the subject. There was no ambiguity in her message: there was a hereafter that awaited us when we passed from earth. Montgomery described the spirit world, not unlike Swedenborg had more than two centuries earlier. There was very little mention of anything scientific, and she disregarded her critics. What she wrote went to the heart of what people most wanted to know: the reassurance of "life hereafter." Writing as she did during and after the Vietnam War era, and while Cold War tensions and fears were still a reality, Montgomery's explanations—even those that had nothing but her word to support them—attracted a large and loyal following.[44]

Several movements achieved prominence in the seventies: the "consciousness movement," the "human potential movement," and the "women's movement." Each triggered a torrent of books, tapes, seminars, workshops, and lectures. During the 1970s, Americans were also introduced to channeling, a New Age variation of mediumship. Edgar Cayce's trance readings, and Ruth Montgomery's channeled messages, paved the way for others to follow.

Belief in the idea that there are walk-ins and spirits that appear to those who have entered a trance state, such as JZ Knight, gained prominence in the latter half of the twentieth century and continued right through to the new millennium. If not a multi-thousand-year-old spirit, it is an extraterrestrial. If not an extraterrestrial, it is an actual angelic figure possessing a human being so as to communicate. Of course, as skeptics argue, anyone can be a prophet of sorts mainly by self-declaration.

Arguably, the New Age's first and most influential discarnate entity to be channeled was "Seth," who became the subject of a series of highly successful books by author Jane Roberts.

One evening toward the end of 1963, Jane Roberts Butts (1929–1984), an upstate New York housewife and writer, and her husband, Robert, were tinkering with a Ouija board. Although long dismissed by skeptics as little more than a toy, the Ouija board has often produced some startling results as the planchette, a wooden pointer, moves from letter to letter, spelling out messages from the afterlife or perhaps another psychic dimension. That's exactly what Roberts said happened to her and her husband. The couple discovered communication taking shape from an entity that identified itself as "Seth." Roberts claimed that prior to then she had no "psychic background." That soon changed when Roberts found she could easily enter a trance state in order to receive messages from Seth.

Presumably a male presence, Seth described himself as "an energy personality essence, no longer in the physical body." At first, Roberts thought the message had originated in her subconscious. However, once she'd repeated aloud what she psychically heard, she realized she "was speaking for Seth while in a trance state." In other words, when Roberts entered an altered state, Seth "borrowed her body" to use it to contact "the world of the living," she wrote, adding that she never referred to Seth as a spirit. He'd "achieved independent status."

So began a relationship between Roberts and Seth, the discarnate entity that would produce a huge amount of channeled messages through Roberts, estimated at six thousand typewritten pages that she called "the Seth material," and first published in 1970. By then, she wrote, "nearly eighty volumes of notebooks [had been] filled with Seth material."

A series of Seth books followed that enthralled New Age readers during the 1970s and 1980s. In hundreds of trance sessions, Seth offered his unique philosophy and psychology on a wide range of subject matter, and also proved to have "clairvoyant abilities." The transcripts and notes of those sessions comprised a prolific, nearly inexhaustible, outpouring of channeled materials about consciousness, the soul, dreams, astral projection, reincarnation, health, the "meaning of religion," and how people relate to the "creator," the architect of the universe. After the first Seth book was published, people from all over the country requested Seth's advice. "We held sessions for those most in need," Roberts explained, and the channeled answers were mailed to those who wrote.

What exactly did Seth communicate through Roberts? "Now

the information in this book [*Seth Speaks*] is being directed to some extent through the inner senses of the woman [Roberts] who is in trance as I write it," Seth said. But, "Seth speaks for himself," Roberts noted.

"Your scientists are finally learning what philosophers have known for centuries, that mind can influence matter. They still have to discover the fact that mind creates and forms matter," Seth explained, adding, "Quite literally, the 'inner self' forms the body by magically transforming thoughts and emotions into physical counterparts. You grow the body."

Because Seth through Jane Roberts channeled a huge amount of material, his communications occurred in numerous sessions that were recorded. Often Seth offered advice, as in this example from a session in April 1970. "Imagine as vividly as you can the existence of inner sense. Clear from your mind all thoughts and worries. Be receptive. Very gently listen, not to physical sounds but to sounds that come through the inner senses."

Roberts said she found it virtually effortless to slip into a self-induced trance state in order that Seth might come forth, and invariably he did. In a session held one evening in May 1970, the entity expounded on the meaning of the soul. "The soul perceives all experience directly," Seth said. "Most experiences of which you are aware come packaged in physical wrappings, and you take the [covering] for the experience itself, and do not think of looking inside. The soul's perceptions are [occurrences] that are mental." Seth continued at some length, elaborating about the nature and potential of the soul: "You continually create your soul as it continually creates you."

In other trance sittings, Seth turned his attention to "after-death choices and the mechanics of transition," saying through Jane Roberts, that there is an endless array of experiences available to us following death. Among them is reincarnation, which Seth described as more complex than merely choosing to endure a new bodily subsistence.

In answer to questions about predestation, Seth replied, "You are not programmed. Nothing happens because it must happen."

In a later session, Seth stated that the external world is an expression of the internal one. The channeled entity gave illustrations that readers could apply to themselves.

"You are not now what you were ten minutes earlier," Seth concluded. "You are not the same being physically, psychologically, spiritually, or psychically, and ten minutes later you will be different again."

The voluminous materials were transcribed and formed the text of the Seth books. Roberts remarked that when she read what she'd said in trance, she was surprised. It is often claimed by psychics and mediums who enter deep trances, that what they say is not remembered when they are no longer in the altered state.

When Roberts entered the trance state so that Seth could utilize her to communicate, her entire persona seemed to transform. Thin with short dark hair and horn-rimmed glasses, Roberts—prim, quiet, and studious-looking—was in her mid-thirties when her adventure with Seth began. However, when the entity imparted his messages through Roberts, there was a noticeable alteration in her appearance. Seth, she said, always had her remove her eyeglasses. Then as the channeled messages began, Roberts's "expressions and gestures changed dramatically to those of Seth." Roberts's eyes were sometimes partially open. Rarely were they closed entirely during the trance sessions. In addition to becoming quite animated as Seth spoke through her, Roberts's voice also changed, becoming deeper and often more assertive.[45]

Roberts was never comfortable with the media attention she and Seth attracted, and she granted few interviews. No one could accuse her of exploiting Seth's recognition. When the *Joel Martin*

Show invited her to appear, Roberts graciously declined, but instead corresponded via mail and adorned her written response with a cartoon, presumably of Seth smoking a cigarette. In fact, it wasn't unusual for Roberts to light up a cigarette while she was in trance.

Skeptics, as you'd expect, ridiculed not only Seth, but also the entire notion of channeling, and rejected out-of-hand that Seth dictated books. A huge number of New Age readers, ignoring debunkers, remained faithful to the Seth books, sending them to the bestseller lists, and into many printings, as well as generating lively debates about them. Roberts died of natural causes in 1984, after a lengthy illness.

Roberts was considered a channeler as opposed to a medium. As a matter of definition, some psychics made a distinction between mediumship and channeling. Mediums claim they can summon the spirits of loved ones related to those who come to them for sittings or séances, as was the case during the great Age of Spiritualism. Channelers, on the other hand, while in trance, more often call upon ancient discarnate entities or "spirit guides" that offer up copious philosophical messages for humankind, as opposed to personal communications from departed loved ones meant for a specific individual. But where in the late nineteenth century, mediums received all the attention, in the late twentieth century, the attention had turned to channelers and their spirit guides. Among the most celebrated of these guides was the entity Ramtha, a discarnate personality who qualified as the most controversial.

Communications from Ramtha came through a channeler named JZ Knight. Together Knight and Ramtha became lightning rods for a storm of debate. When interest in channeling reached its zenith in the mid-1980s, Ramtha rode the crest of the popularity, sharing his brand of New Age philosophy.

Judith Hampton, later known as JZ Knight, was born in 1946

into a poverty-stricken family. Raised with her brothers and sisters in New Mexico, home was a "shanty," and their lives were made immeasurably worse by an abusive and alcoholic father, a long-suffering mother, and a young sister who died tragically. Judy was also a victim of sexual assault at the hands of an uncle. This was an incident that she said left permanent emotional scars, robbed her innocence, and caused her to mistrust men. From that scarred beginning, compounded by a failed marriage and two children, Judy had the rare inner strength to become a successful businesswoman. Her business enterprise took the pretty blonde to Tacoma, Washington, where, in time, she remarried. Judy would become well known as JZ Knight.

At some point, JZ had a psychic reading in which she was told she would someday meet what the psychic called "the One," a message that made no sense to her at the time. However, one day in 1977 when JZ was at home, "to my utter shock and amazement, there stood a giant man at the other end of my kitchen just standing there, aglow. This thing was made [entirely] of light," she recalled. JZ summoned the courage to exclaim, "You are so beautiful. Who are you?"

With a sparkling smile, he answered, "I am Ramtha, the Enlightened One. I have come to help you over the ditch." Although JZ did not understand what was meant by "the ditch," the entity who identified itself as Ramtha captivated her interest, although she admitted she was bewildered and speechless. So began the strange relationship between JZ Knight and the being of light named Ramtha, purporting to be thirty thousand years old.

The experience at first, she said, left her "numb." When she shared the experience with her husband, he was both supportive and understanding. As JZ and her husband thought about what she might have done to precipitate the extraordinary experience, she could recall only that she and her husband had dabbled with the short-lived fad about pyramid power, popular during the 1970s, which claimed that pyramid-shaped objects could preserve meat and sharpen razor blades. The Knights had explored so-called pyramid energy by making small paper pyramids prior to Ramtha's first appearance. However there was no way to draw a conclusion that the events were connected.

When the entity next materialized to JZ he told her, "Beloved woman, you will become a light unto the world." It wasn't long after that when she clearly heard Ramtha's voice, psychically, and began to channel the entity's messages for others who gathered locally, curious to hear what Ramtha had to say. At first, Knight conducted weekly "dialogues" throughout the United States. Then she traveled to Canada, England, Germany, Australia, and New Zealand. Many who heard the channeled communications became fascinated, and soon Ramtha had a sizable following. By the 1980s, Knight had achieved a reputation that established her as the "most successful of the channels that grew up around the New Age movement," according to the *Encyclopedia of Occultism and Parapsychology*.[46] One of those who offered up warm praise about Ramtha's wisdom was the motion picture star Shirley MacLaine.

The Ramtha sessions continued until 1987 when Knight ended the popular "dialogues," and, instead, founded "Ramtha's School of Enlightenment" in Yelm, Washington, on property that was once a ranch. Many of her students relocated to that rustic part of the Pacific Northwest. At one point, some three thousand had joined Knight's school, and those who participated had closer access to her, and therefore Ramtha's teachings. Other interested followers made do by reading published transcripts or purchasing videotapes.

Knight had garnered an enormous amount of public attention, and also became the target of "punishing" media criticism because of the skepticism about whether her channeling was genuine communication from a spirit dimension, a product of Knight's subconscious, or a calculated fraud. Others seized upon the wealth and fame Knight had amassed from channeling Ramtha; some of her harshest critics were past students.

In 1987, facing a torrent of controversy, the forty-year-old channeler decided it was time to tell her side of the story. To answer her detractors Knight wrote her autobiography, *A State of Mind*.[47] But that failed to satisfy opponents, and verbal assaults against Knight continued into the 1990s. The negative attention was exacerbated by a publicized breakup with her second husband, Jeff Knight. Between the mid-1980s and mid-1990s, the channeled "wisdom" of Ramtha was also the subject of several books written by other authors. Knight's school somehow survived, and many of the disputed divorce issues were ultimately settled in her favor.

One other New Age channeler deserving mention is Jach Pursel, who brought forth information from an entity named "Lazaris." Pursel was an insurance-company executive who was meditating one day when he experienced a vision in which he claimed he saw a being that identified itself as Lazaris. Pursel eventually channeled it on a regular basis, offering counsel to family and friends. As word spread and Lazaris became better known, Pursel attracted hundreds of people to his channeling sessions, and soon was traveling throughout the country. Among the celebrities whose interest the channeled messages attracted was Shirley MacLaine.

An interesting question asked of Lazaris was one that many people were curious about: Why had channeled entities made themselves known at this particular time, meaning during the New Age movement of the 1970s and 1980s? Through Pursel, Lazaris answered, "We are here to teach you how to find solutions, to teach you the changes that you need to make in your own consciousness. We're here to teach people how to [transform] negative energy into positive energy to give you knowledge to help you understand yourself and your world more completely." Lazaris explained that long-held conventional answers have failed to accomplish their goals, and channeled entities came at this particular time to guide us as we search for spiritual resolutions. The full text of the spirit guide's answer appeared in the book, *Lazaris Interviews* (1988), from where the above excerpt was taken.[48] During the 1980s, Pursel wrote several books devoted to the teachings of Lazaris. But the reason given for why guides appeared to channelers at the end of the twentieth century was, nevertheless, also another way of saying that when the student is ready, the teacher will come.

Critics and skeptics, of course, regarded all channeling as a hoax, charging that channelers pretended to be deep in trance in order to receive supposed spiritual truths from ancient, wizened entities. In some instances, channelers were accused of simply inventing both the spirit beings and the allegedly profound knowledge from past millennia, going as far as altering their voices and facial expressions. In other cases, channelers were thought to be self-inducing a trance state, and accessing their communications, not from an entity, but from the channeler's own subconscious.

When the channeling craze precipitously declined in popularity by the late 1980s, so did the interest in Ramtha, as well as other channeled beings that had attracted New Age notoriety. Psychic debunkers rushed forward to claim credit for the demise of channeling, but gave themselves more credit than they deserved. The fascination with New Age channeling faded for several other reasons. For one thing, people had grown tired of disembodied or otherworldly entities preaching "ancient wisdom" that was couched in ways that did not apply to individuals, but instead offered generalizations about the dismal state of the world, and the need for peace and love, sensible and timeless advice for humanity that was too often ignored in favor of war, conflict, and hatred.

The spirit guides were offering counsel not unlike centuries of teachings by traditional religions. But many people sought answers to their individual problems and questions. By the time Jane Roberts, author of the *Seth* books, died in 1984, channeled entities had nearly exhausted all they had to say. Growing numbers of New Age types had become increasingly restless. Every channeled spirit purported to be several thousand years old, and offered the same or similar wisdom, or as some critics called them, tired platitudes and clichés, messages that could neither be proven genuine nor be used in a practical way.

The other criticism of channelers had to do with the perception that by offering channeled advice to students about investing, their purpose was as much material as it was spiritual. In the spirit of good old American capitalism, New Age had, for some, become a highly profitable business. It led many to question whether that was the only intention for those invoking channeled entities. Where was the spiritual component in this metaphysical equation? Skeptics and debunkers jumped on the "big business" aspect of New Age.

Still other skeptics, mainly from the psychiatric community, believed that for those self-described channelers who really believed they were inhabited by spirits, it was all a form of delusion or even multiple personality disorder. Channeling, as an auditory hallucination, medical skeptics said, could be controlled by antipsychotic drugs. And still other psychiatrists suggested that although there might be some truly disturbed people who really manifested other personalities, the reinforcement and encouragement they received from followers only convinced them that they were truly inhabited. Others, skeptics said, simply followed the lead of psychotic behavior in hopes of achieving celebrity and the riches that went along with it for themselves.

However, there were still a number of sincere believers who'd also grown uneasy with the lavish lifestyles that channeled spirit entities had apparently provided some, such as Knight. It was not much different from the criticism aimed at certain TV evangelists who ceaselessly pleaded with viewers for their dollars to fight the Devil and his minions, only to learn that millions of dollars in donations went to luxury living for the TV ministers. Just how much a channeler or any psychic practitioner should charge for his or her abilities remains the subject of an ongoing debate.

As channeling fell out of vogue, the continuing interest in communication with the hereafter led to the modern mediumship movement by the late 1980s, with the publication of *We Don't Die*, by Joel Martin and Patricia Romanowski. Mediums provided people with messages from their deceased loved ones rather than arcane philosophy or unknowable prophecies for future centuries proclaimed by allegedly ancient spirit beings.

If prehistoric wisdom and counsel through a trance channeler wasn't your cup of tea, the "explosion" of New Age authors and motivational speakers were ready to provide guidance and direction to the "seekers." Whether the ideas were new or revelatory could be debated, but they certainly found an eager audience. There is no dismissing the change in consciousness brought about by New Age writings. Millions were drawn to the books and lectures offered by the "experts" and gurus, despite the protestations by leaders of traditional religions that maintained the Scriptures provided all that was necessary to guide us through life. It is a debate that continues to this day and shows no sign that it is nearing a resolution.

The late Elizabeth Clare Prophet made her name as head of the controversial Church Universal and Triumphant, founded with her late husband, Mark, who died in 1973. She'd been alternately called a spiritual leader, a guru, or a cult leader, especially after she moved her operations to Montana in 1986, after its years in California. Among the accusations made against Prophet was that she "brainwashed" followers. She built her church, largely motivated by her belief in the "'I AM' Religious Activity," a form of Theosophy that perceives the "Ascended Masters," notably St. Germain, as guiding the world in the direction of a New Age of "light and truth."[49]

There was no disputing Prophet's success, however, when a representative of her movement was interviewed on radio. His answers were convoluted, evasive, and robotlike, as if the responses were programmed in advance. It's been alleged that church adherents were indoctrinated, worked long hours, were deprived of sleep, and ate insufficiently. Yet, some former members had no regrets about joining. Was Prophet running a New Age cult or a religious movement? You decide.

Promoters of the New Age could also be defined as part of a subversive movement, undermining the traditional success-oriented values of the mid-twentieth century. In fact, borrowing from the late 1960s and early 1970s counterculture rebels, authors and promoters even cast themselves as types of conspiratorial prophets proselytizing the New Age values. One of the authors was the influential and critically acclaimed Marilyn Ferguson, who wrote *The Aquarian Conspiracy* in 1980.[50] Her explanation and analysis of the movement was straightforward. She described the Aquarian conspiracy as a "leaderless but powerful network working to bring about radical change in the United States." It had neither a "political doctrine" nor a "manifesto." Ferguson explained that "its members have broken with certain key elements of Western thought."

The "Aquarian Conspirators," as Ferguson defined those who'd embarked on the spiritual journey through the tangle of New Age ideas and beliefs, consisted of a "benign conspiracy for a new human agenda [that] has triggered the most rapid cultural realignment in history." She described it glowingly as a "new mind" and "the ascendance of a startling worldview."

Although there was wide diversity among those engaged in the discovery of New Age ideas, Ferguson also noted that they were connected in their effort to advance to new heights of realization and achievement. Ferguson suggested that the Aquarian Conspirators, as she called them, did not have as a goal some organized overthrow of the establishment, the rallying cry for the 1960s counterculture. But once New Age people made "personal change," they began to consider options for other aspects of their lives. "Work and relationships, health, and political power" were some of the areas of their lives they examined, Ferguson noted. As the New Age or Aquarian Conspiracy grew, it extended to virtually every community across the country, and even reached international dimensions. It was, despite Ferguson's disclaimer, a real politicization of the New Age movement, a transformative philosophy that said that mechanisms of self-empowerment, having derived from the teachings of Theosophy, could be the planks in the platform of a new politics. And this helped define the new millennium.

Those who criticized the New Age as a condemnation of the self-centered "Me Generation" proved mistaken. True, there weren't the strident, sometimes, thunderous protests and angry demonstrations that marked much of the 1960s. But once personal transformations had been made, many who were part of the New Age in the 1970s and 1980s also turned their attention to various causes. As Marilyn Ferguson explained, those who had "shared experiences," "connected with each other," and increasingly with larger numbers of people, to call attention to various social, political, and ecological concerns.

As you can imagine, fundamentalist and evangelic Christian leaders seized upon the book's title. The word "conspiracy" suggested some nefarious plot by hordes of New Age types in league with the dark forces of Satan poised to take over the minds of Americans. The radical religious attack on the tenets of the book are still rampant today, over a decade into the new century, by the political right, which is eager to lay the blame for all the shortcomings in Western society on writers like Ferguson.

In *The Aquarian Conspiracy*, Ferguson foresaw a "radical renewal." That, some critics suggested, went beyond optimism, labeling it an unrealistically utopian scenario of the future. Ferguson's rosy prediction was that as technology and transportation became increasingly sophisticated, communication would become virtually instantaneous and the world would seem much smaller. She believed people would become "increasingly aware of each other, open to each other," and could then "enrich and empower" each other. Ferguson expressed optimism that "from science and from the spiritual experience of millions, we are discovering our capacity for endless awakenings in a universe of endless surprises."[51]

But even Ferguson questioned whether the world's predicaments could be easily solved. In fact, as we have seen, the problems she considered in 1980 have remained dilemmas into the twenty-first century: world hunger, nuclear threats, human rights abuses, and war. That did not even address the further crises faced in the new millennium: global terrorism, ecological concerns, and alarming climate changes. It was a New Age, clad in the wonders of modern science and technology, but with disturbing similarities to the same evils and disasters that have persistently plagued humankind.

9

*Hillary Clinton's
New Age Odyssey*

It was a decade after the notoriety over Nancy Reagan's astrologer Joan Quigley broke into the headlines with Mike Deaver's revelations about an astrologer in the White House, Joan Quigley's own book, and Nancy Reagan's memoirs about the events surrounding President Reagan and the paranormal. In the 1990s, it was First Lady Hillary Clinton's turn to capture headlines across the country to signal another paranormal flap at the White House.

Just in time for Bill Clinton's campaign for a second term in 1996, the question of whether Hillary Rodham Clinton was having personal conversations with the spirit of the late Eleanor Roosevelt broke in the press. Was it true? Was there a medium channeling spirits or divining the future at the White House? Absolutely not, thundered the Clinton spokespeople. But the source of the story had broken major news before, and he stood behind what he said.

It was in the spring of 1996 when Americans first learned that Mrs. Clinton, later Senator Clinton of New York and then Secretary of State Clinton, had delved into the New Age with the help of a psychologist named Jean Houston, characterized by critics as a "psychic philosopher." Reporter Bob Woodward, who investigated the story of Watergate for *The Washington Post* and then wrote *All the President's Men* with fellow reporter Carl Bernstein, first disclosed Mrs. Clinton's "talks" with the late Mrs. Roosevelt in his 1996 book *The Choice*, a behind-the-scenes story of the Clintons.[1]

For those who were unfamiliar with Houston, she'd gained prominence in the human potential movement, was a past president of the Association for Humanistic Psychology, and authored several books related to the subjects she taught, such as the "creative process" and "altered states of consciousness." While still a student, Houston had a mystical experience about the unity of the universe, in the form of a revelation. As a result, she decided to dedicate her life to helping others discover their own strengths and potentials.

Houston was attending college in New York when she lost her sight in an accident. Several months later, she had another supernatural experience in which she saw herself twenty years in the future. Her older self told her not to be concerned with her prospects or expectations; she would find them both exciting and fulfilling. Houston's sight returned, and she began to earnestly study history and philosophy. Later, her studies included archaeology and ancient religions, and travel to Greece. Ultimately, she earned her graduate degrees, including a doctorate in psychology and the philosophy of religion.

By the 1960s, Houston and her husband, Robert Masters, began writing. Their first book dealt with hallucinogenic drugs such as

LSD. One conclusion they presented was that "authentic religious and mystical experiences occur among drug subjects." In the 1970s, Houston and Masters turned their attention to studying altered states that did not require drugs. Among the techniques they researched and wrote about were meditation and visualization. Houston's reputation grew as she wrote and taught about the New Age design for the "transformation" of human consciousness across the entire planet.

Houston detailed much of her hypothesis in *The Possible Human* in 1982. "We have entered upon one of the greatest explorations of all time as we begin to probe the mystery of the brain," she wrote. "It is complex beyond our wildest imaginings. Here is encoded the wisdom of the millennia and the dreams of tomorrow."[2]

Houston met Hillary Clinton at Camp David, the presidential retreat, where the Clintons, who were seeking advice to strengthen the presidency by examining different approaches to problems, had invited a group of well-known self-help authors. Houston, whose approach to solutions was clearly "out-of-the-box thinking," soon became an influence in Mrs. Clinton's life and ultimately a source of controversy. Houston was able to explain to Mrs. Clinton how the first lady "was carrying the burden of five thousand years of history when women were subservient."[3] The two women quickly developed a rapport and explored ways the Clinton presidency could improve society.

Bill and Hillary Clinton belonged to a new generation of thinkers and political leaders. Baby boomers who came of age in the 1960s and who thrived on the New Age approaches to old-time problems, they were in stark—and some would say, frightening—contrast to the Reagans or George H. W. and Barbara Bush. The Clintons were new. Like Kennedy and Nixon in an earlier generation, who spoke to the fact that they were the first presidential candidates born in the twentieth century, a century "tempered by war," the Clintons were a break from the old order. They had been born after the war into a generation that had challenged conventional thinking in the 1960s. As such, they represented a threat to the old order represented by George H. W. Bush, a World War II veteran.

In an alignment of paradigms, probably more typical in America than in most other countries of the world, Bill and Hillary Clinton versus the older generation that feared their coming were much like Barack Obama versus the Clinton generation. In 2008, Senator Obama and Senator Clinton opposed each other for the Democratic Party's presidential nomination. America is a country of immigrants where second and third generations can advance socially through the ranks of power and wealth with an astonishing rapidity. So it was with Bill and Hillary Clinton, both from working-class families, who became Ivy League–trained attorneys and rose to political prominence in Arkansas, New York, and nationally.

They were, indeed, a threat to the established order when Bill Clinton became president, not only because they were young and untested and because Bill and Hillary were more political partners than a typical chief executive and his first lady, but because their ideas posed a challenge to the establishment. Hillary, for example, saw the power of transformational social change, believed in that force not only as an exciting intellectual field of study but as a real political force, especially given the power of the courts in such decisions as the 1954 *Brown v Board of Education* Supreme Court ruling, which ended de jure segregation in American public schools. Hillary, like civil rights leader, attorney, and Supreme Court Justice Thurgood Marshall, believed that true social justice would come from the courts, the protectors of civil rights in the United States.

She had written a senior paper at Wellesley College, one of the elite of the Seven Sisters schools, on so-called neo-Marxist activist Saul Alinsky, whose 1946 *Reveille for Radicals* inspired the quote, "There is only the fight." Alinsky also wrote that "true revolutionaries do not flaunt their radicalism." "They cut their hair," he wrote. And they fight their fight "from within." In other words, true social change comes not only from taking to the streets in peaceful protest, the path of the Reverend Dr. Martin Luther King, Jr., but from revolutionary work inside the bureaucracy, the courts and the legislature, like Thurgood Marshall. This is the path that Hillary Clinton chose both as first lady of Arkansas and of the United States, especially when she advocated a universal federal health care mandate. Revolutionary? Not if you believed that Republican President Teddy Roosevelt was a wild-eyed revolutionary, advocating public health care mandates and busting up the big trusts. Not if you believed that House Speaker Nancy Pelosi was a revolutionary, arguing in 2009 for a "carrier mandate" for health insurance similar to the states' carrier mandate for automobile insurance. Hillary Clinton fought for what she believed was social justice inside the system, but she was taken less than seriously by the Senate and the House, both of which chambers looked upon her as only a first lady and not an advocate for serious legislation. She was marginalized.

However, first ladies, whether of a statehouse or of the White House, were not to be taken lightly, and Hillary Clinton looked to one of our nation's most well-respected and well-loved first ladies, Eleanor Roosevelt. Eleanor, who helped found the United Nations, was tireless. She stood by her husband when he ran for public office as a wheelchair-bound polio victim, vilified by right-wing Republicans as a socialist at best and a neo-communist at worst. But President Franklin D. Roosevelt understood more than most that during the Great Depression, communism was a real threat. In Russia, communism had offered hope to a starving population ravaged not only by the czar but by the financial collapse that was creeping across Europe toward the end of World War I.

At the same time as the Great Depression was engulfing the United States, wiping out the value of entire companies, farms, and homesteads, the Dust Bowl was forcing a migration from Oklahoma and the Texas panhandle to the West Coast where the "Oakies" were subjected to violence and abuse from wealthy California growers. It was a bitter harvest, to be sure.

Across the Atlantic and the Pacific, war clouds were gathering. The Japanese empire was looking at China as a conquest and Southeast Asia as a source of oil. In Europe, the rise to power of Adolf Hitler and the National Socialist Party threatened not only Poland and Czechoslovakia, but France as well. Yet a hostile legislature thwarted Roosevelt's attempts at economic reform and rearmament for the coming war at every turn. The Republicans referred to "that cripple in the White House," and archconservatives not only tried to assassinate the president-elect in 1933, missing him and killing the mayor of Chicago instead, but conspired to overthrow the government in a military coup. Eleanor watched all this with a deep fear for her husband's life.

Through it all, especially through the horrific days of World War II when FDR's gamble—to allow the attack on Pearl Harbor so as to force the Congress's hand in declaring war on Japan, which would result in Hitler's declaring war on the United States—was on the knife-edge between failure and success, Eleanor was steadfast. She supported her husband and fought her own private battles against the right wing of the American political spectrum that opposed him.

So it was that Hillary Clinton, whose husband was facing what she described in a television interview as a "vast right wing conspiracy," ever loyal, looked to Eleanor Roosevelt as a role model. There were other loyal and steadfast first ladies such as Mamie

Eisenhower, Jackie Kennedy, Lady Bird Johnson, and Pat Nixon she could have looked to, but Eleanor Roosevelt, who had become larger than life in the 1950s due to her advocacy for the United Nations, stood out in stark relief. As Speaker Newt Gingrich led the Republican charge to retake Congress from the Democrats, what could Hillary Clinton do to protect Bill Clinton? What would Eleanor Roosevelt have done in a situation like this? There was only one way to find out: Ask her.

Dr. Jean Houston quickly realized that Mrs. Clinton was "really a serious Eleanor Roosevelt aficionado."[4] Mrs. Clinton had long compared herself to Mrs. Roosevelt, and in his book, Bob Woodward noted that, to Mrs. Clinton, Mrs. Roosevelt was "her archetypal, spiritual partner."[5] Eleanor Roosevelt began to redefine the role of first lady, advocating important humanitarian causes aimed at easing the misery of the unemployed and hungry during the Great Depression in the 1930s, and was a strong figure during World War II. She traveled tirelessly, visiting hundreds of thousands of GIs and countless hospitalized servicemen here and abroad. She added to her causes, women's rights and civil rights. After FDR's death in 1945, Mrs. Roosevelt became deeply involved in the newly formed United Nations, and remained active and outspoken until her death in 1962 at the age of seventy-eight. She was the most controversial, idealistic, and socially conscious first lady in the nation's history. Of course, First Lady Hillary Clinton saw her as a role model.

In confidence, Mrs. Clinton told Houston "she had always felt the presence of Eleanor Roosevelt in the White House," wrote Christopher Andersen in *Bill and Hillary: The Marriage*.[6] "I was a huge admirer of [her]. I wanted so much to be like her, to make a real contribution as first lady. But after three years in the White House I felt stymied. I wanted to know what this brilliant woman would have done if she were alive today," Mrs. Clinton said.

And so, Houston urged Mrs. Clinton to "search further and dig deeper for her connections to Mrs. Roosevelt," by engaging in what Houston called "reflective meditation." Mrs. Clinton was encouraged to sit and "talk" to Mrs. Roosevelt, ask questions, and then imagine what her answers would be. Following Houston's instructions, Mrs. Clinton focused on Mrs. Roosevelt's passion, tenacity, and championing of the poverty-stricken. In her dialogues with the late first lady, Mrs. Clinton talked about "the obstacles, the criticism, the loneliness [Mrs. Roosevelt] felt. Hillary's identification with Mrs. Roosevelt was intense and personal," Woodward said.[7]

Houston urged Mrs. Clinton to play the role of Mrs. Roosevelt, to answer as if she were the former first lady. Before long, according to Christopher Andersen, White House staff members heard Mrs. Clinton, "behind closed doors, having animated—if one-sided—conversations with Eleanor's ghost." Mrs. Clinton said she wanted to know what Mrs. Roosevelt would have done in this situation, how she would have handled matters. "She usually responds by telling me to buck up or at least to grow skin as thick as a rhinoceros."[8]

Houston also encouraged Mrs. Clinton to engage in conversations with other great historical figures, such as Gandhi. One figure Mrs. Clinton declined to converse with was Jesus, saying it "would be too personal."[9] Houston also tried to explain that she employed a visualization technique with Mrs. Clinton that teaches how to get in touch with "the wonder of the inner and outer worlds that is our legacy." "There was no séance! There were no spooks!" she declared emphatically.[10] *New Republic* magazine agreed that "Eleanor Roosevelt was not raised from the dead!" And the sessions with Houston were "not a spiritual event," a point that could be argued, considering Houston's long belief and interest in the spirit world and channeling, and the nature of the "reflective meditations" Mrs. Clinton engaged in.[11]

Houston was among the many New Age or human potential figures who believed that a channeler, while in a trance, was in contact with the "collective unconscious," as Carl Jung called it. Or maybe it was a multiverse of quantum entanglement as many theoretical physicists described it. Houston claimed that a "finely tuned mind [could] reach back in time, tapping into the vestiges of our evolutionary ancestors that she says still exist in our brains," said *Newsweek*.[12] It was a form of psychic nonlocality.

Houston believed those in a trance could increase their ESP abilities, including clairvoyance, precognition, and telepathy. In fact, earlier in her career, Houston carried out dream telepathy experiments. And she had connections to Edgar Mitchell, the Apollo 14 astronaut and a respected figure in parapsychology research, who founded his own institute to study extrasensory phenomena. Her denials notwithstanding, Houston clearly had a long history of paranormal interest. Whether Mrs. Clinton embraced all or only some of Houston's beliefs is uncertain.

Likely embarrassed, Mrs. Clinton did her best to play down her "talks" with Mrs. Roosevelt. For her part, Mrs. Clinton issued a written denial that Houston or anyone else was her spiritual adviser. The denials hardly calmed the debate. Rabid right-wing television commentator John McLaughlin, himself a former Jesuit, blasted Mrs. Clinton's "meditative dialogues" with Mrs. Roosevelt's spirit as "spooky, kooky, and dorky." He hollered that, "New Age, quote-unquote, theology is really very un-Christian, very un-Jewish, very untraditional in its genesis and expression." These were the rants of someone who had not read Kabbalah.

Taking a surprisingly softer position was the respected Jesuit magazine *America*, which came to Mrs. Clinton and Houston's defense. "They mock what they do not understand," the magazine concluded about critics of the "conversations" with Mrs. Roosevelt. The Jesuits certainly do not consider themselves New Age, nor would they ever consider engaging in séances, yet they are taught to pray "with an active imagination." Remember, it was the Jesuit Father Malachi Martin who conducted an exorcism on the *Amityville Horror* house on Long Island. *America* also suggested that in raising questions about talking to the departed, critics overlooked the long history of such dialogues within the context of traditional religion, particularly the centuries-old legacy of saints in the Catholic Church.

Some commentators and writers couldn't resist taking swipes at New Age beliefs. Bob Woodward concluded, "Hillary's session with Houston reflected a serious inner turmoil that she had not resolved." Had Mrs. Clinton gone the conventional route of conflict resolution, psychotherapy or counseling from mainstream religion, there would have been little if any criticism. However, once she stepped beyond the narrow strictures of established practices to seek help, tolerance was in short supply. But if Jean Houston's process helped, why not accept it? Might there be many spiritual paths through which we can learn and grow?

When Hillary Rodham was still at Wellesley in the 1960s and law school at Yale in the 1970s, the New Age was on the rise. By the 1990s, the term "New Age" embraced many disparate interests, including alternative health and healing, the belief in the immediate presence of angels, the channeling of spirits, and a host of other metaphysical topics that filled countless books, films, TV programs, and self-help tapes. In 1998, *Life* magazine reported that 80 percent of Americans believed in an afterlife. A 1993 National Opinion Research Council survey from the University of Chicago found four in every ten Americans "reported having experienced some form of communication or contact with the dead." *The New York Times* revealed in 1997 "nearly half of Americans believe in ESP. A hundred forty-five million think they've had a psychic experience." A 1993 *Time*/CNN poll found that 69 percent of responders thought "special guardian angels" exist, and from 1991 to 1995, more than five million angel books were sold. The number doesn't include books about near-death experiences and other stories about what might lie beyond the "veil" of death.[13]

Many described their interest in such phenomena as "nontraditional spiritual searching." Despite the growing popularity, however, disparaging comments in the press weren't hard to find. One newspaper editorial pronounced what they characterized as First Lady Hillary Clinton's attempts to work with spiritual adviser Jean Houston to channel the departed spirit of Eleanor Roosevelt so as to communicate with her "a harmless bit of New Age nonsense."[14]

Say what you will, however, Bill Clinton—with Hillary's support—emerged from an impeachment as one of this country's strongest presidents, turning around the economy, protecting the Bosnian Serb population from genocide, and leaving the incoming George W. Bush with a hefty budget surplus to spend away. Perhaps Hillary's role-playing with First Lady Eleanor Roosevelt did more than most critics will ever realize.

10

The New Age at the End of the Millennium: Fads and Fancies

Once the New Age emerged from what had begun as the "Age of Aquarius" in the 1960s, it was as subject to fad and crazes as any other movement might be. During the 1970s, as we explained earlier, Eastern teachings and philosophy were in vogue as many Americans embraced meditation, yoga, and other Asian spiritual wisdom and practices, apparently ignoring the abysmal living conditions millions faced in such countries as India where poverty was widespread, despite enlightened Hindu religious beliefs.

One of the more interesting New Age fads in the 1970s was "talking to plants."[1] The idea actually dated back to the 1840s in Germany, and among its advocates were such eminent scientists as Charles Darwin and Luther Burbank. The basis of the idea was that plants are "living beings," therefore, plants have nervous systems, and communicate with each other by giving off a particular scent. Burbank believed plants were capable of some level of telepathy. By the 1970s, there were books on the subject, and even a record titled *Music to Grow Plants*. To the surprise of skeptics, there was some "scientific evidence" that music did influence plant growth. Plants preferred classical melodies, and bloomed in the direction of the music, while foliage seemed to wilt when they were exposed to loud rock music. Even Britain's crown prince Charles, the Prince of Wales, has said that he is a farmer at heart and communicating with plants is not an idea to be dismissed lightly.

Then there was John C. Lilly, a medical doctor, who became intrigued with dolphins, and suggested after studying them in the 1960s, and again in the 1980s, that they could learn to communicate telepathically with humans. Lilly insisted dolphins have a "highly developed consciousness." Skeptics dismissed Lilly as a New Age eccentric with weird and unproven theories. However, in 2007, the U.S. Navy announced an idea to use "dolphins for defense," literally to fight terrorism by "training dolphins to protect submarines," especially at night. Scientists had discovered that the unusual mammals were equipped with "built-in sonar." Skeptics didn't get the last laugh; Lilly had been on the right track about dolphin brainpower.[2]

In the 1980s, New Age attention shifted to what were arguably its two most controversial practices: channeling, and the use of crystals. When interest in both began to wane, New Age believers during the 1990s enthusiastically turned to a fascination with angels, especially guardian angels. Borrowing from olden religious beliefs in the celestial beings, all things angelic quickly dominated New Age curiosity, from a plethora of books and magazine articles to angel merchandise, and even so-called angel stores.

The appearance of angels during times of plight was not a New Age belief. As far back as the Continental Army's wintering at

Valley Forge, General George Washington told his staff of a won-drous vision he had when he secluded himself in prayer deep in the woods. A distraught and demoralized Washington, witnessing the decay of his army as sickness and hunger wracked his troops, al-ready weakened from subfreezing temperatures, snow, and sleet, sought refuge from the sights of despair and prayed to the Creator for relief. His answer, the general said, came in the form of an an-gelic being, garbed in white and shining against the stark foliage. The vision, almost like a vision out of poet William Blake, foretold of the success of Washington's endeavors, the eventual victory of the American colonies in the Revolutionary War, and the triumph of the United States of America. Washington's spirit returned, given to him, he told staff, by an angel, and he gave his army the courage to withstand the dreadful winter and go on to fight the British, winning the war at Yorktown, Virginia. In this way, if our first president, who could not tell a lie and had a penchant for cher-ries, is to be believed, it was an angelic presence that helped found the United States.[3]

By the early 1990s, angels had achieved a special place in the New Age movement. They became so immensely popular that in December 1993 they earned a cover story in *Time* magazine. Around then, a *Time*/CNN poll revealed that 69 percent of Amer-icans believed in "special guardian angels." A 1992 Gallup poll reported that 76 percent of teenagers believed in angels; a consid-erable increase from 64 percent in 1978. By 2002, a Scripps How-ard poll found that 20 percent of Americans "believe they have seen angels."

The growing interest in angels led to numerous books about them. Between 1991 and 1995, more than five million angel books were sold. Stores sprung up around the country that specialized in angels—selling everything from books, magazines, and news-letters, to angel jewelry, artwork, and collectibles decorated with depictions of angelic beings, and nearly any other trinket or merchandise one could think of where the image of an angel could be emblazoned. By 1996, there were more than a hundred angel shops in the U.S. and Canada, twenty-nine of them just in California. From coast to coast, angel stores during the 1990s reported brisk business. At the time, four periodicals, at least six religious groups, and no less than five Web sites were devoted to angels, according to *Angels A to Z.*

Even the U.S. Postal Service moved in to profit from the angel fad. In 1995, a popular postage stamp was issued with an illustration of a cherub, the chubby childlike angel familiar on Valentine's Day, and above the cherub was the word LOVE. Many other countries have had angels on their postage stamps; even Vatican City extolled archangels on its airmail stamp, a symbol of winged angels traveling to deliver mail. The origin of the word *angel,* after all, is derived from ancient Greek for "messenger." In a long-held religious belief, angels were messengers of God.

No one can say with certainty why angels captured the enormous attention they did by the 1990s. One theory is that the curiosity may have been motivated by Theosophy's influence on the New Age movement; its ideas about angels were largely drawn from Western religious beliefs. But why would it take two decades from the beginning of the New Age in the early 1970s, until the 1990s for the enthusiasm in angels to fully emerge?

Another conjecture is that people turned to angels in their search for spirituality, hoping for celestial beings that were both powerful and protective. That need was as deep for many people in the late twentieth century as it was for their ancestors in the Middle Ages, during biblical times, and even before that. By believing in angels, we take comfort in there being someone—or something—beyond us that is supernatural, benevolent, and has the strength to aid us in a personal way. Yet a further possibility was that the interest in angels during the 1990s was in anticipation of the millennium; perhaps angelic beings were a significant sign for humanity, such as preparation for the "Second Coming" of Jesus Christ.

"Some Christian writers have speculated that UFOs could well be a part of God's angelic host who preside over the physical affairs of universal creation. UFOs are astonishingly angel-like in some of their reported appearances," wrote Malcolm Godwin in *Angels: An Endangered Species.*

The fact is that whatever theory one holds to, angels have long fascinated people; the number of encounters with the celestial winged beings have been innumerable over the centuries. One of those who dedicated much time attempting to determine why the "angel archetype," as he called it, captured so much attention and interest was the psychologist Carl Jung.

One incongruity was that both New Age and long-established Christianity embraced angels. It was, to say the least, an odd alliance, since New Age thinking and orthodox religious beliefs were typically at opposite ends of the spectrum on nearly every philosophical and theological issue imaginable. To find them on the same side showed that interest in angels was much broader than many realized.

Angels needed no introduction to the New Age movement; they'd been written and spoken about since ancient times, appearing significantly in Christianity, Judaism, and Islam. The Bible includes more than three hundred references to angels, in both the Old and New Testaments. Most of us, in fact, can trace our familiarity with angels to biblical stories. The first time an angel appears in the Bible is when one, bearing a flaming sword, drives Adam from the Garden of Eden for disobeying God (Genesis 3:23–24). In the Old Testament, Jacob wrestled with an angel (Genesis 32:24–28). An angel was sent to guide and protect Moses (Exodus 23:20). God also sent an angel to save Daniel when he was in the lion's den (Daniel 6:22). Angels appeared to Mary, Joseph, and the shepherds to announce the birth of Jesus; and later, in the Garden of Gethsemane, an angel comforted Jesus. Guardian angels also materialized in order to help the apostles Paul and Peter.

Moroni, the "Mormon Angel of God" came to earth as God's messenger, and guided Joseph Smith to initiate the Mormon religion, during the early nineteenth century in upstate New York, from where it spread across the country.[4]

Angels were believed to have come to earth to act as "guardians and guides," although most remained invisible, were immortal, and often appeared mysteriously. There is no accurate count of how many angels there might be; some accept that the number might be in the billions. There is no attempt in the Bible to provide evidence that angels exist; it "just takes them for granted," Hope Price wrote in her book *Angels*.[5] Curiously, no one really knows what angels look like—they take many forms as specific situations require. Nor are they male or female, angels are androgynous, meaning genderless. The beautiful being in white robes with large wings, gleaming halo, and harp or sword is a depiction taken largely from artists' renditions, although over the centuries, many witnesses have claimed that was how angels appeared to them.

Theologians say angels are "shining proof of God's divine love," according to Price.[6] No one who is deeply religious takes issue with the biblical description; but what was the New Age version of angels? The foremost belief was in guardian angels. Others considered that channeling and reports of extraterrestrials were forms of angelic contact. Credence in each person having a "personal" guardian angel, from the moment of birth, is a conviction that dates back through history, known in Judaism, Christianity, and Islam, and now accepted as a New Age precept.[7] The idea of guardian angels actually dates back to between 3000 and 4000 BCE.

Long before the New Age, history recorded encounters by the famous with guardian angels. The best known such incident in America occurred when a despairing General George Washington was visited by an angel at Valley Forge in the brutal winter of 1777 during the Revolutionary War. Washington described "an apparition of a beautiful lady" dressed in white, and accompanied by a "bright angel with a crown of light." The experience was believed instrumental in bolstering Washington's faith through the bitter cold and ice with his freezing and starving ragtag troops, as they fought the well-equipped British army, and ultimately— miraculously—defeated them.[8]

Washington's experience resembled many accounts by soldiers and officers of so-called angels on the battlefield that have been reported over the centuries.[9] Significant instances of this sort were reported during World War I and World War II. One of the most famous occurred at the Battle of Mons, Belgium, in 1914.[10] "The German attack against allied forces [Great Britain, France, and Belgium] was heavy," Matthew Merta wrote in *Angels A to Z*. Then a "troop of angels" in white robes with "arms outstretched" appeared and repelled the stunned Germans. In this case, there were many witnesses to the same angelic episode, making it much harder to refute than instances in which an angel is seen or felt by a single individual.

Skeptics dismiss battlefield angel scenarios as imaginary or hallucinatory, an understandable result of terror occurring in combat conditions. However, thousands who've told of angel sightings during battle strongly disagree, and insist their encounters were genuine. No less a figure than Charles Lindbergh said he felt an "angelic presence" with him during his historic solo transatlantic flight in 1927. He believed the angel protected him when he unintentionally "dozed off" while piloting his famed airplane.[11]

There have been numerous descriptions of incidents with angels reported by a wide cross-section of people, leading New Age authors and experts on the subject to conclude that an angel could appear to anyone, of any age, rich or poor, and regardless of race, gender, or religious belief. When the celestial beings make themselves known to very young children, it's difficult to argue that angels are mere flights of fancy. In fact, children report "more angel experiences than adults," author Patrick Wans noted. Consider the following true story from our files, sent by a young child's mother.

Danny, nearly two years old, would often look above him as if he were watching something moving across the ceiling over his crib. "Mama," the little boy often happily exclaimed to his mother as he pointed upward. The remainder of whatever words he was trying to express was garbled, typical for a child his age. His mother, Angela, saw nothing, and chalked up the frequent incidents to her son's imagination, but he joyfully persisted.

One day in her kitchen, Angela held Danny in her arms as she walked to the refrigerator, on which were several magnets, a few paste-on notes, and a new calendar. Suddenly, Danny excitedly pointed to the picture on the calendar that he'd never seen before. "Mama. Mama," he repeated excitedly and waved his fingers as high as he could, then touched the illustration. At first, Angela did not understand what Danny was trying to say. Then, after giving the incident some thought, she realized what her little boy might have meant. The calendar artwork was of a beautiful angel, dressed in a white gown, with wings and a halo. Had Danny pointed to the painting of the angel as a way of telling his mother that he'd seen a similar angelic figure when he so often gestured as he gazed intently above his bed?[12]

Other times, reports of angels are not descriptions of the winged being with halo and harp that we've grown accustomed to seeing in popular or classic artwork, including some of the world's great paintings. The celestial beings, many believe, can take a human form when they act as guardian angels, as in the following example from the files of the Parapsychology Institute of America, founded in New York in 1971.

Karen was driving on an open stretch of highway after a day spent visiting relatives. The ride was uneventful until, at a turn in the road, she lost control of the car, and tumbled down a grassy embankment. She was injured, in pain, and unable to move. Shaken and frightened, she sat trapped in the disabled car, dazed and uncertain what to do next. She needed to be extricated from the automobile, but no one could catch sight of her from the highway in order to come to her assistance.

Suddenly, a figure approached, although it was difficult to determine who it was in the glare of the late-afternoon sun. As the person came closer, Karen could see it was a boy of about twelve or thirteen. Without saying a word, the youngster gently but firmly freed the injured woman from the damaged and dented automobile; then helped her up the embankment. The young boy remained by her side, quiet and expressionless, until a state trooper's car came down the road, and the officer saw Karen and the crippled automobile. As she turned to thank the boy, he vanished as unexpectedly as he first appeared. Karen was rushed to a nearby hospital where she recovered from her injuries. Later, she wondered if the child who mysteriously came to her aid was actually a guardian angel. Had he been sent to help because she was in peril?[13]

Jack was driving home in a blinding snowstorm that approached blizzard conditions when his car stalled and he was left helpless as the weather worsened. He ventured ahead on foot, but soon became too disoriented and chilled to walk farther. Then, unexpectedly, he saw another man walking toward him. The stranger took hold of Jack's arm and soon the pair were plodding together through mounting snow and worsening visibility. Jack could not recall how long they'd trekked, but eventually they arrived at Jack's home, although he had no idea how the stranger knew the directions so accurately. Once Jack was safely in his house, and greeted by his worried wife, the couple turned to thank the stranger and invite him in to warm up. However, to their amazement, the man was gone. Had this been a guardian angel experience? It could never be proven, but Jack and his wife believed it had all the characteristics of such an encounter.[14]

Laurie, not a strong swimmer, faced nearly certain disaster when she fell from a small boat that had been caught in the wake of a larger passing boat. Laurie plunged overboard. She was panicky and fearful of drowning before her boyfriend could jump in the water to save her. But, she said she suddenly had the strange sensation that something unseen was lifting her, keeping her buoyant until her friend could grab her hand and pull her back to their boat. Badly shaken, she nonetheless was certain that someone, although invisible, had carried her through the ordeal. Had she been saved by an angel?[15]

During the New Age, as in prior years, many told of similar personal experiences with what they believed were guardian angels that inexplicably appeared when there was difficulty or danger. However, in some instances, deceased loved ones act as guardian angels, but are not actually angels in the traditional sense, since celestial angels are not humans. The following incident from our files is one example.

Peter, at eighteen, had already been touched by personal tragedy when his older brother Gary was shot and killed in a hunting accident. One day as Peter walked by the room of his youngest brother, ten-year-old Jimmy, he was stopped short by what he recognized as Gary's voice. "Hurry! Get Jimmy. Grab Jimmy!" the voice clearly demanded. Peter hurriedly raced to his brother's room where the little boy was playing with a video game. As Peter wondered what the message in his head was trying to tell him, suddenly he noticed that a bookshelf had broken loose from a wall bracket, and was about to fall. Peter darted toward Jimmy just in time. Moments later, the shelf broke free, and crashed to the floor. Had Peter not quickly moved Jimmy from harm's way, the plummeting shelf would have struck the child's head. This is one true example of many thousands of instances in which a departed loved one communicated to someone on earth to warn him or her of impending peril. In this type of situation, the spirit of a deceased loved one acts as a guardian angel.

Even the most enthusiastic New Age author or angel expert would agree that guardian angels are not superheroes, nor do they magically appear in every instance of danger. Despite thousands of unsolicited reports of angelic interventions, in most instances, people had to work out or fulfill their own destiny without heavenly help. Guardian angels do not interfere with "free will."

The New Age, as we said earlier, brought together disparate beliefs. In the case of angels, religion and the paranormal overlapped in some unexpected settings. As just one example, the Archangel Michael often appears as a psychic symbol to a well-known medium in readings when the spirit of a police officer killed in the line of duty communicated to a loved one. From a theological perspective, the discussion of angels in the context of a psychic reading is anathema.

However, within New Age, it was not considered unusual to introduce the "chief of the archangels," Michael, into a medium's reading. The archangel's influence is accepted in Judaism, Christianity, and Islam. While Michael is recognized in religious studies for the magnitude of his powers, including his heavenly battle against Satan, for mediums who claim they psychically see or sense Michael, the symbolism is apparent: Michael the Archangel was long ago declared the guardian or "patron" of police officers by the

Roman Catholic Church. In addition to St. Michael, the hierarchy of archangels includes Raphael, Gabriel, and Uriel.[16]

Angels also made their impact in the major media, just as they had for centuries in art, including the famed paintings of the artist Raphael (1483–1520). In classic literature, the writer John Milton (1608–1674) made angels the focal point of his poetic epic *Paradise Lost,* considering them spirits and "sons of God."

TV viewers in more recent years will recall at least two well-received series about angels: *Highway to Heaven* in the 1980s and *Touched by an Angel* in the 1990s. The celestial beings have been the subject of several dozen motion pictures; perhaps none as enduring as Clarence, the angel in the Christmas classic, *It's a Wonderful Life,* a perennial favorite. By the 1990s, network TV stations had caught up with their viewers' interest in angels; soon there were documentaries, news segments, and talk shows all devoted to angels and people's experiences with them. The decade also produced a number of successful authors who wrote about angels, including Sophy Burnham, Eileen Elias Freeman, Linda Georgian, and Tim Wylie;[17] all agreed humans could learn from angels.

An enormous amount has been written and studied concerning angelology, far more than can be included here; but there is no lack of resources available for those who wish to learn further. During the New Age, the angel fad reached its high point during the 1990s. However, unlike crystals, which became trendy in the 1980s and then had their popularity steadily decline, angels have had a far different and more long-lasting appeal. There is every reason to believe they will continue to hold attention in both the worlds of theology and metaphysics, for angels represent the fulfillment of a deep human need for help from commanding, otherworldly beings. In a world fraught with random and unexpected dangers, fear is sufficient for people to yearn for something powerful to guide and protect them through the dark and unknown. As the

New Age revealed, the sheer numbers of guardian angel experiences make these heartening and even life-saving encounters difficult to dismiss.[18]

With angels as an omnipresent inspiration also came a belief in what became the epitome of the New Age craze, crystals. The interest in crystals peaked during the 1980s. Crystal healing became synonymous with the New Age movement. The idea was that quartz crystals had the power to heal "mental, emotional, physical, and spiritual health," wrote Dael Walker in *The Crystal Book*.[19]

Although there was no scientific evidence to support that crystal healing was genuine, it was offered "as an experimental alternative tool for natural healing," Walker explained. Proponents of the unorthodox technique said they considered the "human body as a series of energy systems with crystals as a device for adjusting and balancing these systems."[20] The big question, of course, was whether being treated with crystals, by holding, wearing, or placing them on a person who was ill, actually worked.

The history of crystals dated back to ancient times when a variety of gemstones were used in religious rituals, and there are several hundred references to crystals in the Bible, and who of us hasn't heard of the crystal ball, used as a divination tool, to predict the future.

Amethyst, also a quartz crystal that came in several different colors, was known in ancient Egypt, and was often placed on the body of someone who'd died. The Catholic Church regarded amethyst quartz as a sign of "spiritual power." The early Greeks found a practical use for amethyst; they believed it warded off drunkenness.

Much of the modern New Age interest in crystals can be traced back to the assertions of the famed clairvoyant Edgar Cayce. Although countless books had been written about the inhabitants of Atlantis, only a small number made reference to their use of crystal energy. One exception was Ruth Montgomery, who wrote in *The World Before* that crystals were employed in both Atlantis and Lemuria.

You may recall that in many of Cayce's past life trance readings, subjects were told they'd had earlier incarnations in the ancient, lost civilization of Atlantis. According to Cayce, huge crystals powered Atlantis, much as our society has long generated electricity for its energy needs. In Atlantis, crystals were employed to amass and transform solar power into electrical energy that was then provided free. Cayce's trance sessions also told how Atlanteans made use of crystals for a variety of individual purposes. Of course, this presupposed that Cayce's details about the existence of Atlantis as a highly advanced culture thousands of years ago were accurate. According to Cayce, some evil-minded Atlanteans eventually misused crystal power, instead of applying it to benefit others, there were those who exploited the power for negativity and destruction. What followed was an enormous discharge of energies that caused a devastating earthquake and the complete extinction of Atlantis.

Back in the 1960s, many became intrigued by Cayce's ideas, largely motivated by the bestselling book *The Sleeping Prophet,* which earned Cayce the title of "a prophet of the New Age," wrote Mary Ellen Carter, and revived the interest in crystals, although Cayce's pronouncements about Atlantis were untraceable. Was there validity to the theory that the stone held special healing properties? Throughout the 1980s there would be considerable debate between those who taught and advocated "crystal science," maintaining crystal healing was a "tool," and traditional scientists and physicians who scoffed at and dismissed crystal healing as ineffective and worthless.

Inevitably, debate developed in the 1980s about whether energy fields measured around quartz crystal had any scientific meaning.

Doctors concluded that any positive or salutary effect a patient experienced from a crystal was psychosomatic, raising the question of the placebo effect. In other words, might the belief in crystals and other gemstones have caused their effectiveness by activating potent brain chemicals?

Geologically, crystals are actually "fossilized water," a natural mineral produced by activity within the earth's crust. "Quartz amplifies, transforms, stores, focuses, and transfers energy," Dael Walker wrote. The claims made for crystals ranged from nearly miraculous to outlandish. One theory was that crystal energy was used in the construction of one or more Egyptian pyramids. Bringing its uses more up to date, advocates declared that charged crystals could improve gasoline mileage, no small promise during the energy shortages during the 1970s and 1980s. Another assertion was that crystals had the capacity to alter consciousness, since they could supposedly "stimulate the energy centers [in the brain]," Walker wrote, adding, "Clear quartz is the overall body energizer. . . . Linking the crystal to visualization you can direct the subconscious mind to move energy where you want it."

Crystals could also be used to manifest one's reality, advocates insisted. If, for example, one was desirous of a material possession, relationship, particular talent, career choice, or money, crystal energy was supposed to help make that dream come true by helping people somehow tap into their subconscious mind to "create something in your life you want or need," Walker explained.

Some believed crystal energy had the capacity to enhance such psychic powers as clairvoyance. One theory was that a crystal was a device used as a "focus to help awaken the subconscious, intuitive, or psychic mind," according to *Psychic World* magazine.[21] Crystal gazing had long been considered a way to strengthen the ability to visualize, a component of clairvoyance or psychic sight.

Clear quartz was most prized and was used to make crystal balls for gazing into the future, a long-disputed and stereotyped method known as scrying. Crystals were also supposedly able to boost the effectiveness of meditation and prayer. Another claim was that these amazing stones could make possible contact with "spiritual guides," angels, as well as highly evolved masters, and spirits of the departed. As if that wasn't enough, crystal teachers purported that the stones helped increase "intuition and creativity." A further assertion was that crystals improved or motivated better performance in school and study.

In order for crystals to work, proponents explained, they had to be "charged." There were several methods suggested, one borrowed from another popular 1970s New Age fad called "pyramid power." The instructions were to place your quartz crystal in a wire-frame model of the Great Pyramid of Egypt. If you preferred, crystals could also be charged by magnets, the uninitiated were advised, or an already charged crystal could be used to energize additional crystals. Another suggestion from so-called experts was to hold the stone in the left hand in order to strengthen the "body's energy field." Supposedly, that would enable the crystal to be employed as a healing tool.[22]

It was advised that if a crystal were worn as jewelry, particularly as a necklace, ring, or earrings, the gemstone would continue to be "energized." A crystal worn as a pendant, it was claimed, might influence the body's chakras or energy centers, a New Age idea borrowed from a long-held Hindu belief. The various colors of quartz stones were supposed to be related to the body's dozen chakras. Certain colors were said to influence specific chakras, therefore restoring physical and emotional health, Dael Walker noted. Some people wore or carried their crystal for what Walker called "psychic protection," explaining that the stone acted as a shield or "force field" to impede "most negative or imbalanced thoughts and emotions."

Quite apart from the fascination with crystals during the New Age, quartz crystals have a long and separate history in communications. Crystals were used at one time in broadcasting. Among the first radios in the 1920s were "crystal sets," often homemade from a round cereal box, wrapped with wire, and a quartz crystal positioned on it for tuning in and listening to whatever radio stations were on the air at the time.[23]

Healing was the most controversial use of the stones during the New Age. Traditional medicine railed against crystal healing, but advocates held fast to their theory that the body is a "series of energy systems that crystals interact with, and in combination with the mind, create functional changes which then manifest in the physical body," Walker explained. "Since the human body is electronic in nature, it responds to the crystal. The physical body is the end result of energy [and] the crystal amplifies energy." Purveyors suggested a crystal could be held by an individual as a means of increasing or improving contact with one's own mind, a kind of internal communication.

No crystal energy teacher, author, or alleged expert was foolish enough to propose that crystal healing was meant to replace traditional medicine. However, the public attention that crystal healing received raised the most significant question: did quartz crystals have the extraordinary powers to do all, or even some of, what its advocates claimed?

The answer, as physicians and scientists who examined crystal healing and many who turned to stones for help found out, was that the quartz crystals and other gems, such as sapphires, produced no measurable health improvements. Although crystal healing might have been useful for some psychologically, and would retain a number of adherents, once sufficient numbers of people realized "crystal energy" failed to deliver on its promises, the crystal craze fizzled. A lot of people who'd purchased "healing" crystals felt they were left holding sparkly gems; that's all.[24] That led some overly optimistic skeptics to prematurely conclude the New Age movement had ended. It did not. Instead, the New Age transformed even as the new millennium brought economic disaster for many around the world.

11

New Age and Music: The Power of Tonality

The power of tonality, organized successions of sounds, melodic or harmonic as opposed to noise, has been recognized by civilizations since the dawn of human culture.[1] In ancient cultures, sounds could invoke fear, awareness, or calls to arms. The sound of the shofar, for example, is not only an integral part of the religious services on the Jewish high holy days, but listening to the sound of the shofar is an obligation for Jewish people.

In one of the most poignant scenes of the Bible, the Israelites, led by Joshua, surrounded the walls of the city of Jericho, marched around it chanting a prayer and playing the shofar, and kept on marching and playing until the walls came tumbling down. The Bible tells us that it was the hand of the Creator who destroyed the walls so the Israelites could overwhelm the defenders and claim the promised land as their own, but is that the truth? Or did the Creator impart to Joshua and his warriors what amounted to a secret weapon, a sonic weapon the vibrations from which could weaken and eventually bring down thick and heavy fortifications? Clearly, the deployment of a sonic weapon was successful from a military perspective.

Even today, sonic weapons, ultrasound beams, and loud sonic cannons, used for crowd control when law enforcement needs to rely on nonlethal weapons, are in common use. We have all seen how sound waves of specific frequencies can shatter crystal. Why, therefore, would it be beyond the range of normal experience for people to doubt the effects of directed sound?

On the edge of paranormal conspiracy are the stories of the mysterious project of the High Frequency Active Auroral Research Program (HAARP), which officially defines itself as the study of the ionosphere through high-energy radio frequency waves. But others have said that HAARP was intended to control not just radio frequencies, but to use radio frequencies to send concealed communications or, worse, to control individuals for the purpose of conditioning them as a test of mass population control or turning on bio-psychological switches to deploy preprogrammed people to perform acts of violence or sabotage. These are some of the conspiracies surrounding HAARP, but also point to the relationship of sound, tonality, and the paranormal.[2]

New Age infused popular culture as well as motivated far-reaching changes in America's consciousness. It even became a type of music that was as difficult to characterize or define as was the New Age movement itself. These were mainly instrumental pieces that did not fit easily into any of the popular musical genres that most of us are familiar with: rock, country, hip-hop, jazz, folk, and so on. "New Age music" as a description was more about evoking a feeling or mood than placing an emphasis on lyrics, recognizable melodies, or messages. As one New Age catalog described it, this is "music to create an environment with." Some fans considered it "otherworldly" while others portrayed it as "uplifting" and "calming." The compositions included such instruments as flute, harp, and keyboard, as well as synthesizer.

Musicians and composers, inspired by their own interest or involvement in New Age ideas, developed New Age music.[3] One of the more popular New Age singers and musicians in recent years has been the Irish artist Enya, whose songs have been described as sounding ethereal, and even angelic.[4] As background music, people who meditate often play New Age songs, as do many holistic practitioners in their offices. "Meditation music," in fact, became quite popular; some believed it helped attain an "altered state of consciousness" that increased the depth of the meditative state.

"The right music can calm the spirit, energize the body, speed healing, boost immunity, and relieve headaches," wrote Adrienne Warren in *Psychic World* magazine. With New Age music, "sound has become a more widely appreciated healing therapy," she noted.[5]

New Age compositions appeared to reflect the composers' own sensitivities, with little concern for what category the music fit into. For that reason, major companies largely ignored the New Age genre, not certain of its commercial appeal. That initially forced many New Age performers to create their own labels. However, once the music became successful, to the tune of a hundred million dollars a year in sales, leading recording companies took notice. By the 1990s, many radio stations began to play New Age songs, and some stations, mainly college outlets, devoted weekly programs specifically to New Age music.

Among other well-known New Age artists were Jean-Michel Jarre and Steve Halpern.[6] During a radio interview, one interesting metaphysical subject was raised concerning "channeled music," when some New Age composers, including Halpern, claimed they'd received music or lyrics from "highly evolved spirit guides." In other words, the artists said, the music they wrote came from somewhere above or outside them.[7]

Halpern, a former jazz musician, received considerable attention in New Age circles. He explained that the idea of music as "therapy" originally came to him as he meditated. He'd studied the "psychology of music," and applied his knowledge and inspiration to creating compositions that were meant to help people relax; they were not pop tunes that one could sing along to. Halpern has long contended that music and sounds have consequences for people's mental and physical health, a theory disputed by some critics who argued that he overstated what his "spiritual music" could accomplish.

On August 16 and 17, 1987, more than 144,000 people assembled at eleven so-called power points throughout the world. The mega-event was billed as the Harmonic Convergence, and its intention was "to save planet Earth." Among the gathering places designated were specific locations in California, Hawaii, Arizona, South Dakota, New York, Mexico, Peru, Greece, Japan, India, and Egypt. Those who took part joined hands, danced, and "hummed" or chanted to create something called "vibrational toning." Its purpose was to accomplish "inner peace." The event attracted celebrities identified with the Age of Aquarius, or the later New Age, including Shirley MacLaine, Timothy Leary, and folksinger John Denver.[8]

The credit for creating and leading this surreal spectacle was a California artist and writer, Jose Arguelles. He persuaded Americans that August 1987 was to be "a turning point of historic magnitude exceeding anything we've ever known." Arguelles argued that people needed to come together for the sake of the planet, and spelled out the story in a book he wrote, *The Mayan Factor.* He explained that he arrived at the correct time for the Harmonic Convergence by calculating the dates based on the ancient Aztec calendar and a Hopi Indian tale, and because nine planets would be lined up in a highly unusual formation. The Hopi saga foretold that "enlightened teachers" on that date would "awaken the rest of humanity," wrote Frank W. Hoffmann in *Mind & Society Fads.*[9]

Arguelles felt certain that "some of the mysteries of life" would be disclosed at the time of the Harmonic Convergence. The result of the coming together was supposed to produce "an unprecedented amount of energy to converge in one place and harmonize with itself, creating an energy greater than any experienced on earth to date," Arguelles insisted.[10] In order for Earth to be saved, it was necessary to pray and "hum" as a way of showing what Hoffman called "good faith [to the] cosmic powers." The actual transformation would occur twenty-five years after the Harmonic Convergence in 1987. That meant it was to take place in the year 2012, based on the calculations derived from the Mayan calendar. On the day of the Convergence in 1987, Arguelles predicted there would be a wave of UFO activity, resulting from the belief that the ancient Mayans were, in fact, extraterrestrials.

1987 was indeed a heavy year for UFO activity, with perhaps the most notable encounter in Gulf Breeze, Florida, by Ed Walters. Other UFO sighting events took place that year over Nashville, Alaska, Orange County in New York, and over Waterbury, Connecticut. Indeed those who participated agreed the event was worthwhile, and that it inspired peace and harmony. But there were also numerous critics, especially in the major media, who either ridiculed or criticized the participants for doing nothing concrete or practical to help the troubled planet Earth, Frank Hoffman noted.[11]

One of the eleven "power point" locations chosen for the Harmonic Convergence was Sedona, Arizona, a community that has drawn so many New Age types to visit or live there that it's been called "the Southwest's most mystical city," noted Dennis William Hauck. By the mid-1990s, the small town of about twelve thousand assumed a special place for New Age devotees, especially following the Convergence in 1987.[12]

It grew rapidly, attracting some three million visitors a year.[13] Sedona, about 120 miles north of Phoenix, and less than thirty miles southwest of Flagstaff, is located in what remains one of the most beautiful and unspoiled parts of the United States.[14] The majestic beauty of ancient canyons and cliffs surround Sedona, and beyond the crags and rock faces is a place that became famous during the New Age for its energy "vortexes," best described as "whirlwinds of concentrated psychic energy," explained Pat McDonald in *Psychic World* magazine.[15]

For centuries, Native Americans regarded the area as "sacred," and came there to conduct "medicine and magic rituals," McDonald said.[16] By the 1970s, the area's natural grandeur attracted many, and after the 1987 Harmonic Convergence, a number of people who'd gathered for the event insisted they sensed the "powers" of Sedona's vortexes. The bell rocks around Sedona resonate with sound, literally vibrating like bells.

Once word spread through New Age circles, Sedona became known as a place where "earth energies" could be united, and people were able to work on their own individual development. For those interested in New Age teachings, practices, and merchandise, Sedona has many centers and bookstores. Visitors can gain knowledge concerning everything from the workings of sweat lodges and medicine wheels, to learning about astrology, auras, chakras, divination, spirit communication, and yoga, to name a few.[17]

Sedona has four vortexes, special locations that are said to contain psychic energies. These "energies affect both your physical and spiritual natures. They increase your awareness, calm, and cleanse your body," Pat McDonald wrote.[18] They are also able to "balance psychic energies," Dennis Hauck explained.

Many visitors confirm they've felt "strange forces and receive[d] otherworldly communications," and the vortexes are also said to have produced changes in people's outlooks and feelings. Nearby Oak Creek Canyon is "believed to cleanse people both physically and spiritually," and the Chapel of the Holy Cross is where many claim they've had "visionary experiences" while they meditated, according to Hauck.[19] Few places could match Sedona's reputation for New Age thinking.

12 *Toward a New Frontier of Awareness*

Simply looking at the progression of cultural beliefs and consumer proclivities as they relate to the New Age, it is clear that there was a palpable change in attitudes toward the paranormal and metaphysics between the late 1960s and the 1990s. There was a significant transformation in consciousness as a move toward open-mindedness was taking place, despite skeptics and religious fundamentalists to whom the New Age movement remained both an abomination and growing competition.

Even as interest in channeling dwindled by the late 1980s, and questions were raised about the scientific worth of crystal healing,[1] there were elements of the New Age that seemed well rooted for a long life: the flood of inspirational and self-help books continued, as did the idea of self-discovery. And there was growing attentiveness to holistic health, healing, and alternative medicine, a trend evident by the 1970s.

Although New Age embraced far more than the paranormal, psychic phenomena was no less an interest than it had ever been. In the early 1980s, an important breakthrough occurred with the beginning of the modern mediumship movement. Through the astounding abilities of a young Long Island man, George Anderson. With the publication of his story *We Don't Die,* mediumship returned prominently, on a national scale. For many grieving people, messages from departed loved ones proved deeply meaningful.[2]

In the 1990s, there was another important New Age trend, as we explained earlier, when everything about angels was in vogue. The overlap between metaphysics and traditional religion, to some an unsettling association, was unmistakable as millions of angels captivated the attention of millions of people.

By the mid-1990s, the Internet revolution was upon us, and it joined the New Age in a most unusual way.[3] Computers, of course, are machines. We don't think of turning to them as a source of comfort when we lose a loved one. However, in 1995, the World Wide Cemetery was created. It wasn't an actual cemetery. This one was navigated on the Internet at a Web site called www.cem etery.org. This was a "virtual cemetery," where "Internet users, their families and friends, can erect permanent monuments to our dead. Another Web site founded around the same time was named Virtual Memorial Garden. Still one more was called Virtual Memorials. Founded in 1996, it described itself as a Web site "created to honor, remember, and share stories and photos of those we love and have lost."

If online memorials at first seemed odd, recall that as far back as the nineteenth century, with the invention of photography, it was not unusual to have a picture taken of a deceased loved one laid out in a casket. Prior to that, for centuries, many prominent people were immortalized in plaster "death masks" made of the person immediately after passing. For years, memorials in words and pictures have appeared in countless newspapers, often on or near the obituary page. Now the grieving were given the use of the latest technology to create public tributes with photos of loved ones who've died, with the knowledge that the images, names, and written thoughts about the departed will always be there to see and read. This was a new age in which technology had made possible, as one bereaved person remarked, a place for "souls in cyberspace." It also helped the living to maintain "continuing bonds with the dead," concluded *Omega: Journal of Death and Dying*. Incidentally, there were also Web sites for "pet memorials."

Within the New Age movement, those who considered themselves in the vanguard became aware of changing attitudes toward many of their ideas and beliefs for global harmony. The lofty dreams and promises of New Age writers for a revolutionary change in thinking and behavior wrapped in peace, love, and compassion ran smack into harsh reality that was often quite contradictory, with no signs of massive changes for the better, despite New Age optimism in the face of seemingly intractable world crises and never-ending tragedies. To maintain its credibility, the New Age response was to proclaim that its efforts had consistently been about "personal transformation," not magically changing the world. In other words, New Age shed what many of its followers had originally considered the movement's "social vision," largely rooted in the 1960s Age of Aquarius and counterculture.

The New Age also faced another problem: the very name, "New Age." By the 1990s, it was falling out of favor even with many who'd once embraced it. In fact, some authors and others within the movement distanced themselves and asked that neither they nor their books be referred to as "New Age." In addition to the ongoing difficulty with its definition, the term had increasingly become something of a stereotype for those who never quite grabbed its meaning.

A 1997 article in the respected and leading trade magazine *Publishers Weekly (PW)*, titled "New Age Is All the Rage," described it as an "irksome label." One New Age publishing trade group executive, Marilyn McGuire, said, "I keep urging our members to change the name, but nobody comes up with anything to replace it." She added, "I wouldn't dare to define it."[4]

"For all its inadequacy, the term New Age [linked] the wide variety of philosophies, religions, and other disciplines that have both formed and reflected a particular worldview," wrote Lynn Garrett in the same article. "If [it] is sometimes criticized for including too much and joining traditions and practices that don't seem to coexist logically, that may be its appeal. People pick and choose, to cobble together personal belief systems what strikes one person as flaky may seem like revelation to another."[5]

By the mid-1990s, there were a number of bestselling books that could fit into New Age if they wished to: *Embraced by the Light*, *The Celestine Prophecy*, *The Seven Spiritual Laws of Success*, and *Conversations with God*. *PW* magazine raised the question of whether alternative health and Eastern religions belonged with New Age books, or in separate categories. When the movement began, any book that did not fit within the "mainstream" went directly to the New Age section. By the 1990s, the bookstore dynamic had changed, and despite the discomfort with the New Age category, no one had yet found a suitable substitute. Should books about spirituality, the paranormal, and a mix of religion, self-improvement, alternative medicine, Eastern philosophy, and the occult all be placed together under the heading "New Age"? Was there a better description? At the time, no one could think of any.

In 1997, *Publishers Weekly* reported, "New Age bookstores were elated that spirituality had become a hot topic." By the 1990s, stores that specialized in metaphysical, spiritual, and occult subjects were thriving, such as Bodhi Tree in Los Angeles, and Transitions in Chicago—two of the larger stores.[6] Other locations were in places such as Boston; Atlanta; Columbus, Ohio; Flint, Michigan; San Francisco; cities in Texas and Arizona; and even tiny and touristy New Hope, Pennsylvania. Each store carried up to thousands of titles, as well as other related merchandise from audiobooks to videos, amulets, incense, candles, and oils. There was also a bookstore for Edgar Cayce materials and remedies at the late psychic's foundation in Virginia Beach, as well as an ample library there, devoted to psychic phenomena, healing, and related subjects.

It was a far cry from circa 1900 when the Occult Bookstore in midtown Manhattan was one of the few of its kind: There were also substantial New Age sections in the major book chains, including Borders[7] and Barnes & Noble, and on the Internet, at Web sites such as the online bookseller, Amazon.com. In New York City, for many years, the Weiser Bookstore filled the need, selling new and old occult and metaphysical books, and by the 1980s began catering to the New Age readership. The Weiser Bookstore has since closed; however, Samuel Weiser Inc. continued to publish esoteric and occult titles. The bookshops weren't only an American phenomenon. Other Western countries have such stores, including several in London, England.

By 2001, *Publishers Weekly* was telling readers that New Age books had become a "crowded field." The magazine added that New Age "has become among the publishing world's hottest tickets in recent years." As well, there were a growing number of "New Age–oriented Web sites." Readers [had] become more sophisticated and "New Age offerings have become increasingly specialized." For example, there had long been books available about astrology; now there were "astrology-related subcategories" such as Chinese and Vedic astrology.[8]

The next year, *Publishers Weekly* quoted the head of Llewellyn Publishing Company, Carl Weschcke: "I actively believe there is such a thing as a New Age. The New Age, in my concept, is far more than ancient wisdom in new dress," he said.[9]

But New Age, the industry magazine pointed out, had increasingly become a moniker that carried a stigma, although the subjects it included had been "embraced by the mainstream," according to an industry book buyer. One publisher commented, "The baby boomer generation is a generation of people seeking answers." Books were where many of those answers appeared. "The New Age continues to cast a spell over publishers."[10]

Several classic metaphysics books were reissued, including *Mental Radio* by Upton Sinclair (1930), with its preface written by none other than Albert Einstein. Others, such as *Remember, Be Here Now* written by Ram Dass in 1971, were still selling in 2002, thirty-one years later. There were also reprints of books that were originally published fifty, even a hundred and more years ago, such as Emanuel Swedenborg's eighteenth-century writings. The new technologies that had become familiar to twenty-first-century readers provided new means of access to ideas, with Internet sites and e-books as examples, as well as CDs and DVDs.[11]

The publishing industry is, as are all forms of media industries, a fast-paced business, subject to the ups and downs of readers' tastes and interests. By 2004, *Publishers Weekly* reported that New Age books were continuing to "change and develop." Readers were becoming more specialized, moving from introductory to more "advanced books." For example, one trend was an interest in "books about secret societies, freemasons, [and] alternate religions."[12]

A blockbuster bestseller was *The Da Vinci Code* by Dan Brown, published in 2003. Although it was a work of fiction, many readers believed portions of it, at least, they thought it had a ring of truth.

It was described as a "theological thriller," that touched upon conspiracy theories, and with some highly "controversial interpretations of Christianity." Specifically, there was the suggestion that Jesus Christ had a secret "tryst" with Mary Magdalene from which a child was born. Consider that if Jesus really existed—and historian Flavius Josephus, writing at the time, says that he did—he would have been a rabbi belonging to an extreme Jewish sect, probably one having custody of the Ark of the Covenant. As a rabbi, he would have had to have been married and had children. These are historical arguments.

In Dan Brown's work, deciphering a complex code left by a dying museum curator led the story's heroes on a trail to Da Vinci's renowned fresco *The Last Supper* with plot twists that include the Knights Templar, the early clandestine history of the Roman Catholic Church, the furtive and ultra-conservative Catholic group, Opus Dei, and the search for the elusive Holy Grail, or "sacred vessel." The Holy Grail, of course, was a medieval fiction, a translation of *sangraal*, or "holy blood," the bloodline of Jesus.

Questions are raised about the church's alleged cover-up of its true record, supposedly contained in secret scrolls. Especially shocking is Brown's detail of *The Last Supper*, specifically that Mary Magdalene, wrongly vilified as a prostitute, is seated near Jesus, along with his Apostles.

Brown's criticism of church and biblical teachings aroused the ire of many Christians when the book was released. Apparently, there were readers unable, or unwilling, to separate fact from fiction.

Also, not to be ignored was the phenomenal success of the seven Harry Potter books by J. K. Rowling. Although they were not officially New Age, by the late 1990s and beyond, the wildly popular Harry Potter books and movies owed much to the change in consciousness that occurred over the last decades of the twentieth century. The young-adult books about the boy wizard, his magical powers, and sorcery, were a worldwide sensation, and hundreds of millions of copies were in print.[13]

At the heart of the increased interest in New Age and related subjects, "People were trying to find new answers as they search for something bigger than themselves," one publishing industry executive commented in a *PW* interview. Not surprisingly, Christian leaders were appalled; from their perspective, biblical teachings represented the Word of God, and therefore contained all the answers a person required for a "God-centered spiritual life." However, the admonitions from clergy failed to consider the negative impact that widely reported Catholic Church sexual abuse scandals had on many people. There was also the fact that increasing numbers of Americans wanted answers to concerns which traditional religion either ignored or derided, including queries about the afterlife, and other questions regarding individual paranormal experiences.

As Americans became better educated, and their thinking evolved, they were less willing to accept blanket condemnation by orthodox clergy that attributed every unapproved supernatural event to the work of Satan. In some fundamentalist denominations, such medically accepted methods as hypnotism, and widely practiced techniques including yoga and transcendental meditation, were condemned to the same forbidden precincts as witchcraft, sorcery, and animal sacrifices. However, most people had become sufficiently discerning to recognize the difference between ESP and Satanism. Having a vivid and comforting dream of a deceased loved one, or a life-saving premonition, is not the same as casting evil spells or summoning "magical powers." Prohibiting everything as if they were identical and beneath the sinister cloud of the "occult," only raised doubts about the credibility of many traditional Christian and Catholic teachings.[14]

Increasing numbers of Americans maintained their belief in God, over 90 percent, but saw little or no conflict between that and perusing a book about communicating with the departed, as just one example. Perhaps, that's why surveys and polls in recent years have reported that more people considered themselves spiritual, rather than religious, and that leads us back to why millions sought answers in a wide range of inspirational and metaphysical books and other materials. In September 2004, a publishing magazine article described readers of New Age as "seekers"; indeed, that's what they were.[15] *The New York Times* took note that the paranormal had even become the subject for romance novels, whose audience was primarily women, "where characters have ethereal powers or inhabit fantasy worlds."

By 2004, New Age booksellers and publishers, with their eye constantly attuned to trends, and the bottom line, found less reader interest in Eastern religions, and an increased demand for books about Wicca, "earth-based religions, animal communication, and psychic healing," according to one publishing company executive. Not everything changed. Faith in celestial influences was unmoved, despite the best efforts of professional debunkers and clergy, and so astrology books held fast to their seemingly never-ending grip on the popular imagination.[16] Likewise, *Publishers Weekly* magazine noted the enduring "appeal of self-help books" in the "religion/spirituality category." Llewellyn publisher Carl Weschcke pointed out that self-help and New Age were very similar. "Improving yourself is the essence of everything we do," he said. "You cannot separate your higher self from the self you deal with every day. It's all spiritual self-help."

In 2005, *PW* magazine reported there were four "books by New Age authors and spiritualists among its top ten bestselling books of the nineties," a trend that showed no signs of abating.[17] Other newspapers and magazines observed the continuing hunger for books about the afterlife. For many, they'd provided tremendous comfort in times of bereavement and grief. The subject even came to the attention of the business-oriented *Wall Street Journal* (*WSJ*). An article in March 2006 noted the "huge popularity of books written by mediums about psychic phenomena."[18]

Millions of readers had become familiar with a new generation of books by, or about, George Anderson, John Edward, James Van Praagh, Allison Dubois, Jeffrey Wands, Rosemary Altea, Suzane Northrop, and many others, all of them, nationally known mediums. The *Wall Street Journal* article focused its attention on Sylvia Browne, who'd become something of a publishing phenomenon.[19] Between 1998 and 2006, Browne, described as a "leading psychic author," had written thirteen successful books about various aspects of psychic and spiritual phenomena. Many had become bestsellers on such subjects as angels, spirit guides, the afterlife, past lives, and prophecy. She'd been helped immensely by frequent TV appearances on the nationally syndicated *Montel Williams Show*. When you added her book revenues to the money Browne made from private readings, at several hundred dollars a session, and public appearances, for Sylvia Browne, the New Age had turned into a golden age, literally, despite withering criticism from a swarm of debunkers.

At one time or another, Anderson, Edward, and Van Praagh had all hosted TV shows, demonstrating their psychic talents. Prior to the 1980s, such prime media exposure for psychic-mediums was all but unthinkable.

The public is "fascinated by life's mysteries and feel[s] that organized religion doesn't offer all the answers," the book buyer for Barnes & Noble commented in the *WSJ* article. The skeptics and debunkers saw the picture very differently, of course. One said, "that people are looking for nonrational explanations for the world around them."

Perhaps it wasn't the American people who were irrational. Possibly they were seeking reasonable explanations and guidance for the events around them that seemed illogical and wildly beyond their ability to alter or control. In September 2006, *Publishers Weekly* ran an article titled "A New Age for Mind/Body/Spirit? Publishers reflect on staying relevant in a troubled world."[20]

In just the first several years of the first decade of the new millennium, the piece pointed out, we'd faced the deadly and numbing calamity of the 9/11 terrorist attack, wars in Iraq and Afghanistan, the persistently ticking time bomb that is the Middle East, the ever-present danger posed by global terrorism, threats of nuclear proliferation from Iran and North Korea, a catastrophic tsunami in Asia, the ravages of Hurricane Katrina in New Orleans and the Gulf Coast, and the "inconvenient truth" about global warming. Since the beginning of this century, there have been the worst mass murder in the country's history at Virginia Tech, the slaughter of students in a peaceful Amish country school, the murders of twenty-six people, including twenty young children, at the Sandy Hook Elementary School in Newtown, Connecticut, and who knows what tomorrow. Is it any wonder that so many Americans continued to turn to psychic, spiritual, and inspirational sources for answers, or at least some consolation and reassurance?

The *PW* article, written by Donna Freitas, raised that point, noting that more and more people had begun to look "inward" seeking answers, "turning to the Mind/Body/Spirit shelf for books that promise comfort and individual enlightenment." In a TV interview, rap music mogul Russell Simmons talked about "our inner voice; turning inward for the answers that are within us. We are all connected to the 'Source,' God, Allah, Krishna."

The next obvious question was whether these books were of genuine help? Not everyone thought so. *PW* cited a number of detractors who regarded the genre of New Age self-help, spiritual, and inspirational books to be just another profit-making enterprise that "like Prozac give the impression of making life better, while hiding the real underlying problems of society," quoting Jeremy Carrette and Richard King in *Selling Spirituality: The Silent Takeover of Religion*. Cited in the *PW* article in September 2006, Carrette and King argued that the perpetrators were "New Age capitalists repackaging ancient religion and philosophy for profit."[21]

Another warning offered by critics was against those New Age authors, teachers, and gurus who whipped up fears of the world in turmoil, and promoted an impending doomsday scenario, then rushed in with their grand theories to save the very people they'd needlessly frightened. It wasn't unusual to read self-help books in, say, 1978 and be told, "We are living in the worst of times." Jump to the mid-1980s, and there were other New Age gurus warning, "This generation has more to fear than any before it." Move ahead to the 1990s and you'd find variations of the same darkly pessimistic scenario by yet other supposedly all-knowing and "enlightened" authors and lecturers.

In their defense, New Age publishers maintained that self-help and inspirational books do provide worthwhile advice to readers facing various difficulties, and some defenders added that the goal of New Age is not to "tell people what to do," noted *Publishers Weekly*.[22] New Age purveyors argued their aim was to help people facilitate personal change; then an individual can have a positive effect on humankind and the well-being of the planet.

PW added: "It's clear that an industry that's often been derided for encouraging self-centeredness is aiming to enable readers to help themselves and the world." What was also clear by 2006 was that the term "New Age" had all but been removed. Publishers of books about the paranormal, as well as spirituality, inspiration, holistic health, and even the occult finally found an acceptable replacement: "Mind/Body/Spirit."[23] Many who'd distanced themselves from New Age were clearly more comfortable with the new title, Mind/Body/Spirit that covered the same range of subjects, but without the stigma attached to New Age. As many in the publishing industry noted, Mind/Body/Spirit was "more marketable." Now psychic phenomena, spirituality, UFOs, alternative health, even quantum physics, Eastern philosophy, Wicca, and many other topics could fit comfortably within the new category.[24]

Suddenly, "New Age" sounded terribly dated while Mind/Body/Spirit, noted *Publishers Weekly*, seemed a more mainstream heading, as it moved beyond the traditional psychic and so-called occult subjects. Another change had also come about: people by the new millennium had become far more open-minded than those of earlier generations. Mind/Body/Spirit had "helped the [publishing] industry, wooing readers who wouldn't be caught in New Age sections but are perfectly comfortable buying books to enhance their minds, bodies, and spirits," Donna Freitas wrote in a *Publishers Weekly* cover story in September 2006.[25] Between 2002 and 2005, sales of books about spirituality grew a "whopping" 28 percent, according to M2PressWIRE. By 2002, "self-help" had become a "$7 billion-a-year industry," reported *Business Leaders Profiles*.

In 2005, books, audiovisual, software, and other products about religious subjects reported sales figures of $7.5 billion; sales by 2010 were expected to rise to $9 billion. Industry analysts attributed much of that increase to books such as *The Purpose Driven Life* and *The Da Vinci Code*, while the motion picture *The Passion of the Christ* also drove much interest.

Self-help has not and probably would not ever lose its appeal. Proof of that was the response to a book published in early 2007 simply titled *The Secret* by Rhonda Byrne. It zoomed to the top of the bestseller lists with the promise that if you want something badly enough, you can really have it. The "Secret" was a concept known as the "law of attraction." It was an idea rooted in ancient religious belief, and in the 1950s, a variation of it was offered in the widely read book, *The Power of Positive Thinking* by the Reverend Norman Vincent Peale. Some may also see the comparison with the long-held principle "like attracts like." *The Secret* noted that the "entire universe emerged from thought."

There were twenty-four contributors to the book. Among them were such prominent figures as John Gray, author of *Men Are from Mars, Women Are from Venus;* Lisa Nichols, coauthor of *Chicken Soup for the African American Soul;* and Hale Dwoskin, author of the bestseller *The Sedona Method.*

Dressed up for the post–New Age era of the twenty-first century, *The Secret* told its readers "that everything that's coming to you in your life, you are attracting. And, it's attracted to you by virtue of the images you're holding in your mind; it's what you are thinking. Whatever is going on in your mind you are attracting to you."

The book pointed out that some of the world's great inventors "knew The Secret," such as Thomas Edison, Alexander Graham Bell, the Wright Brothers. "The Secret means that we are creators of our universe." Some critics claimed that *The Secret* raised "false expectations," others charged that it replaced God, and a number of critics took issue with what seemed to be an appeal to materialism. But this was no longer the 1960s and the Age of Aquarius. The simple, or simplistic, premise of *The Secret*—"Ask, believe, receive"—seemed more appropriate to the new millennium.

In June 2006, *Newsweek* featured an article about LOHAS, an acronym for Lifestyles of Health and Sustainability, "the term for twenty-first-century New Agers. Lohasians, which are LOHAS consumers, are dedicated to personal and planetary health," according to a study by the National Marketing Institute. *Newsweek* noted the term was "created by marketers on the West Coast." The term "Lohasians" referred to LOHAS consumers, according to Beliefnet.com. "They also shop widely for spiritual practices, from Buddhism to paganism; believe in a spirit world; and many perceive themselves as spiritual, not religious," and "ecologically minded," explained *Newsweek*. Seventeen percent of Americans were estimated to fit into the oddly named category.

However, the idea that the term "Lohasians" would ever become universally accepted, even by people who fit the definition, seemed remote. If New Age became stereotyped, can you imagine someone describing him or herself as a Lohasian? To someone unfamiliar with the word, it sounds as if it might be a cult, or perhaps, extraterrestrial visitors from another galaxy.

There's no question that the New Age brought about an evolution in people's thinking, notably open-mindedness to new ideas, even if the original dream of world peace and harmony seemed as elusive as ever. In fact, many people worried when the incessant predictions of doomsday might plunge us into biblical Armageddon. We could only hope that a collective social conscience would prevail.

Perhaps the most significant contributions of the New Age were the impetus given to the environmental movement, dubbed by many as "living green," and the immense interest spurred in alternative medicine, holistic health, and unorthodox healing techniques. In the twenty-first century, despite the most sophisticated medical technology the world has ever known, millions of Americans were moving forward by going back to a number of the oldest healing methods: acupuncture, faith and psychic healing, herbal medicine, even prayer. It may have seemed anachronistic to some. For many others, it was part of a continuing search for improved health by understanding the relationship between body, mind, and spirit.

In the twenty-first century, we are about to come full circle. From the myths and beliefs of the ancients, through the rationalism of Western thought and the industrial age, but then back, as the culture of spiritualism, the belief in the paranormal, and the advances of science all merge into what can be called a fourth type of culture. It's a culture in which we discover that the paranormal is just another category of normal, only this time science can explain it.

As we discover portals to other dimensions, portals in time, and other forms of life somewhere not on our plane of reality, the Mars Curiosity rover scans ancient Martian rocks for indications of life forms after it has already established the evidence for past water flows, and even as the Vatican has publicly announced that it has embraced the potential for life elsewhere in the universe, we recognize that the New Age is already upon us in science as well as in belief, and here on Earth, we will come to understand that the ancients seers of thousands of years ago truly saw what we will discover as reality. As Shakespeare might predict, we will find that there are more things in heaven and earth than were dreamt of in our philosophy.

Introduction: The Paranormal and the Attack of the Debunkers

1. Laurence J. Peter, *Peter's Quotations: Ideas for Our Time* (New York: Bantam Books, 1979), 383.

2. Ibid, 382.

3. Williams J. Birnes and Joel Martin, *The Haunting of America: From the Salem Witch Trials to Harry Houdini* (New York: Forge, 2009), 154–175.

4. Paul Kurtz died in October 2012 at the age of eighty-six. (Source: Associated Press.)

1. Uri Geller, the Paranormal, and Psychokinesis

1. The sources used to compile this chapter include books, articles, online materials, and author interviews, including with Uri Geller and James Randi.

2. In the 1940s, when J. B. Rhine published a report compiling his PK research and experiments, it was met with much criticism and derision from many scientists and psychic debunkers. For a long-ago harsh criticism of Rhine's PK (and ESP) research, one source is the book *Sixty Years of Psychical Research* by Joseph F. Rinn (New York: Truth Seekers Publishers, 1950). Rinn, a psychic debunker, was a close friend of Harry Houdini, the famed magician and debunker.

3. Jonathan Margolis, *Uri Geller Magician or Mystic?* (New York: Welcome Rain Publishers, 1999), 27.

4. For more about Shipi Shtrang, see Margolis, 81–86.

5. Margolis, 103.

6. Richard S. Broughton, *Parapsychology: The Controversial Science* (New York: Ballantine Books, 1991), 157–165; Margolis, 160–170; James "The Amazing" Randi, *The Magic of Uri Geller* (New York: Ballantine Books, 1975), 32–44; Lois Duncan and William Roll, *Psychic Connections: A Journey into*

the Mysterious World of Psi (New York: Delacorte Press, 1995), 154–157, 222, 224.

7. Harry Houdini, *A Magician Among the Spirits* (New York: Harper and Row, 1924).

8. Randi, 117–128.

9. Ibid, 4.

10. Ibid, 4.

11. Author interview with Randi, 1975; Randi, *The Magic of Uri Geller*, 4.

12. Author interview with Puharich, 1970s.

13. One of Puharich's better-known connections was the former astronaut, Dr. Edgar Mitchell. Geller's 1972 visit to Stanford Research Institute (SRI) "was arranged by . . . Mitchell," Charles Panati (ed.) *The Geller Papers* (Boston: Houghton Mifflin, 1976), 1. It was Puharich who brought Geller to the United States.

14. Panati, 1.

15. Ibid, 31–34.

16. Andrija Puharich, *Uri: A Journal of the Mystery of Uri Geller* (New York: Anchor Press, 1974) 263–271; Randi, 42–44; Margolis, 163–164, 166; Panati, 61–66.

17. Randi, 64.

18. Margolis, 134–136. "Mass hypnotism" has been used by debunkers when they run out of specious explanations for paranormal events. When an *Omni* magazine reporter insisted on the skeptics' group providing an answer for the success of paranormal experiments involving coauthor Joel Martin, the debunkers' reply was predictable. The head of CSICOP, the debunkers group, Paul Kurtz answered that Martin's mediumship tests were successful because of "mass hypnotism." It was a ludicrous answer.

19. For the story of Arigo, those interested may want to read *Arigo: Surgeon of the Rusty Knife* by John G. Fuller (T. Y. Crowell, 1974).

20. Margolis, 125–133, 214.

21. Panati.

22. Although *My Story* is credited entirely to Uri Geller's authorship, the book was written largely by the accomplished writer, John G. Fuller. Fuller told this to Joel Martin in a private conversation.

23. Chris Moleta was the longtime producer and engineer for the *Joel Martin Show*.

24. Randi, xii; Leon Jaroff of *Time* magazine was not exactly an objective

observer of Geller. Jaroff intensely disliked the paranormal, mistakenly confusing it with the occult (Margolis, 168).

25. Margolis, 53.

26. Ibid, 242–243.

27. John Taylor was a professor of mathematics at King's College, London. He is credited as the "first British scientist to study Geller's phenomena." He initially concluded Uri Geller had genuine PK ability, which he explained in *Superminds* (New York: Viking Press, 1975). However, Taylor later changed his opinion for reasons still unclear, as he wrote in *Science and the Supernatural* (London: Temple Smith, 1980). Had he suspected fraud on Geller's part—or had he given in to scientific and skeptical peer pressure? Another theory suggested that "John Taylor's new position stemmed for his failure to find an electromagnetic explanation for paranormal phenomena," *Encyclopedia of Occultism Parapsychology*, 1287. Also see Randi, 155–156; Broughton, 159, 161; Uri said he did not know why "Taylor just switched off one day," Margolis, 204.

28. See also Birnes and Martin, *The Haunting of Twentieth-Century America* (New York: Forge Books, 2011), 287–291; *Fate Magazine*, October 1981.

29. Joel Martin and Patricia Romanowski, *We Don't Die: George Anderson's Conversations with the Other Side* (New York: G. P. Putnam's Sons, 1988).

30. See also note 18 in this chapter for reference to the "mass hypnosis" explanation often advanced by psychic debunkers.

31. Russell Targ and Keith Harary, *The Mind Race: Understanding and Using Psychic Abilities* (New York: Villard Books, 1984), 157.

32. Kurtz made similar remarks to Joel Martin in radio interviews during the 1980s.

33. Joel Martin, "Who Believes in the Paranormal and Why?" *Psychic World Magazine*: Summer 1997.

34. Some polls and surveys report that the number of Americans in 2012 was closer to *eight* out of ten who believe in God. That does not affect the millions of paranormal events experienced by Americans as reported in polls and surveys. In other words, even many who now describe themselves as "nonreligious" accept spirituality (a broader term) and the paranormal, exclusive of religion.

35. Randi, *The Magic of Uri Geller*, 298–299.

36. Truzzi founded his own organization, the Center for Scientific Anomalies Research. He also coauthored a highly regarded book about using the

paranormal to solve crimes, *The Blue Sense: Psychic Detectives and Crime* (New York: Warner Books, 1991).

37. For example, it's generally accepted that no less than 15 percent of people have had an unexplainable psi experience (Broughton); four out of ten people report an after-death communication; eight million claim near-death experiences.

38. The authors have had the opportunity to both observe and participate in a range of tests and experiments examining psi, many of them employing devices and technology that provided startling, positive results. As just one example, see the book *We Are Not Forgotten* (Martin and Romanowski), Appendix One: The Electroencephalogram Test, 303–309.

39. Deborah Blum, *Ghost Hunters: William James and the Search for Scientific Proof of Life After Death* (New York: Penguin Press, 2006).

2. *Candy Jones, Long John Nebel, and MK-ULTRA*

Except as noted, this chapter is compiled from sources including author interviews with Donald Bain, on radio and in private conversation; audio recordings of Candy Jones made by her late husband, John Nebel; authors' research including several private conversations/interviews with spy technology experts and retired military and intelligence personnel.

1. Donald Bain, *The Control of Candy Jones* (Chicago: Playboy Press, 1976).

2. Donald Bain, *Long John Nebel: Radio Talk King, Master Salesman, Magnificent Charlatan* (New York: Macmillan, 1974).

3. Richard S. Broughton, *Parapsychology: The Controversial Science* (New York: Ballantine Books, 1991), 266–267.

4. Ibid, 266.

5. Jon E. Lewis, *The Mammoth Book of Cover-Ups*, 344–355; H. Keith Melton and Robert Wallace, *The Official C.I.A. Manual of Trickery and Deception* (New York: HarperCollins, 2009), 1–65; John Marks, *The Search for the "Manchurian Candidate"* (New York: Times Books, 1979), 57–61, 67–69, 71–72, 98, 114–116.

6. Gordon Thomas, *Journey into Madness: The True Story of Secret CIA Mind Control and Medical Abuse* (New York: Bantam Books, 1989).

7. In 1975, Senator Frank Church chaired a Senate committee probing CIA activities, including secret experiments toward "mind control," many using mind-altering drugs such as LSD.

3. *The Weaponization of Mind Control and LSD*

1. Wilder Penfield, *The Mystery of the Mind* "Cerebral Cortex and Consciousness," 111; Memories 31, 35, 63.

2. For those interested in more about Dr. Cameron, see John Marks, *The Search for the "Manchurian Candidate"* (New York: Times Books, 1979), 131–141.

3. William Birnes coauthored with Lt. Col. Philip J. Corso, the bestselling book *The Day After Roswell*. Birnes had many private conversations with Corso about his life and career.

4. Among many books about the CIA and its efforts at mind control, the authors found helpful John Marks, *The Search for the "Manchurian Candidate,"* and H. Keith Melton and Robert Wallace, *The Official C.I.A. Manual of Trickery and Deception* (New York: HarperCollins, 2009).

5. Although not directly about LSD, there are some curious, and likely little-known historical accounts of interest in "drugs and physic phenomena." One such article in the *Journal of the American Society for Psychical Research (JASPR)* from 1937 suggested "Drugs offer a fruitful field of research of the student of psychic states." One drug mentioned was mescaline from the peyote plant. "There are many stimulants the effects of which out to be studied," the article concluded. Obviously, despite a degree of prescience, the author could not foresee the government's interest in LSD and mind control, *JASPR,* volume XXXI, July 1937 Number 7, pages 219–221. The author was the late Nandor Fodor, a well-known psychic researcher and author for many years. See also John Marks, *The Search for the "Manchurian Candidate,"* Chapter 4, LSD, 53–72.

6. G. H. Estabrooks, *Hypnotism* (New York: E. P. Dutton & Company, 1943, 1957), 193–213.

7. Ibid, 193.

8. Ibid, 195.

9. Ibid, 200–201, 202.

10. Ibid, 202.

11. Bain, 263–267.

12. Marks, 73–86; Jon E. Lewis, *The Mammoth Book of Cover-Ups* (Philadelphia: Running Press, 2007), 344–347.

13. Mark Zepezauer, *The CIA's Greatest Hits* (Tucson, AZ: Odonian Press, 1994).

14. Marks, 48.

15. Ibid, 8.

16. *Amplified Bible*: I Samuel 28.

17. Ronald McRae, *Mind Wars: The True Story of Government Research into the Military Potential of Psychic Weapons* (New York: St. Martin's Press, 1984), 24.

18. Mary Gordon, *Joan of Arc* (New York: Viking/Penguin Books, 2000).

19. McRae, 25.

20. Martin and Birnes, *The Haunting of the Presidents* (New York: Signet, 2003).

21. William Kalush and Larry Sloman, *The Secret Life of Houdini: The Making of America's First Superhero* (New York: Atria Books, 2006).

4. *Harry Houdini*

1. William Kalush and Larry Sloman, *The Secret Life of Houdini: The Making of America's First Superhero* (New York: Atria Books, 2006), 71.

2. Ibid, 70–71.

3. Ibid, 97–99.

4. Ibid, 94–95.

5. Ibid, 99.

6. Ibid, 101.

7. Ibid, 72.

8. Ibid, 125.

9. Ibid, 127–128.

10. Ibid, 109–111.

11. An excellent example of a "manual on trickery" commissioned by the CIA is H. Keith Melton and Robert Wallace, *The Official C.I.A. Manual of Trickery and Deception* (New York: William Morrow, 2009). During the Cold War in 1953, the CIA undertook MK-ULTRA. It was "top secret." MK-ULTRA was an effort to create mind-control methods to challenge Soviet mind-control techniques. The CIA employed a top magician, John Mulholland, to author two manuals. (Source: book jacket, CIA manual referenced above).

12. In 1973, then CIA director Richard Helms ordered all MK-ULTRA documents destroyed. However, some files survived, and provide us with a glimpse of top-secret "behavior modification or mind control" methods (*C.I.A. Manual of Trickery*, viii). Marks noted that the CIA's "parapsychology goals" appeared in a *Washington Post* article (1977), titled "Psychic Spying?" (Marks, 230).

13. Joel Martin and William J. Birnes, *The Haunting of the Presidents: A Paranormal History of the U.S. Presidents* (New York: Signet Books, 2003), 77–80; Ruth Montgomery, *Gift of Prophecy: The Phenomenal Jean Dixon* (New York: Morrow, 1965).

14. Comments from the late army officer Philip J. Corso are drawn from extensive interviews between Corso and William Birnes.

15. Briefly, from what is known now about the CIA's top-secret programs delving into "behavior modification/mind control methods," many seem startling, even bizarre. Many included experiments with mind-altering drugs such as LSD and other hallucinogenics. Other "research" involved radio and electrical stimulation of the brain; even the use of radiation and microwaves. There were animal studies, as well as hypnosis, and parapsychology experiments, including ESP, remote viewing, and psychokinesis; even the use of magicians and trickery. For more detail some sources include John Marks, *The Search for the "Manchurian Candidate"* (New York: Times Books, 1979); Jon E. Lewis, *The Mammoth Book of Cover-Ups* (Philadelphia: Running Press, 2007); Melton and Wallace, *The Official C.I.A. Manual of Trickery and Deception*; Donald Bain, *The Control of Candy Jones* (Chicago: Playboy Press, 1976); Broughton, 326.

16. Martin and Birnes, *The Haunting of the Presidents*, 222.

17. Kalush and Sloman, 491, 498, 500.

18. Martin and Birnes, 222–223.

19. Kalush and Sloman, 506.

20. Beryl Williams and Samuel Epstein, *The Great Houdini* (New York: Scholastic Books, 1962), 241–242; Kalush and Sloman, 508–511, 512–515.

21. The Houdini battle against well-known Boston medium Mina Crandon (known professionally as Margery) boiled into a major—and very controversial—news story in 1924. When Houdini learned Margery was about to be awarded a $2,500 prize from the prestigious *Scientific American* magazine for her psychic mediumship gifts, Houdini was in a rage. He proceeded to "test" her, and, not surprisingly, exposed her as a fraud. Margery lost the award, of course. Only many years later did a Houdini assistant confess that when Houdini could not debunk Margery, he secretly "sabotaged" her; in other words, *he* used trickery. Charges and countercharges continued for years with no resolve. There are many books that provide detail about the Houdini and Margery battle. A few sources we used: Kalush and Sloman, 405–421, 427–450; Arthur Ford, *Unknown But*

Known, (New York: Signet, 1969), 14; Joel Martin and Patricia Romanowski, *We Don't Die*, (New York: G. P. Putnam's Sons, 1988), 280–281; Janice Weaver, *Harry Houdini: The Legend of the World's Greatest Escape Artist* (New York: Abrams, 2011), 38–39; Tom Lalicki, *Spellbinder: The Life of Harry Houdini*, (New York: Holiday House, 2000). For some detail about experiences involving the paranormal, specifically about Houdini in the afterlife, and his alleged spirit communications, see: Kalush and Sloman, chapter 26, "There Is No Death," 537–549; Kalush and Sloman include discussion about the medium Arthur Ford's controversial séance for Mrs. Houdini in the hope of receiving a secret from Houdini's spirit, 538–548; Arthur Ford, 14; Martin and Romanowski, 281–282. Interview with D. C. Webster, friend of Arthur Ford. Other sources for this chapter included interviews with the late magician Milbourne Christopher, also an author and collector of Houdini memorabilia. He gave Martin a tour of his "Houdini Collection" in his then Manhattan home.

5. *Hitler, the Paranormal, and the CIA*

1. John Marks, *The Search for the "Manchurian Candidate,"* 12, 13.
2. Ibid, 12.
3. Ibid, 13.
4. Ibid.
5. John Toland, *Adolf Hitler* (Garden City, NY: Doubleday, 1976); author interviews with John Toland, both broadcast and privately; William J. Birnes and Joel Martin, *The Haunting of Twentieth-Century America: From the Nazis to the New Millennium* (New York: Tor/Forge Books, 2011), 19–60; Paul Roland, *The Nazis and the Occult* (Edison, NJ: Chartwell Books, 2009).
6. Roland, 25–26.
7. Ibid, 40–46, 48–49.
8. John Marks, 11.
9. Mark Zepezauer, *The CIA's Greatest Hits* (Tucson, AZ: Odonian Press, 1994).
10. Ibid.
11. Marks, 211.
12. Sheila Ostrander and Lynn Schroeder, *Psychic Discoveries Behind the Iron Curtain* (Englewood Cliffs, NJ: Prentice Hall, 1970).
13. Marks, 11.

14. Author interview with Lynn Schroeder.

15. Russell Targ and Keith Harary, *The Mind Race: Understanding and Using Psychic Abilities* (New York: Villard Books, 1984), 5.

16. Ibid.

17. Ibid.

18. Ibid, 26–32.

19. Ibid, 35–37.

20. Ibid, 41–42.

21. This quote attributed to Albert Einstein can be found in many books and articles, as well as Targ and Harary, 53.

22. In *The Mind Race* there is a thoughtful chapter about precognition, 53–68; Broughton, *Parapsychology the Controversial Science* (New York: Ballantine Books, 1991), 18–24; Lois Duncan and William Roll, Ph.D., *Psychic Connections: A Journey into the Mysterious World of Psi* (New York: Delacorte Press, 1995), 125–145; Larry Dossey, *The Science of Premonitions* (New York: Plume Books, 2009).

23. Targ and Harary, 46, 56–59, 178.

24. Ron McRae, *Mind Wars* (New York: St. Martin's Press, 1984), xxv–xxviii (Introduction by Jack Anderson).

25. Jim Marrs, *Psi Spies: The True Story of America's Psychic Warfare Program* (Franklin Lakes, NJ: New Page Books, 2007), 120–121.

26. Targ and Harary, 15–17, 59; Duncan and Roll, 121.

27. This "discovery" has a long history. In hundreds of tests of psychic-mediumship the author (Joel Martin) found that psychics and mediums were far more accurate when motivated by a deceased (spirit) communication, or some emotional component that they can make a psychic connection to. The late medium Eileen Garrett held the same opinion; she was bored by tests using cards as J. B. Rhine had done at Duke University throughout the 1930s.

28. Many recent books about parapsychology devote mention to the Ganzfield method (pro and con). Several sources include: Targ and Harary, 22–23, 151–152; Broughton, 99–105; Roll, 122–124; McRae, 58, 60.

29. *Encyclopedia of Occultism and Parapsychology* (J. Gordon Melton, ed.), 1267–1268; Ingo Swann, *Natural ESP: A Layman's Guide to Unlocking the Extrasensory Power of Your Mind* (New York: Bantam Books, 1987); Targ and Harary, 48–50, McRae, 55, 94–95, 101–102.

30. Targ and Harary, 17.

31. Jim Marrs, *Psi Spies: The True Story of America's Psychic Warfare Program* (Franklin Lakes, NJ: New Page Books, 2007), 140, 176, 220.

32. Marks, *The Search for the "Manchurian Candidate,"* 9.

33. Boughton, 115–116, 119.

34. Ibid, 319–321.

35. Ibid, 320n.

36. Sheila Ostrander and Lynn Schroeder, *Psychic Discoveries Behind the Iron Curtain* (New York: Bantam, 1971), 248–249, 40–41.

37. Nandor Fodor, *Between Two Worlds* (West Nyack, NY: Parker Publishing Company), 24–29.

38. Ostrander and Schroeder, 136–137.

39. Joel Martin and Patricia Romanowski, *We Don't Die: George Anderson's Conversations with the Other Side* (New York: G. P. Putnam's Sons, 1988), 192–208.

40. Targ and Harary, *The Mind Race*, 80, 253–255.

41. Ostrander and Schroeder, 200–213.

42. Ibid, 56.

43. Even more puzzling about Rhine's remarks in his 1957 *Journal of Parapsychology* article was the fact that "the Army began funding some of Rhine's work at Duke University as early as 1952," noted Broughton, 326.

44. Ostrander and Schroeder, 6, 7, 38–41, 59; Broughton, 143; Targ and Harary, 75–76, 77.

45. Author interviews with Dr. Rus; Ostrader and Schroeder, 402.

46. Ostrander and Schroeder, 328–331.

47. Ibid, 344.

48. Ibid, 368–372, 390.

49. Max Toth and Greg Nielson, *Pyramid Power* (New York: Warner Books, 1974); author interviews with Max Toth.

50. Quotes attributed to Uri Geller concerning his CIA work, capture of Iraqi dictator Saddam Hussein, and remote viewers are from 2006 Reuters news account.

51. For another reference to the 1982 kidnapping and subsequent rescue of Captain James Dozier, see Ron McRae, *Mind Wars*, 16.

52. Jon E. Lewis, *The Mammoth Book of Cover-Ups* (Philadelphia: Running Press, 2007), 511–512; Jon Ronson, *The Men Who Stare at Goats*, 2004; Joseph McMoneagle, *Remote Viewing Secrets: A Handbook* (Charlottesville, VA: Hampton Roads, 200), 202–203.

6. Remote Influencing and Paranormal Warfare

This chapter is a combination, as follows: The sources used for this chapter include Ron McRae, *Mind Wars* (New York: St. Martin's Press, 1984), 114–130; James Channon interview with William J. Birnes in *UFO Magazine*; Jon Ronson, *The Men Who Stare at Goats* (New York: Simon and Schuster, 2004), chapter 3, "The First Earth Battalion," 27–53; also selected online sources for James Channon; *First Earth Battalion*; Jon Ronson; Stewart Brand's *Whole Earth Catalog*; Guy Savelli; Dr. John Alexander; Lt. James Rowe; Paul H. Smith. Smith authored *Reading the Enemy's Mind* (New York: Forge, 2004); Alexander wrote *The Warrior's Edge* (New York: Morrow, 1990); Ostrander and Schroeder, *Psychic Discoveries Behind the Iron Curtain* (New York: Bantam, 1970), 42–58, 114 (story of Soviet psychic Wolf Messing). Alexander also interviewed by William Birnes (radio).

7. The Light Beckons: Near-Death Experiences

1. Amchu, One of Us: The Story of Sam Goldberg- from author files (William Birnes).
2. Elise's Story-from author files (Joel Martin).
3. James R. Lewis, *Encyclopedia of Afterlife Beliefs,* (Detroit: Gale Research, 1994), 258; Raymond A. Moody, Jr., *Life After Life* (Covington, Georgia: Mockingbird Books, 1975); Craig R. Lundahl (ed.), *A Collection of Near-Death Research Readings,* (Chicago: Nelson-Hall, Inc, 1982) 89–109.
4. Joel Martin and Patricia Romanowski, *Love Beyond Life: The Healing Power of After-Death Communications* (New York: HarperCollins, 1997), 70–71.
5. Elisabeth Kübler-Ross, *On Death and Dying* (New York: Macmillan, 1969), 2.
6. "Life, Letters and Journals of Louisa May Alcott" as excerpted in the *Journal of the American Society for Psychical Research,* Number 7 (July 1913); Birnes and Martin, *The Haunting of America: From the Salem Witch Trials to Harry Houdini* (Tor/Forge Books, 2009), 178–189.
7. Elisabeth Kübler-Ross, *On Death and Dying,* 5.
8. In *On Death and Dying,* Kübler-Ross devotes a chapter to each of what she explains are the "fire stages of death."
9. Martin interview (radio) and in-person appearance with Moody, 1999. Martin's private conversation with Kübler-Ross during 1980s.
10. Lewis, *Encyclopedia of Afterlife Beliefs and Phenomena,* 198–199, 259.

11. LANDS founders and highlights of their efforts with NDE Research explained in this paragraph are taken from Brad Steiger and Sherry Hansen Steiger, *Children of the Light* (New York: Signet, 1995).

12. The research, personal observations, and interviews conducted by Martin and Birnes (authors) revealed the same conclusion: the common characteristics of NDES are too many to ignore. The NDE is a universal phenomenon deserving serious attention.

13. Carl G. Jung, *Memories, Dreams, Reflections* (New York: Vintage Books, 1965).

14. Herbert Greenhouse, *The Astral Journey* (Garden City, NY: Doubleday, 1975). Author interview with Greenhouse.

15. Betty Eadie, *Embraced by the Light* (Placerville, CA: Gold Leaf Press 1992); *The Awakening Heart* (NY: Pocket Books 1996). Author interview with Eadie, 1993.

16. Don Piper, *90 Minutes in Heaven* (Grand Rapids, MI: Revell, 2004).

17. Joel Marin, guest with Dannion Brinkley on *Alan Handleman Show* (natinally syndicated radio), 1977. (Brinkley, *Saved by the Light* (New York: Villard, 1994).

18. Maurice Rawlings, *Beyond Death's Door* (New York: Bantam Books, 1979).

19. Kenneth Ring, *Life at Death: A Scientific Investigation of Near-Death Experiences* (New York: Coward, McCann & Geoghegan, 1980).

20. Author interview with Reverend Ralph Wilkerson on *Joel Martin Show* (radio).

21. From author files.

22. *The Lancet* report of the NDE study conducted by medical doctors in the Netherlands (*The Lancet,* Volume 358, December 15, 2001).

23. From author files.

24. From author files.

25. From author files.

26. Author (Martin) witnessed this out-of-body experiment.

27. From author files.

28. Maurice Rawlings, *Beyond Death's Door*, 30.

29. Robert Van de Castle, *Our Dreaming Mind* (New York: Ballantine Books, 1994).

30. As an example of "halos and the radiant light" in religious art, those interested might look at Nancy Grubb, *Angels in Art* (New York: Abbeville Press, 1995). The book contains reproductions of great art/paintings

from centuries ago. There are often halos and light surrounding the angels portrayed by countless artists, especially in the Middle Ages. Likewise, religious art, especially of Catholic saints, show a halo, light or aura—often around the saint.

31. Lewis, *Afterlife Beliefs,* 167–68, 289–91.

32. Ibid, 62–63, 83, 309.

33. Greenhouse, *The Astral Journey.*

34. Author interviews with D. Scott Rogo on radio (*Joel Martin Show*). Rogo wrote the books *Miracles: A Parascientific Inquiry into Wondrous Phenomena* (New York: Dial Press, 1982); *Who Is Padre Pio,* TAN Books and Publishers, 1974.

35. Lewis, *Afterlife Beliefs,* 347–49, 359.

36. Birnes and Martin, *The Haunting of America From the Salem Witch Trials to Harry Houdini,* 104–106; Lewis, *Afterlife Beliefs,* 347–349; *Encyclopedia of Occultism & Parapsychology,* 1269–1271.

37. Birnes and Martin, *The Haunting of the Presidents,* 49–56.

38. Lewis, *Afterlife Beliefs,* 102–104, 258.

39. From author files.

40. Author (Martin) witnessed this psychic reading by a well-known medium for the parents of the deceased child. Author later interviewed parents to verify details and accuracy.

41. Karlis Osis and Erlendur Haraldsson, *At the Hour of Death*—originally published in 1977 rev. ed. New York Hastings House, 1986). Author's private conversations with Dr. Osis.

42. Lewis, *Afterlife Beliefs,* 104.

43. Ibid, 34.

44. Ibid, 258, 243, 277; *Encyclopedia of Occultism and Parapsychology,* 871.

45. Eileen Garrett was one of the best-known and frequently studied psychic—mediums of the twentieth century (1892–1970). She was written about in many books and articles. Some of the sources include John G. Fuller, *The Airmen Who Would Not Die;* Lawrence LeShan, *The Medium, the Mystic, and the Physicist: Toward a General Theory of the Paranormal*; Eileen Garrett, *Many Voices,* written by her in 1968; *Reader's Digest Into the Unknown* (1981), page 193, among many others. Author (Martin) interviewed a close friend of Mrs. Garrett, Ben Weaster, founder, Toronto Society for Psychical Research. He showed Martin letters he and Mrs. Garrett exchanged, and answered many question about her life and work.

46. Morse is a pediatrician by training. Melvin Morse, M.D. *Closer to the Light* (New York: Villard Books, 1990); *Transformed by the Light* (New York; Villard Books, 1992). Author interviews with Morse about his NDE research with young children. Morse has been a frequent national TV guest.

47. Arthur Ford, *Unknown but Known* (New York: Signet Books), 53.

48. Ibid.

49. From author files.

50. Joel Martin and Patricia Romanowski, *Love Beyond Life: The Healing Power of After-Death Communications* (New York: HarperCollins, 1997).

51. Underlining this last point consider the continuing interest in near—death experiences, represented by two more best selling books about NDEs: Todd Burpo and Lynn Vincent, *Heaven Is for Real* (Nashville, TN: Thomas Nelson, 2010); Burpo is a minister. Dr. Eben Alexander, *Proof of Heaven* (New York: Simon & Schuster, 2012). It should be noted that Alexander is a respected medical doctor, a neurosurgeon.

8. *The New Age Becomes Big Business*

1. William J. Birnes and Joel Martin, *The Haunting of America: From the Salem Witch Trials to Harry Houdini* (Tor/Forge Books, 2009). This book devotes detail to the "Great Age of Spiritualism."

2. J. Gordon Melton, Jerome Clark, and Aidan Kelly, eds. *New Age Encyclopedia* (Detroit: Gale Research, 1990).

3. *Encyclopedia of Occultism and Parapsychology*, 119.

4. "The number of Americans who do not identify with any religion continues to grow at a rapid pace. One-fifth of the U.S. public—and a third of adults under thirty—are religiously unaffiliated today, the highest percentages ever in Pew Research Center polling" (Pew Research, October 9, 2012). What's more, of the 46 million unaffiliated adults, a third (47 percent) classify themselves as "spiritual" but not "religious."

5. Modern Times was a controversial "socialist community" founded on Long Island, New York, in 1851. Many of its members were spiritualists. The utopian community was tolerant of "nearly everything," and with no government it came to an end during the turmoil of the Civil War, in 1864. Source: *Encyclopedia of Occultism and Parapsychology*, 868. The similarities between the experimental utopian communities of the 1830s–1850s bear striking similarities to the hippie communes during the 1960s.

6. Richard Woods, *The Occult Revolution* (New York: Herder and Herder, 1971). This book's author, shaken by the "alienated youth" who turned to new ways of thinking during the 1960s, saw a major threat to traditional religious beliefs. In stating his case, Woods mistakenly lumps together yoga, ESP, UFOs, astrology, telepathy, and "devil worship," as the—dreaded—"occult revolution."

7. Michael York writing in *New Religions: A Guide*, edited by Christopher Partridge (New York: Oxford University Press, 2004).

8. Ibid.

9. Richard Woods, *The Occult Revolution* (New York: Herder and Herder, 1971).

10. D. Scott Rogo, *Miracles: A Parascientific Inquiry into Wonderous Phenomena* (New York: Dial Press, 1982). Also, author interview (radio) with Rogo.

11. Michael York writing in *New Religions: A Guide*.

12. *Encyclopedia of Occultism and Parapsychology*, 927.

13. Mary Olsen Kelly, ed. *The Fireside Treasury of Light* (New York: Fireside/Simon & Schuster, 1990).

14. Michael York writing in *New Religions: A Guide*.

15. Author interview with Dr. Brian Weiss, 1999.

16. Dick Sutphen, *You Were Born to Be Together* (New York: Pocket Books, 1976), 15.

17. Jess Stearn, *Soul Mates* (New York: Bantam Books, 1984). Author interviews with Stearn (1990s).

18. Michael York writing in *New Religions: A Guide*.

19. Mary Olsen Kelly, *The Fireside Treasury of Light*, 25.

20. Author interview with Dr. Bernie Siegel, on radio (1993).

21. *New Religions: A Guide*, 194–95, 173–75, 172–73, 327–29, 248–49.

22. Article by Elizabeth Puttick in *New Religions: A Guide*, Christopher Partridge (ed.), 399–402.

23. Jess Stearn and Edgar Cayce, *The Sleeping Prophet* (New York: Doubleday, 1967); see also Birnes and Martin, *The Haunting of Twentieth-Century America* (New York: Forge Books, 2011) Chapter 4: *Edgar Cayce: The Sleeping Psychic*, 135–166.

24. Author interview with Dr. Leo Buscaglia (1983).

25. Mary Olsen Kelly, *The Fireside Treasury of Light*. Excerpt of Ken Keyes's *Handbook of Higher Consciousness*, 73–76.

26. Mary Olsen Kelly. Excerpt of Shakti Gawan's writing, 28–29; Shakti Gawan with Laurel King, *Living in the Light* (San Rafael, CA: New World Library, 1978).

27. Christopher Partridge, *New Religions: A Guide*. "ISKON: The International Society for Krishna Consciousness (Hare Krishna Movement)" by Malory Nye, 187–189; Nathaniel Lande, *Mindstyles/Lifestyles* (Los Angeles: Price/Stern/Sloan, 1976). Author interviews with Krishna members.

28. Mary Olsen Kelly. Excerpts of M. Scott Peck's writing, 89–90; M. Scott Peck, M.D., *The Road Less Traveled* (New York: Simon & Schuster, 1978).

29. "Anthony J. Robbins." *Contemporary Authors Online*. Detroit: Gale, 2005. *Biography in Context*; www.tonyrobbins.com (official website); en.wikipedia.org/wiki/Tony_Robbins; *Awaken the Giant Within*, (New York: Simon & Schuster, 1992).

30. "Marianne Williamson." *Religious Leaders of America* (Gale, 1999); *Almanac of Famous People* (Gale, 2011); *Time*, July 29, 1991.

31. *A Course in Miracles* as explained in the *New Age Encyclopedia* by J. Gordon Melton (Detroit: Gale, 1990).

32. Gary Zukav, *The Seat of the Soul* (New York: Fireside/Simon & Schuster, 1989), 27.

33. Ibid.

34. Ibid, 13–14.

35. Ibid, 38–39.

36. Caroline Myss, *Anatomy of the Spirit* (New York: Harmony Books, 1996).

37. Orloff was not alone. In the course of our research, by the 1980s we had found a number of psychologists and therapists open to incorporating their patients' paranormal experiences within traditional psychotherapy.

38. Melton, *New Age Encyclopedia*, 270–72; *Encyclopedia of Occultism and Parapsychology*, 790; Kelly, *The Fireside Treasury of Light*, 36–38; *New Religions: A Guide*, 311; Shirley MacLaine, *Out on a Limb* (New York: Bantam Books, 1983); MacLaine, *Dancing in the Light* (New York: Bantam Books, 1985).

39. *New Age Encyclopedia*, 253–254; *Encyclopedia of Occultism and Parapsychology*, 716; J.Z. Knight, *A State of Mind: My Story: Ramtha, the Adventure Begins* (New York: Warner Books, 1987).

40. Melton, *New Age Encyclopedia*, 401–402; *Encyclopedia of Occultism and Parapsychology*, 1117. Ryerson is referred to in three MacLaine books

written during the 1980s and was portrayed in the motion picture *Out on a Limb* (1987), based on MacLaine's 1983 bestselling book by the same title.

41. Coauthor Joel Martin had private interview with Peter Cameron (1996). The late Mr. Cameron, theatrical agent was a friend of Peter Sellers. Cameron showed Martin many of the books about Jewish mysticism that he'd shared with Sellers to study Kabbalah, and explained the actor's interest.

42. *New Age Encyclopedia,* 271; Charles Silva, *Date with the Gods* (Long Island, NY: Coleman Graphics, 1977). Joel Martin interviewed Silva on radio.

43. MacLaine's suggestion about gender and the New Age was not far-fetched. A century earlier, women mediums dominated the séance tables during America's Great Age of Spiritualism. (For more about the subject, see Birnes and Martin, *The Haunting of America: From the Salem Witch Trials to Harry Houdini,* chapter 6, "Women at the Séance Table" (246–281). In 1999, *The Atlas of the New Age* reported that "witches and natural magic are now experiencing more serious interest." It was predominantly women who were the market for the "revival in Wicca." It should be noted that the paranormal and Wicca (and natural magic) are *not* the same. Parapsychologists generally avoid Wicca, yet under the umbrella of New Age, books about psychics, mediums, and witches are—wrongly—lumped together.

44. Author interview (radio) with Ruth Montgomery (1979). Other interviews with Montgomery during 1970s and 1980s. Of her many books, one was autobiographical: Ruth Montgomery, *Herald of the New Age* (Garden City, NY: Doubleday, 1986).

45. Jane Roberts, *Seth Speaks* (Englewood Cliffs, NJ: Prentice-Hall, 1972); *The Seth Material* (Englewood Cliffs, NJ: Prentice-Hall, 1970); *The "Unknown" Reality: A Seth Book, Volume One* (Prentice-Hall, 1977). "Seth" quotes for this chapter are from *Seth Speaks,* including xvi, xvii, 90–91, 79–108, 167–191.

46. *Encyclopedia of Occultism and Parapsychology,* 716.

47. JZ Knight, *A State of Mind: My Story* (New York: Warner Books, 1987).

48. Jach Pursel, *Lazaris Interviews* (2 vols.), (Beverly Hills, CA: Concept Synergy, 1988).

49. Christopher Partridge (ed.) *New Religions: A Guide*, 311, 330, 334; *New Age Encyclopedia*, 361–362.

50. *New Religions*, 312; Marilyn Ferguson, *The Aquarian Conspiracy* (Los Angeles: J. B. Tarcher, 1980).

51. Kelly, *Treasury of Light*, 32.

9. *Hillary Clinton's New Age Odyssey*

1. Bob Woodward, *The Choice* (New York: Simon & Schuster, 1996).

2. Jean Houston, *The Possible Human* (Los Angeles, CA: Jeremy P. Tarcher, 1982). This quote also appears in Kelly, *Treasury of Light*, 57.

3. Woodward, *The Choice*, 56.

4. Ibid, 129–130.

5. Ibid, 130.

6. Christopher Andersen, *Bill and Hillary: The Marriage* (New York: Morrow, 1999).

7. Woodward, 130.

8. Ibid; Martin and Birnes, *The Haunting of the Presidents*, 330.

9. Andersen, quoted by Martin and Birnes, 330.

10. Woodward, 132.

11. Martin and Birnes, *The Haunting of the Presidents*, 331.

12. *Newsweek* magazine article, quoted by Martin and Birnes, *Presidents*, 331.

13. Martin and Birnes, *Presidents*, 328.

14. "New Age nonsense"—or perhaps something more. Could Hillary Clinton have had actual contact with Mrs. Roosevelt? Was she the only one? Apparently not. See the true story of sculptor Penelope Jencks who had her own similar experience, Martin and Birnes, 332–334.

10. *The New Age at the End of the Millennium:*
Fads and Fancies

1. *Into the Unknown* (Pleasantville, NY: Reader's Digest Association, 1981), 250–251; Frank Hoffmann and William Bailey, *Mind and Society Fads* (New York: Haworth Press, 1992), 249–251; *Encyclopedia of Occultism and Parapsychology*, 1018–1020; *Psychic World*, "Communicating with Plants" by Isa Duncan (Spring 1998), 73–79.

2. *New Age Encyclopedia*, 263–264, 150–153; *The World Almanac Book of the Strange*, 90–91.

3. Martin and Birnes, *The Haunting of the Presidents*, 16–32.

4. *The Essential Joseph Smith* (Salt Lake City: Signature Books, 1995), 2, 226.

5. Hope Price, *Angels* (New York: Avon Books, 1993), 216.

6. Ibid, 204.

7. Authors' research, observations of readings by mediums, many interviews with men, women, children suggest the belief in "guardian angels," regardless of age, gender, ethnicity, religion.

8. Gustav Davidson, *A Dictionary of Angels* (New York: Free Press, 1967), 127–228.

9. See also note 3, this chapter.

10. Daniel Cohen, *The Ghosts of War* (New York: G. P. Putnam's Sons), 26–29.

11. Brad Steiger, *Guardian Angels and Spirit Guides* (New York: Plume, 1995), xi.

12. Also, author interview with this family (1995).

13. Author files.

14. Author files.

15. Author files.

16. Brad Steiger, *Wisdom Teachings of Archangel Michael* (New York: Signet, 1997); *Saint Michael and the Angels* (Rockford, IL: Tan Books and Publishers, 1983).

17. Author interview (radio) with Tim Wylie (early 1990s).

18. George Noory and William J. Birnes, *Journey to the Light* New York: Forge Books/Tom Doherty Associates, 2009); Eileen Elias Freeman, *Touched by Angels* (New York: Warner Books, 1993); Sophy Burnham, *A Book of Angels* (New York: Ballantine Books, 1990); Jerry and Lorin Biederman, *Earth Angels* (New York: Broadway Books, 1997).

19. Dael Walker, *The Crystal Book* (Sunol, CA: The Crystal Company, 1983).

20. Adrienne Warren, "Crystal Gazing" (*Psychic World*, Spring 1997), 58–61, 104–105 (specifically about "crystal ball gazing, key to revealing your future").

21. "Gemstone Essences" (*Psychic World*, Spring 1997), 81.

22. *Encyclopedia of Occultism and Parapsychology*, 92–93 (Cayce and Atlantis), 289 (Crystal healing); *New Age Encyclopedia*, 46–48; Edgar Cayce, *Atlantis: Fact or Fiction* (Virginia Beach, VA: ARE Press, 1962); Birnes and Martin, *The Haunting of Twentieth-Century America*, 135–166.

23. The author's father (Martin) built "crystal sets" during the 1920s. "Crystal set" radios are still sold in some specialty stores and through selected mail-order catalogs.

24. *New Age Encyclopedia*, 138–142.

11. *New Age and Music: The Power of Tonality*

1. Tonality—Wikipedia (see online sources).

2. Jon E. Lewis, *The Mammoth Book of Cover-Ups* (Philadelphia: Running Press, 2007), 158–160.

3. New Age music—Wikipedia (see online sources).

4. Enya—Wikipedia (see online sources).

5. Adrienna Warren, "The Soothing Sounds of Music," *Psychic World* (Winter 1997), 74–76, 115–116.

6. Author interview (radio) with Steve Halpern; author interview (radio) with Jean-Michael Jarre.

7. In the authors' experiences, this is not an unusual answer from songwriters of many genres.

8. Frank W. Hoffmann and William G. Bailey, *Mind and Society Fads* (New York: The Haworth Press, 1992), 159; *New Age Encyclopedia*, 204–205.

9. Ibid, 159–160; Harmonic Convergence—Wikipedia (see online sources); *New Age Encyclopedia*, 28–30.

10. Hoffmann and Bailey, 159.

11. Ibid, 160.

12. Depending on the source, "power points" are also described as "power spots" or "power centers."

13. Hoffmann and Bailey, 160; Harmonic Convergence—Wikipedia (see online sources).

14. Dennis William Hauck, *Haunted Places: The National Directory* (New York: Penguin Books, 1996).

15. Pat McDonald, "Sedona Place of Magic and Mystery" (*Psychic World*, Spring 1997), 42.

16. Ibid, 40.

17. There are a number of excellent travel books as well as online sources describing Sedona, its accommodations and sights, including vortexes, *Explorer's Guide (Sedona)* by Christine Bailey, 2011; *Explorer's Guide (Arizona)* by Christine Maxa, 2011; Sedona, Arizona—Wikipedia, The Spiritual Side of Sedona.

18. Pat McDonald, 42–43.
19. Hauck, *Haunted Places* (see Sedona, Arizona).

12. *Toward a New Frontier of Awareness*

1. Not helping the "crystal craze" were several nationally reported gem scams perpetrated by dishonest, self-appointed New Age gurus.
2. Martin and Romanowski, *We Don't Die* (New York: G. P. Putnam's Sons, 1988).
3. Many astrologers also embraced the "new technology" employing computer programs to prepare astrological charts/horoscopes for clients.
4. "New Age Is All the Rage," *Publishers Weekly,* March 10, 1997.
5. Ibid.
6. Bodhi Tree in Los Angeles has since closed. Several other New Age bookstores have also gone out of business. Some publishing industry experts attribute the closings to the poor national economy.
7. Borders chain of bookstores has since closed.
8. *Publishers Weekly,* May 21, 2001.
9. Ibid.
10. Ibid.
11. Ibid, May 21, 2001.
12. Ibid, September 6, 2004.
13. Harry Potter also had his enemies; among them Christian fundamentalist denominations, and even Pope Benedict in 2003, when he was a Cardinal. Benedict said that the Harry Potter books "distort Christianity in the soul" (Reuters, July 14, 2005). The Harry Potter books also created confusion for some readers. Because the J. K. Rowling character is a "boy wizard," and the stories delve in magic, sorcery, and the supernatural, many mistook the fictional themes for New Age or the paranormal; a too-frequent mistake. The Potter books are technically *not* New Age or paranormal.
14. As one example, the authors referred to *Angels, Demons, and the End Times,* published by the Christian Broadcasting Network, Virginia Beach, VA (2006). In it is a section entitled "Do Séances, Ouija Boards, and Fortune-Telling lead to Demonic Possession?" There are many other books, video and in-person sermons condemning the New Age and the paranormal. Their impact has steadily weakened in recent years, despite the best efforts of some conservative clergy.

15. *Publishers Weekly*, September 6, 2004.

16. Ibid.

17. Ibid, August 15, 2005.

18. *Wall Street Journal*, March 2006.

19. Ibid.

20. Ibid.

21. A commonly repeated conclusion from debunkers in such publications as *Skeptical Inquirer*, books, TV, and radio appearances.

22. *Publishers Weekly*, September 4, 2006.

23. Ibid.

24. Jeremy Carrette and Richard King, *Selling Spirituality: The Silent Take-over of Religion* (Routledge, 2005), quoted in *Publishers Weekly*, September 4, 2006.

25. *Publishers Weekly*, September 2006, cover story by Donna Freitas.

Alexander, Eben. *Proof of Heaven: A Neurosurgeon's Journey into the Afterlife.* New York: Simon & Schuster, 2012.

Atwater, P. M. H. *Beyond the Light: The Mysteries and Revelations of Near-Death Experiences.* New York: Avon Books, 1997.

———. *Coming Back to Life: The After-Effects of the Near-Death Experience.* New York: Dodd Mead, 1988.

———. *Near-Death Experiences, the Rest of the Story: What They Teach Us About Living, Dying, and Our True Purpose.* Charlottesville, Vir.: Hampton Roads Publishing, 2011.

Bain, Donald. *The Control of Candy Jones.* Chicago: Playboy Press, 1976.

———. *Long John Nebel: Radio Talk King, Master Salesman, and Magnificent Charlatan.* New York: Macmillan, 1974.

Beauregard, Mario, and Denyse O'Leary. *The Spiritual Brain: A Neuroscientist's Case for the Existence of the Soul.* New York: HarperOne, 2007.

Berne, Eric. *The Games People Play: The Psychology of Human Relationships.* New York: Grove Press, 1964.

Birnes, William J., and Joel Martin. *The Haunting of America: From the Salem Witch Trials to Harry Houdini.* New York: Tom Doherty Associates, 2009.

———. *The Haunting of Twentieth-Century America: From the Nazis to the New Millennium.* New York: Tom Doherty Associates, 2011.

Blum, Deborah. *Ghost Hunters: William James and the Search for Scientific Proof of Life After Death.* New York: Penguin Press, 2006.

Bohm, David. *Changing Consciousness.* San Francisco: HarperSanFrancisco, 1991.

Brandon, Ruth. *The Spiritualists: The Passion for the Occult in the Nineteenth and Twentieth Centuries.* New York: Alfred A. Knopf, 1983.

Brinkley, Dannion, with Paul Perry. *At Peace with the Light.* New York: HarperCollins, 1995.

———. *Saved by the Light.* New York: Villard Books, 1994.

Broughton, Richard S. *Parapsychology: The Controversial Science*. New York: Ballantine Books, 1991.

Burpo, Todd, with Lynn Vincent. *Heaven Is for Real: A Little Boy's Astounding Story of His Trip to Heaven and Back*. Nashville, Tenn.: Thomas Nelson, 2010.

Buscaglia, Leo. *Living, Loving, and Learning*. New York: Holt, Rinehart, and Winston, 1982.

Chopra, Deepak. *Ageless Body, Timeless Mind*. New York: Harmony Books, 1993.

———. *Life After Death: The Burden of Proof*. New York: Harmony Books, 2006.

———. *Spiritual Solutions: Answers to Life's Greatest Challenges*. New York: Harmony Books, 2012.

———. *War of the Worldviews: Science Vs. Spirituality*. New York: Harmony Books, 2011.

Christopher, Milbourne. *Houdini: A Pictorial Life*. New York: Thomas Y. Crowell, 1976.

Cooper, John Charles. *Religion in the Age of Aquarius*. Philadelphia: Westminster Press, 1971.

Corso, Philip J., with William J. Birnes. *The Day After Roswell*. New York: Pocket Books, 1997.

Crick, Francis. *The Astonishing Hypothesis: The Scientific Search for the Soul*. New York: Maxwell Macmillan, 1994.

Dossey, Larry. *Be Careful What You Pray For—You Just Might Get It*. San Francisco: HarperSanFrancisco, 1997.

———. *Healing Words*. San Francisco: HarperSanFrancisco, 1993.

———. *The Power of Premonitions*. New York: Dutton, 2009.

———. *Recovering the Soul: A Scientific and Spiritual Search*. New York: Bantam Books, 1989.

Dreher, Diane. *The Tao of Inner Peace*. New York: HarperPerennial, 1991.

Duncan, Lois, and William Roll, Ph.D. *Psychic Connections: A Journey Into the Mysterious World of Psi*. New York: Delacorte Press, 1995.

Dyer, Wayne W. *Your Erroneous Zones*. New York: T. Y. Crowell, 1976.

Eadie, Betty J. *The Awakening Heart*. New York: Pocket Books, 1996.

———. *Embraced by the Light*. Placerville, Calif.: Gold Leaf Press, 1992.

Ebon, Martin (ed). *The Amazing Uri Geller*. New York: New American Library, 1975.

———. *Communicating with the Dead*. New York: New American Library, 1981.

———. *The Evidence for Life After Death*. New York: New American Library, 1977.

———. *Psychic Warfare: Threat or Illusion?* New York: McGraw-Hill, 1983.

Elliston, Jon. *Interrogation: The CIA's Secret Manual on Coercive Questioning*. [S.I.]-Parascope, 1997.

———. *Psywar on Cuba: The Declassified History of U.S. Anti-Castro Propaganda*. New York: Ocean Press, 1999.

Ellwood, Robert S. Jr. *Religious and Spiritual Groups in Modern America*. Englewood Cliffs, NJ: Prentice Hall, 1972.

Estabrooks, George Hoben. *Hypnotism*. New York: Dutton, 1957.

Estep, Sarah Wilson. *Voices of Eternity*. New York: Fawcett Gold Medal Books, 1988.

Fodor, Nandor. *Between Two Worlds*. West Nyack, NY: Parker Publishing, 1964.

Ford, Arthur. *Unknown but Known*. New York: Signet Mystic Books, 1969.

Frattaroli, Elio. *Healing the Soul in the Age of the Brain: Becoming Conscious in an Unconscious World*. New York: Penguin Putnam, 2001.

Fuller, John G. *The Airmen Who Would Not Die*. New York: G. P. Putnam's Sons, 1979.

Garrison, Omar V. *The Hidden Story of Scientology*. Secaucus, N.J.: Citadel Press, 1974.

Gawain, Shakti. *Living in the Light: A Guide to Personal and Planetary Transformation*. New York: Bantam Books, 1986.

Gibson, Walter B., and Morris N. Young. *Houdini on Magic*. New York: Dover Publications, 1953.

Godwin, Malcolm. *Angels: An Endangered Species*. New York: Simon & Schuster, 1990.

Greenhouse, Herbert B. *The Astral Journey*. Garden City, NY: Doubleday, 1975.

Greer, Jane. *The Afterlife Connection: A Therapist Reveals How to Communicate With Departed Loved Ones*. New York: St. Martin's Press, 2003.

Guggenheim, Bill, and Judy Guggenheim. *Hello from Heaven!* New York: Bantam Books, 1996.

Harris, Thomas A. *I'm O.K., You're O.K.* New York: Harper & Row, 1969.

Hayden, Tom. *The Long Sixties: From 1960 to Barack Obama*. Boulder, Colo.: Paradigm, 2009.

Heath, Pamela Rae, and Jon Kilmo. *Suicide: What Really Happens in the After-life?* Berkeley, Calif.: North Atlantic Books, 2006.

Hoffmann, Frank W., and William G. Bailey. *Mind and Society Fads.* New York: The Haworth Press, 1992.

Holzer, Hans. *Murder in Amityville.* New York: Belmont Tower Books, 1979.

Houdini, Harry. *A Magician Among the Spirits.* 1924. Reprint. New York: Arno Press, 1972.

Houston, Jean. *The Possible Human.* New York: G. P. Putnam's Sons, 1982.

Howard, Michael. *The Occult Conspiracy.* Rochester, Vt.: Destiny Books, 1989.

Kaiser, David. *How the Hippies Saved Physics: Science, Counterculture, and the Quantum Revival.* New York: W. W. Norton, 2011.

Kalush, William, and Larry Sloman. *The Secret Life of Houdini: The Making of America's First Superhero.* New York: Atria Books, 2006.

Kaplan, Stephen, and Roxanne Salch Kaplan. *Amityville Horror Conspiracy.* Laceyville, Pa.: Belfry Books, 1995.

Kelly, Mary Olsen (ed). *The Fireside Treasury of Light.* New York: Fireside/ Simon & Schuster, 1990.

Keyes, Ken Jr. *Handbook to Higher Consciousness.* Berkeley, Calif.: Living Love Center, 1973.

Knight, JZ *A State of Mind: My Story: Ramtha, the Adventure Begins.* New York: Warner Books, 1987.

Kripal, Jeffrey J. *Esalen: America and the Religion of No Religion.* Chicago: University of Chicago Press, 2007.

Krishnamurti, Jiddhu. *The Krishnamurti Reader.* Boston: Shambhala, 2011.

Kübler-Ross, Elisabeth. *Living with Death and Dying.* New York: Collier Books/Macmillan, 1981.

————. *On Death and Dying.* New York: Macmillan, 1969.

Kurtz, Paul. *A Skeptic's Handbook of Parapsychology.* Buffalo, N.Y.: Prometheus Books, 1985.

Leary, Timothy, Richard Alpert, and Ralph Metzner. *The Psychedelic Experience: A Manual Based on the Tibetan Book of the Dead.* Secaucus, N.J.: Citadel Press, 1964.

Leshan, Lawrence. *The Medium, the Mystic, and the Physicist.* New York: Viking Press, 1974.

Lewis, James R. *Encyclopedia of Afterlife Beliefs and Phenomena.* Detroit: Gale Research, 1994.

Lewis, Jon E. *The Mammoth Books of Cover-Ups: An Encyclopedia of Conspiracy Theories.* Philadelphia: Running Press, 2007.

Long, Jeffrey, with Paul Perry. *Evidence of the Afterlife: The Science of Near-Death Experiences.* New York: HarperOne, 2010.

Lundahl, Craig R. *A Collection of Near-Death Research Readings.* Chicago: Nelson-Hall Publishers, 1982.

MacLaine, Shirley. *Out on a Limb.* New York: Bantam Books, 1983.

Malarkey, Kevin, and Alex Malarkey. *The Boy Who Came Back from Heaven.* Carol Stream, Ill.: Tyndale House Publishers, 2010.

Margolis, Jonathan. *Uri Geller: Magician or Mystic?* New York: Welcome Rain Publishers, 1999.

Marks, John. *The Search for the "Manchurian Candidate": The CIA and Mind Control.* New York: Times Books, 1979.

Marrs, Jim. *PSI: The True Story of America's Psychic Warfare Program.* Franklin Lakes, N.J.: New Page Books, 2007.

———. *Rule by Secrecy: The Hidden History that Connects the Trilateral Commission, the Freemasons, and the Great Pyramids.* New York: Perennial, 2000.

Martin, Joel, and William J. Birnes. *The Haunting of the Presidents: A Paranormal History of the U.S. Presidency.* New York: Signet, 2003.

Martin, Joel, and Patricia Romanowski. *Love Beyond Life: The Healing Power of After-Death Communications.* New York: HarperCollins, 1997.

———. *We Don't Die: George Anderson's Conversations with the Other Side.* New York: G. P. Putnam's Sons, 1988.

Maslow, Abraham H. *Toward a Psychology of Being.* New York: Van Nostrand Reinhold, 1968.

McMoneagle, Joseph. *Mind Trek: Exploring Consciousness, Time, and Space Through Remote Viewing.* Charlottesville, Va.: Hampton Roads Publishing Company, 1993.

———. *Remote Viewing Secrets: A Handbook.* Charlottesville, Va.: Hampton Roads, 2000.

———. *The Stargate Chronicles: Memories of a Psychic Spy.* Charlottesville, Va.: Hampton Roads, 2002.

———. *The Ultimate Time Machine: A Remote Viewer's Perception of Time and Predictions for the New Millennium.* Charlottesville, Va.: Hampton Roads, 1998.

McRae, Ron. *Mind Wars: The True Story of Government Research into the Military Potential of Psychic Weapons*. New York: St. Martin's Press, 1984.

Melton, H. Keith and Robert Wallace. *The Official CIA Manual of Trickery and Deception*. New York: William Morrow, 2009.

Melton, J. Gordon. *New Age Encyclopedia*. Detroit: Gale, 1990.

Mitchell, Edgar D. *Psychic Exploration: A Challenge for Science*. New York: G. P. Putnam's Sons, 1974.

Mitford, Jessica. *The American Way of Death*. New York: Simon and Schuster, 1963.

Monroe, Robert. *Journeys Out of the Body*. Garden City, N.Y.: Anchor Press, 1977.

Montgomery, Ruth. *A World Beyond*. New York: Ballantine Books, 1988.

———. *Gift of Prophecy: The Phenomenal Jean Dixon*. New York: Morrow, 1965.

———. *Herald of the New Age*. Garden City, N.Y.: Doubleday, 1986.

———. *Here and Hereafter*. New York: Coward-McCann, 1968.

———. *Strangers Among Us*. New York: Coward, McCann, and Geoghegan, 1979.

Moody, Raymond Jr. *Life After Life*. New York: Bantam Books/Mockingbird Books, 1975.

Moorjani, Anita. *Dying to Be Me*. Carlsbad, Calif.: Hay House, 2012.

Morehouse, David. *Psychic Warrior: Inside the CIA's Stargate Program*. New York: St. Martin's Press, 1996.

Morse, Melvin, and Paul Perry. *Closer to the Light: Learning from Children's Near-Death Experiences*. New York: Villard, 1990.

———. *Parting Visions: Uses and Meanings of Pre-Death, Psychic, and Spiritual Experiences*. New York: Villard, 1994.

———. *Transformed by Light: A Study of the Powerful Effect of Near-Death Experiences on People's Lives*. New York: Villard, 1992.

Myss, Caroline. *Anatomy of the Spirit*. New York: Harmony Books, 1996.

Newberg, Andrew. *Why We Believe What We Believe*. New York: Simon and Schuster, 2006.

Noory, George, and Rosemary Ellen Guiley. *Talking to the Dead*. New York: Forge Books, 2011.

Noory, George, and William J. Birnes. *Journey to the Light*. New York: Forge Books, 2009.

Orloff, Judith. *Second Sight*. New York: Warner Books, 1996.

Osis, Kärlis and Erlendur Haraldsson. *At the Hour of Death*. New York: Hastings House, 1977.

Ostrander, Sheila and Lynn Schroeder. *Psychic Discoveries Behind the Iron Curtain*. Englewood Cliffs, NJ: Prentice Hall, 1970.

Panati, Charles, ed. *The Geller Papers*. Boston: Houghton Mifflin, 1976.

Paramahansa, Yoganda. *Autobiography of a Yogi*. Los Angeles: Self-Realization Fellowship, 1971.

Parnia, Sam. *What Happens When We Die: A Groundbreaking Study into the Nature of Life and Death*. Carlsbad, Calif.: Hay House, 2006.

Partridge, Christopher. *New Religions: A Guide: New Religious Movements, Sects, and Alternative Spiritualties*. New York: Oxford University Press, 2004.

Penfield, Wilder. *The Mystery of the Mind*. Princeton, N.J.: Princeton University Press, 1975.

Piper, Don, with Cecil Murphey. *90 Minutes in Heaven: A True Story of Death and Life*. Grand Rapids, Mich.: Revell, 2004.

Price, Hope. *Angels: True Stories of How They Touch Our Lives*. New York: Avon Books, 1993.

Puharich, Andrija. *Uri: A Journal of the Mystery of Uri Geller*. New York: Anchor Press, 1974.

Radin, Dean I. *The Conscious Universe: The Scientific Truth of Psychic Phenomena*. New York: HarperCollins, 1997.

Randi, James. *Flim-Flam!: Psychics, ESP, Unicorns, and Other Delusions*. Buffalo, NY: Prometheus Books, 1982.

———. *The Magic of Uri Geller*. New York: Ballantine Books, 1975.

Randle, Kevin D. *To Touch the Light*. New York: Pinnacle Books, 1994.

Rawlings, Maurice. *Beyond Death's Door*. Nashville, Tenn.: Thomas Nelson, 1978.

Rhine, J. B. *New Frontiers of the Mind*. New York: Farrar and Rhinehart, 1937.

———. *The Reach of the Mind*. New York: William Sloane Associates, 1947.

Ring, Kenneth. *Heading Toward Omega: In Search of the Meaning of the Near-Death Experience*. New York: William Morrow, 1984.

———. *Life at Death: A Scientific Investigation of the Near-Death Experience*. New York: Coward, McCann, and Geoghegan, 1980.

Ring, Kenneth, and Evelyn Elsaesser Valarino. *Lessons from the Light: What We Can Learn from the Near-Death Experience*. New York: Insight Books/ Plenum Press, 1998.

Ritchie, George G., Jr., *My Life After Dying*. Norfolk, VA: Hampton Roads Publishing Co., 1991.

Ritchie, George G., Jr., with Elizabeth Sherrill. *Return from Tomorrow*. Old Tappan, N.J.: Fleming Revell, 1978.

Robbins, Anthony. *Awaken the Giant Within*. New York: Simon & Schuster/Fireside Books, 1986.

Roberts, Jane. *Seth Speaks*. Englewood Cliffs, NJ: Prentice-Hall, 1972.

Rogo, D. Scott. *Psychic Breakthroughs Today*. UK: Aquarian Press; New York, Sterling, 1987.

Roland, Paul. *The Nazis and the Occult: The Dark Forces Unleashed by the Third Reich*. Edison, NJ: Chartwell Books, 2007.

Ronson, Jon. *The Men Who Stare at Goats*. New York: Simon & Schuster, 2006.

Russell, Jeffrey Burton. *A History of Heaven*. Princeton, NJ: Princeton University, 1997.

Sabom, Michael B. *Recollections of Death: A Medical Investigation*. New York: Harper & Row, 1982.

Schindler, Mary and Robert Schindler. *A Life that Matters: The Legacy of Terri Schiavo—A Lesson for Us All*. New York: Warner Books, 2006.

Shermer, Michael. *Why People Believe Weird Things: Pseudoscience, Superstition, and Other Confusions of Our Time*. New York: W. H. Freeman, 1977.

Siegel, Bernie S. *Love, Medicine, and Miracles*. New York: Harper & Row, 1986.

Silverman, Kenneth. *Houdini!: The Career of Ehrich Weiss*. New York: HarperCollins, 1996.

Simonton, O. Carl. *Getting Well Again*. Los Angeles: J. P. Tarcher, 1978.

Smith, Paul H. *Reading the Enemy's Mind: Inside Stargate—America's Psychic Espionage Program*. New York: Tom Doherty Associates, 2005.

Stearn, Jess. *A Matter of Immortality*. New York: Atheneum, 1976.

———. *Soul Mates*. New York: Bantam Books, 1984.

Swann, Ingo. *Natural ESP*. New York: Bantam Books, 1987.

Swedenborg, Emanuel. *Heaven and Hell*. New York: Swedenborg Foundation, 1972. (Originally published in Latin, London, 1758.)

Targ, Russell, and Harold Puthoff. *Mind Reach*. New York: Delacorte, 1977.

Targ, Russell, and Keith Harary. *The Mind Race: Understanding and Using Psychic Abilities*. New York: Villard Books, 1984.

Taylor, John. *Science and the Supernatural*. London: Temple Smith, 1980.

————. *Superminds: A Scientist Looks at the Paranormal*. New York: Viking Press, 1975.

Thomas, Gordon. *Journey into Madness: The True Story of Secret CIA Mind Control and Medical Abuse*. New York: Bantam Books, 1989.

Toth, Max and Greg Nielson. *Pyramid Power*. New York: Warner Books, 1974.

Van de Castle, Robert. *Our Dreaming Mind*. New York: Ballantine Books, 1994.

Williams, Beryl, and Samuel Epstein. *The Great Houdini*. New York: Pocket Books, 1951.

Williams, Mary E. (ed). *Paranormal Phenomena: Opposing Viewpoints*. New York: Thomson Learning, 2003.

Williamson, Marianne. *A Return to Love: Reflections on the Course of Miracles*. New York: HarperCollins, 1992.

Wise, David. *Nightmover: How Aldrich Ames Sold the CIA to the KGB for $4.6 Million*. New York: HarperCollins, 1995.

Woods, Richard. *The Occult Revolution*. New York: Herder and Herder, 1971.

Zepezauer, Mark. *The CIA's Greatest Hits*. Tucson, AZ: Odonian Press, 1994.